A TREASURY OF

 THE ART OF LIVING

Edited by SIDNEY GREENBERG

with a Foreword by HARRY GOLDEN

Published by
Melvin Powers
WILSHIRE BOOK COMPANY
12015 Sherman Road
No. Hollywood, California 91605
Telephone: (213) 875-1711

Printed by

HAL LEIGHTON PRINTING COMPANY
P.O. Box 3952
North Hollywood, California 91605
Telephone: (213) 983-1105

Affectionately Dedicated

To

Evelyn and Phil
Ruth and Sam
Sarah and Jack
Eunice and Joseph

and to their children
my nephews and nieces

FOREWORD

We are going to the moon. We may very well have a man there within the decade. Within the lifetimes of our children, we shall have charted many of the vast corners of outer space. Perhaps in our own lifetime, we shall know homes heated by atomic energy, and drive cars powered by tiny transistors.

But I wonder how much any of these things will change us? I wonder if they will make us better men, more knowledgeable? I doubt it seriously. Technological and scientific advances rarely make improvements upon our nature.

It is now considered a cliche to say that the humanities have not kept pace with the technological advances, but for all that, it is still true. A rolling stone gathers no moss is the oldest of all cliches, and the oldest of all truths.

The ever-advancing accomplishments of science simply bewilder us. While we are presented daily with more and more creature comforts, and wider and wider horizons, ethics is still where Aristotle and Spinoza left off; men still spend their lives in work and worry. It is no coincidence that at the bottom of the great economic depression, Carl Sandburg wrote, "The People, Yes." The Editor of A Treasury of the Art of Living understands this too. We know that from the selections Dr. Greenberg has made for this valuable book. The people, "Yes"—which means that the human story remains the same. It is still the most complex of all stories and there are no easy solutions or wider horizons for understanding ourselves.

The Editor in producing this book has provided us with the valuable insights into our everyday lives. Whether our wives cook in an all-steel kitchen or our own work-day is spent in computing the number of electrical circuits needed for a missile, we know that

that which really survives, that which is not transient are *words,* good *words,* the *words* of thinkers and the ideas these thinkers have generated.

Because of the terrible disparity between science and our own humanity, we have evolved no formulas for easing the tension that invades our modern living.

We live in an age of increasing industrialization and urbanization. The "family gathering," as we knew it in the previous generation, is all but gone today. A brother is in Pasadena and the lively uncle lives in Miami. A sister lives in Dallas and nephews and nieces are discreetly scattered from Bangor to Butte. And let us face up to the fact that we are not going to be "reunited." Our lives will not suddenly be made integral; we must begin to live with the prospect they will not be made integral at all.

The Founding Fathers had no idea that we would one day discover the Mesabi Range in Minnesota which would become the steel industry and change an agrarian, rural civilization into an urban-industrial society. There are a million new challenges, and one of the most important of those challenges is our need to find "roots," if possible, to live in and with this vast mobility and somehow achieve a formula by which to reduce our tension.

A Treasury of the Art of Living, so brilliantly put together by Dr. Greenberg, can help some of us. The book can help some of us to unclutch our fingers from our heart and find a method of relaxation in a society that is rapidly running away from us.

Harry Golden
Charlotte, N.C.

INTRODUCTION

It is told of Balzac, the great French author, that he once spent a long and unrewarding evening in the company of people who had nothing particularly vital to say. When he returned to his home, he proceeded at once to his study, removed his coat, rubbed his hands and, as he permitted his eyes to rove over the masters whose works lined his shelves, he said aloud: "Now for some real people!"

We in our time are the heirs of all that the "real people" have ever thought and written. Their literary harvest is more accessible than ever before, it is more abundant than ever before and it is more desperately needed than ever before.

Our generation has discovered a terrifying capacity for destroying human life. Only recently the President of our country declared in an address to the nation that the two great nuclear powers could annihilate three hundred million lives in one hour of warfare! Trembling on the brink of atomic holocaust, we need the distilled wisdom of the "real people" to speak to us before it is too late.

Deep is our need for guidance, for courage, for strength, for inspiration. Our moral values are being honored more in the breach than in the observance. Ethical standards are being corroded in our public life. The terrifying rise in our crime statistics poses a problem of unprecedented dimensions. The democratic way of life is under open attack from without, it is being flaunted in many sectors of our corporate life at home. We can disregard the voices of the "real people" only at our very great collective peril.

In addition, there are always a host of personal problems on which we need the wisest counsel available. What values shall we pursue? How shall we face the advancing years? How shall we use the present? Where is happiness to be found? How shall we measure our wealth, our progress, our stature? How shall we face sorrow? How shall we best discharge our obligations as parents, as mates, as citizens? These are only a few of the many crucial areas of deep and immediate concern on which we should like to hear from the "real people."

A Treasury of the Art of Living has brought together the keenest observations of the "real people." "Great men taken in any way" wrote Thomas Carlyle, "are profitable company." They are perhaps most profitable when they speak to us about the dilemmas, the problems, the anxieties that weigh heavily upon our hearts and minds.

This volume was begun in my first year at the Seminary, exactly a quarter of a century ago. When the direction my life would take became fixed, I realized that I would need all the accumulated spiritual and cultural resources of the human family in order to be able to minister effectively in the myriad ways that contemporary spiritual leader is called upon to serve. He is a preacher and teacher, a pastor and personal counselor, a writer and molder of public opinion. Any one of these tasks are for others full time occupations. Taken together they constitute an almost impossible assignment. The very least one could do was to prepare oneself as thoroughly as possible. Part of that preparation was to seek out the wisdom of the "real people." Thus was started a card file of thoughts which has grown over the years. A Treasury of the Art of Living is a product of that file.

"The best books" said Israel Abrahams, "are those which best teach men how to live." I have tried to create such a book. Here, of course, the editor's judgment came into play. I have included only those thoughts which I felt are constructive, calculated to bring out the best in us and to deepen our commitment to the enduring moral and ethical values. And I have tried to be especially sensitive to the literary merit of the selection. The thoughts that were included were chosen for the compelling manner in which they were phrased as well as for their intrinsic merit.

A Treasury of the Art of Living is obviously not a book to be swallowed in one gulp. It should be read at intervals with adequate time allowed for a thought to be digested and evaluated. What one reads will depend on the emotional or psychological or intellectual need of the moment. The organization of the book should help guide the reader to the desired section.

One of the strongest motivations that prompted the publication of this volume was the hope that it will be of special help to my colleagues in the rabbinate and the ministry and others who are constantly in need of fresh inspiration and stimulation.

George McDonald has left us one added reason for the appearance of A Treasury of the Art of Living. "Instead of a gem or a flower" he advised, "cast the gift of a lovely thought into the heart of a friend." To the many friends who have enriched my twenty-one years at Temple Sinai I offer this collection of lovely thoughts.

SIDNEY GREENBERG

September, 1963
Temple Sinai
Philadelphia, Pennsylvania

CONTENTS

THE ART OF LIVING

1. LIVING AS AN ART

If you have known how to compose your life, you have accomplished a great deal more than the man who knows how to compose a book. Have you been able to take your stride? You have done more than the man who has taken cities and empires. The great and glorious masterpiece of man is to live to the point. All other things—to reign, to hoard, to build—are, at most, but inconsiderate props and appendages.

Michel de Montaigne

The one essential thing is that we strive to have light in ourselves. Our strivings will be recognized by others, and when people have light in themselves, it will shine out from them. Then we get to know each other as we walk together in the darkness, without needing to pass our hands over each other's faces, or to intrude into each other's hearts.

Albert Schweitzer

The art of living successfully consists of being able to hold two opposite ideas in tension at the same time: first, to make long-term plans as if we were going to live forever; and, second, to conduct ourselves daily as if we were going to die tomorrow.

Sydney J. Harris

A man who does not learn to live while he is getting a living, is a poorer man after his wealth is won, than he was before.

John G. Holland

Many will know the story of the fish in Mammoth Cave, Kentucky. These fish have lived for generations in the dark, so that at last the optic nerve has atrophied and they are quite blind. Similarly Darwin tells us that he lost completely his love of poetry and music, once very strong within him, simply because he ceased to develop it. This is true of all our powers, memory, concentration, capacity for hard work. We must use them or lose them.

Harold Nicholson

It is perfectly true, as philosophers say, that life must be understood backwards. But they forget the other proposition, that it must be lived forwards.

Sören Kierkegaard

Life is easier to take than you'd think. All that is necessary is to accept the impossible, do without the indispensable, and bear the intolerable.

Kathleen Norris

The lesson of life is to believe what the years and centuries say against the hours.

Ralph Waldo Emerson

Life is action and passion. It is expected of a man that he share in the action and passion of his time under penalty of being judged not to have lived!

Oliver Wendell Holmes

I am convinced that my life belongs to the whole community; and as long as I live, it is my privilege to do for it whatever I can, for the harder I work the more I live. I rejoice in life for its own sake. Life is no brief candle for me. It is a sort of splendid torch which I got hold of for a moment, and I want to make it burn as brightly as possible before turning it over to future generations.

George Bernard Shaw

Grandmother, about eighty, is visiting in the East and sends home things she has bought for her house. "I don't suppose I shall live forever," she says, "but while I do live I don't see why I shouldn't live as if I expected to."

Charles Horton Cooley

Is life worth living? This is a question for an embryo, not for a man.

Samuel Butler

The minute you know that you are not afraid to die, is the minute you begin to know how to live.

H. F. White

Too many believe life is a crib from which they are privileged to feed. Out of it they demand clothing and food and money and power. That isn't living at all. Life is an altar, and the things that go on altars are sacrifices.

Preston Bradley

Every year that I live I am more convinced that the waste of life lies in the love we have not given, the powers we have not used, the selfish prudence which will risk nothing, and which, shirking pain, misses happiness as well.

John B. Tabb

May you live all the days of your life.

Jonathan Swift

How few our real wants, and how vast our imaginary ones!

John Casper Lavater

Live your life each day as you would climb a mountain. An occasional glance toward the summit keeps the goal in mind, but many beautiful scenes are to be observed from each new vantage point. Climb slowly, steadily, enjoying each passing moment; and the view from the summit will serve as a fitting climax for the journey.

Harold V. Melchert

Life is not a having and a getting, but a being and a becoming.

Matthew Arnold

However mean your life is, meet it and live it; do not shun it and call it hard names. It is not so bad as you are. It looks poorest when you are richest. The fault-finder will find faults even in paradise. Love your life.

Henry Thoreau

Make yourself an honest man and then you may be sure that there is one less rascal in the world.

Thomas Carlyle

Be such a man, and live such a life, that if every man were such as you, and every life a life like yours, this earth would be God's Paradise.

Phillips Brooks

Make the best use of what is in your power, and take the rest as it happens.

Epictetus

As yesterday is history, and tomorrow may never come, I have resolved that from this day on, I will do all the business I can honestly, have all the fun I can reasonably, do all the good I can willingly, and save my digestion by thinking pleasantly.

Robert Louis Stevenson

I have three precious things which I hold fast and prize. The first is gentleness; the second is frugality; the third is humility, which keeps me from putting myself before others. Be gentle and you can be bold; be frugal and you can be liberal; avoid putting yourself before others and you can become a leader among men.

Lao Tzu

When a certain religious group took as a motto some years ago these words, "Millions now living will never die," someone commented, "Yes, but the tragedy is that millions now living are already dead and don't know it."

Charles L. Wallis

We took to ourselves the old farmer's saying, "Live as though you would die tonight. Farm as though you would live forever."

Peter Howard

The secret of life is not to do what you like, but to like what you do.

Author Unknown

Man cannot live by bread alone. The making of money, the accumulation of material power, is not all there is to living. Life is something more than these, and the man who misses this truth misses the greatest joy and satisfaction that can come into his life—service for others.

Edward Bok

Men love to risk their lives, conquering pinnacles. They love the spice of danger in it. And that's what life is.

Leon Harrison

A child asked a man to pick a flower for her. That was simple enough. But when she said, "Now put it back," the man experienced a baffling helplessness he never knew before. "How can you explain that it cannot be done?" he asked. "How can one make clear to young people that there are some things which, when once broken, once mutilated, can never be replaced or mended?"

Marcia Borowsky

Resolved to live with all my might while I do live, and as I shall wish I had done ten thousand ages hence.

Jonathan Edwards

In today's crowded civilization and in this busy and active society, man is finding it increasingly difficult to indulge one of the most priceless luxuries which life can give: occasional total solitude. Being alone does not mean being lonely. It means cutting off the external, the superficial and the superfluous, and seeking instead the inner strength which one finds best in solitude. It enriches the spirit and ennobles the man, and one who denies himself its refuge is not living life to its fullest.

Henry King

Nothing in life is to be feared. It is only to be understood.

Marie Curie

The great use of life is to spend it for something that outlasts it.

William James

The art of living is more like that of wrestling than of dancing; the main thing is to stand firm and be ready for an unforeseen attack.

Marcus Aurelius

He most lives who thinks most, who feels the noblest, and who acts the best.

Philip James Bailey

I not only bow to the inevitable; I am fortified by it.

Thornton Wilder

When anyone has offended me, I try to raise my soul so high that the offence cannot reach it.

Descartes

A saint is one who makes goodness attractive.

Lawrence Housman

Every man is tasked to make his life, even in its details, worthy of the contemplation of his most elevated and critical hour.

Henry Thoreau

Teach us that wealth is not elegance, that profusion is not magnificence, that splendor is not beauty.

Benjamin Disraeli

We are always getting ready to live, but never living.

Ralph Waldo Emerson

A long life may not be good enough but a good life is long enough.

Benjamin Franklin

The art of living consists in keeping earthly step to heavenly music.

Ivan N. Panin

There are obviously two educations. One should teach us how to make a living. The other should teach us how to live.

James Truslow Adams

When men speak ill of thee, so live that nobody will believe them.

Plato

A straight line is the shortest in morals as in geometry.

Rachel

I am not bound to win but I am bound to be true. I am not bound to succeed but I am bound to live up to what light I have. I must stand with anybody that stands right: stand with him while he is right and part with him when he goes wrong.

Abraham Lincoln

Life's greatest achievement is the continual remaking of yourself so that at last you know how to live.

Author Unknown

Live with men as if God saw you; converse with God as if men heard you.

Seneca

On Arturo Toscanini's eightieth birthday, someone asked his son, Walter, what his father ranked as his most important achievement. The son replied, "For him there can be no such thing. Whatever he happens to be doing at the moment is the biggest thing in his life—whether it is conducting a symphony or peeling an orange."

Ardis Whitman

Bear well thy heart against the assaults of envy, which kills even sooner than death itself; and know no envy at all, save such envy of the merits of virtuous men as shall lead these to emulate the beauty of their lives.

Eleazar Rokëach

Short is the little that remains to thee of life. Live as on a mountain!

Marcus Aurelius

Life is long if it is full.

Seneca

Solitude is important to man. It is necessary to his achievement of peace and contentment. It is a well into which he dips for refreshment for his soul. It is his laboratory in which he distills the pure essence of worth from the raw materials of his experiences. It is his refuge when the very foundations of his life are being shaken by disastrous events.

Margaret E. Mulac

To be sure, a man does not live without bread, but he does not live at all if bread is all he gets.

Russell Frank Auman

It is better to light one small candle than to curse the darkness.

Confucius

Make sure the thing you're living for is worth dying for.

Charles Mayes

Fear not that thy life shall come to an end, but rather fear that it shall never have a beginning.

John Henry Newman

We cannot control the evil tongues of others; but a good life enables us to disregard them.

Cato

It is not enough that men shall know. They must be.

Henry Ward Beecher

I will govern my life, and my thought, as if the whole world were to see the one, and to read the other.

Seneca

So live that you would not be ashamed to sell the family parrot to the town gossip.

Will Rogers

A friend of Ivan Turgenev once wrote to him, "It seems to me that to put oneself in the second place is the whole significance of life." To this the great Russian author replied: "It seems to me to discover what to put before oneself in the first place is the whole problem of life."

Robert E. Luccock

Far more than we need an intercontinental missile or a moral rearmament or a religious revival, we need to come alive again, to recover the virility of the imagination on which all earlier civilizations have been based.

Archibald MacLeish

"I accept the universe," is reported to have been a favorite utterance of our New England transcendentalist, Margaret Fuller; and when someone repeated this phrase to Thomas Carlyle, his sardonic comment is said to have been: "Gad! she'd better!"

William James

The art of life lies in a constant readjustment to our surroundings.

Okakura Kakuzo

Learn as if you were to live for ever; live as if you were to die tomorrow.

Author Unknown

Only a life lived for others is a life worth while.

Albert Einstein

There once lived a wondrous good and wise man named Socrates. But he gave offense to those who were in power, and they jailed him; told him that he would have to die. Socrates received the news with a smile.

"You should prepare for death," they told him, but he shook his head and kept on smiling.

"I have been preparing for death all my life," he said.

"In what way?" they asked.

And Socrates said, "I have never, secretly or openly, done a wrong to any man."

Quentin Reynolds

To live well we must have a faith fit to live by, a self fit to live with, and a work fit to live for.

Joseph Fort Newton

As long as a man does not sin, he is feared; as soon as he sins, he himself is in fear.

The Midrash

Life, happy or unhappy, successful or unsuccessful, is extraordinarily interesting.

George Bernard Shaw

Near the body of a young man who had taken his life this note was found: "I leave to society a bad example. I leave to my friends the memory of a misspent life. I leave to my father and mother all the sorrow they can bear in their old age. I leave to my wife a broken heart, and to my children the name of a drunkard and a suicide. I leave to God a lost soul who has insulted his mercy."

Harry Emerson Fosdick

A gambler always loses. He loses money, dignity, and time. And if he wins he weaves a spider's web round himself.

Moses Maimonides

Let us endeavor so to live that when we come to die, even the undertaker will be sorry.

Mark Twain

Many phrases and words sound alike but are very different. For instance, "standard of living" and "standard of life." The first puts its emphasis upon material comforts, the second on spiritual idealism. In our day there is a tendency to confuse success with achievement, to accept a man of distinction as a distinguished man. Unless we have a standard of life, all else is sounding brass and cymbals and history will probe our ruins for the answer.

Ralph McGill

Life is like a camel. You can make it do anything except back up.

Marcelene Cox

We have received the world as a legacy which none of us is allowed to impair, but which, on the contrary, every generation is bound to bequeath in a better state to its posterity.

Joseph Joubert

2. REFLECTIONS ON AGE

The whole secret of remaining young in spite of years, and even of gray hairs, is to cherish enthusiasm in oneself, by poetry, by contemplation, by charity,—that is, in fewer words, by the maintenance of harmony in the soul. When everything is in its right place within us, we ourselves are in its right place within us, we ourselves are in equilibrium with the whole work of God. Deep and grave enthusiasm for the eternal beauty and the eternal order, reason touched with emotion and a serene tenderness of heart—these surely are the foundations of wisdom.

Henri F. Amiel

Maturity, we now know, need be no dull routine of a defeated and resigned adulthood. It can rather be the triumphant use of powers that all through our childhood and youth have been in preparation.

Harry A. Overstreet

Death comes not to the living soul, nor age to the loving heart.

Phoebe Cary

To be seventy years young is sometimes far more cheerful and hopeful than to be forty years old.

Oliver Wendell Holmes

Be old while you are young and stay young when you are old.

Chinese Proverb

When I was young I was amazed at Plutarch's statement that the elder Cato began at the age of eighty to learn Greek. I am amazed no longer. Old age is ready to undertake tasks that youth shirked because they would take too long.

W. Somerset Maugham

Old age is a tyrant, which forbids the pleasures of youth on pain of death.

François Rochefoucauld

When one finds company in himself and his pursuits, he cannot feel old, no matter what his years may be.

A. B. Alcott

If we keep well and cheerful we are always young, and at last die in youth, even when years would count us old.

Tryon Edwards

We grow with years more fragile in body, but morally stouter, and can throw off the chill of a bad conscience almost at once.

Logan Pearsall Smith

It is a man's own fault, it is from want of use, if his mind grows torpid in old age.

Samuel Johnson

A diplomat is a man who remembers a lady's birthday but forgets her age.

Author Unknown

Nearly two-thirds of all the greatest deeds ever performed by human beings—the victories in battle, the greatest books, the greatest pictures and statues—have been accomplished after the age of sixty.

Albert Edward Wiggam

A man's age is as unimportant as the size of his shoes if his interest in life is not impaired, if he is compassionate and if time has mellowed his prejudices.

Douglas Meador

Let me grow lovely, growing old
So many fine things do;
Laces, and ivory, and gold,
And silks need not be new.
And there is healing in old trees,
Old streets a glamour hold;
Why may not I, as well as these,
Grow lovely, growing old?

Karle Wilson Baker

The evening of life brings with it its lamp.

Joseph Joubert

As you grow old you have fewer joys but more interests.

Francoise Sagan

We have added years to man's life. Now we face an even greater challenge—adding life to these years. In other words, we have given the American people the opportunity to enjoy nearly twice as many years as did their ancestors and now we have the obligation to help turn old age into something more than a chronological period of life.

Louis M. Orr

Their ages are a most
  Peculiar fact—
Which women won't admit,
  And men won't act.

Leonard K. Schiff

Youth thinks intelligence a good substitute for experience, and his elders think experience a substitute for intelligence.

Lyman Bryson

In youth the days are short and the years are long; in old age the years are short and the days long.

Ivan N. Panin

Growing old is no more than a bad habit which a busy man has no time to form.

Andre Maurois

As for old age, embrace and love it. It abounds with pleasure if you know how to use it. The gradually declining years are among the sweetest in a man's life; and I maintain that even when they have reached the extreme limit, they have their pleasure still.

Seneca

It is not by the gray of the hair that one knows the age of the heart.

Edward Bulwer-Lytton

I wish not the pangs, and the aches and loneliness of youth, but I crave the comfort, and the calm and the certainty that increases with each passing year. . . . And yet I would be pleased if, when I am an old man sitting in the sun, something would stir in my ancient blood and for just one instant I felt again the aching, unsatisfied loneliness of youth.

Richard O. Boyer

Whatever a man's age, he can reduce it several years by putting a bright-colored flower in his button-hole.

Mark Twain

Age appears to be best in four things,—old wood best to burn, old wine to drink, old friends to trust, and old authors to read.

Francis Bacon

The secret of remaining young is never to have an emotion that is unbecoming.

Oscar Wilde

It's not how old you are but how you are old.

Marie Dressler

To keep young, every day read a poem, hear a choice piece of music, view a fine painting, and if possible, do a good action.

Johann Wolfgang von Goethe

Time is a dressmaker specializing in alterations.

Faith Baldwin

To know how to grow old is the masterwork of wisdom, and one of the most difficult chapters in the great art of living.

Henri F. Amiel

The only way any woman may remain forever young is to grow old gracefully.

W. Beran Wolfe

It is magnificent to grow old, if one keeps young.

Harry Emerson Fosdick

He who would pass his declining years with honor and comfort, should, when young, consider that he may one day become old, and remember when he is old, that he has once been young.

Joseph Addison

To be interested in the changing seasons is a happier state of mind than to be hopelessly in love with spring.

George Santayana

I have often thought what a melancholy world this would be without children, and what an inhuman world without the aged.

Samuel Taylor Coleridge

Think of what the world would have missed had a retirement age, even at 70, been universally enforced. Gladstone was Prime Minister of England at 83; Benjamin Franklin helped frame the Constitution of the U.S. at 80; Oliver Wendell Holmes retired from the Supreme Court bench at 91; Henry Ford, when past 80, took up the presidency of the Ford Motor Co. for the second time; and Alonzo Stagg was named the "Football Man of the Year" at 81. Dr. Lillien J. Martin learned to drive an automobile when she was 76 years old, and at the same age founded the Old Age Center in San Francisco, where she received aged people as students. She continued to direct it until her death at 91.

Wingate M. Johnson

It's not miserable to be old; it's miserable not to be capable of *living your age*.

Eugene P. Bertin

You are as young as your faith, as old as your doubt; as young as your self-confidence, as old as your fear; as young as your hope, as old as you despair.

Samuel Ullman

Each part of life has its own pleasures. Each has its own abundant harvest, to be garnered in season. We may grow old in body, but we need never grow old in mind and spirit. We must make a stand against old age. We must atone for its faults by activity. We must exercise the mind as we exercise the body, to keep it supple and buoyant. Life may be short, but it is long enough to live honorably and well. Old age is the consummation of life, rich in blessings.

Cicero

Age should not have its face lifted but it should rather teach the world to admire wrinkles as the etchings of experience and the firm lines of character.

Ralph Barton Perry

The passions of youth are vices in age.

Joseph Joubert

When John Quincy Adams, at 80, was asked how he was, he answered:

"John Quincy Adams himself is very well, thank you. But the house he lives in is sadly dilapidated. It is tottering on its foundations. The walls are badly shattered and the roof is worn; the building trembles with every wind, and I think John Quincy Adams will have to move out of it before long. But he himself is very well."

Author Unknown

Youth is happy because it has the ability to see beauty. Anyone who keeps the ability to see beauty never grows old.

Franz Kafka

The young man who has not wept is a savage, and the old man who will not laugh is a fool.

George Santayana

An elderly lady who was asked by a child if she were young or old said: "My dear, I have been young a very long time."

Author Unknown

The thing to do is neither to fear old age nor to fight it, but to accept it without tension and use it. When I say "use it," I do not mean bear it, accommodate yourself to it, but take hold of it and make something beautiful out of it. That's what nature does—she does not die drably; she puts on her most gorgeous robes in autumn, her yellows and her flaming reds, and dies gloriously.

E. Stanley Jones

Nature gives to every time and season some beauties of its own;

and from morning to night, as from the cradle to the grave, is but a succession of changes so gentle and easy that we can scarcely mark their progress.

Charles Dickens

Why do we look old? Because we remember the weight of the burden of last year's experiences. There is no other reason. Instead of lifting our faces, we should discover that the thing to lift is our thought. It is the mind, not the physical body, which has the stamp of age and reflects it in the body.

Ernest Holmes

A man is not old as long as he is seeking something.

Jean Rostand

If wrinkles must be written upon our brows, let them not be written upon the heart. The spirit should not grow old.

James A. Garfield

Unless we bank some intellectual and cultural resources in middle age, we are left barren and destitute as we grow older, with little to sustain us except prattle about our symptoms and wistful sighs for the past.

Sydney J. Harris

---

3. THE ART OF USING TIME

One ought every day to hear a little music, read a good poem, see a fine picture and, if possible, speak a few reasonable words.

Johann Wolfgang von Goethe

There is an American proverb which I think is not only false but pernicious in its implication. America prides itself on having coined the saying "Time is money." This is a false statement and leads to serious error. The only case in which time and money are alike, is that there are some people who do not know what to do with their time and some who do not know what to do with their money, and still others who are so unfortunate as not to know what to do with either. But, otherwise, time is infinitely more precious than money, and there is nothing common between them. You cannot accumu-

late time; you cannot regain time lost; you cannot borrow time; you can never tell how much time you have left in the Bank of Life. Time is life . . .

Israel Davidson

I cannot afford to waste my time making money.

Louis Agassiz

"This is the day which the Lord hath made." We shall never overtake tomorrow. Wherever we are, it will always be today. So if ever we are to be glad we are alive, and relaxed in a childlike gala mood of appreciation for all the things we have to enjoy, and of gratitude to their Giver, now is the time to begin. "This is the day which the Lord hath made; we will rejoice and be glad in it." That is common sense. And, even if we try, we can-

not fret and worry at the same time
we are rejoicing and being glad.
Russell Henry Stafford

We ask for long life, but 'tis deep
life or grand moments that signify.
Let the measure of time be spiritual not mechanical.
Ralph Waldo Emerson

The time which we have at our
disposal every day is elastic.
Marcel Proust

Killing time is suicide on the installment plan.
T. E. Burke

You have not lived a perfect day,
even though you have earned your
money, unless you have done something for someone who will never
be able to repay you.
Ruth Smeltzer

It is now and in this world that
we must live.
Andre Gide

What is time?—the shadow on
the dial,—the striking of the clock,
—the running of the sand,—day
and night,—summer and winter,—
months, years, centuries? These are
but arbitrary and outward signs,—
the measure of time, not time itself. Time is the life of the soul. If
not this,—then tell me, what is
time?
Author Unknown

He that hopes hereafter to look
back with satisfaction upon past
years, must learn to know the present value of single minutes, and endeavor to let no particle of time fall
useless to the ground.
Samuel Johnson

Ordinary people think merely
how they shall spend their time; a
man of intellect tries to use it.
Arthur Schopenhauer

If we are ever to enjoy life, now
is the time—not tomorrow, nor next
year, nor in some future life after
we have died. The best preparation
for a better life next year is a full,
complete, harmonious, joyous life
this year. Our beliefs in a rich future life are of little importance unless we coin them into a rich present life. Today should always be
our most wonderful day.
Thomas Dreier

You are not born for fame if you
don't know the value of time.
Vauvenargues

There was once a group of ladies
in Brooklyn that seemed to want to
do something for me. They thought
maybe it was too hard to be a poet
and that they could help. They had
me down to read to them and they
asked me, "How do you find time
to be a poet?"
I looked them over—there were
about five hundred of them—and I
asked them if they could keep a
confidence. All five hundred said
they could, so I told them where I
got the time for it.
"Like a sneak," I said, "I stole
some of it. Like a man, I seized
some of it.—And I had a little in
my tin cup to begin with."
Robert Frost

Some 25 years ago a London
physician declared there is a disease more devastating than tuberculosis or cancer. Since his day we
have taken most of the terror from
tuberculosis and made some strides

in preventing cancer. But this other ailment seems to be increasing. It is called by various names, but the most common one is boredom. . . . True, not many deaths are due to boredom. But if we think of the time it kills, the vitality it lowers and the productive power it lessens we see that it takes a terrific toll.

Ralph W. Sockman

Write it on your heart that every day is the best day in the year. No man has earned anything rightly until he knows that every day is doomsday. Today is a king in disguise. Today always looks mean to the thoughtless, in the face of a uniform experience that all good and great and happy actions are made up precisely of these blank todays. Let us not be deceived, let us unmask the king as he passes.

Ralph Waldo Emerson

Little drops of water,
  Little grains of sand,
Make a mighty ocean,
  And the pleasant land.

Thus the little minutes,
  Humble though they be,
Make the mighty ages
  Of eternity.

E. C. Brewer

There is nothing of which we are apt to be so lavish as of time, and about which we ought to be more solicitous; since without it we can do nothing in this world.

William Penn

Everyone is criticizing and belittling the times. Yet I think that our times, like all times, are very good times, if only we know what to do with them.

Ralph Waldo Emerson

Our days are like identical suitcases; all the same size but some people can pack more into them than others.

P. L. Andarr

Who forces time is pushed back by time; who yields to time finds time on his side.

The Talmud

Why fear to-morrow, timid heart?
  Why tread the future's way?
We only need to do our part,
  To-day, dear child, to-day.

The past is written! Close the book
  On pages sad and gay;
Within the future do not look,
  But live to-day—to-day.

'Tis this one hour God has given;
  His Now we must obey;
And it will make our earth his
    heaven
  To live to-day—to-day.

Lydia Avery Coonley Ward

Time is a man's most precious possession—his most precious commodity. To take a man's time, is to take a portion of his life. To give a man some of your time, is to give him a portion of yours.

Margaret E. Mulac

After we come to mature years, there is nothing of which we are so vividly conscious as of the swiftness of time. Its brevity and littleness are the theme of poets, moralists and preachers. Yet there is nothing of which there is so much—nor day nor night, ocean nor sky, winter nor summer equal it. It is a perpetual flow from the inexhaustible fountains of eternity:—And we have no adequate conception of our earthly life until we think of it and live in it as a part of forever.

Now is eternity, and will be, tomorrow and next day, through the endless years of God.

Stebbins

Since time is not a person we can overtake when he is gone, let us honor him with mirth and cheerfulness of heart while he is passing.

Johann Wolfgang von Goethe

The whole life of man is but a point of time; let us enjoy it, therefore, while it lasts, and not spend it to no purpose.

Plutarch

Dost thou love life? Then do not squander time; for that's the stuff life is made of.

If time be of all things the most precious, wasting time must be the greatest prodigality; since lost time is never found again and what we call time enough always proves little enough. Let us then be up and doing, and doing to the purpose; so by diligence shall we do more with less perplexity. Sloth makes all things difficult, but industry all things easy.

Employ thy time well, if thou meanest to gain leisure. Since thou art not sure of a minute, throw not away an hour.

Benjamin Franklin

Money and time are the heaviest burdens of life, and the unhappiest of all mortals are those who have more of either than they know how to use.

Samuel Johnson

We die daily. Happy those who daily come to life as well.

George MacDonald

He enjoys true leisure who has time to improve his soul's estate.

Henry David Thoreau

I have no Yesterdays,
Time took them away;
Tomorrow may not be
But I have Today.

Pearl Yeadon McGinnis

Nothing really belongs to us but time, which even he has who has nothing else.

Baltasar Gracian

Finish every day and be done with it. You have done what you could. Some blunders and absurdities no doubt crept in; forget them as soon as you can. Tomorrow is a new day; begin it well and serenely and with too high a spirit to be cumbered with your old nonsense. This day is all that is good and fair. It is too dear, with its hopes and invitations, to waste a moment on the yesterdays.

Ralph Waldo Emerson

Let every dawn of morning be to you as the beginning of life and every setting sun be to you as its close; then let every one of these short lives leave its sure record of some kindly thing done for others, some goodly strength or knowledge gained for yourself.

John Ruskin

The best inheritance a parent can give his children is a few minutes of his time each day.

O. A. Battista

If one were given five minutes' warning before sudden death, five minutes to say what it had all meant to us, every telephone booth would be occupied by people trying to call up other people to stammer that they loved them.

Christopher Morley

Time was is past—thou canst it not recall.
Time is thou hast—employ thy portion small.
Time future is not, and may never be.
Time present is the only time for thee!

Inscription on an ancient sun dial.

One hour of life, crowded to the full with glorious action, and filled with noble risks, is worth whole years of those mean observances of paltry decorum, in which men steal through existence, like sluggish waters through a marsh, without either honour or observation.

Sir Walter Scott

Waiting until we older grow and richer grow before we redirect our lives, may mean waving all hope for the sustaining comfort that our faith alone can supply us. Our teachers point out that when God was about to reveal himself to Moses at the burning bush, when Moses was still a young man, Moses hid his face. When Moses grew older and prayed to see God's countenance, God told him, "No man shall see me and live. When I sought to reveal Myself, thou hiddest thy face. Now when thou seekest Me, I hide myself." He who will not when he may, perhaps may not when he will.

Joseph L. Fink

You cannot kill time without injuring eternity.

Henry Thoreau

The load of tomorrow, added to that of yesterday, carried today, makes the strongest falter. We must learn to shut off the future as tightly as the past.

William Osler

Lost: Somewhere between sunrise and sunset, two golden hours, each set with sixty diamond minutes. No reward is offered, for they are gone forever.

Horace Mann

I send you my best wishes for a year in which you will have pleasure in living every day without waiting for the days to be gone before finding charm in them, and without putting all hope of pleasure in the days to come.

Mme. Marie Curie

Happy the man, and happy he alone,
He, who can call today his own;
He who, secure within, can say:
"Tomorrow, do thy worst, for I have liv'd today."

Horace

A time of quietude brings things into proportion and gives us strength. We all need to take time from the busyness of living, even if it be only 10 minutes to watch the sun go down or the city lights blossom against a canyoned sky. We need time to dream, time to remember, and time to reach toward the infinite. Time to be.

Gladys Taber

We live in deeds, not years; in thoughts, not breaths; in feelings, not in figures on the dial; we should count time by heart throbs.

Philip James Bailey

To be able to fill leisure intelligently is the last product of civilization.

Bertrand Russell

Know the true value of time. Snatch, seize, and enjoy every moment of it. No idleness, no laziness, no procrastination. Never put off till tomorrow what you can do today.

Lord Chesterfield

If you sit down at set of sun
And count the acts that you have done,
And, counting find
One self-denying deed, one word
That eased the heart of him who heard;
One glance most kind,
That fell like sunshine where it went—
Then you may count that day well spent.

But if, through all the livelong day,
You've cheered no heart, by yea or nay—
If, through it all
You've nothing done that you can trace
That brought the sunshine to one face—
No act most small
That helped some soul and nothing cost—
Then count that day as worse than lost.

George Eliot

A fresh mind keeps the body fresh. Take in the ideas of the day, drain off those of yesterday. As to the morrow, time enough to consider it when it becomes today.

Edward George Bulwer-Lytton

He who waits to do a great deal of good at once, will never do anything.

Samuel Johnson

Life is too brief
Between the budding and the falling leaf.
Between the seed time and the golden sheaf,
For hate and spite.
We have no time for malice and for greed:
Therefore, with love make beautiful the deed;
Fast speeds the night.

W. M. Vories

The future is hidden even from those who make it.

Anatole France

Very few men, properly speaking, live at present, but are providing to live another time.

Jonathan Swift

Preoccupation with immortality is for the upper classes, particularly ladies with nothing to do. An able man, who has a regular job and must toil and produce day by day, leaves the future world to itself, and is active and useful in this one.

Johann Wolfgang von Goethe

We are but minutes, little things,
Each one furnished with sixty wings
With which we fly on our unseen track
And not a one of us ever comes back.

We are but minutes, use us well,
For how we are used we must someday tell;
Who uses minutes has hours to use,

Who loses minutes—whole years
must lose.
Author Unknown

Life is too short to be little.
Benjamin Disraeli

You better live your best and
act your best and think your best
today; for today is the sure preparation for tomorrow and all the
other tomorrows that follow.
James Martineau

The clock of life is wound but
once,
And no man has the power
To tell just when the hands will
stop—
At late or early hour.
Now is the only time you own:
Live, love, work with a will.
Place no faith in tomorrow, for—
The clock may then be still.
George H. Candler

Every day should be passed as
if it were to be our last.
Publius Syrus

If you have hard work to do,
Do it now.
Today the skies are clear and blue,
Tomorrow clouds may come in
view,
Yesterday is not for you;
Do it now.

If you have a song to sing,
Sing it now.
Let the notes of gladness ring
Clear as song of bird in Spring,
Let every day some music bring;
Sing it now.

If you have kind words to say,
Say them now.
Tomorrow may not come your way.
Do a kindness while you may,

Loved ones will not always stay;
Say them now.
If you have a smile to show,
Show it now.
Make hearts happy, roses grow,
Let the friends around you know
The love you have before they go;
Show it now.
Author Unknown

The supply of time is a daily
miracle. You wake up in the morning and lo! Your purse is magically
filled with 24 hours of the unmanu-
factured tissue of the universe of
life. It is yours! The most precious
of your possessions.
Arnold Bennett

All our seeming contradictions
arise between the today that is
merely a bridge to tomorrow and
the today that is a springboard to
eternity.
Franz Rosenzweig

Count that day lost whose low
descending sun
Views from thy hand no worthy
action done.
Jacob Bobart

Modern man's main occupation
at least in America, seems to be
leisure. What he does in his free
time may in the end determine
the fate of his civilization more
decisively than what he produces
in his working hours.
William S. Schlamm

Resolved never to do anything
which I should be afraid to do if it
were the last hour of my life.
Jonathan Edwards

Without fullness of experience,
length of days is nothing. When
fullness of life has been achieved,

shortness of days is nothing. That is perhaps why the young, ... have usually so little fear of death; they live by intensities that the elderly have forgotten.

Lewis Mumford

There is nothing of which we are so fond and with which we are so careless as life.

La Bruyere

Friends, in this world of hurry
And work and sudden end
If a thought comes quick of doing
A kindness to a friend
Do it this very instant!
Don't put it off—don't wait;
What's the use of doing a kindness
If you do it a day too late?

Author Unknown

There is something higher than modernity, and that is eternity.

Solomon Schechter

The flowers of all the tomorrows are in the seeds of today.

Chinese Proverb

So brief the hour
For work or play,
Why grieve the night
Or waste the day?

Frances M. Lipp

It isn't so much what you do dear,
As the things you leave undone
That leaves a bit of heartache
At the setting of the sun.

Margaret Sangster

The days hover like shadows about man. Each day, in which no good was done, returns to its Creator in disgrace.

Hillel Zeitlin

It is one of the illusions, that the present hour is not the critical, decisive hour. Write it on your heart that every day is the best day in the year. No man has learned anything rightly until he knows that every day is Doomsday.

Ralph Waldo Emerson

Lo, here hath been dawning
    another blue day;
Think, wilt thou let it slip useless
    away?
Out of eternity this new day is
    born,
Into eternity at night will return.
Behold it aforetime no eye ever
    did;
So soon it forever from all eyes is
    hid.
Here hath been dawning another
    blue day;
Think, wilt thou let it slip useless
    away?

Thomas Carlyle

For my own part, I live every day as if this were the first day I had ever seen and the last I were going to see.

William Lyon Phelps

Let every day be a day of humility; condescend to all the weaknesses and infirmities of your fellow-creatures, cover their frailties, love their excellencies, encourage their virtues, relieve their wants, rejoice in their prosperities, compassionate their distress, receive their friendship, overlook their unkindness, forgive their malice, be a servant of servants, and condescend to do the lowest offices to the lowest of mankind.

William Law

Time was never meant to be killed. It was meant to be used with intelligence and common sense. It is as alive as you are, moving on its ordered way, something to be cherished, not strangled to death.

Charles Hanson Towne

Men spend their lives in anticipation, in determining to be vastly happy at some period or other, when they have time. But the present time has one advantage over every other; it is our own.

Caleb C. Colton

If you are losing your leisure, look out! You may be losing your soul.

Logan Pearsall Smith

It is good for one to appreciate that life is now. Whatever it offers, little or much, life is now—this day —this hour—and is probably the only experience of the kind one is to have. As the doctor said to the woman who complained that she did not like the night air: "Madam, during certain hours of the twenty-four, night air is the only air there is."

Charles Macomb Flandrau

Bad habits are easier to abandon today than tomorrow.

Yiddish Proverb

Hors d'oeuvres have always a pathetic interest for me: they remind me of one's childhood that one goes through, wondering what the next course is going to be like—

and during the rest of the menu one wishes one had eaten more of the hors d'oeuvres.

Saki

Spend your time in nothing which you know must be repented of; in nothing on which you might not pray for the blessing of God; in nothing which you could not review with a quiet conscience on your dying bed; in nothing which you might not safely and properly be found doing if death should surprise you in the act.

Richard Baxter

Putting off an easy thing makes it difficult; putting off a hard one makes it impossible.

G. H. Lorimer

We are always complaining that our days are few, and acting as though there would be no end to them.

Seneca

Nothing lies on our hands with such uneasiness as time. Wretched and thoughtless creatures! In the only place where covetousness were a virtue we turn prodigals.

Joseph Addison

Unfaithfulness in the keeping of an appointment is an act of dishonesty. You may as well borrow a person's money as his time.

Horace Mann

---

4. THE ART OF REMEMBERING AND FORGETTING

He who receives a benefit should never forget it; he who bestows should never remember it.

Pierre Charron

Memory is a master painter, lining indelible pictures upon the mind's canvas. Time pilfers our years, our hopes, even our griefs.

But it cannot cross the threshold that leads to the domain of Memory. Here we resuscitate the past. Here we gather once more water lilies that died, but came to life again in the pool of remembrance.

Alexander A. Steinbach

A retentive memory may be a good thing, but the ability to forget is the true token of greatness.

Elbert Hubbard

Forget injuries, never forget kindnesses.

Confucius

Waste not your strength trying to push shut doors which God is opening. Neither wear yourself out in keeping open doors which ought to be forever sealed. Some episode in your life, over which you are anxious, is closed. It is in the past. Whatever its memory, you cannot change it. But you can shut the door. Go into some silent place of thought. Test your self-respect. Ask your soul, "Have I emerged from this experience with honor, or if not, can honor be retrieved?" And if your soul answers "Yes," close then the door to that Past; hang a garland over the portal if you will, but come away without tarrying. The east is aflame with the radiance of the morning, and before you stands many another door, held open by the hand of God.

Oscar Edward Maurer

The things we remember best are those better forgotten.

Baltasar Gracian

What the heart has once owned and had, it shall never lose.

Henry Ward Beecher

According to an ancient Greek legend, a woman came down to the River Styx to be ferried across to the region of departed spirits. Charon, the kindly ferryman, reminded her that it was her privilege to drink of the waters of Lethe, and thus forget the life she was leaving. Eagerly she said, "I will forget how I have suffered." "And," added Charon, "remember too that you will forget how you have rejoiced." The woman said, "I will forget my failures." The old ferryman added, "And also your victories." She continued, "I will forget how I have been hated." "And also how you have been loved," added Charon. Then she paused to consider the whole matter, and the end of the story is that she left the draught of Lethe untasted, preferring to retain the memory even of sorrow and failure rather than to give up the memory of life's loves and joys.

Ralph W. Sockman

Remembrance is a form of meeting.

Kahlil Gibran

The value of anything is what the next day's memory of it shall be.

Author Unknown

There is a noble forgetfulness—that which does not remember injuries.

Charles Simmons

If an unkind word appears,
  File the thing away.
If some novelty in jeers,
  File the thing away.
If some clever little bit
Of a sharp and pointed wit,
Carrying a sting with it—
  File the thing away.

If some bit of gossip come,
    File the thing away.
Scandalously spicy crumb,
    File the thing away.
If suspicion comes to you
That your neighbor isn't true
Let me tell you what to do—
    File the thing away.
Do this for a little while,
Then go out and burn the file.

John Kendrick Bangs

A good memory is a very nice thing to have, but a perfect memory—absolutely and unqualifiedly perfect—God forbid: It would crowd our minds like an office where nothing ever gets thrown out, neither third class mail nor fifth class nor junk.

Alexander Gode

The best repentance is to up and act for righteousness, and forget that you ever had relations with sin.

William James

Those deserve not to be forgotten who have forgotten themselves.

Gustave Vapereau

Habit is memory in action.

Comtesse Diane

In the very depths of your soul, dig a grave; let it be as some forgotten spot to which no path leads; and there in the eternal silence bury the wrongs which you have suffered. Your heart will feel as if a load had fallen from it, and a divine peace come to abide with you.

Author Unknown

So many people go through life filling the storeroom of their minds with odds and ends of a grudge here, a jealousy there, a pettiness, a selfishness—all ignoble. The true task of a man is to create a noble memory, a mind filled with grandeur, forgiveness, restless ideals, and the dynamic ethical ferment, preached by all religions at their best.

Leo Baeck

To remember much is not necessarily to be wise.

Samuel David Luzzatto

It is the lot of man to suffer, it is also his fortune to forget.

Benjamin Disraeli

Memory is a crazy woman that hoards colored rags and throws away food.

Austin O'Malley

Memory tempers prosperity, consoles adversity, cautions youth, and delights old age.

Author Unknown

Could we know what men are most apt to remember, we might know what they are most apt to do.

Lord Halifax

When a man does a noble act, date him from that. Forget his faults. Let his noble act be the standpoint from which you regard him.

Henry Whitney Bellows

His heart was as great as the world but there was no room in it to hold the memory of a wrong.

Ralph Waldo Emerson

5. THE MEASURE OF A MAN

Show me the man you honor, and I will know what kind of a man you are, for it shows me what your ideal of manhood is, and what kind of a man you long to be.

Thomas Carlyle

He is noble who both nobly feels and acts.

Heinrich Heine

I am the inferior to any man whose rights I trample under foot.

Ralph Ingersoll

It is not what he has, nor even what he does, which directly expresses the worth of a man, but what he is.

Henri F. Amiel

Qualities we look for in a liberally educated person: He is one who is deeply interested in life and enjoys it; who is sympathetic and generous in his attitude to other people, cultures, and countries; who accepts his world and himself as a growing, changing enterprise; who is sensitive to the beautiful and the ugly in actions and objects; who believes in human rights and freedom; who has a degree of knowledge and knows how to get the knowledge he does not have and who has at least a moderate skill in the art of living.

Harold L. Taylor

When God measures a man, He puts the tape around the heart instead of the head.

Author Unknown

High birth is a thing which I never knew anyone to disparage except those who had it not; and I never knew anyone to make a boast of it who had anything else to be proud of.

William Warburton

The fame of great men ought always to be estimated by the means used to acquire it.

François Rochefoucauld

What a man has is too often the standard of worth while a man is living; what he has done is the ultimate standard of the world; what he has been is God's standard.

Edward Capel Cure

The greatest want of the world is the want of men—men who will not be bought or sold; men who in their inmost souls are true and honest; men who do not fear to call sin by its right name; men whose conscience is as true to duty as the needle to the pole; men who will stand for the right though the heavens fall.

E. G. White

The pine hath a thousand years,
The rose but a day
But the pine with its thousand years
Glories not o'er the rose with its day,
If each but serves its purpose
Ere it passes away.

Japanese Proverb

We ought to call noble only those who are temperate and just, even though they belong to the class of domestic slaves.

Philo

Whether a man lives or dies in vain can be measured only by the way he faces his own problems, by the success or failure of the inner conflict within his own soul. And of this no one may know save God.

James Conant

There is gold in the golden rule for the man who does not estimate others by the rule of gold.

Elmer G. Leterman

Perhaps the strongest character in the whole Bible is the one who had the most misfortune, the one who went through untold trials. He was a man who said about God, "Though He slay me yet will I trust him." It was Job. The strong man does not always ride the wave of success. The strong man is the one who can turn the misfortune of life into character; the one who is committed to the essential and not to the superficial. He faces and overcomes inner challenges and depends not on outer acclaim.

Ensworth Reisner

I have sometimes asked myself whether my country is the better for my having lived at all.

Thomas Jefferson

One cannot always be a hero, but one can always be a man.

Johann Wolfgang von Goethe

A eulogy is customary, which is a sort of laudatory biography. But I am always aware when listening to the remarks of the mourners and looking into their thoughtful faces that the true life story of the deceased, including his mistakes as well as his good deeds, is engraved deep in the memory of his friends, and that he wrote it there himself.

Charles Francis Potter

The divine test of a man's worth is not his theology but his life.

Morris Joseph

Wealth, notoriety, place and power are no measure of success whatever. The only true measure of success is the ratio between what we might have done on the one hand and the thing we have made of ourselves on the other.

H. G. Wells

There are two kinds of men who never amount to much: those who cannot do what they are told, and those who can do nothing else.

C. H. K. Curtis

A person who is going to commit an inhuman act invariably excuses himself by saying, "I'm only human, after all."

Sydney Harris

The question is not what a man can scorn, or disparage, or find fault with, but what he can love and value and appreciate.

John Ruskin

A man is simple when his chief care is the wish to be what he ought to be, that is, honestly and naturally human.

Charles Wagner

It is the content of our lives that determines their value. If we limit ourselves to supply the means of living, in what way have we placed ourselves above the cattle that graze the fields? Cattle can live in comfort. Their every need is amply supplied. Is it not when one exercises his reason, his love of beauty, his desire for friendship, his selection of the good from that which is not so good, that he earns the right to call himself a man? I should be inclined to claim that the person who limits his interests to the means of living without consideration of the content or meaning of his life is defeating God's great purpose when he brought into existence a creature with the intelligent and godlike powers that are found in man. It is in living wisely and fully that one's soul grows.

Arthur H. Compton

A man is known through his purse, pleasure and pique.

The Talmud

I like to see a man proud of the place in which he lives. I like to see a man live so that his place will be proud of him.

Abraham Lincoln

That person is cultured who is able to put himself in the place of the greatest number of other persons.

Jane Addams

A man's treatment of money is the most decisive test of his character—how he makes it and how he spends it.

James Moffatt

If a man is interested in himself only, he is very small; if he is interested in his family, he is larger; if he is interested in his community, he is larger still.

Aristotle

What a man is in himself, what accompanies him when he is alone, what no one can give or take away, is obviously more essential to him than everything he has in the way of possessions, or even what he may be in the eyes of the world.

Arthur Schopenhauer

My point of view is that we sin in falling short of such efficiency as nature may expect according to her gifts to us.

Emil Ludwig

Where there are no men, you try to be a man.

Hillel

We do not know a nation until we know its pleasures of life, just as we do not know a man until we know how he spends his leisure. It is when a man ceases to do the things he has to do, and does the things he likes to do, that the character is revealed. It is when the repressions of society and business are gone and when the goads of money and fame and ambition are lifted, and man's spirit wanders where it listeth, that we see the inner man, his real self.

Lin Yutang

The measure of a man is not according to the number of his servants, but according to the number of people whom he serves.

Eugene Overton

I should say sincerity, a deep, great, genuine sincerity, is the characteristic of all men in any way heroic.

Thomas Carlyle

Consider whether we ought not to be more in the habit of seeking honor from our descendants than from our ancestors; thinking it better to be nobly remembered than nobly born; and striving so to live, that our sons, and our sons' sons, for ages to come, might still lead their children reverently to the doors out of which we had been carried to the grave, saying, "Look, this was his house, this was his chamber."

John Ruskin

Every man is worth just as much as the things are worth about which he is concerned.

Marcus Aurelius

The measure of a man is the way he bears up under misfortune.

Plutarch

Reputation is in itself only a farthing candle, of a wavering and uncertain flame, and easily blown out, but it is the light by which the world looks for and finds merit.

James Russell Lowell

Goodness consists not in the outward things we do, but in the inward things we are.

E. H. Chapin

Our children should be fitted for bread-winning, but they should be taught that bread-winning is only a means, not the purpose of life, and that the value of life is to be judged . . . by the good and the service to God with which it is filled.

Samson R. Hirsch

---

6. THE MARKS OF GREATNESS

Nothing is more simple than greatness; indeed, to be simple is to be great.

Ralph Waldo Emerson

One of the marks of true greatness is the ability to develop greatness in others.

J. C. Macaulay

Genius is the capacity for taking infinite pains.

Thomas Carlyle

Little minds are too much hurt by little things. Great minds perceive them all, and are not touched by them.

François Rochefoucauld

Doing easily what others find difficult is talent; doing what is impossible for talent is genius.

Henri F. Amiel

Genius is one per cent inspiration and ninety-nine per cent perspiration.

Thomas A. Edison

It is great to be great, but it is greater to be human.

Will Rogers

There are three marks of a superior man: being virtuous, he is free from anxiety; being wise, he is free from perplexity; being brave, he is free from fear.

Confucius

There are stars whose light reaches the earth only after they themselves have disintegrated and are no more. And there are men whose scintillating memory lights the world after they have passed from it. These lights which shine in the darkest night are those which illumine for us the path. . . .

Hannah Senesh

Truly great persons are more interested in controlling themselves than in controlling others. If monuments are put up to honor persons less worthy than themselves, they do not mind, for humility is one of their traits. It is probable that Einstein, acclaimed as the greatest scientist of his time, was more humble than most of the students at the university where he taught. Greatness is modest; it avoids publicity.

Clinton E. Bernard

Genius is initiative on fire.

Holbrook Jackson

What makes greatness is starting something that lives after you. That is what our great of today think and do.

Ralph W. Sockman

All times are great exactly in proportion as men feel, profoundly, their indebtedness to something or other. . . . A feeling of immeasurable obligation puts life into a man, and fight into him, and joy into him.

David Grayson

This is the final test of a gentleman: His respect for those who can be of no possible service to him.

William Lyon Phelps

He is great enough that is his own master.

Joseph Hall

Greatness of soul consists not so much in soaring high and in pressing forward, as in knowing how to adapt and limit oneself.

Michel de Montaigne

No great man ever complains of want of opportunity.

Ralph Waldo Emerson

In character, in manners, in style, in all things the supreme excellence is simplicity.

Henry Wadsworth Longfellow

No man has come to true greatness who has not felt in some degree that his life belongs to his race, and that what God gives him he gives him for mankind.

Phillips Brooks

The superior man is the providence of the inferior. He is eyes for the blind, strength for the weak, and a shield for the defenseless. He stands erect by bending above the fallen. He rises by lifting others.

Robert G. Ingersoll

Greatness consists not in holding some high office; Greatness really consists in doing some great deed with little means; in the accomplishment of vast purposes from the private ranks of life.

Russell H. Conwell

Whom, then, do I call educated? First, those who control circumstances instead of being mastered by them; those who meet all occasions manfully and act in accordance with intelligent thinking; those who are honorable in all dealings, who treat good-naturedly persons and things that are disagreeable; and furthermore, those who hold their pleasure under control and are not overcome by misfortune; finally those who are not spoiled by success.

Socrates

To bear up under loss; to fight the bitterness of defeat and the weakness of grief; to be victor over anger, to smile when tears are close; to resist disease and evil men and base instincts; to hate hate, and to love love; to go on when it would seem good to die; to look up with unquenchable faith in something ever more about to be—that is what any man can do, and be great.

Zane Grey

Greatness flees from him who seeks it, and follows him who flees from it.

The Talmud

The world turns aside to let any man pass who knows whither he is going.

David Starr Jordan

There was never yet a truly great man that was not at the same time truly virtuous.

Benjamin Franklin

Great men are the true men, the men in whom nature has succeeded. They are not extraordinary—they are in the true order. It is the other species of men who are not what they ought to be.

Henri F. Amiel

A great man is he who has not lost the heart of a child.

Mencius

The truly great consider first, how they may gain the approbation of God; and secondly, that of their own conscience; having done this, they would then willingly conciliate the good opinion of their fellowmen.

Caleb C. Colton

Great men are they who see that spiritual is stronger than any material force; that thoughts rule the world.

Ralph Waldo Emerson

The greatest achievement of the human spirit is to live up to one's opportunities and make the most of one's resources.

Vauvenargues

A great man is one who has conquered himself. He has brought order, discipline and meaning into his life and prevented it from becoming the aimless, self-centered, repulsive existence to which he is drawn by his inherited weaknesses. The process begins when a man brings a center of interest into his life. This interest must be something inspiring and elevating. If you push these requirements far enough, the center of his life can only be God.

Harold Oxley

The true test of civilization is not the census, nor the size of cities, nor the crops, but the kind of man that the country turns out.

Ralph Waldo Emerson

It is the essence of genius to make use of the simplest ideas.

Charles Peguy

No great man lives in vain. The History of the world is but the Biography of great men.

Thomas Carlyle

The great man is he who towers by half an inch above the heads of the crowd.

Felix Adler

The secret of greatness is simple: Do better work than any other man in your field—and keep on doing it.

Wilfred A. Peterson

Great minds have purposes, others have wishes.

Washington Irving

He is greatest who is most often in men's good thoughts.

Samuel Butler

Not a day passes over the earth but men and women of no note do great deeds, speak great words, and suffer noble sorrows. Of these obscure heroes, philosophers, and martyrs the greater part will never be known till that hour when many that were great shall be small, and the small great.

Charles Reade

The man who does his work, any work, conscientiously, must always be in one sense a great man.

Dinah Maria Mulock

Greatness, after all, in spite of its name, appears to be not so much a certain size as a certain quality in human lives. It may be present in lives whose range is very small.

Phillips Brooks

If we win men's hearts throughout the world, it will not be because we are a big country but because we are a great country. Bigness is imposing. But greatness is enduring.

Adlai E. Stevenson

Reverence for superiors, respect for equals, regard for inferiors— these form the supreme trinity of the virtues.

Felix Adler

No saint, no hero, no discoverer, no prophet, no leader ever did his work cheaply and easily, comfortably and painlessly, and no people was ever great which did not pass through the valley of the shadow of death on its way to greatness.

Walter Lippmann

There is a great man who makes every man feel small. But the real great man is the man who makes every man feel great.

G. K. Chesterton

To dwell in the wise house of the world,
To stand in true attitude therein,
To walk in the wide path of men,
In success to share one's principles with the people,
In failure to live them out alone,
To be incorruptible by riches or honors,
Unchangeable by poverty,
Unmoved by perils or power:
These I call the qualities of a great man.

Mencius

Let us say again that the lessons of great men are lost unless they reenforce upon our minds the highest demands which we make upon ourselves; that they are lost unless they drive our sluggish wills forward in the direction of their highest ideals.

Jane Addams

How majestic is naturalness. I have never met a man whom I really considered a great man who was not always natural and simple. Affectation is inevitably the mark of one not sure of himself.

Charles G. Dawes

The hero is one who kindles a great light in the world, who sets up blazing torches in the dark streets of life for men to see by. The saint is the man who walks through the dark paths of the world, himself a "light."

Felix Adler

There is no such thing as a little country. The greatness of a people is no more determined by their number than the greatness of a man is determined by his height.

Victor Hugo

All men are ordinary men: the extraordinary men are those who know it.

G. K. Chesterton

The most illiterate man who is touched with devotion, and uses frequent exercises of it, contracts a certain greatness of mind, mingled with a noble simplicity, that raises him above others of the same condition.

Samuel Johnson

A contemplation of God's works, a generous concern for the good of mankind, and the unfeigned exercise of humility—these only, denominate men great and glorious.

Joseph Addison

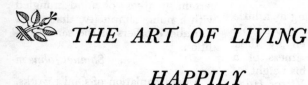

THE ART OF LIVING

HAPPILY

7. THE QUEST FOR HAPPINESS

The fountain of content must spring up in the mind, and he who has so little knowledge of human nature as to seek happiness by changing anything but his own disposition will waste his life in fruitless efforts and multiply the griefs which he purposes to remove.

Samuel Johnson

One of the finest sides to living is liking people and wanting to share activities in the human enterprise. The greatest pleasures come by giving pleasure to those who work with us, to the person who lives next door, and to those who live under the same roof. Entering into this human enterprise, feeling oneself a part of the community, is a very important element which generates happiness.

Fred J. Hafling

Unless we think of others and do something for them, we miss one of the greatest sources of happiness.

Ray Lyman Wilbur

The happy people are those who are producing something; the bored people are those who are consuming much and producing nothing.

William Ralph Inge

Most people have the idea that happiness is something that can be manufactured. They do not realize that it can no more be manufactured than wheat or corn can be manufactured. It must grow; and the harvest will be like the seed. It will take every moment that we have lived of life's probation day to think on the true, honest, just, pure and lovely things of life. These are the things that will make us contented.

Author Unknown

Amusement is the happiness of those that cannot think.

Alexander Pope

Getters generally don't get happiness; givers get it. You simply give to others a bit of yourself—a thoughtful act, a helpful idea, a word of appreciation, a lift over a rough spot, a sense of understanding, a timely suggestion. You take something out of your mind, garnished in kindness out of your heart, and put it into the other fellow's mind and heart.

Charles H. Burr

Get your happiness out of your work or you may never know what happiness is.

Elbert Hubbard

Above all, let us never forget that an act of goodness is in itself an act of happiness. It is the flower of a long inner life of joy and contentment; it tells of peaceful hours and days on the sunniest heights of our soul.

Maurice Maeterlinck

Happiness is the sense that one matters. Happiness is an abiding enthusiasm. Happiness is single-mindedness. Happiness is whole-heartedness. Happiness is a by-product. Happiness is faith.

Samuel M. Shoemaker

A multitude of small delights constitute happiness.

Charles Baudelaire

To me there is in happiness an element of self-forgetfulness. You lose yourself in something outside yourself when you are happy; just as when you are desperately miserable you are intensely conscious of yourself, are a solid little lump of ego weighing a ton.

J. B. Priestley

The grand essentials to happiness in this life are something to do, something to love, and something to hope for.

Joseph Addison

A contributing factor to happiness is to be able to enjoy the gifts of nature. The poorest man living can enjoy these, for such blessings are free. Everybody can take pleasure in a glorious sunset. You would have to pay a great sum for a painting by a skilled artist. Only the wealthy can afford it, but almost any evening we can look at a brilliant western sky, and each one of us can say, "That's mine!"

David O. McKay

Happiness in this world, when it comes, comes incidentally. Make it the object of pursuit, and it leads us a wild-goose chase, and is never attained. Follow some other object, and very possibly we may find that we have caught happiness without dreaming of it.

Nathaniel Hawthorne

The habit of being happy enables one to be freed, or largely freed, from the domination of outward conditions.

Robert Louis Stevenson

The way to be happy is to make others so.

Ralph Ingersoll

We can only have the highest happiness, such as goes along with being a great man, by having wide thoughts and much feeling for the rest of the world as well as ourselves; and this sort of happiness often brings much pain with it. . . . There are so many things wrong and difficult in the world, that no man can be great unless he gives up thinking much about pleasure and rewards, and gets strength to endure what is hard and painful.

George Eliot

In order that people may be happy in their work, these three things are needed: They must be fit for it: They must not do too much of it: And they must have a sense of success in it.

John Ruskin

Your success and happiness lie in you. External conditions are the accidents of life. The great enduring realities are love and service. Joy is the holy fire that keeps our purpose warm and our intelligence aglow. Resolve to keep happy and your joy in you shall form an invincible host against difficulty.

Helen Keller

Few persons realize how much of their happiness is dependent upon their work, upon the fact that they are kept busy and not left to feed upon themselves. Happiness comes most to persons who seek her least, and think least about it. It is not an object to be sought; it is a state to be induced. It must follow and not lead. It must overtake you, and not you overtake it.

John Burroughs

In every part and corner of our life, to lose oneself is to be gainer; to forget oneself is to be happy.

Robert Louis Stevenson

Happiness has little to do with age, circumstances, health, wealth, learning or status. It follows as you become a part of life's *solution* rather than its *problem*.

Roy C. McLain

Happiness is not the end of life; character is.

Henry Ward Beecher

God has so constituted our nature that we cannot be happy unless we are, or think we are, the means of good to others. We can scarcely conceive of greater wretchedness than must be felt by him who knows he is wholly useless in the world.

Erskine Mason

The foolish man seeks happiness in the distance;
The wise grows it under his feet.

James Oppenheim

The world would be better and brighter if our teachers would dwell on the Duty of Happiness as well as on the Happiness of Duty, for we ought to be as cheerful as we can, if only because to be happy ourselves is the most effectual contribution to the happiness of others.

John Lubbock Avebury

Anything you're good at contributes to happiness.

Bertrand Russell

Civilization, in the real sense of the term, consists not in the multiplication, but in the deliberate and voluntary reduction of wants. This alone promotes real happiness and contentment, and increases the capacity for service.

Mohandas K. Gandhi

That person lives in hell who gets what he desires too soon. Whether he finds his happiness in wealth, power, fame or women, or in a combination of all, that happiness will be meaningless if it robs him of his desire. Heaven is a country through which we are permitted to search eagerly and with hope for what we want.

Thomas Dreier

I have learned to seek my happiness by limiting my desires, rather than in attempting to satisfy them.

John Stuart Mill

The secret of being miserable is to have leisure to bother about whether you are happy or not.

George Bernard Shaw

Never mind your happiness; do your duty.

Will Durant

One day my life will end; and lest
Some whim should prompt you to review it,
Let her who knows the subject best
Tell you the shortest way to do it:
Then say, "Here lies one doubly blest."
Say, "She was happy." Say, "She knew it."

Jan Struther

The best way to attain happiness is not to seek it.

Claude G. Montefiore

We act as though comfort and luxury were the chief requirements of life, when all that we need to make us really happy is something to be enthusiastic about.

Charles Kingsley

The purpose of life is not to be happy—but to *matter,* to be productive, to be useful, to have it make some difference that you lived at all.

Leo Rosten

He who enjoys doing and enjoys what he has done is happy.

Johann Wolfgang von Goethe

Goodness does not more certainly make men happy than happiness makes them good.

W. S. Landor

A man who has had his way is seldom happy, for generally he finds that the way does not lead very far on this earth of desires which can never be fully satisfied.

Joseph Conrad

The belief that youth is the happiest time of life is founded on a fallacy. The happiest person is the person who thinks the most interesting thoughts, and we grow happier as we grow older.

William Lyon Phelps

If one only wished to be happy, this could be easily accomplished; but we wish to be happier than other people, and this is always difficult, for we believe others to be happier than they are.

Montesquieu

The fact is that we can find happiness only in serving others. Just as a car is designed to move, so is a man designed to serve. And if he looks for happiness in anything other than service and sacrifice, he will always be disappointed.

Harold Oxley

The harvest of happiness is most often reaped by the hands of helpfulness.

Author Unknown

Happiness is in the taste, and not in the things themselves; we are happy from possessing what we like, not from possessing what others like.

François Rochefoucauld

Happiness! It is useless to seek it elsewhere than in this warmth of human relations. Our sordid interests imprison us within their walls. Only a comrade can grasp us by the hand and haul us free.

Antoine De Saint Exupery

The only true happiness comes from squandering ourselves for a purpose.

John Mason Brown

Happiness is like coke—something you get as a by-product in the process of making something else.

Aldous Huxley

This is the true joy of life, the being used for a purpose recognized by yourself as a mighty one; the being thoroughly worn out before you are thrown on the scrap heap; the being a force of Nature instead of a feverish selfish little clod of ailments and grievances complaining that the world will not devote itself to making you happy.

George Bernard Shaw

To be happy is not the purpose of our being, but to deserve happiness.

Immanuel Hermann Fichte

What happiness is, no person can say for another. But no one, I am convinced, can be happy who lives only for himself. The joy of living comes from immersion in something that we know to be bigger, better, more enduring and worthier than we are.

John Mason Brown

Happiness is not found in self-contemplation, it is perceived only when it is reflected from another.

Samuel Johnson

Man is meant for happiness and this happiness is in him, in the satisfaction of the daily needs of his existence.

Leo Tolstoi

You never see the stock called Happiness quoted on the exchange.

Henry Van Dyke

A brook is going somewhere. It is water-on-a-mission. About to present itself to other waters at its destination, it never neglects little wayside opportunities. On its way to make its final offering, it gaily gives itself all along the way. Deer drink of its refreshing coolness with a deep content. Boys of seven years and of seventy probe its pools and eddies with their lures and return home at day's end with the brook's gift of speckled trout. Fish, crustaceans, mollusks, and water insects are given a home in its swirling currents and tranquil pools. From its birth in bubbling springs to its arrival at its final goal the brook is selfless and a happy appearing thing. Service and happiness belong together.

Harold E. Kohn

The real secret of happiness is simply this: To be willing to live and let live, and to know very clearly in one's own mind that the unpardonable sin is to be an unpleasant person.

Galen Starr Ross

If I could show you the cabbages which I have planted here with my own hands, you would not urge me to relinquish the joys of happiness for the pursuit of power.

Diocletian

He who harbors a slight will miss the haven of happiness.

Author Unknown

The great point is to know one's own inconsistencies, and to keep those which are the most conducive to happiness.

Jean J. Rosseau

Most folks are about as happy as they make up their minds to be.

Abraham Lincoln

The best way to secure future happiness is to be as happy as is rightfully possible to-day.

Charles W. Eliot

The happiest people seem to be those who have no particular cause for being happy except that they are so.

William Ralph Inge

I always give much away, and so gather happiness instead of pleasure.

Rachel Levin Varnhagen

There is this difference between happiness and wisdom, that he that thinks himself the happiest man, really is so; but he that thinks himself the wisest, is generally the greatest fool.

Caleb C. Colton

Happiness is not so much in having as sharing. We make a living by what we get, but we make a life by what we give.

Norman MacEwan

Happiness is a rebound from hard work. One of the follies of man is to assume that he can enjoy mere emotion. As well try to eat beauty! Happiness must be tricked. She loves to see men work. She loves sweat, weariness, self-sacrifice. She will not be found in palaces, but lurking in cornfields and factories, and hovering over littered desks. She crowns the unconscious head of the busy child.

David Grayson

No one has any more right to go about unhappy than he has to go about ill-bred.

Lillian Whiting

He owes it to himself, to his friends, to society and to the community in general to live up to his best spiritual possibilities.

Lillian Whiting

Happiness sneaks in through a door you didn't know you left open.

John Barrymore

Happiness is a sunbeam which may pass through a thousand bosoms without losing a particle of its original ray; nay, when it strikes on a kindred heart, like the converged light on a mirror, it reflects itself with redoubled brightness.—It is not perfected till it is shared.

Jane Porter

The envious are not happy unless they are making other people envious.

Comtesse Diane

Happiness grows at our own firesides, and is not to be picked in strangers' gardens.

Douglas Jerrold

To look fearlessly upon life; to accept the laws of nature, not with meek resignation, but as her sons, who dare to search and question; to have peace and confidence within our souls—these are the beliefs that make for happiness.

Maurice Maeterlinck

A man who finds no satisfaction in himself, seeks for it in vain elsewhere.

Francois Rochefoucauld

A man's felicity consists not in the outward and visible blessings of fortune, but in the inward and unseen perfections and riches of the mind.

Anacharsis

Pleasure is very seldom found where it is sought. Our brightest blazes are commonly kindled by unexpected sparks.

Samuel Johnson

Happiness is a perfume you cannot pour on others without getting a few drops on yourself.

Ralph Waldo Emerson

Happiness can be built only on virtue, and must of necessity have truth for its foundation.

Samuel T. Coleridge

Many persons have a wrong idea about what constitutes true happiness. It is not attained through self-gratification, but through fidelity to a worthy purpose.

Helen Keller

Unhappiness lies in not knowing what we want out of life and killing ourselves to get it.

Author Unknown

In our frantic search for happiness we assume it resides in something that we can possess or manipulate: a spacious home, smart clothes, powerful automobiles or a huge bank account; we think of expensive vacations or costly amusements. We are sorely mistaken. If we have material comforts and at the same time possess happiness, it means that our happiness stems from within ourselves. It resides in something we are, not in what we have.

Kenneth Hildebrand

Happiness is not in our circumstances but in ourselves. It is not something we see, like a rainbow, or feel, like the heat of a fire. Happiness is something we are.

John B. Sheerin

The art of being happy lies in the power of extracting happiness from common things.

Henry Ward Beecher

A man may lose his strength; he may lose his money; he may lose every earthly thing which he possesses. Yet he may still attain and control his happiness if it stems from service to others.

He who makes service to others his method of obtaining happiness has in his possession something which comes from within his own mind, from within his own soul, and which is controlled largely by his own will or desire. Most other things are beyond control of an individual, and circumstances may deprive him of them.

George E. Mathieu

Only one thing I know. The only ones among you who will be really happy are those who will have sought and found how to serve.

Albert Schweitzer

To be of use in the world is the only way to be happy.

Hans Christian Andersen

The man who is born with a talent which he is meant to use finds his greatest happiness in using it.

Johann Wolfgang von Goethe

Those only are happy who have their minds fixed on some object other than their own happiness; on the happiness of others, on the improvement of mankind, even on some art or pursuit, followed not as a means but as itself an ideal end. Aiming thus at something else, they find happiness by the way. . . . Ask yourself whether you are happy, and you cease to be so. The only chance is to treat, not happiness, but some end external to it, as the purpose of life.

John Stuart Mill

Happiness and beauty are by-products. Folly is the direct pursuit of happiness and beauty.

George Bernard Shaw

Success is getting what you want; happiness is wanting what you get.

Author Unknown

They must often change who would be constant in happiness or wisdom.

Oliver Goldsmith

Search for a single, inclusive good is doomed to failure. Such happiness as life is capable of comes from the full participation of all our powers in the endeavor to wrest from each changing situation of experience its own full and unique meaning.

John Dewey

Happiness is a way station between too little and too much.

Channing Pollock

Happiness is not found, it is made. One can only give the seed of happiness to another. Each one must make it grow within himself.

Marciso Irala

Happiness is not given but exchanged.

Author Unknown

He who seeks only for applause from without has all his happiness in another's keeping.

Oliver Goldsmith

We cannot have happiness until we forget to seek for it.

Henry Van Dyke

Happiness is where it is found, and seldom where it is sought.

Josh Billings

Happiness is not a station you arrive at, but a manner of traveling.

Margaret Lee Runbeck

That kind of life is most happy which affords us most opportunities of gaining our own esteem.

Samuel Johnson

I believe the root of all happiness on this earth to lie in the realization of a spiritual life with a consciousness of something wider than materialism; in the capacity to live in a world that makes you unselfish because you are not overanxious about your personal place; that makes you tolerant because you realize your own comic fallibilities; that gives you tranquillity without complacency because you believe in something so much larger than yourself.

Sir Hugh Walpole

To awaken each morning with a smile brightening my face; to greet the day with reverence for the opportunities it contains; to approach my work with a clean mind; to hold ever before me, even in the doing of little things, the Ultimate Purpose toward which I am working; to meet men and women with laughter on my lips and love in my heart; to be gentle, kind, and courteous through all the hours; to approach the night with weariness that ever woos sleep and the joy that comes from work well done—this is how I desire to waste wisely my days.

Thomas Dekker

It is one of the many paradoxes of psychology that the pursuit of happiness defeats its own purpose. We find happiness only when we do not directly seek it. An analogy will make this clear. In listening to music at a concert, we experience pleasurable feelings only so long as our attention is directed towards the music. But if in order to increase our happiness we give all our attention to our subjective feeling of happiness, it vanishes. Nature contrives to make it impossible for anyone to attain happiness by turning into himself.

J. Arthur Hadfield

Happiness is not given but exchanged.

Comtesse Diane

If you observe a really happy man, you will find him building a boat, writing a symphony, educating his son, growing double dahlias or looking for dinosaur eggs in the Gobi Desert. He will not be searching for happiness as if it were a collar button that had rolled under the radiator, striving for it as a

goal in itself. He will have become aware that he is happy in the course of living life twenty-four crowded hours of each day.

W. Beram Wolfe

To be happy is easy enough if we give ourselves, forgive others, and live with thanksgiving. No self-centered person, no ungrateful soul can ever be happy, much less make anyone else happy. Life is giving, not getting.

Joseph Fort Newton

If you ever find happiness by hunting for it, you will find it as the old woman did her lost spectacles —on her own nose all the time.

Josh Billings

To be happy, we must be true to nature, and carry our age along with us.

William Hazlitt

The secret of happiness is renunciation.

Andrew Carnegie

An honest reputation is within the reach of all men; they obtain it by social virtues, and by doing their duty. This kind of reputation, it is true, is neither brilliant nor startling, but it is often the most useful for happiness.

Charles Pinot Duclos

Happiness is a habit—cultivate it.

Elbert Hubbard

A big dog saw a little dog chasing its tail and asked, "Why are you chasing your tail so?" Said the puppy, "I have mastered philosophy; I have solved the problems of the universe which no dog before me has rightly solved; I have learned that the best thing for a dog is happiness, and that happiness is my tail. Therefore I am chasing it; and when I catch it I shall have happiness."

Said the old dog, "My son, I, too, have paid attention to the problems of the universe in my weak way, and I have formed some opinions. I, too, have judged that happiness is a fine thing for a dog, and that happiness is in my tail. But I have noticed that when I chase after it, it keeps running away from me, but when I go about my business, it comes after me."

C. L. James

We have no more right to consume happiness without producing it than to consume wealth without producing it.

George Bernard Shaw

Happiness? It is an illusion to think that more comfort means more happiness. Happiness comes of the capacity to feel deeply, to enjoy simply, to think freely, to risk life, to be needed.

Storm Jameson

Happiness does not come from possessions, but from our appreciation of them. It does not come from our work, but from our attitude toward that work. It does not come from success, but from the spiritual growth we attain in achieving that success.

Author Unknown

The supreme happiness of life is the conviction of being loved for yourself, or, more correctly, being loved in spite of yourself.

Victor Hugo

---

8. THE JOY OF LIVING

There is no cure for birth and death save to enjoy the interval.

George Santayana

Oh, the wild joys of living! the leaping from rock to rock,
The strong rending of boughs from the fir-tree, the cool silver shock
Of the plunge in the pool's living water, the hunt of the bear,
And the sultriness showing the lion is couched in his lair.
And the meal, the rich dates yellowed over the gold dust divine,
And the locust-flesh steeped in the pitcher, the full draft of wine,
And the sleep in the dried river-channel where bulrushes tell

That the water was wont to go warbling so softly and well.
How good is man's life, the mere living! how fit to employ
All the heart and the soul and the senses forever in joy!

Robert Browning

Life is most enjoy'd,
When courted least; most worth, when disesteemed.

Edward Young

On the whole I am on the side of the unregenerate who affirm the worth of life as an end in itself as against the saints who deny it.

Oliver Wendell Holmes, Jr.

It is untrue to say a man has made his fortune when he is not capable of enjoying it.

Vauvenargues

A greater poverty than that caused by lack of money is the poverty of unawareness. Men and women go about the world unaware of the beauty, the goodness, the glories in it. Their souls are poor. It is better to have a poor pocket-book than to suffer from a poor soul.

Thomas Dreier

Sunshine is delicious, rain is refreshing, wind braces up, snow is exhilarating; there is no such thing as bad weather, only different kinds of weather.

John Ruskin

All the wonderful things in life are so simple that one is not aware of their wonder until they are beyond touch. Never have I felt the wonder and beauty and joy of life so keenly as now in my grief that Johnny is not here to enjoy them. Today, when I see parents impatient or tired or bored with their children, I wish I could say to them, But they are alive, think of the wonder of that! They may be a care and a burden, but think, they are alive! You can touch them— what a miracle! All parents who have lost a child will feel what I mean. Others, luckily, cannot. But I hope they will embrace them with a little added rapture and a keener awareness of joy.

Frances Gunther

If your morals make you dreary, depend upon it they are wrong.

Robert Louis Stevenson

Nothing is so contagious as enthusiasm. It is the real allegory of the tale of Orpheus; it moves stones and charms brutes. It is the genius of sincerity and truth accomplishes no victories without it.

Edward Bulwer-Lytton

When a man dies, if he can pass enthusiasm along to his children, he has left them an estate of incalculable value.

Thomas A. Edison

Years wrinkle the skin, but to give up enthusiasm wrinkles the soul.

Samuel Ullman

Nature, in zeal for human amity,
Denies or damps an undivided joy.
Joy is an import; joy is an exchange;
Joy flies monopolists: it calls for two.

Edward Young

Every great and commanding movement in the annals of the world is the triumph of enthusiasm.

Ralph Waldo Emerson

Birth, the commonest of all occurrences, never ceases to be the most wonderful.

George Moore

Enthusiasm is like having two right hands.

Elbert Hubbard

A man can succeed at almost anything for which he has unlimited enthusiasm.

Charles Schwab

There is a pleasure in the pathless woods,
There is a rapture on the lonely shore,

There is society where none intrudes
By the deep sea, and music in its roar:
I love not man the less but nature more
From these our interviews, in which I steal
From all I may be or have been before
To mingle with the universe and feel
What I can ne'er express, yet cannot all conceal.

Lord Byron

'Tis much the doctrine of the times, that men should not please themselves, but deny themselves everything they take delight in; not look upon beauty, wear no good clothes, eat no good meat, etc., which seems the greatest accusation that can be upon the maker of all good things. If they be not to be used, why did God make them?

John Selden

We men are always complaining that our happy hours are so few and our sad hours so many, and yet it is we who are to blame. If we opened our hearts to enjoy the good that God offers us every day we should have strength enough to bear the evil in its turn when it does come.

Johann Wolfgang von Goethe

Optimism is the chemical ingredient which we can use daily in our lives to transform the clouds of discouragement to the harbinger of hope that the sun may again appear before our vision.

Earl G. Stanza

It is a glorious privilege to live, to know, to act, to listen, to behold, to love. To look up at the blue summer sky; to see the sun sink slowly belond the line of the horizon; to watch the worlds come twinkling into view, first one by one, and the myriads that no man can count, and lo! the universe is white with them; and you and I are here.

Marco Morrow

There are two things to aim at in life: first, to get what you want; and, after that, to enjoy it. Only the wisest of mankind achieve the second.

Logan Pearsall Smith

Life is not to be spent anticipating a reward or not, or endured, or anything of the kind, but it is to be enjoyed to the last detail.

Theodore Dreiser

9. THE ART OF CONTENTMENT

All the discontented people I know are trying sedulously to be something they are not, to do something they cannot do.

David Grayson

The secret of contentment is knowing how to enjoy what you have, and to be able to lose all desire for things beyond your reach.

Lin Yutang

Nor hell nor heaven shall that soul
  surprise,
Who loves the rain,
And loves his home,
And looks on life with quiet eyes.
Frances Shaw

The City of Contentment is in
the State of Mind.
Author Unknown

When you are disposed to be
vain of your mental acquirements,
look up to those who are more accomplished than yourself, that you
may be fired with emulation; but
when you feel dissatisfied with your
circumstances, look down on those
beneath you, that you may learn
contentment.
Hannah More

Happy the man, of mortals happiest he,
Whose quiet mind from vain desires is free;
Whom neither hopes deceive, nor
  fears torment,
But lives at peace, within himself
  content.
George Granville

A harvest of peace is produced
from a seed of contentment.
Author Unknown

Envy deserves pity more than
anger, for it hurts nobody so much
as itself. It is a distemper rather
than a vice: for nobody would feel
envy if he could help it. Whoever
envies another, secretly allows that
person's superiority.
Horace Walpole

It is not miserable to be blind; it
is miserable to be incapable of enduring blindness.
John Milton

I am always content with that
which happens, for I think that
which God chooses is better than
what I choose.
Epictetus

The truest kinship with humanity
would lie in doing as humanity has
always done, accepting with sports-
manlike relish the estate to which
we are called, the star of our happiness, and the fortunes of the land
of our birth.
G. K. Chesterton

Serenity comes to the man who
lives with an unfaltering faith in an
unfailing God. The person who
lives with eternity in his heart will
find a strange calm in his spirit.
Joseph R. Sizoo

You traverse the world in search
of happiness, which is within reach
of every man: a contented mind
confers it on all.
Horace

The man who consecrates his hours
By vig'rous effort and an honest
  aim,
At once he draws the sting of life
  and death;
He walks with nature; and her
  paths are peace.
Edward Young

As I watch my fellow citizens, I
realize it's not easy to be content
with little. But it seems much
harder to be content with a great
deal.
Burton Hillis

Happiness consists not in having
much, but in being content with
little.
Lady Marguerite Blessington

When Pyrrhus was about to sail for Italy, Cineas, a wise and good man, asked him what were his intentions and expectations. "To conquer Rome," said Pyrrhus.

"And after that?"

"We will subdue Carthage, Macedonia, all Africa and all Greece."

"And when we have conquered all we can, what shall we do?"

"Do? Why, then we will sit down and spend our time in peace and comfort."

"Ah, my Lord," said the wise Cineas, "what prevents our being in peace and comfort now?"

George Lincoln Walton

Those who are at war with others are not at peace with themselves.

William Hazlitt

Do not despise your situation; in it you must act, suffer, and conquer. From every point on earth we are equally near to heaven and to the infinite.

Henri F. Amiel

A man must seek his happiness and inward peace from objects which cannot be taken away from him.

Alexander Humboldt

Envy, like flame, blackens that which is above it, and which it cannot reach.

Jean Antoine Petit-Senn

A man whose heart is not content is like a snake which tries to swallow an elephant.

Chinese Proverb

Nothing can bring you peace but yourself. Nothing can bring you peace but the triumph of principle.

Ralph Waldo Emerson

My crown is in my heart, not on my head;
Not deck'd with diamonds and Indian stones,
Nor to be seen: my crown is called content.

William Shakespeare

A contented mind is the greatest blessing a man can enjoy in this world.

Joseph Addison

Whatever your career may be, do not let yourselves become tainted by a deprecating and barren skepticism, do not let yourselves be discouraged by the sadness of certain hours which pass over nations. Live in the serene peace of laboratories and libraries. Say to yourselves first, "What have I done for my instruction?" and as you gradually advance, "What have I done for my country?" until the time comes when you may have the immense happiness of thinking that you have contributed in some way to the progress and to the good of humanity. But whether our efforts are, or not, favored by life, let us be able to say, when we come near the great goal, "I have done what I could."

Louis Pasteur

True contentment depends not upon what we have; a tub was large enough for Diogenes, but a world was too little for Alexander.

Caleb C. Colton

The fountain of content must spring up in the mind; and he who has so little knowledge of human nature as to seek happiness by changing anything but his own disposition, will waste his life in fruitless efforts, and multiply the griefs which he purposes to remove.

Samuel Johnson

The mind is a river; upon its water thoughts float through in a constant procession every conscious moment. It is a narrow river, however, and you stand on a bridge over it and can stop and turn back any thought that comes along, and they can come only single file, one at a time. The art of contentment is to let no thought pass that is going to disturb you.

Frank Crane

To be of service is a solid foundation for contentment in the world.

Charles W. Eliot

Great tranquillity of heart is his who cares for neither praise nor blame.

Thomas à Kempis

Nothing is enough for the man to whom enough is too little.

Epicurus

All men believe they deserve the best places; but nature not having made them fit to fill them contrives that they fill the lowest very happily.

Vauvenargues

Content makes poor men rich; discontent makes rich men poor.

Author Unknown

When God sorts out the weather and sends rain,
Why rain's my choice.

James Whitcomb Riley

When the camel demanded horns, they cut off his ears.

The Talmud

When a man is sure that all he wants is happiness, then most grievously he deceives himself. All men desire happiness, but they need something far different, compared to which happiness is trivial, and in the lack of which happiness turns to bitterness in the mouth. There are many names for that which men need—"the one thing needful"—but the simplest is "wholeness."

John Middleton Murry

The usual fortune of complaint is to excite contempt more than pity.

Samuel Johnson

A strong determination to get the best out of life; a keen desire to enjoy what one has, and no regrets if one fails: this is the secret of the Chinese genius for contentment.

Lin Yutang

Dig a big hole in the garden of your thoughts. Into it put all your disillusions, disappointments, regrets, worries, troubles, doubts and fears—and forget. Cover well with the earth of fruitfulness. Water it from the well of content. Sow on top the seeds of hope, courage, strength, patience and love. Then, when the time of gathering comes, may your harvest be a rich and fruitful one.

Author Unknown

It is our duty to compose our character, not to compose books, and to win, not battles and provinces, but order and tranquillity for our conduct of life.

Michel de Montaigne

He that always complains is never pitied.

Author Unknown

Joy is indeed a precious quality which very few experience in their lives. The person who knows how to enjoy life will never grow old no matter how many years he can call his own. It is easy to be happy at specific times, but there is a certain art in being happy and contented every day.

Ora Capelli

Those who complain most are most to be complained of.

Matthew Henry

I have often observed that resignation is never so perfect as when the blessing denied begins to lose somewhat of its value in our eyes.

Jane Austen

When people complain of life, it is almost always because they have asked impossible things from it.

Ernest Renan

There is but one way to tranquillity of mind and happiness, and that is to account no external things thine own, but to commit all to God.

Epictetus

Peace of mind may transform a cottage into a spacious manor hall; the want of it can make a regal park an imprisoning nutshell.

Joshua Loth Liebman

Who seeks more than he has hinders himself from enjoying what he has.

Solomon Ibn Gabirol

Envy cannot be concealed. Envy accuses and judges without proof, makes defects seem bigger than they are, and has tremendous epithets for the smallest faults; its speech is full of gall, exaggeration, and insult; it fastens upon merit with a desperate rage and pertinacity; it is blind, furious, insensate, and savage.

Vauvenargues

He will easily be content and at peace, whose conscience is pure.

Thomas à Kempis

When we cannot find contentment in ourselves, it is useless to seek it elsewhere.

Francois Rochefoucauld

He is happy whose circumstances suit his temper; but he is more excellent who can suit his temper to any circumstances.

David Hume

The crop always seems better in our neighbor's field, and our neighbor's cow gives more milk.

Ovid

It is right to be contented with what we have, never with what we are.

Sir James Mackintosh

Quiet minds cannot be perplexed or frightened, but go on in fortune or misfortune at their own private pace, like a clock during a thunderstorm.

Robert Louis Stevenson

10. THE ART OF LAUGHTER

Health and cheerfulness mutually beget each other.

Joseph Addison

If only men could be induced to laugh more they might hate less, and find more serenity here on earth. If they cannot worship together, or accept the same laws, or tolerate the wonderful diversity of thought and behavior and physique with which they have been blessed, at least they can laugh together.

Malcolm Muggeridge

Learn to laugh. And most of all, learn to laugh at yourself. The person who can give a riotous account of his own faux pas, will never have to listen to another's embarrassing account of it. He will rarely know the sting of humiliation. He is a delight to be with; but more important, he is enjoying his own life, and applying to his ills and errors the most soothing balm the human spirit has devised—laughter.

Margaret M. Butts

Laughter should dimple the cheek, not furrow the brow. A jest should be such that all shall be able to join in the laugh which it occasions; but if it bears hard upon one of the company, like the crack of a string, it makes a stop in the music.

Owen Feltham

Life pays a bonus to those who learn that laughter is a vital part of living. It is one of God's richest gifts. The Lord loves a cheerful giver; but He also loves the cheerful—period. And so does everyone else.

Edwin Davis

Strange, when you come to think of it, that of all countless folk who have lived on this planet not one is known in history or in legend as having died of laughter.

Sir Max Beerbohm

With the fearful strain that is on me night and day, if I did not laugh I should die.

Abraham Lincoln

Religion, in whatever form, is consolation for the pain of life. Humor is the instinct for taking pain playfully. They both are inseparable.

Max Eastman

The laughter of man is the contentment of God.

Eugene P. Bertin

A nation that knows how to laugh at itself is stronger and has greater survival value than one that takes itself with ponderous solemnity; the weakness of Germany, since Bismarck's day, lay not in its arms but in its incapacity to make fun of its own institutions.

Sydney J. Harris

There is the laughter which is born out of the pure joy of living, the spontaneous expression of health and energy—the sweet laughter of the child. This is a gift of God. There is the warm laughter of the kindly soul which heartens the discouraged, gives health to the sick and comfort to the dying . . .

There is, above all, the laughter that comes from the eternal joy of creation, the joy of making the world new, the joy of expressing the inner riches of the soul—laughter that triumphs over pain and hardship in the passion for an enduring ideal, the joy of bringing the light of happiness, of truth and beauty into a dark world. This is divine laughter par excellence.

J. E. Boodin

The laughter of satire is contemptuous; of comedy, courteous; of humor, loving.

Austin O'Malley

One should take good care not to grow too wise for so great a pleasure of life as laughter.

Joseph Addison

'Tis easy enough to be pleasant,
When life flows along like a song;
But the man worth while is the
one who will smile
When everything goes dead wrong.

Ella Wheeler Wilcox

True humor springs not more from the head than from the heart; it is not contempt, its essence is love.

Thomas Carlyle

The freedom of any society varies proportionately with the volume of its laughter.

Zero Mostel

This old, old world is a dreary place
For the man whose pass is a frowning face;
Who looks for the shadows instead of the light,
For the sordid and dull instead of the bright;

Who sees but the worry and labor and strife
Instead of the glory and sunshine of life.

But for him who possesses the saving grace
Of a laughing heart and a smiling face,
Who sings at his work and laughs at defeat,
And looks for the good and the bright and the sweet,
Who cheers on his fellows by word and by deed,
This world is a pleasant place indeed.

Emil Carl Aurin

Smiles are as catchin' as the measles and a whole lot more pleasant.

Harvey Hamlyn

Smile a smile. While you smile, another smiles,
And soon there's miles and miles of smiles,
And life's worth while if you but smile.

Author Unknown

Jests that give pain are no jests.

Cervantes

Weep before God—laugh before people.

Yiddish Proverb

While there is infection in disease and sorrow, there is nothing in the world quite so irresistibly contagious as laughter and good humor.

Charles Dickens

Laughter is a green semaphore on the road of human relationship; it is a hand in the darkness, a

whisper of courage in the storm.
Douglas Meador

A man without mirth is like a wagon without springs. He is jolted disagreeably by every pebble in the road.
Henry Ward Beecher

Laughter is an integral part of life, one that we could ill afford to lose. If I were asked what single quality every human being needs more than any other, I would answer, the ability to laugh at himself. When we see our own grotesqueries, how droll our ambitions are, how comical we are in almost all respects, we automatically become more sane, less self-centered, more humble, more wholesome. To laugh at ourselves we have to stand outside ourselves—and that is an immense benefit. Our puffed-up pride and touchy self-importance vanish; a clean and sweet humility begins to take possession of us. We are on the way to growing a soul.
A. Powell Davies

The men whom I have seen succeed best in life have always been cheerful and hopeful men who went about their business with a smile on their faces and took the changes and chances of this mortal life like men, facing rough and smooth alike as it came.
Charles Kingsley

Nothing on earth can smile but man. Gems may flash reflected light, but what is a diamond-flash compared to an eye-flash and a mirth-flash? Flowers cannot smile; this is a charm that even they cannot claim. It is the prerogative of man; it is the color which love

wears, and cheerfulness, and joy—these three. It is a light in the windows of the face by which the heart signifies it is at home and waiting. A face that cannot smile is like a bud that cannot blossom, and dries up on the stalk. Laughter is day, and sobriety is night, and a smile is the twilight that hovers gently between both—more bewitching than either.
Henry Ward Beecher

Are you worsted in a fight?
Laugh it off.
Are you cheated of your right?
Laugh it off.
Don't make tragedy of trifles,
Don't shoot butterflies with rifles—
Laugh it off.

Does your work get into kinks?
Laugh it off.
Are you near all sorts of brinks?
Laugh it off.
If it's sanity you're after
There's no recipe like laughter—
Laugh it off.
Henry Rutherford Elliot

Laughter, of course, is an activity not of the jaw muscles, but of the mind; indeed, silent laughter is usually the most fitting and satisfied form of mirth with which to confront matters of the profoundest import. The ability to laugh, silently or aloud, at moments of ultimate crisis is a sublime attribute: an expression of everything in us that is human and most civilized.
Julius Novick

For health and the constant enjoyment of life, give me a keen and ever present sense of humor; it is the next best thing to an abiding faith in providence.
George B. Cheever

Frame your mind to mirth and merriment
Which bar a thousand harms and lengthen life.

William Shakespeare

Humor is an affirmation of dignity, a declaration of man's superiority to all that befalls him.

Romain Gary

The most wasted of all days is that during which one has not laughed.

Sebastian Chamfort

Cheerfulness is the best promoter of health, and is as friendly to the mind as to the body.

Joseph Addison

The young man who has not wept is a savage, and the old man who will not laugh is a fool.

George Santayana

When the first baby laughed for the first time, the laugh broke into a million pieces, and they all went skipping about. That was the beginning of fairies.

James Barrie

I have always noticed that deeply and truly religious persons are fond of a joke, and I am suspicious of those who aren't.

Alfred North Whitehead

It takes thirty-four muscles to frown, and only thirteen to smile. Why make the extra effort?

Author Unknown

That laughter costs too much which is purchased by the sacrifice of decency.

Quintilian

Optimism: A cheerful frame of mind that enables a tea kettle to sing though in hot water up to its nose.

Anonymous

Laughter is one of the best things that God has given us, and with hearty laughter neither malice nor indecency can exist.

Stanley Baldwin

A sense of humor is a sense of proportion.

Kahlil Gibran

A smile on your lips;
Cheers your heart,
Keeps you in good humor,
Preserves peace in your soul,
Promotes your health,
Beautifies your face
Induces kindly thoughts,
Inspires kindly deeds.

Author Unknown

Laughter, even if its edge is bitter, is the safety-valve. We can counter evil so long as we can discover in it some element that can be brought to ridicule. But when laughter is snuffed out, we are forced into a retreat from which there seems no possibility of escape.

John O'London

Imagination was given to man to compensate him for what he is not; and a sense of humor was provided to console him for what he is.

Author Unknown

God is the creator of laughter that is good.

Philo

If we consider the frequent reliefs we receive from laughter, and how often it breaks the gloom which is apt to depress the mind, one would take care not to grow too wise for so great a pleasure of life.

Joseph Addison

To smile at the jest which plants a thorn in another's breast is to become a principal in the mischief.

Richard B. Sheridan

You grow up the day you have your first real laugh—at yourself.

Ethel Barrymore

An ounce of cheerfulness is worth a pound of sadness to serve God with.

Thomas Fuller

Proper to man is the smile. It is the cheapest luxury he enjoys. It is full of optimistic vitamins— the lubricant of zestful living. It purifies the mind and soul.

Eugene P. Bertin

A laugh is just like sunshine,
It freshens all the day,
It tips the peak of life with light,
And drives the clouds away;
The soul grows glad that hears it,
And feels its courage strong;
A laugh is just like sunshine
For cheering folks along.

A laugh is just like music,
It lingers in the heart,
And where its melody is heard,
The ills of life depart;
And happy thoughts come crowding
Its joyful notes to greet;
A laugh is just like music
For making living sweet.

Author Unknown

Men show their characters in nothing more clearly than in what they think laughable.

Johann Wolfgang von Goethe

The gift of gaiety may itself be the greatest good fortune, and the most serious step toward maturity.

Irwin Edman

What sunshine is to flowers, smiles are to humanity. They are but trifles, to be sure; but, scattered along life's pathway, the good they do is inconceivable.

Joseph Addison

A baby smiled in its mother's face
The mother caught it, and gave it then
To the baby's father—serious case—
Who carried it out to the other men;
And every one of them went straight away
Scattering sunshine through the day.

Louis De Louk

You've all seen the machine a physician uses to take a patient's blood pressure. It indicates something about physical health. Someday, perhaps, someone will invent a laugh-pressure machine to show how sick or how healthy a sense of humor is. That will really indicate a lot about *mental* health.

Murray Banks

There is very little success where there is little laughter.

Andrew Carnegie

I am persuaded that every time a man smiles, but much more often when he laughs, it adds something to his fragment of life.

Lawrence Sterne

If you can't crown yourself with laurels, you can wreathe your face in smiles.

Author Unknown

Fate used me meanly; but I looked at her and laughed,
That none might know how bitter was the cup I quaffed.

Along came Joy, and paused beside me where I sat,
Saying, "I came to see what you were laughing at."

Ella Wheeler Wilcox

Humor is the brother, and often the synonym of comedy. It is an important and necessary antidote for the realities of the laboring for bread, the paying of taxes, and the irritants of daily life.

Author Unknown

---

11. THE MEASURE OF WEALTH

The want of goods is easily repaired: but the poverty of the soul is irreparable.

Michel de Montaigne

What a man is in himself, what accompanies him when he is alone, what no one can give him or take away, is obviously more essential to him than everything he has in the way of possessions, or even what he may be in the eyes of the world.

Arthur Schopenhauer

We need not be rich to be generous, nor have all wisdom to be understanding. Our influence may not be great, but it can be good. Our speech may not be eloquent, but it can be truthful and sincere. We cannot all have good looks, but we can have good conscience, and, having that, we shall have peace of mind and need fear no man.

Author Unknown

The writings of the wise are the only riches our posterity cannot squander.

Walter Savage Landor

Wealth makes everything easy—honesty most of all.

Comtesse Diane

That man is the richest whose pleasures are the cheapest.

Henry David Thoreau

Prosperity is only an instrument to be used; not a deity to be worshipped.

Calvin Coolidge

To be rich in admiration and free from envy; to rejoice greatly in the good of others; to love with such generosity of heart that your love is still a dear possession in absence; these are the gifts of fortune which money cannot buy and without which money can buy nothing. He who has such a treasury of riches, being happy and valiant himself, in his own nature, will enjoy the universe as if it were his own estate; and help the man to whom he lends a hand to enjoy it with him.

Robert Louis Stevenson

No man can tell whether he is rich or poor by turning to his ledger. It is the heart that makes a man rich. He is rich according to what he is, not according to what he has.

Henry Ward Beecher

Good name in man and woman,
    dear my lord,
Is the immediate jewel of their
    souls; . . .
William Shakespeare

The best definition of wealth—the only true definition, I think—is the possession of whatever gives us happiness, contentment or a sense of one's significance in the scheme of things.
Ernest W. Watson

A man is poor when he has lost the confidence of his friends; when people who are nearest to him do not believe in him; when his character is handicapped by deceit and punctured by his dishonesty. He is poor when he makes money at the expense of his character, when principle does not stand out supreme in his ideals. When ideals are clouded he is in danger of the worst kind of poverty. To be in the poorhouse is not necessarily to be poor if one has maintained his integrity of character and stands foursquare to the world. If one has not bent the knee of principle to avarice he is not poor though he may be compelled to beg bread.
Author Unknown

The real wealth, not only of America, but of the world, is in the resources of the ground we stand on, and in the resources of the human mind.
Norman Cousins

Money is not required to buy one necessity of the soul.
Henry David Thoreau

Remember, what you possess in the world will be found at the day of your death to belong to someone else, but what you are will be yours forever.
Henry van Dyke

Wealth is not only what you have but it is also what you are.
Sterling W. Sill

To have what we want is riches, but to be able to do without is power.

George MacDonald

A man is rich in proportion to the number of things he can do without. Beware of all enterprises that require new clothes.
Henry David Thoreau

I am happy in having learned to distinguish between ownership and possession. Books, pictures, and all the beauty of the world belong to those who love and understand them—not usually to those who possess them. All of these things that I am entitled to have I have—I own by divine right. So I care not a bit who possesses them.

James Howard Kehler

Not what you possess but what you do with what you have, determines your true worth.

Thomas Carlyle

Who is rich? He who rejoices in his lot.

The Mishnah

If you want to know how rich you really are, find out what would be left of you tomorrow if you should lose every dollar you own tonight.

Wm. J. H. Boetcker

No legacy is so rich as honesty.

William Shakespeare

Rudyard Kipling, English poet, speaking to a graduating class at McGill University, advised the graduates not to care too much for money or power or fame; for, he said in effect, "Someday you will meet a man who cares for none of these things . . . and then you will know how poor you are."

George A. Buttrick

It's good to have money and the things that money can buy, but it's good, too, to check up once in a while and make sure you haven't lost the things that money can't buy.

George Horace Lorimer

Property has its duties as well as its rights.

Benjamin Disraeli

Money buys everything except love, personality, freedom, immortality, silence, peace.

Carl Sandburg

To purchase heaven has gold the power?
Can gold remove the mortal hour?
In life can love be bought with gold?
Are friendship's pleasures to be sold?
No—all that's worth a wish—a thought,
Fair Virtue gives unbrib'd, unbought.
Cease then on trash thy hopes to bind,

Let nobler views engage thy mind.

Samuel Johnson

It is not poverty that we praise, it is the man whom poverty cannot humble or bend.

Seneca

If all the gold in the world were melted down into a solid cube, it would be about the size of an eight-room house. If a man got possession of all that gold—billions of dollars' worth, he could not buy a friend, character, peace of mind, clear conscience, or a sense of eternity.

Charles F. Banning

As a man grows older, he values the voice of experience more and the voice of prophecy less. He finds more of life's wealth in the common pleasures—home, health, children. He thinks more about worth of men and less about their wealth. He boasts less and boosts more. He hurries less, and usually makes more progress. He esteems the friendship of God a little higher.

Roy L. Smith

The real measure of our wealth is how much we should be worth if we lost our money.

J. H. Jowett

What greater ornament to a son than a father's glory, or to a father than a son's honorable conduct?

Sophocles

Money isn't the most important thing to save. It is the least. Better to save your self-respect, your honor, your individual independence, your pride in being, and your health. These, and many more, are far better than gold. And their dividends are never passed!

George Matthew Adams

A king said to the sage, "Wert thou to make such a request of me, thou wouldst have sufficient for thy needs throughout thy life." The sage replied, "Why should I make such a request of thee, seeing that I am richer than thou!" The king asked, "But how art thou richer than I?" He answered, "Because I am more content with the little I possess than thou art with thy greater wealth."

Solomon Ibn Gabirol

To crave more than you need—that is poverty.

Ivan N. Panin

Wealth consists not in having great possessions, but in having few wants.

Epicurus

Man is not the master of what he has, but only its guardian.

Jacob ben Asher

There is nothing that makes men rich and strong but that which they carry inside of them. True wealth is of the heart, not of the hand.

John Milton

I would rather be a beggar and spend my money like a king, than be a king and spend money like a beggar.

Robert G. Ingersoll

A wise man will desire no more than what he may get justly, use soberly, distribute cheerfully and leave contentedly.

Author Unknown

All good things are cheap; all bad very dear.

Henry David Thoreau

The best condition in life is not to be so rich as to be envied nor so poor as to be damned.

Josh Billings

In finances, be strict with yourself, generous with others.

Moses Maimonides

Do you know what real poverty is? It is never to have a big thought or a generous impulse.

Jerome P. Fleishman

All our money has a moral stamp. It is coined over again in an inward mint. The uses we put it to, the spirit in which we spend it, give it a character which is plainly perceptible to the eye of God.

Thomas Starr King

Augur said, "Give me neither poverty nor riches"; and this will ever be the prayer of the wise. Our incomes should be like our shoes: if too small, they will gall and pinch us, but if too large, they will cause us to stumble and to trip. But wealth, after all, is a relative thing, since he that has little, and wants less, is richer than he that has much, but wants more.

Caleb C. Colton

A little house well fill'd, a little land well till'd, and a little wife well will'd, are great riches.

John Ray

In the sphere of material things, giving means being rich. Not he who *has* much is rich, but he who *gives* much. The hoarder who is anxiously worried about losing something is, psychologically speaking, the poor impoverished man, regardless of how much he has. Whoever is capable of giving of himself is rich.

Erich Fromm

All our possessions are as nothing compared to health, strength and a clear conscience.

Hosea Ballou

The wealth of a nation cannot be stored in gold bars. It must remain in the spirit and attitude of the people; wholesome, hopeful and reverent.

Douglas Meador

---

12. THE PERILS OF WEALTH AND POVERTY

No dust affects the eyes so much as gold dust.

Lady Marguerite Blessington

A man who shows me his wealth is like the beggar who shows me his poverty; they are both looking for alms, the rich man for the alms of my envy, the poor man for the alms of my guilt.

Ben Hecht

It requires a strong constitution to withstand repeated attacks of prosperity.

J. L. Basford

There is only one class in the community that thinks more about money than the rich, and that is the poor. The poor can think of nothing else. That is the misery of being poor.

Oscar Wilde

Prosperity too often has the same effect on its possessor, that a calm at sea has on the Dutch mariner, who frequently, it is said, in these circumstances, ties up the rudder, gets drunk, and goes to sleep.

George Horne

Dug from the mountainside, washed from the glen
Servant am I or master of men.
Steal me, I curse you;
Earn me, I bless you;
Grasp me and hoard me, a fiend shall possess you;
Live for me, die for me,
Covet me, take me,
Angel or devil, I am what you make me.

Author Unknown

Two things are required of a well: it must not freeze in winter, it must not run dry in summer. Two things are required of piety: it must not be chilled by adversity, it must not wither in prosperity.

Ivan N. Panin

For the poor, the economic is the spiritual.

Mohandas K. Gandhi

Riches get their value from the mind of their possessor. They are blessings to those who know how to use them; curses to those who do not.

Terence

Money was made not to command
our will,
But all our lawful pleasures to fulfill;
Shame and woe to us, if we our
wealth obey—
The horse doth with the horseman
run away.

Abraham Cowley

The more a man possesses over
and above what he uses, the more
careworn he becomes.

George Bernard Shaw

One is never more on trial than
in the moment of excessive good
fortune.

Lew Wallace

In the Temple at Jerusalem
there was a flute fashioned out of
reeds, and old flute, having come
down from the days of Moses. The
sound of the flute was sweet and
beautiful, ravishing the soul of the
worshippers. But one day the
priests of the sanctuary decided to
decorate the flute and they covered
it with gold. The flute was never
the same again. Its sweet, clear,
cool tones were now harsh, metal-
lic and jarring. Gold had coarsened
its melody.

Abba Hillel Silver

Poverty is an anomaly to rich
people. It is very difficult to make
out why people who want dinner
do not ring the bell.

Walter Bagehot

Poverty does not produce unhappiness: it produces degradation.

George Bernard Shaw

There is often less danger in the
things we fear than in the things
we desire.

John Churton Collins

There are two things needed in
these days; first, for rich men to
find out how poor men live; and,
second, for poor men to know how
rich men work.

Edward Atkinson

If you run after fortune, you may
be running away from contentment.

Yiddish Proverb

Among us English-speaking peoples especially do the praises of
poverty need once more to be
boldly sung. We have grown literally afraid to be poor. We despise
anyone who elects to be poor in
order to simplify and save his
inner life. If he does not join the
general scramble, we deem him
spiritless and lacking in ambition.
We have lost the power even of
imagining what the ancient realization of poverty could have meant;
the liberation from material attach-
ments, the unbribed soul, the man-
lier indifference, the paving our
way by what we are and not by
what we have, the right to fling
away our life at any moment irre-
sponsibly,—the more athletic trim,
in short, the fighting shape.

William James

Anybody can sympathize with
the sufferings of a friend, but it
requires a very fine nature to sympathize with a friend's success.

Oscar Wilde

Money will buy a pretty good
dog, but it won't buy the wag of
his tail.

Josh Billings

One realizes the full importance
of time only when there is little
of it left. Every man's greatest

capital asset is his unexpired years of productive life.

P. W. Litchfield

The darkest hour of any man's life is when he sits down to plan how to get money without earning it.

Horace Greeley

We see how much a man has, and therefore we envy him; did we see how little he enjoys, we should rather pity him.

Jeremiah Seed

What is bought is cheaper than a gift.

Cervantes

No one can love his neighbor on an empty stomach.

Woodrow Wilson

We get more profit than pleasure out of honesty, and those who have won their money at the cost of their honour would often gladly win back their honour at the cost of their money.

Comtesse Diane

Gold is the most useless metal in the world, for it is good only for plugging teeth and tormenting fools.

Benjamin Franklin

Money may buy the husk of things, but not the kernel. It brings you food but not appetite, medicine but not health, acquaintances but not friends, servants but not faithfulness, days of joy but not peace or happiness.

Henrik Ibsen

From poverty our own power can save us, from riches only divine grace.

Ludwig Boerne

We have lost the habit of thinking quietly, of trying to know ourselves and our friends, and the world around us, and the God who is above and within us. We are looking in the wrong places for happiness. We are so exclusively occupied with material things and with their accumulation that the higher values are crowded out.

Robert J. McCracken

One who believes that anything can be accomplished by money is likely to do anything for money.

Hasidic Saying

The Chinese tell of a man of Peiping who dreamed of gold, much gold, his heart's desire. He rose one day and when the sun was high he dressed in his finest garments and went to the crowded market place. He stepped directly to the booth of a gold dealer, snatched a bag full of gold coins, and walked calmly away. The officials who arrested him were puzzled: "Why did you rob the gold dealer in broad daylight?" they asked. "And in the presence of so many people?"

"I did not see any people," the man replied. "I saw only gold."

Louis Binstock

There is a burden of care in getting riches; fear in keeping them; temptation in using them; guilt in abusing them; sorrow in losing them; and a burden of account at last to be given concerning them.

Matthew Henry

Why snatch at wealth, and hoard and stock it?

Your shroud, you know, will have no pocket!

Betty Paoli

To get his wealth he spent his health
And then with might and main
He turned around and spent his wealth
To get his health again.

Author Unknown

Sir, all the arguments which are brought to represent poverty as no evil show it to be evidently a great evil. You never find people laboring to convince you that you may live very happily upon a plentiful fortune.

Samuel Johnson

Few of us can stand prosperity. Another man's, I mean.

Mark Twain

For every talent that poverty has stimulated it has blighted a hundred.

John W. Gardner

Poverty is very good in poems but very bad in the house; very good in maxims and sermons but very bad in practical life.

Henry Ward Beecher

The greedy search for money or success will almost always lead men into unhappiness. Why? Because that kind of life makes them depend upon things outside themselves.

Andre Maurois

They who are of the opinion that money will do everything may very well be suspected to do everything for money.

Lord Halifax

To appear rich, we become poor.

Lady Marguerite Blessington

The miser does not own his wealth; his wealth owns him.

Judah Jeiteles

Wisdom leads to tranquillity, gold and silver to anxiety.

Solomon Ibn Gabirol

A baby enters the world with hands clenched, as if to say, "The world is mine; I shall grab it." A man leaves with hands open, as if to say, "I can take nothing with me."

The Midrash

Prosperity is only an instrument to be used, not a deity to be worshipped.

Calvin Coolidge

My God, give me neither poverty nor riches, but whatsoever it may be thy will to give, give me, with it, a heart that knows humbly to acquiesce in what is thy will.

Christian Scriver Gotthold

THE ART OF LIVING

WITH THE HIGHEST

13. THE ART OF ASPIRATION

The significance of a man is not in what he attains, but rather in what he longs to attain.

Kahlil Gibran

What we truly and earnestly aspire to be, that in some sense we are. The mere aspiration, by changing the frame of the mind, for the moment realizes itself.

Anna Jameson

To live in the presence of great truths and eternal laws—that is what keeps a man patient when the world ignores him and calm and unspoiled when the world praises him.

Honoré de Balzac

No man has earned the right to intellectual ambition until he has learned to lay his course by a star which he has never seen, to dig by the divining rod for springs which he may never reach.

Oliver Wendell Holmes, Jr.

Education is a persistent dream often interrupted by the nightmare of a sobering actuality. We should not be afraid to dream, for today's dream of a better world may be tomorrow's reality.

Frederick Mayer

The finest qualities of our characters do not come from trying but from that mysterious and yet most effective capacity to be inspired.

Harry Emerson Fosdick

Moral education is impossible without the habitual vision of greatness.

Alfred North Whitehead

Not failure, but low aim, is crime.

James Russell Lowell

A map of the world that does not include Utopia is not worth glancing at.

Oscar Wilde

If I shoot at the sun, I may hit a star.

P. T. Barnum

Whether a man accepts from fortune her spade and will look

downward and dig, or from aspiration her axe and cord, and will scale the ice, the one and only success which it is his to command is to bring to his work a mighty heart.

Oliver Wendell Holmes

Those who bestow too much application on trifling things, become generally incapable of great ones.

Francois Rochefoucauld

The men who try to do something and fail are infinitely better than those who try to do nothing and succeed.

Lloyd Jones

It seems to me we can never give up longing and wishing while we are thoroughly alive. There are certain things we feel to be beautiful and good, and we must hunger after them.

George Eliot

That men have climbed the Matterhorn and McKinley means little. That they should *want* to climb them and *try* to climb them means everything. For it is the ultimate wisdom of the mountains that a man is never more a man than when he is striving for what is beyond his grasp, and that there is no conquest worth winning save that over his own weakness and fear.

James Ramsey Ullman

This world cannot finally satisfy a man. There is deep-seated in the make-up of the ordinary person a craving for flowers that do not fade and pleasures that do not pass away. Deep down inside of every human being there is a desire for the genuine—the lasting quality of real life.

Warren Walker

Join the great company of those who make the barren places of life fruitful with kindness. Carry a vision of heaven in your heart, and make the world-correspond to that vision.

Helen Keller

Those who live on the mountain have a longer day than those who live in the valley. Sometimes all we need to brighten our day is to rise a little higher.

Author Unknown

You may not always attain every ambition; but by having a higher aim you will come closer to it than if you pin yourself to the ground by thinking low thoughts. You can afford the most extravagant ambitions in the world. Aim at the moon. No one can stop you from having such ambitions. And no one except one person can prevent you from attaining them. You are that person.

Charles B. Roth

The ideal life is in our blood and never will be still. We feel the things to be beating beneath the things we are.

Phillips Brooks

Too low they build who build beneath the stars.

Edward Young

Ah, but a man's reach should exceed his grasp. Or what's a heaven for?

Robert Browning

High aims form high characters, and great objects bring out great minds.

Tyron Edwards

In great attempts it is glorious even to fail.

Cassius Longinus

Ideals are like stars: you will not succeed in touching them with your hands, but like the seafaring man on the ocean desert of waters, you choose them as your guides, and, following them, you reach your destiny.

Carl Schurz

I never cut my neighbor's throat;
My neighbor's gold I never stole;
I never spoiled his house and land;
But God have mercy on my soul!

For I am haunted night and day
By all the deeds I have not done;
O unattempted loveliness!
O costly valor never won!

Marguerite Wilkinson

Beware what you set your heart upon. For it shall surely be yours.

Ralph Waldo Emerson

God never permitted any man to hold an ideal too beautiful for His power to make it practicable.

Wendell Phillips

The place where men meet to seek the highest is holy ground.

Felix Adler

You must have long-range goals to keep from being frustrated by short-range failures.

Charles C. Noble

I want to soar the boundless blue
Where winds and tempests have their birth,

And let the clouds conceal for me
Not heaven, but the earth.

I. L. Peretz

Perpetual inspiration is as necessary to the life of goodness, holiness and happiness as perpetual respiration is necessary to animal life.

William Law

Aim at the sun, and you may not reach it; but your arrow will fly higher than if aimed at an object on a level with yourself.

J. Hawes

Humanity cannot be measured by what it is; only by what it is trying to become.

John Ciardi

Did you ever hear of a man who has striven all his life faithfully toward an object and in no measure obtained it? If a man constantly aspires, is he not elevated? Did ever a man try heroism, magnanimity, truth, sincerity, and find that there was no advantage in them— that it was a vain endeavor?

Henry David Thoreau

The highest flights of charity, devotion, trust, patience, bravery to which the wings of human nature have spread themselves have been flown for religious ideals.

William James

Every man ought to be inquisitive through every hour of his great adventure down to the day when he shall no longer cast a shadow in the sun. For if he dies without a question in his heart, what excuse is there for his continuance?

Frank Moore Colby

Hitch your wagon to a star. Let us not fag in paltry works which serve our pot and bag alone.

Ralph Waldo Emerson

Far better it is to dare mighty things, to win glorious triumphs, even though checkered by failure, than to take rank with those poor spirits who neither enjoy much nor suffer much, because they live in the grey twilight that knows not victory nor defeat.

Theodore Roosevelt

A good intention clothes itself with power.

Ralph Waldo Emerson

The golden thread in the mind of man is the light that leads towards excellence as a human objective. If perfection is a divine attribute, excellence is a human incentive and a healthy aim, even when we fall short of the target.

A. M. Sullivan

It is for us to pray not for tasks equal to our powers, but for powers equal to our tasks, to go forward with a great desire forever beating at the door of our hearts as we travel towards our distant goal.

Helen Keller

A noble man compares and estimates himself by an idea which is higher than himself; and a mean man, by one lower than himself. The one produces aspiration; the other ambition, which is the way in which a vulgar man aspires.

Henry Ward Beecher

The dust's for crawling, heaven's for flying,

Wherefore, O Soul, whose wings are grown,
Soar upward to the sun!

Edgar Lee Masters

An ideal is a port toward which we resolve to steer.

Felix Adler

Psychology has its Gresham's Law; its bad money drives out the good. Most people tend to perform the actions that require least effort, to think the thoughts that are easiest, to feel the emotions that are most vulgarly commonplace, to give the rein to desires that are most nearly animal.

Aldous Huxley

On a mural Francis Scott Bradford has depicted the life of man. A heroic figure of man is painted as chained to the skyscrapers of his cities, rearing up, stretching his chains, peering onward into the stars and planets of the heavens. And the scroll inscribes the summary: "Man, though chained to earth, looks across time and space toward an unknown perfection which he may never reach but will forever seek."

Rollo May

Far away there in the sunshine are my highest aspirations. I may not reach them, but I can look up and see their beauty, believe in them, and try to follow where they lead.

Louisa May Alcott

Aspiration is achievement.

Israel Zangwill

There is not a heart but has its moments of longing, yearning for something better, nobler, holier than it knows now.

Henry Ward Beecher

Obstacles are those frightful things you see when you take your eyes off the goal.

Hannah More

We cannot swing up a rope that is attached only to our belt.

William Ernest Hocking

14. DREAMS AND THE DREAMER

Existence would be intolerable if we were never to dream.

Anatole France

'Tis not what man does which exalts him, but what man would do!

Robert Browning

The power of ideals is incalculable. We see no power in a drop of water. But let it get into a crack in the rock and be turned into ice, and it splits the rock; turned into steam, it drives the pistons of the most powerful engines. Something has happened to it which makes active and effective the power that is latent in it.

Albert Schweitzer

Vision is the Aladdin's lamp of the soul. It is the divine spark that lights the lamp of progress. It is the hand that pushes aside the curtains of night to let the sunrise in. It is vision that guides a log-cabin boy to the presidency of our Republic. Vision gave wings to man, pulled atomic energy from the sun, subdued the forces of nature, making them the soulless and untiring slaves of those whom such powers held in bondage since time began.

Author Unknown

Live in contact with dreams, and you will get something of their charm; live in contact with facts, and you will get something of their brutality. I wish I could find a country where the facts were not brutal, and the dreams not unreal.

George Bernard Shaw

Dreamers are the architects of greatness. Their brains have wrought all human miracles. . . . Your homes are set upon a land a dreamer found. The pictures on its walls are visions from a dreamer's soul. A dreamer's pain wails from your violin. They are the chosen few—the Blazers of the Way—who never wear Doubt's bandage on their eyes—who starve and chill and hurt, but hold to courage and to hope, because they know that there is always proof of truth for them who try—that only cowardice and lack of faith can keep the seeker from his chosen goal; but if his heart be strong and if he dream enough and dream it hard enough, he can attain, no matter where men failed before.

Walls crumble and empires fall. The tidal wave sweeps from the sea and tears a fortress from its rocks. The rotting nations drop off

Time's bough, and only things the dreamers make live on.

Herbert Kaufman

The greatest achievement was at first and for a time a dream. The oak sleeps in the acorn; the bird waits in the egg; and in the highest vision of the soul a waking angel stirs. Dreams are the seedlings of realities.

James Allen

When Socrates was describing the ideal way of life and the ideal society, Glaucon countered: "Socrates, I do not believe that there is such a City of God anywhere on earth." Socrates answered, "Whether such a city exists in heaven or ever will exist on earth, the wise men will live after the manner of that city, having nothing to do with any other, and in so looking upon it, will set his own house in order."

Rollo May

Behind every advance of the human race is a germ of creation growing in the mind of some lone individual. An individual whose dreams waken him in the night while others lie contentedly asleep.

Crawford H. Greenewalt

I prefer a dream to an illusion. In a dream I know my eyes are closed; in an illusion I think they are open.

Comtesse Diane

Give thanks, O heart, for the high souls
That point us to the deathless goals:

Brave souls that took the perilous trail
And felt the vision could not fail.

Edwin Markham

We had needs invent heaven if it had not been revealed to us.

Robert Louis Stevenson

Man knows his littleness; his own mountains remind him; but the dreams of man make up for our faults and failings; for the brevity of our lives, for the narrowness of our scope; they leap over boundaries and are away and away.

Lord Dunsany

Those who dream by day are cognizant of many things which escape those who dream only by night.

Edgar Allan Poe

Hold fast your dreams!
Within your heart
Keep one still, secret spot
Where dreams may go,
And, sheltered so,
May thrive and grow
Where doubt and fear are not.
O keep a place apart,
Within your heart,
For little dreams to go!

Louise Driscoll

You see things; and you say "Why?" But I dream things that never were; and I say "Why not?"

George Bernard Shaw

Some Indian braves were challenged to climb to the highest peak to see a sea beyond the mountains. Most of them brought back leaves or moss or a certain flower, or some kind of token to prove the height to which they had climbed; but one came back breathless without anything except an expression of joy on his face, and the glory of vision in his eye. All he said was, "I have seen the crystal sea," and no one doubted it.

Louise Harrison McCraw

The glory of the star, the glory of the sun—we must not lose either in the other. We must not be so full of the hope of heaven that we cannot do our work on the earth; we must not be so lost in the work of the earth that we shall not be inspired by the hope of heaven.

Phillips Brooks

A child, awakened out of a deep sleep, expressed all the crying babies and all the weeping idealists in the world. "Oh, dear," he said, "I have lost my place in my dream."

Lincoln Steffens

We grow great by dreams. All big men are dreamers. They see things in the soft haze of a spring day or in the red fire of a long winter's evening. Some of us let these great dreams die, but others nourish and protect them; nurse them through bad days till they bring them to the sunshine and light which comes always to those who sincerely hope that their dreams will come true.

Woodrow Wilson

We are haunted by an ideal life, and it is because we have within us the beginning and the possibility of it.

Phillips Brooks

The indelicate hand of necessity is forever leaving its fingerprints on the fragile crystal of dreams.

Douglas Meador

Humanity certainly needs practical men, who get the most out of their work, and, without forgetting the general good, safeguard their own interests. But humanity also needs dreamers, for whom the disinterested development of an enterprise is so captivating that it becomes impossible for them to devote their care to their own material profit.

Marie Curie

It was a Spring that never came, but we have lived enough to know what we have never had, remains. It is the things we have that go.

Sara Teasdale

A task without a vision is drudgery; a vision without a task is a dream; a task with a vision is victory.

Author Unknown

If age is strictly honest with youth it has to tell it things that are not altogether good for youth to take to heart. The experience of the years is largely made up of vanished dreams, deluded hopes and frustrated ambitions. But it is the very dreams, hopes and ambitions of youth that accomplish so many things that age in its wisdom knows to be impossible. Where would the world be if wisdom ruled youth and power rested in age?

Thomas F. Woodlock

If one advances confidently in the direction of his dreams, and endeavours to live the life which he has imagined, he will meet with a success unexpected in common hours. . . . If you have built castles in the air, your work need not be lost; that is where they should be. Now put the foundations under them.

Henry David Thoreau

15. THE GOALS OF LIFE

If I can stop one heart from breaking,
I shall not live in vain;
If I can ease one life the aching,
Or cool one pain,
Or help one fainting robin
Unto his nest again,
I shall not live in vain.

Emily Dickinson

After a teacher had told his students how they should play the game of life, one puzzled student asked: "But how can we play the game when we don't know where the goal posts are?"

Charles L. Wallis

All the great things are simple, and many can be expressed in a single word: freedom; justice; honor; duty; mercy; hope.

Winston S. Churchill

Men need nothing so much in these modern days as they need a working philosophy of life, an adequate way to live. Loosed from their moorings that have held life, many are now adrift. They have thrown overboard the chart, compass, steering wheel, and the consciousness of destination. They are free from everything except rocks and storms.

E. Stanley Jones

There is in nature what is within reach and what is beyond reach.

He who is unaware of the distinction may waste himself in lifelong toil trying to get at the inaccessible without ever getting close to truth. But he who knows it and is wise will stick to what is accessible; and in exploring this region in all directions and confirming his gains he will even push back the confines of the inaccessible.

Johann Wolfgang von Goethe

Luther Burbank fell in love with plants; Edison fell in love with invention; Ford fell in love with motor cars; Kettering fell in love with research; John Patterson fell in love with salesmanship; the Wright brothers fell in love with airplanes. Someone has truly said: "Be careful what you set your heart on for it will surely come true." The men who harness their hearts to mighty tasks often see their dreams become realities.

Author Unknown

To toil for a hard master is bitter, but to have no master to toil for is more bitter still.

Everybody wants something. The practical man is the man who knows how to get what he wants. The philosopher is the man who knows what man ought to want. The ideal man is the man who

Oscar Wilde

knows how to get what he ought to want.

Edgar S. Brightman

The notion of making money by popular work, and then retiring to do good work on the proceeds, is the most familiar of all the devil's traps for artists.

Logan Pearsall Smith

One of the purest and most enduring of human pleasures is to be found in the possession of a good name among one's neighbors and acquaintances.

Charles W. Eliot

While I have always recognized that the object of business is to make money in an honorable manner, I have endeavored to remember that the object of life is to do good.

Peter Cooper

Perhaps it would be a good idea, fantastic as it sounds, to muffle every telephone, stop every motor and halt all activity for an hour some day to give people a chance to ponder for a few minutes on what it is all about, why they are living and what they really want.

John Truslow Adams

If you mean to act nobly and seek to know the best things God has put within reach of men, you must learn to fix your mind on that end, and not on what will happen to you because of it.

George Eliot

Fanaticism consists in redoubling your effort when you have forgotten your aim.

George Santayana

The means may be likened to a seed, the end to a tree; and there is just the same inviolable connection between the means and the end as there is between the seed and the tree.

Mohandas K. Gandhi

Before we set our hearts too much upon any thing let us examine how happy those are who already possess it.

François Rochefoucauld

Resolved first, that every man should live, always and everywhere, at his highest and best for God. Resolved second, whether any other man in the world strives to do so or not, I will, so help me God.

Jonathan Edwards

The purpose of man's life is not happiness, but worthiness.

Felix Adler

I used to be anxious to accomplish much good in the world. I am now content if I do but little harm.

Ivan N. Panin

Life is an arrow—therefore you must know
What mark to aim at, how to use the bow—
Then draw it to the head and let it go!

Henry Van Dyke

Because we can synthesize rubber, span the earth with sound, and spin wool from peanuts, we think we know the answers to all the riddles which have puzzled philosophers since time began. But there comes a moment when man wearies of the things he has won; when he suspects with bewilderment and dismay that there is another purpose, some profound and eternal purpose in his being.

It is then he discovers that beyond the kingdom of the world there exists a kingdom of the soul.

A. J. Cronin

Of the thousands of mentally and emotionally abnormal people I have observed over a number of years, I believe that the one most frequent denominator among them has been lack of worthy purpose in life, a lack of ambition or lack of opportunity to be of some definite purpose in society, to make some definite and at least partially unselfish contribution to the world.

James T. Fisher and Lowell S. Hawley

Best law—Golden Rule
Best education—Self-knowledge
Best philosophy—A contented mind
Best music—Laughter of a child
Best medicine—Cheerfulness and temperance
Best war—Fight against one's own weakness
Best science—Extracting sunshine from a cloudy day
Best telegraphy—Flashing a ray of sunshine into a gloomy heart
Best biography—The life that writes charity in largest letters.

Henry F. Kobe

When people have something worth while to live for, they discover that they have enough to live on.

Julian E. Stuart

All ambitions are lawful except those which climb upward on the miseries or credulities of mankind.

Joseph Conrad

Your purpose in life is simply to help on the purpose of the universe.

George Bernard Shaw

There is a loftier ambition than merely to stand high in the world. It is to stoop down and lift mankind a little higher.

Henry Van Dyke

O, do not pray for easy lives. Pray to be stronger men. Do not pray for tasks equal to your powers. Pray for powers equal to your tasks.

Phillips Brooks

16. THE ART OF GROWING UP

Our business in life is not to get ahead of other people, but to get ahead of ourselves. To break our own record, to outstrip our yesterdays by todays, to bear our trials more beautifully than we ever dreamed we could, to whip the tempter inside and out as we never whipped him before, to give as we have never given, to do our work with more force and a finer finish than ever,—this is the true idea,—to get ahead of ourselves. To beat some one else in a game, or to be beaten, may mean much or little. To beat our own game means a great deal. Whether we win or not, we are playing better than we ever did before, and that's the point after all—to play a better game of life.

Maltie D. Babcock

I held it truth, with him who sings
To one clear harp in divers tones
That men may rise on stepping-stones
Of their dead selves to higher things.

Alfred Lord Tennyson

The rung of a ladder was never meant to rest upon, but only to hold a man's foot long enough to enable him to put the other somewhat higher.

Thomas Henry Huxley

A man should never be ashamed to own he has been in the wrong, which is but saying in other words that he is wiser today than he was yesterday.

Alexander Pope

Undertake something that is difficult; it will do you good. Unless you try to do something beyond what you have already mastered, you will never grow.

Ronald E. Osborn

Maturing is the process by which the individual becomes conscious of the equal importance of each of his fellow men.

Alvin H. Goeser

Life affords no higher pleasure than that of surmounting difficulties, passing from one step of success to another, forming new wishes and seeing them gratified. He that labors in any great or laudable undertaking has his fatigues first supported by hope and afterwards rewarded by joy.

Samuel Johnson

Each year, one vicious habit rooted out in time ought to make the worst man good.

Benjamin Franklin

Experience is a good school, but the fees are high.

Heinrich Heine

It is very dangerous to go into eternity with possibilities which one has oneself prevented from becoming realities. A possibility is a hint from God. One must follow it. In every man there is latent the highest possibility; one must follow it. If God does not wish it, then let Him prevent it, but one must not hinder oneself. Trusting to God I have dared, but I was not successful; in that is to be found peace, calm, a confidence in God. I have not dared; that is a woeful thought, a torment in eternity.

Sören Kierkegaard

If we devoted as much energy to getting away from sin as we do to getting away with sin, how much nobler we would become.

Sidney Greenberg

A person remains immature, whatever his age, as long as he thinks of himself as an exception to the human race.

Harry A. Overstreet

I find the great thing in this world is not so much where we stand, as in what direction we are moving.

Oliver Wendell Holmes

It is also said of me that I now and then contradict myself. Yes, I improve wonderfully as time goes on.

George Jean Nathan

What is happiness other than the grace of being permitted to unfold to their fullest bloom all the spiritual powers planted within us.

Franz Werfel

Life's greatest achievement is the continual remaking of yourself so that at last you know how to live.

Winfred Rhoades

One of the best sermons I have ever heard was delivered by a country preacher in a little country church. He said: "People talk to me about the problem of evil, but I will tell you an even greater problem: the problem of goodness. How do you account for the fact that in such a world as this there should be so much self-sacrifice, so much unselfishness, so much love? By what miracle has man, who only a few thousand years ago was living on the level of the beasts, risen to a point where he will literally 'lay down his life' for his family, for a cause, for a friend?"

As the years accumulate do you find yourself more sympathetic and tolerant, with a higher reverence for the nobility of your fellow men? That is the essential test of growth.

Bruce Barton

A person is not mature until he has both an ability and a willingness to see himself as one among others and to do unto those others as he would have them do to him.

Harry A. Overstreet

It is the content of our lives that determines their value. If we limit ourselves to supply the means of living, in what way have we placed ourselves above the cattle that graze in the fields? Cattle can live in comfort. Their every need is amply supplied. Is it not when one exercises his reason, his love of beauty, his desire for friendship, his selection of the good from that which is not so good, that he earns the right to call himself a man? I should be inclined to claim that the person who limits his interests to the means of living without consideration of the content or meaning of his life is defeating God's great purpose when he brought into existence a creature with the intelligence and godlike powers that are found in man. It is in living wisely and fully that one's soul grows.

Arthur H. Compton

No man has ever risen to the real stature of spiritual manhood until he has found that it is finer to serve somebody else than it is to serve himself.

Woodrow Wilson

One sign of maturity is the ability to be comfortable with people who are not like us.

Virgil A. Kraft

We gain nothing by being with such as ourselves; we encourage each other in mediocrity. I am always longing to be with men more excellent than myself.

Charles Lamb

There is one person whom it is my duty to make good and that is myself.

Robert Louis Stevenson

Bad will be the day for every man when he becomes absolutely contented with the life that he is living, with the thoughts that he is thinking, with the deeds that he is doing, when there is not forever beating at the doors of his soul some great desire to do something larger, which he knows that he was meant and made to do because he is still, in spite of all, the child of God.

Phillips Brooks

And ah for a man to arise in me,
That the man that I am
May cease to be.

Alfred Lord Tennyson

"A tragedy with a happy ending" is exactly what the child wants before he goes to sleep; the reassurance that "all's well with the world" as he lies in his cosy nursery. It is a good thing that the child should receive this reassurance; but as long as he needs it he remains a child, and the world he lives in is a nursery-world. Things are not always and everywhere well with the world, and each man has to find it out as he grows up. It is the finding out that makes him grow, and until he has faced the fact and digested the lesson he is not grown up—he is still in the nursery.

Edith Wharton

He only is advancing in life whose heart is getting softer, whose blood warmer, whose brain quicker, whose spirit is entering into living peace.

John Ruskin

Human beings are not born with human nature—they develop it.
Ashley Montagu

The mature man knows that he is likely to make mistakes. He wants to take responsibility for them. Only by facing his mistakes does he learn to act more responsibly.

Richard H. Rice

Man is always trying to make something for himself rather than something of himself.

Moses Heifetz

Growth and progress are the only possible goals of life. I believe that the clue to man's destiny lies in his relentless training toward independence, not only political, but also in the psychological sense.

Ernest Dichter

For the human mind is seldom at stay: If you do not grow better, you will most undoubtedly grow worse.

Richardson

The author who penetrates the deepest into the human soul is the one who has the strongest respect for the awakening power of conscience and the stretching power of commitment.

Norman Cousins

New occasions teach new duties,
    time makes ancient good uncouth;
They must upward still and onward,
    who would keep abreast of truth.
James Russell Lowell

A boy becomes an adult three years before his parents think he does—and about two years after he thinks he does.

Lewis Hershey

Build thee more stately mansions,
  O my soul,
As the swift seasons roll!
Leave thy low-vaulted past!

Let each new temple, nobler than
the last,
Shut thee from heaven with a dome
more vast,
Till thou at length are free,
Leaving thine outgrown shell by
life's unresting sea!
Oliver Wendell Holmes

We never become truly spiritual
by sitting down and wishing to become so. You must undertake something so great that you cannot accomplish it unaided.
Phillips Brooks

Though his beginnings be but poor
and low,
Thank God, a man can grow.
Florence Earle Coates

There is one rule for minds and
bodies: they can only be preserved
by continual nourishment.
Vauvenargues

He who attends to his greater
self becomes a great man and he
who attends his smaller self becomes a small man.
Mencius

If seeds in the black earth can
turn into such beautiful roses, what
might not the heart of man become
in its long journey toward the stars.
G. K. Chesterton

It is easier to abandon evil traits
today than tomorrow.
Hasidic Saying

Experience is not what happens
to a man. It is what a man does
with what happens to him.
Aldous Huxley

One of the saddest experiences
which can ever come to a human
being is to awaken, gray-haired and
wrinkled near the close of an un-
productive career, to the fact that
all through the years he has been
using only a small part of himself!
V. M. Burrows

Security means inner harmony of
the personality with the environment. Man must learn how to balance emotional stress against his
own emotional supports. And he
must be mature.
William C. Menninger

The warm loves and fears, that
swept over us as clouds, must lose
their finite character and blend
with God, to attain their own perfection. But we need not fear that
we can lose anything by the progress of the soul. The soul may be
trusted to the end. That which is so
beautiful and attractive as these
relations, must be succeeded and
supplanted only by what is more
beautiful and so on for ever.
Ralph Waldo Emerson

A friend said of Hendrick Van
Loon, the writer: "He lived as some
people eat—ravenously—and with
an ever-increasing appetite. All
around him people were growing
old, but he grew up."
J. Richard Sneed

Tinnius Rufus asked, "Why did
not God make man exactly as He
wants him to be?" Akiba replied,
"For the very reason that man's
duty is to perfect himself."
The Midrash

He who asks of life nothing but
the improvement of his own nature,
and a continuous moral progress
toward inward contentment and religious submission, is less liable

than anyone else to miss and waste life.

Henri F. Amiel

Three men are my friends—he that loves me, he that hates me and he that is indifferent to me. Who loves me, teaches me tenderness; who hates me, teaches me caution; who is indifferent to me, teaches me self-reliance.

J. E. Dinger

There comes a time in the development of ourselves, when receiving from others, which is the essence of selfishness, gives way to the irresistible urge to give to others—to grow beyond the limits of one's skin.

Joshua Loth Liebman

The speed of a runaway horse counts for nothing.

Jean Cocteau

To pass from a mirror-mind to a mind with windows is an essential element in the development of real personality.

Harry Emerson Fosdick

Make the most of yourself, for that is all there is of you.

Ralph Waldo Emerson

To exist is to change, to change is to mature.

Henri Bergson

The great developer is responsibility.

Louis D. Brandeis

The mark of the immature man is that he wants to die nobly for a cause, while the mark of the mature man is that he wants to live humbly for one.

William Stekel

17. THE ART OF BUILDING CHARACTER

Character is the beginning and the end of all things. Without it, we have only the ashes of a people's failure; with it, we have the rainbow of civilization's desires.

Eric A. Johnston

The qualities of character, hidden or buried, are revealed eventually even as the quality of a building is revealed under the stress of time and storm. When we do less than our best we cheat ourselves. We are the architects and builders of our own characters and must of necessity dwell within them.

George E. Mayo

Have patience with all things, but chiefly have patience with yourself. Do not lose courage in considering your own imperfections, but instantly set about remedying them—every day begin the task anew.

Sir Francis De Sales

Happiness is not the end of life; character is.

Henry Ward Beecher

The crown and glory of life is character. It is the noblest possession of a man, constituting a rank in itself, and estate in the general good will; dignifying every station, and exalting every position in society. It exercises a greater power than wealth and secures all the honor without the jealousies of fame. It carries with it an influence which always tells; for it is the result of proved honor, rectitude, and consistency-qualities which, perhaps more than any others, command the general confidence and respect of mankind.

Samuel Smiles

The problem of life is not to make life easier, but to make men stronger.

Author Unknown

Character is made by what you stand for; reputation by what you fall for.

Alexander Woollcott

Every temptation that is resisted, every noble aspiration that is encouraged, every sinful thought that is repressed, every bitter word that is withheld, adds its little item to the impetus of that great movement which is bearing humanity onward toward a richer life and higher character.

John Fiske

Character building begins in our infancy and continues until our death.

Eleanor Roosevelt

You will find, if you think for a moment, that the people who influence you are people who believe in you. In an atmosphere of suspicion men shrivel up; but in that atmosphere they expand, and find encouragement and educative fellowship. For the respect of another is the first restoration of the self-respect a man has lost; our ideal of what he is becomes to him the hope and pattern of what he may become.

Henry Drummond

A state can be no better than the citizens of which it is composed. Our labor is not to mold states but to make citizens.

John Morley

Parents can't change the color of their child's eyes, but they can help give the eyes the light of understanding and warmth of sympathy. They can't much alter the child's features, but they can in many ways help endow it with the glow of humaneness, kindness, friendliness . . . which may in the long run bring a lot more happiness than the perfection that wins beauty contests.

Aram Scheinfield

An honest man is the noblest work of God.

Pope

The end and aim of all education is the development of character.

Francis W. Parker

Children are unlikely to follow exactly in their parents' footsteps, but children will travel more easily over bridges which the parents regularly use.

Goodwin Watson

The reputation of a thousand years may be determined by the conduct of one hour.

Japanese Proverb

Fame is a vapor, popularity an accident, riches take wings. Only one thing endures, and that is character.

Horace Greeley

Put more trust in nobility of character than in an oath.

Solon

Reputation is what men and women think of us;
Character is what God and the angels know of us.

Thomas Paine

Character is that which can do without success.

Ralph Waldo Emerson

If we work upon marble, it will perish; if we work upon bronze, time will efface it; if we build temples, they will crumble into dust; but if we work upon immortal souls, if we imbue them with just principles of action, with fear of wrong and love of right, we engrave on those tables something which no time can obliterate, and which will brighten and brighten through all eternity.

Daniel Webster

One of the saddest and most foolish superstitions of the modern world is that people can arrive at righteousness without will power, that we can build good characters without effort. If we are to change, it will have to be by resolving upon it.

A. Powell Davies

There has never been a great or beautiful character which has not become so by filling well the ordinary and smaller offices appointed by God.

Horace Bushnell

Life is a quarry, out of which we are to mold and chisel and complete a character.

Johann Wolfgang von Goethe

Firmness of purpose is one of the most necessary sinews of character, and one of the best instruments of success. Without it genius wastes its efforts in a maze of inconsistencies.

Lord Chesterfield

A regenerated society can only be composed of regenerated men. To expect a change in human nature may be an act of faith; but to expect a change in human society without it is an act of lunacy.

Lord Eustace Percy

Character is a by-product; it is produced in the great manufacture of daily duty.

Woodrow Wilson

Our character is but the stamp on our souls of the free choices of good and evil we have made through life.

Cunningham Geikie

I pray thee O God, that I may be beautiful within.

Socrates

Character is built out of circumstances—from exactly the same materials one man builds palaces, while another builds hovels.

G. H. Lewes

A man is what he is, not what men say he is. His character no man can touch. His character is what he is before God. His reputation is what men say he is. That can be damaged. For reputation is for time. Character is for eternity.

John B. Gough

Talent is nurtured in solitude; character is formed in the stormy billows of the world.

Johann Wolfgang von Goethe

Truthfulness is a corner-stone of character, and if it be not firmly laid in youth, there will ever after be a weak spot in the foundation.

Jackson Davis

Men of character are the conscience of the society to which they belong.

Ralph Waldo Emerson

Not education, but character, is man's greatest need and man's greatest safeguard.

Herbert Spencer

I would rather be adorned by beauty of character than by jewels. Jewels are the gift of fortune, while character comes from within.

Plautus

Character is like a rifle; it cannot shoot higher than it is aimed.

Alexander Animator

Sow a thought, reap an act;
Sow an act, reap a habit;
Sow a habit, reap a character;
Sow a character, reap a destiny.

Author Unknown

You cannot dream yourself into a character; you must hammer and forge yourself one.

James A. Froude

Nothing stands but character— real, simple, transparent, solid character. That will bear a thousand blasts of opposition and hostility, and at the end will seem the richer, the chaster, for the rude discipline through which it has passed.

Joseph Parker

Character is what a man is in the dark.

Dwight L. Moody

One never knows himself till he has denied himself. The altar of sacrifice is the touchstone of character.

O. P. Gifford

Trust that man in nothing who has not a conscience in everything.

Laurence Sterne

Character is the best dowry for your children.

Arnold H. Glasow

Character can be tested in various ways. In the business world the test is integrity. On a journey to the North Pole it would be dogged determination. In marriage, it is loyalty.

David R. Mace

Character is like a tree, and reputation like its shadow. The shadow is what we think of it; the tree is the real thing.

Abraham Lincoln

Just as an oak tree grows from a little acorn so does great character grow from a great many decisions that may at the time seem very minor.

Ben M. Herbster

Personality has the power to open many doors, but character must keep them open.

Author Unknown

Remove the chance to fail and we shall miss one of the best means of developing character.

Harold Stonier

When we develop character we acquire lovely personalities, for personality is character shining through everything we do and everything we say.

E. Maude Gardner

To educate a man in mind and not in morals is to educate a menace to society.

Theodore Roosevelt

Every man has in himself a continent of undiscovered character. Happy is he who acts the Columbus to his own soul.

Sir J. Stevens

Learning is the raising of character by the broadening of vision and the deepening of feeling.

Mayer Sulzberger

Character isn't built on ease, success, a million dollars or a happy life. Mainly through pain, sorrow and adversity are the bricks fashioned which can erect an enduring edifice.

Faith Baldwin

In the end, we are all the sum total of our actions. Character cannot be counterfeited, nor can it be put on and cast off as if it were a garment to meet the whim of the moment. Like the markings on wood which are ingrained in the very heart of the tree, character requires time and nurture for growth and development.

Thus also, day by day, we write our own destiny; for inexorably we become what we do. This I believe, is the supreme logic and the law of life.

Madame Chiang Kai-Shek

Character must stand behind and back up everything—the sermon, the poem, the picture, the play. None of them is worth a straw without it.

Josiah Gilbert Holland

In the destiny of every moral being there is an object more worthy of God than happiness. It is character. And the great aim of man's creation is the development of a grand character and grand character is, by its very nature, the product of probationary discipline.

Austin Phelps

There is nothing so fatal to character as half finished tasks.

David Lloyd George

---

18. AS A MAN THINKETH

If either man or woman would realize the full power of personal beauty, it must be by cherishing noble thoughts and hopes and purposes; by having something to do and something to live for that is worthy of humanity, and which, by expanding the capacities of the soul, gives expansion and symmetry to the body which contains it.

James Bailey Upham

Nurture your mind with great thoughts; to believe in the heroic makes heroes.

Benjamin Disraeli

I hold it true that thoughts are things
Endowed with body, breath, and wings.
And that we send them forth to fill
The world with good results or ill.

That what we call our secret
  thought
Flies to the earth's remotest spot,
Leaving its blessings or its woes
Like tracks behind it as it goes.
Author Unknown

Almost all the trouble in the world is created by things people think, say, and write. Words of anger, malice, hatred, resentment, jealousy, like physical blows, cause people to hit back. Over-bearing, demanding words create determined resistance. And the attitudes of mind back of them, even though we do not speak the words, are sensed by others. For the telepathic power of thought is no longer merely a theory. Thoughts are things.
Wilfred A. Peterson

Good thoughts and actions can never produce bad results; bad thoughts and actions can never produce good results. This is but saying that nothing can come from corn but corn, nothing from nettles but nettles.
James Allen

Life consists in what a man is thinking of all day.
Ralph Waldo Emerson

If you think you are beaten, you
  are;
  If you think you dare not, you
    don't.
If you'd like to win, but think you
    can't,
  It's almost a cinch you won't.
If you think you'll lose, you're lost,
  For out in the world we find
Success begins with a fellow's will;
  It's all in the state of mind.

If you think you're outclassed, you
  are;
  You've got to think high to rise.
You've got to be sure of yourself
    before
  You can ever win a prize.
Life's battles don't always go
  To the stronger or faster man;
But soon or late the man who wins
  Is the one who thinks he can.
Walter D. Wintle

Brainpower is now the greatest commodity we can contribute to the world. Democracy was never intended to be a breeding place for mediocrity. We must engage in the business of stimulating brainpower lest we fail in producing leaders of consequence. In a period of speed, space and hemispheric spasms we dare not treat new thoughts as if they were unwelcome relatives.
Dean F. Berkley

They are never alone that are accompanied with noble thoughts.
Sir Philip Sidney

Man is but a reed, the weakest in nature, but he is a thinking reed.
Blaise Pascal

The great conquerors, from Alexander to Caesar, and from Caesar to Napoleon, influenced profoundly the lives of subsequent generations. But the total effect of this influence shrinks to insignificance if compared to the entire transformation of human habits and human mentality produced by the long line of men of thought, from Thales to the present day, men individually powerless, but ultimately the rulers of the world.
Alfred N. Whitehead

There is a basic law that like attracts like. That which you mentally project reproduces in kind and negative thoughts definitely attract negative results. Conversely, if a person habitually thinks optimistically and hopefully he activates life around him positively and thereby attracts to himself positive results. His positive thinking sets in motion creative forces, and success instead of eluding him flows toward him.

Norman Vincent Peale

You are today where your thoughts have brought you; you will be tomorrow where your thoughts take you.

James Allen

All that we are is the result of what we have thought. The mind is everything. What we think, we become.

Buddha

Think like a man of action and act like a man of thought.

Henri Bergson

This journey through life can be a pleasant and rewarding experience if we have the right attitude. A good attitude is like cork—it can hold you up. A poor attitude is like lead—it can sink you.

L. Kenneth Wright

I am incurably convinced that the object of opening the mind as of opening the mouth is to shut it again on something solid.

G. K. Chesterton

A closed mind is a dying mind.

Edna Ferber

When the file cabinets of the mind are filled with thoughts of strength, health, beauty, honesty, efficiency, economy, and prosperity, their God-designed energy constantly attunes every fiber of your being to respond to and express these positive, perfect qualities in every department of your life. You cannot help manifesting the good that you think!

Clifton J. Noble

The key to every man is his thought. Sturdy and defying though he look, he has a helm which he obeys, which is the idea after which all his facts are classified. He can only be reformed by showing him a new idea which commands his own.

Ralph Waldo Emerson

Most men are so closely confined to the orbit of their wordly station that they have not even the courage to escape it by their ideas; and if there are some whom speculating on great matters unfits for small ones, there are yet more who by constant handling of small matters have lost the very sense of what is great.

Vauvenargues

The happiness of your life depends upon the quality of your thoughts, therefore guard accordingly; and take care that you entertain no notions unsuitable to virtue and reasonable nature.

Marcus Antoninus

Mind is the great lever of all things.

Daniel Webster

If we are to succeed, we must think success. If we are to be happy, we must think happily. If we are to be well, we must think healthful, constructive thoughts. If we are to get over confusion, we must think peace. The mind can never accept what it rejects.

Ernest Holmes

Life does not consist mainly— or even largely—of facts and happenings. It consists mainly of the storm of thoughts that is forever blowing through one's head.

Mark Twain

The weak-minded change their opinions because they are easily influenced by others, and the strong-minded change their opinions because they have complete mastery of their opinions.

Jacob Klatzkin

We may take Fancy for a companion, but must follow Reason as our guide.

Samuel Johnson

In many cases people are what you make them. A scornful look turns into a complete fool a man of average intelligence. A contemptuous indifference turns into an enemy a woman who, well treated, might have been an angel.

Andre Maurois

Our personalities are not merely mirrors giving back reflections of our thoughts. We are shaped, molded, colored, and defined by our thoughts. They work within us to make us what we are as organically as the life impulse within an acorn determines the form and glory of the oak.

Elmer G. Leterman

It is the mind that maketh good or ill, that maketh wretch or happy, rich or poor.

Edmund Spenser

Instead of a gem or a flower, cast the gift of a lovely thought into the heart of a friend.

George McDonald

Associate reverently, and as much as you can, with your loftiest thoughts.

Henry Thoreau

Strength of mind is exercise, not rest.

Alexander Pope

Ideas are precious. An idea is the only lever which really moves the world.

Arthur F. Corey

It is a romantic myth that the country is pure and the city foul, that a merchant is essentially and necessarily more ignoble than he who cultivates the soil, that the work of the hand has a moral value which the work of the mind lacks. In a complicated modern civilization, whatever its specific economic forms, every function is as necessary as every other.

Ludwig Lewisohn

Why should we think upon things that are lovely? Because thinking determines life. It is a common habit to blame life upon environment. Environment modifies life but does not govern life. The soul is stronger than its surroundings.

William James

The thought that is beautiful is the thought to cherish. The word that is beautiful is worthy to endure. The act that is beautiful is eternally and always true and right. Only beware that your appreciation of beauty is just and true; and to that end, I urge you to live intimately with beauty of the highest type, until it has become a part of you, until you have within you that fineness, that order, that calm, which puts you in tune with the finest things of the universe, and which links you with that spirit that is the enduring life of the world.

Bertha Bailey

Great thoughts are blessed guests, and should be heartily welcomed, well fed and much sought after. Like rose leaves, they give out a sweet smell if laid up in the jar of memory.

Charles Haddon Spurgeon

All that a man does outwardly is but the expression and completion of his inward thought. To work effectively, he must think clearly; to act nobly, he must think nobly.

William E. Channing

Reason is a barrier, but a barrier that tells us why we cannot pass through.

Comtesse Diane

Thoughts are indestructible, as real as radio and television waves, as powerful as life, and they are never lost. While it is true that thoughts may come unbidden, you can cast out thoughts that are harmful and substitute good thoughts instead.

Ruth Barrick Golden

The pleasures of the senses pass quickly; those of the heart become sorrow; but those of the mind are with us even to the end of our journey.

Spanish Proverb

The greatest discovery of my generation is that human beings can alter their lives by altering their attitudes.

William James

Beware when the great God lets loose a thinker on this planet.

Ralph Waldo Emerson

There are some people—and I am one of them—who think that the most practical and important thing about a man is still his view of the universe. We think that for a landlady considering a lodger it is important to know his income, but still more important to know his philosophy. We think that for a general who is about to fight an enemy it is important to know the enemy's numbers, but still more important to know the enemy's philosophy. We think the question is not whether the theory of the cosmos matters, but whether in the long run anything else affects it.

G. K. Chesterton

Thought takes man out of servitude, into freedom.

Henry W. Longfellow

A mind filled with thoughts of God cannot entertain evil thoughts.

A. Nicholas

By your thoughts you are daily, even hourly, building your life, just as surely as the mason builds a wall by placing brick upon brick, or stone upon stone. By your thoughts you are erecting the temple of your life; you are carving your destiny, as the sculptor with his chisel and hammer, chip by chap, creates the finished statue from a block of marble or from a rough stone.

Ruth Barrick Golden

Our life is what our thoughts make it.

Marcus Aurelius

Intellect is to emotion as our clothes are to our bodies: we could not very well have civilized life without clothes, but we would be in a poor way if we had only clothes without bodies.

Alfred North Whitehead

The ideas and images in men's minds are the invisible powers that constantly govern them; and to these they all pay universally a ready submission.

Jonathan Edwards

Thought is, perhaps, the forerunner and even the mother of ideas, and ideas are the most powerful and the most useful things in the world.

George Gardner

Right thinking is a prerequisite to right living . . . In truth the destiny of any life is determined by what fills that mind. Brain power can be, and often is, prostituted to selfish and unworthy aims in life. When forces of evil invade a people's land, it must first shackle the minds of those people. Dictators have worked their cruel power upon nations in this way. Realizing that destiny is determined by thinking, great care should be taken as to what is put into the mind.

Roy I. Bagley

I gave a beggar from my little store
Of well earned gold.

He spent the shining ore, and came
again and yet again
Still cold and hungry as before.
I gave a thought, and through that
thought of mine
He found himself, the man, supreme, divine!
Fed, clothed and crowned with
blessings manifold,
And now he begs no more.

Ella Wheeler Wilcox

The thoughts we think are like deposits made in a bank, and sooner or later they go through habit grooves and spring into action. To see how thought responds to the great law of habit, you might think of your mind as a plastic, pliable surface. Each time you think a new thought, it cuts a groove in that surface. When you again think the same thought or one very much like it, it cuts the groove a little deeper, until it becomes like a wagon rut in a country road. Once these thought grooves, or patterns, are established, our thoughts have a tendency to slip into them, whether they be good thought patterns or bad.

M. D. Hannah

The world stands on ideas, not on iron or cotton.

Ralph Waldo Emerson

Beautiful thoughts make a beautiful soul, and a beautiful soul makes a beautiful face.

Author Unknown

Until there be correct thought, there cannot be right action and when there is correct thought, right action will follow.

Henry George

Because of the law of gravitation the apple falls to the ground. Because of the law of growth the acorn becomes a mighty oak. Because of the law of causation, a man is "as he thinketh in his heart." Nothing can happen without its adequate cause.

Don Carlos Musser

A thought,—good or evil,—an act, in time a habit,—so runs life's law.

Ralph Waldo Trine

Every person in the world has it in him to become far more than he is. "Men habitually use only a small part of the powers which they possess," said the eminent psychologist, William James. Great unused reservoirs of power lie buried deep within us all. Psychologists tell us that about one tenth of the mind is the conscious mind and nine tenths the unconscious mind. The conscious mind is that part with which we reason, selecting or rejecting what seems to us to be good or bad, as the case may be. What our reasoned judgment dwells upon sinks into the unconscious mind and becomes a part of us. If we train ourselves to dwell upon what is true and good and beautiful, we gradually build integrated, poised, power-filled lives. If we indulge in negative, undisciplined, greedy, lustful thinking we become tense, unhappy, depressed, fear-ridden individuals—derelicts helplessly afloat upon the rough seas of life. "As a man thinketh in his heart, so is he," says the Bible.

L. L. Dunnington

Those who use their reason do not reach the same conclusions as those who obey their prejudices.

Walter Lippmann

There are gems of thought that are ageless and eternal.

Cicero

One-story intellects, two-story intellects with skylights. All fact-collectors are one-story men. Two-story men compare, reason, generalize. Three-story men idealize, imagine, predict; their best illumination comes from above, through the skylight.

Oliver Wendell Holmes

That man proves his worth who can make us listen when he is by, and think when he has gone.

Comtesse Diane

Let a man strive to purify his thoughts. What a man thinketh, that is he; this is the eternal mystery. Dwelling within his Self with thoughts serene, he will obtain imperishable happiness. Man becomes that of which he thinks.

Upanishads

Every revolution was first a thought in one man's mind.

Ralph Waldo Emerson

A man's mind stretched by a new idea can never go back to its original dimensions.

Oliver Wendell Holmes

The fingers of your thoughts are molding your face ceaselessly.

Charles Reznikoff

The world is what we think it is. If we can change our thoughts, we can change the world. And that is our hope.

H. M. Tomlinson

A great many people think they are thinking when they are merely rearranging their prejudices.

William James

19. THE ART OF DISCONTENT

I believe in the challenging mind, in the unreconciled heart and in the will toward perfection.

Ellen Glasgow

Should a person accept poverty with stoicism? Should he accept being unloved, being a political prisoner? Should he accept the annihilation of his self-respect and his integrity! The dictum of accepting the inevitable can be destructive of all human hope and freedom. It is a wonderful tool in the hands of those in positions of dominance who do not want those in subordinate roles to overthrow the applecart. Dante said "In God's will lies our peace," but we better first make sure that it is God's will we are obeying, and not that of a frail human being, his whim or prejudice, or our own fear.

George Lawton

One who is contented with what he has done will never become famous for what he will do. He has lain down to die, and the grass is already over him.

C. N. Bovee

The predominant aim of education in the United States is to adjust the young to their environment. But the best object of education, in my view, is rather to enable young people to change their environment, to induce them to do so, to provide them with incentives, and to suggest how the environment should be changed. We came into the world, not to adjust ourselves to it, but to alter it.

Robert M. Hutchins

Many a man might have become great in later years if he had not in his younger years believed himself to be that already.

Daniel Sanders

Be satisfied with life always but never with one's self.

George Jean Nathan

The noblest within us is brought forth not in contentment but in discontent, not in truce but in fight.

Baruch Charney Vladeck

The well-adjusted make poor prophets.

Eric Hoffer

Discontent is the first step in the progress of a man or a nation.

Oscar Wilde

Who is not satisfied with himself will grow; who is not sure of his own correctness will learn many things.

Chinese Proverb

This life were brutish did we not sometimes
Have intimations clear of wider scope,
Hints of occasion infinite, to keep
The soul alert with noble discontent

And onward yearnings of unstilled
  desire;
Fruitless, except we now and then
  divined
A mystery of Purpose, gleaming
  through
The secular confusions of the
  world,
Whose will we darkly accomplish,
  doing ours.

James Russell Lowell

Man is the only animal that
laughs and weeps; for he is the
animal that is struck with the difference between what things are,
and what they ought to be.

William Hazlitt

There are two kinds of discontent in this world: the discontent
that works, and the discontent
that wrings its hands. The first gets
what it wants, and the second loses
what it has. There's no cure for
the first but success; and there's
no cure at all for the second.

Gordon Graham

Aristotle said that all creative
people are dissatisfied because they
are all looking for happiness in
perfection and seeking for things
that do not exist. This is one of
the hopes of the world. There is
no progress where people are satisfied. Discontent is perhaps the most
potent challenge to improvement.

Clarence Edwin Flynn

May we, like our fathers, still
stand out against the multitude,
protesting with all our might
against its follies and its fears. May
a divine discontent give color to
our dreams, and a passion for holy
heresy set the tone of our thoughts.
May the soul of the rebel still

throb in us as it throbbed in our
forefathers, that today and forever
we may still be a light unto those
who stumble in darkness.

Lewis Browne

The religious person at his best
is never wholly content with himself and at peace with the world,
for he knows how far he falls short
of what he ought to be and can be.
There is a positive and healthy
tension between what is and what
ought to be that forbids complacency and incites to action.

Harry C. Meserve

I would define man as the unfinished animal, the radically dissatisfied and maladjusted animal
who comes up with a dozen different answers to each of Nature's
proposals. Man is the only animal
who is not content to remain in
the original state of nature.

Lewis Mumford

Noble discontent is the path to
heaven.

Thomas Wentworth Higginson

Ever insurgent let me be,
Make me more daring than devout;
From sleek contentment keep me
  free
And fill me with a buoyant doubt.

Louis Untermeyer

The capacity of indignation
makes an essential part of the outfit
of every honest man.

James Russell Lowell

To be forbearing to all—that
is love; to be relentless toward self
—that is wisdom; to be content
with what one has—that is riches;
to be discontented with what one
is—that is piety.

Ivan N. Panin

The reasonable man adapts himself to the world. The unreasonable one persists in trying to adapt the world to himself. Therefore all progress depends on the unreasonable man.

George Bernard Shaw

The man who is hard to satisfy moves forward. The man who sits back comfortably and is satisfied with what he has accomplished moves backward. If I were to bequeath to every young man one virtue, I would give him the spirit of divine dissatisfaction, for without it, the world would stand still.

Charles P. Steinmetz

Bad will be the day for every man when he becomes absolutely contented with the life that he is living, with the thoughts that he is thinking, with the deeds that he is doing, when there is not forever beating at the doors of his soul some great desire to do something larger, which he knows that he was meant and made to do because he is still, in spite of all, the child of God.

Phillips Brooks

In all men there must arise a spark of the dissenter if civilization is to survive. Society has less to lose from these subversive individuals who are willing to pervert the right of free inquiry than it has by denying freedom to the host of honest men and women who are genuinely concerned to learn what is not now known, to create knowledge now sorely needed.

Richard B. Ballou

Those who are quite satisfied, sit still and do nothing; those who are not quite satisfied, are the sole benefactors of the world.

Walter Savage Landor

Self-complacency is the companion of ignorance.

Solomon Schechter

20. CREEDS TO LIVE BY

Faithfully faithful to every trust,
Honestly honest in every deed,
Righteously righteous and justly just;
This is the whole of the good man's creed.

Author Unknown

Whatever may happen in the future, I know that I have learned three things which will remain forever convictions of my heart as well as my mind. Life, even the hardest life, is the most beautiful, wonderful and miraculous treasure in the world. Fulfilment of duty is another beautiful thing, making life happy and giving to the soul an unconquerable force to sustain ideals. This is my second conviction, and my third is that cruelty, hatred, and injustice never can and never will be able to create a mental, moral, or material millennium.

Peter A. Sorokin

Do all the good you can,
In all the ways you can,
In all the places you can,
At all the times you can,

To all the people you can,
As long as ever you can.
                    John Wesley

We come into this world crying
while all around us are smiling.
May we so live that we go out of
this world smiling while everybody
around us is weeping.
                Persian Proverb

Somebody did a golden deed;
Somebody proved a friend in need;
Somebody sang a beautiful song;
Somebody smiled the whole day
    long;
Somebody thought " 'Tis sweet to
    live";
Somebody said "I'm glad to give";
Somebody fought a valiant fight;
Somebody lived to shield the right;
    Was that "somebody" you?
                Author Unknown

To love the beautiful, to desire
the good, to do the best.
                Moses Mendelssohn

I expect to pass through this
world but once. Any good thing,
therefore, that I can do, or any
kindness that I can show a fellow
being, let me do it now. Let me
not defer or neglect it, for I shall
not pass this way again.
                Stephen Grellet

Justice is the only worship;
Love is the only priest;
Ignorance is the only slavery;
Happiness is the only good;
The time to be happy is now
The place to be happy is here,
The way to be happy is to make
    others so.
                Ralph Ingersoll

Lift where you stand.
                Edward Everett

To keep my health!
To do my work!
To live!
To see to it I grow and gain and
    give!
Never to look behind me for an
    hour!
To wait in weakness and to walk in
    power.
But always fronting onward toward
    the light,
Always and always facing toward
    the right,
Robbed, starved, defeated, fallen,
    wide astray—
On with what strength I have
Back to the way!
                Charlotte P. Gilman

Be displeased with what thou
art, if thou desirest to attain to
what thou art not; for where thou
hast pleased thyself, there thou
abidest, and if thou sayest I have
enough, thou perishest.
                Saint Augustine

I would be true, for there are those
    that trust me;
    I would be pure, for there are
        those who care;
I would be strong, for there is much
    to suffer;
    I would be brave, for there is
        much to dare.
I would be friend of all—the foe—
    the friendless;
    I would be giving, and forget
        the gift;
I would be humble, for I know my
    weakness;
    I would look up—and laugh—
        and love—and lift.
                Harold Arnold Walters

To live content with small
means; to seek elegance rather than

luxury, and refinement rather than fashion; to be worthy, not respectable, and wealthy, not rich; to study hard, think quietly, talk gently, act grandly; to listen to the stars and birds, to babes and sages, with open heart; to bear all cheerfully, do all bravely, await occasions, hurry never; in a word to let the spiritual, unbidden and unconscious, grow up through the common.

William Henry Channing

Let me be a little kinder, let me be a little blinder
To the faults of those about me; let me praise a little more.
Let me be, when I am weary, just a little bit more cheery:
Let me serve a little better those that I am striving for.
Let me be a little braver, when temptation bids me waver;
Let me strive a little harder to be all that I should be.
Let me be a little meeker with the brother that is weaker;
Let me think more of my neighbor and a little less of me.

Author Unknown

Be amongst the persecuted rather than the persecutors.

The Talmud

Would any man be strong, let him work; or wise, let him observe and think; or happy, let him help; or influential, let him sacrifice and serve.

John Ruskin

What can I do? I can talk out when others are silent. I can say man when others say money. I can stay up when others are asleep. I can keep working when others have stopped to play. I can give life big meanings when others give life little meanings. I can say love when others say hate. I can say every man when others say one man. What can I do? I can give myself to life when other men refuse themselves to life.

Horace Traubel

To be honest, to be kind;
To earn a little and to spend a little less;
To make upon the whole a family happier for his presence;
To renounce when that shall be necessary and not to be embittered;
To keep a few friends, but those without capitulation,
Above all, on the same grim conditions, to keep friends with himself—
Here is a task for all that a man has of fortitude and delicacy.

Robert Louis Stevenson

So here's my creed—
And how I love it!—
Beauty in earth,
And God above it.

Thomas Curtis Clark

THE ART OF LIVING

AT OUR BEST

---

21. THE ART OF SUCCEEDING

Self-trust is the first secret of success.

Ralph Waldo Emerson

I divide the world into three classes: the few who make things happen; the many who watch things happen; and the vast majority who have no idea of what happens: We need more people who make things happen.

Nicholas Murray Butler

Next to knowing when to seize an opportunity, the most important thing in life is to know when to forego an advantage.

Benjamin Disraeli

A friend of mine says that every man who takes office in Washington either grows or swells, and when I give a man an office, I watch him carefully to see whether he is swelling or growing.

Woodrow Wilson

It is provided in the essence of things that from any fruition of success, no matter what, shall come forth something to make a greater struggle necessary.

Walt Whitman

If you wish success in life, make perseverance your bosom friend, experience your wise counselor, caution your elder brother, and hope your guardian genius.

Joseph Addison

The reason most people do not succeed is that they will not do the things that successful people must do. The successful scientist must follow a formula. The tourist follows a road map. The builder follows a blueprint. The successful cook follows a recipe. . . . It is not important that you merely want to succeed, unless you want to badly enough that you are willing to do certain things.

Author Unknown

The heights by great men reached
    and kept
Were not attained by sudden
    flight,

But they while their companions slept
Were toiling upward in the night.

Henry Wadsworth Longfellow

I have learned that success is to be measured not so much by the position that one has reached in life as by the obstacles which he has overcome while trying to succeed.

Booker T. Washington

To have faith where you cannot see; to be willing to work on in the dark; to be conscious of the fact that, so long as you strive for the best, there are better things on the way, this in itself is success.

Katherine Logan

Success and suffering are vitally and organically linked. If you succeed without suffering, it is because someone has suffered for you; if you suffer without succeeding, it is in order that someone else may succeed after you.

Edward Judson

Nothing will ever be attempted if all possible objections must be first overcome.

Samuel Johnson

One half of knowing what you want is knowing what you must give up before you get it.

Sidney Howard

Only he is successful in his business who makes that pursuit which affords him the highest pleasure sustain him.

Henry David Thoreau

Success is full of promise till men get it; and then it is a last year's nest from which the birds have flown.

Henry Ward Beecher

According to the theory of aerodynamics, and as may be readily demonstrated thru laboratory tests and wind tunnel experiments, the bumble bee is unable to fly. This is because the size, weight and shape of its body in relation to the total wing spread make flying impossible. But the bumble bee, being ignorant of these profound scientific truths, goes ahead and flies anyway and manages to make a little honey every day.

Author Unknown

He who attracts luck carries with him the magnet of preparation.

William A. Ward

Success slips away from you like sand through the fingers, like water through a leaky pail, unless success is held tight by hard work, day by day, night by night, year in and year out. Everyone who is not looking forward to going to seed looks forward to working harder and harder and more fruitfully as long as he lasts.

Stuart Sherman

What is victory? Victory is that which must be bought with the lives of young men to retrieve the errors of the old. Victory is a battered thing courage must salvage out of the wreckage which stupidity has wrought. Victory is redemption purchased for men's hope at a cost so terrible that only defeat could be more bitter.

Gordon R. Munnoch

Providence has nothing good or high in store for one who does not resolutely aim at something high or good. A purpose is the eternal condition of success.

Theodore T. Munger

The conditions of conquest, are always easy. We have but to toil awhile, endure awhile, believe always, and never turn back.

William Gilmore Simms

Opportunities do not come with their values stamped upon them. Every one must be challenged. A day dawns, quite like other days; in it a single hour comes, quite like other hours; but in that day and in that hour the chance of a lifetime faces us. To face every opportunity of life thoughtfully and ask its meaning bravely and earnestly, is the only way to meet the supreme opportunities when they come, whether open-faced or disguised.

Maltbie V. Babcock

This is the foundation of success nine times out of ten—having confidence in yourself and applying yourself with all your might to your work.

Thomas E. Wilson

The will to succeed in any endeavor depends upon concentrating mind and muscle upon those routines necessary to success.

L. L. Moorman

A man can be as truly a saint in a factory as in a monastery, and there is as much need of him in the one as in the other.

Robert J. McCracken

The roots of true achievement lie in the will to become the best that you can become.

Harold Taylor

There are two kinds of success. One is the very rare kind that comes to the man who has the power to do what no one else has the power to do. That is genius. But the average man who wins what we call success is not a genius. He is a man who has merely the ordinary qualities that he shares with his fellows, but who has developed those ordinary qualities to a more than ordinary degree.

Theodore Roosevelt

For threescore years I have been analyzing the causes of success and failure. Experience has taught me that financial success, job success, and happiness in human relations are, in the main, the result of (a) physical well-being; (b) constant effort to develop one's personal assets; (c) setting up and working toward a series of life goals; (d) allowing time for meditation and spiritual regeneration.

Roger W. Babson

It is not enough to have great qualities, we should also have the management of them.

François Rochefoucauld

The common idea that success spoils people by making them vain, egotistic, and self-complacent is erroneous; on the contrary it makes them, for the most part, humble, tolerant, and kind. Failure makes people bitter and cruel.

W. Somerset Maugham

Man is at his best when stimulated by hope of reward, fear of failure, and the light of a star.

Erwin H. Schell

One of the chief reasons for success in life is the ability to maintain a daily interest in one's work, to have a chronic enthusiasm, to regard each day as important.

William Lyon Phelps

The great secret of success is to go through life as a man who never gets used up. That is possible for him who never argues and strives with men and facts, but in all experiences retires upon himself, and looks for the ultimate cause of things in himself.

Albert Schweitzer

The greatest obstacle to being heroic is the doubt whether one may not be going to prove one's self a fool; the truest heroism is to resist the doubt, and the profoundest wisdom is to know when it ought to be resisted and when to be obeyed.

Nathaniel Hawthorne

When a resolute young fellow steps up to the great bully, the world, and takes him boldly by the beard, he is often surprised to find it comes off in his hand, and that it was only tied on to scare away timid adventurers.

Ralph Waldo Emerson

One wide-awake persistent enemy may be worth twenty friends. Friends point out all the good things you do. You know all about that. Your enemies point out your mistakes. Get yourself a first-class enemy, cultivate him, and when you achieve success thank him.

Harold Hobbs, Sr.

Coming together is a beginning; keeping together is progress; working together is success.

Henry Ford

Formula for achievement: Congregate, coordinate, cooperate.

Gretchen Schenk

Before everything else, getting ready is the secret of success.

Henry Ford

There are two significant characteristics of every great life. The first is capacity to make a good beginning and the second is courage to push on to a good ending. One of the saddest things in life is to see a man begin some worthy venture revealing great promise and then to watch him flounder into failure for lack of courage to push on through frustration and disappointment. . . . A life of triumph hinges on a firm faith for rugged times.

Harold Blake Walker

To be born a gentleman is an accident, but to die one is an achievement.

H. P. Kaye

The most powerful weapon on earth is the human soul on fire.

Marshal Foch

The difference between failure and success is doing a thing nearly right and doing it exactly right.

Edward C. Simmons

Success will come to the individual who seeks it and is willing to do more than is necessary.

Walter Mason

One of the follies of youth is to expect success without patient preparation.

Arnold H. Glasow

Little successes can prevent greater successes if we settle back and rest on the laurels already won.

Jesse Mercer Gehman

He has achieved success who has lived well, laughed often, and loved much; who has gained the respect of intelligent men, the trust of pure women and the love of little children; who has left the world a better place than he found it, whether by an improved poppy, a perfect poem or a rescued soul; who has never lacked appreciation of earth's beauty or failed to express it; who has looked for the best in others and given them the best he had; whose life was an inspiration; whose memory a benediction.

Bessie A. Stanley

He that is good for making excuses, is seldom good for anything else.

Benjamin Franklin

Our chief want in life is somebody who shall make us do what we can.

Ralph Waldo Emerson

Being famous is like having a string of pearls given you. It's nice, but after a while, if you think of it at all, it's only to wonder if they're real or cultured.

W. Somerset Maugham

The greatest superstition now entertained by public men is that hypocrisy is the royal road to success.

Robert G. Ingersoll

A successful man is he who receives a great deal from his fellow-men, usually incomparably more than corresponds to his service to them.

Albert Einstein

Firm must be the will, patient the heart, passionate the aspiration, to secure the fulfillment of some high and lonely purpose, when reverie spreads always its bed of roses on the one side, and practical work summons to its treadmill on the other.

Samuel Smiles

To do for the world more than the world does for you—that is success.

Henry Ford

There is something in each of us that resents restraints, repressions, and controls but we forget that nothing left loose ever does anything creative. No horse gets anywhere until he is harnessed. No steam or gas ever drives anything until it is confined. No Niagara is ever turned into light and power until it is tunneled. No life ever grows great until it is dedicated, focused, disciplined.

Harry E. Fosdick

You must have long-range goals to keep you from being frustrated by short-range failures.

Charles C. Noble

When a person alibies that he could have amounted to something if it had not been for his race, creed or religion, one should call attention to Epictetus, the slave who lived in the first century in Greece, and became one of the world's most profound scholars and philosophers. He should be reminded that Disraeli, the despised Jew, became Prime Minister of Great Britain; that Booker T. Washington, who was born in slavery in this country became one of the nation's greatest educators; and that another Negro slave, George Washington Carver, became one of the greatest scientists of his generation. Lincoln, born of illiterate parents in a log cabin in Kentucky, lived to be acclaimed one of the greatest statesmen of all time.

Phil Conley

No true and permanent Fame can be founded except in labors which promote the happiness of mankind.

Charles Sumner

Don't be misled into believing that somehow the world owes you a living. The boy who believes that his parents, or the government, or anyone else owes him a livelihood and that he can collect it without labor will wake up one day and find himself working for another boy who did not have that belief and, therefore, earned the right to have others work for him.

David Sarnoff

I am only one, but I am one. I cannot do everything, but I can do something. And I will not let what I cannot do interfere with what I can do.

Edward Everett Hale

It does not take great men to do great things; it only takes consecrated men.

Phillips Brooks

The world is moving so fast these days that the man who says it can't be done is generally interrupted by someone doing it.

Harry Emerson Fosdick

The drive to achieve advances not only gifted persons, but the average person as well. The person of only average ability is likely to get where he wants to go if he wants to badly enough.

Leslie J. Nason

Fame is climbing a greasy pole for $10 and ruining trousers worth $15.

Josh Billings

There is hardly one in three of us who live in the cities who is not sick with unused self.

Ben Hecht

To accomplish great things, we must not only act but also dream, not only plan but also believe.

Anatole France

Isn't it strange
That princes and kings,
And clowns that caper
In sawdust rings,
And common people
Like you and me
Are builders for eternity?

Each is given a bag of tools,
A shapeless mass,
A book of rules;
And each must make—
Ere life is flown—
A stumbling block
Or a steppingstone.

R. L. Sharpe

Every man is enthusiastic at times. One man has enthusiasm for 30 minutes—another for 30 days, but it is the man who has it for 30 years who makes a success in life.

Edward Butler

Education means drawing forth from the mind latent powers and developing them, so that in mature years one may apply these powers not merely to success in one's occupation, but to success in the greatest of all arts—the art of living.

William Lyon Phelps

---

22. THE ART OF MASTERING FATE

There is no chance, no destiny, no fate,
Can circumvent or hinder or control
The firm resolve of a determined soul.
Gift counts for nothing; will alone is great;
All things give way before it, soon or late.
What obstacle can stay the mighty force
Of the sea-seeking river in its course,
Or cause the ascending orb of day to wait?
Each wellborn soul must win what it deserves
Let the fool prate of luck. The fortunate
Is he whose earnest purpose never swerves,
Whose slightest action or inaction serves
The one great aim. Why, even Death stands still,
And waits an hour sometimes for such a will.

Ella Wheeler Wilcox

There is a tide in the affairs of men, which, taken at the flood, leads on to fortune; omitted, all the voyage of their life is bound in shallows and in miseries; and we must take the current when it serves, or lose our ventures.

William Shakespeare

Destiny is an invention of the cowardly and the resigned.

Ignazio Silone

Chiefly, the mould of a man's fortune is in his own hands.

Francis Bacon

We make our fortunes and we call them fate.

Benjamin Disraeli

Life consists not simply in what heredity and environment do to us but in what we make out of what they do to us.

Harry Emerson Fosdick

Every man is his own ancestor, and every man is his own heir. He devises his own future, and he inherits his own past.

H. F. Hedge

The wind that fills my sails
Propels; but I am helmsman.

George Meredith

A man can live well even in a palace.

Marcus Aurelius

A man's own character is the arbiter of his fortune.

Syrus

Man is not the creature of circumstances, circumstances are the creatures of men.

Benjamin Disraeli

Fatalism is always apt to be a double-edged philsophy; for while, on the one hand, it reveals the minutest occurrences as the immutable result of a rigid chain of infinitely predestined causes, on the other, it invests the wildest incoherencies of conduct or of circumstance with the sanctity of eternal law.

Lytton Strachey

People are always blaming their circumstances for what they are. I don't believe in circumstances. The people who get on in this world are the people who get up and look for the circumstances they want, and, if they can't find them, make them.

George Bernard Shaw

As long as a man stands in his own way, everything seems to be in his way, governments, society, and even the sun and moon and stars, as astrology may testify.

Henry David Thoreau

Circumstances are the rulers of the weak; they are but the instruments of the wise.

Samuel Lover

Most of the shadows of this life are caused by standing in our own sunshine.

Ralph Waldo Emerson

Man is born with a tendency to detect a maximum of contributory negligence in other people's misfortunes, and nothing but blind chance in his own.

Arthur Schnitzler

Men at some times are masters of their fates;
The fault is not in our stars,

But in ourselves, that we are underlings.

William Shakespeare

We pass our life in forging fetters for ourselves, and in complaining of having to wear them.

Gustav Vapereau

It matters not how strait the gate,
How charged with punishments the scroll,
I am the master of my fate:
I am the captain of my soul.

William Ernest Henley

Fatalism, whether pious or pessimistic, stands flatly discredited. It serves as an excuse for practical inaction or mental indolence. To believe that the future is predestined by non-human causes saves men from the trouble of doing; to believe that conscious will is merely a mask for irrational impulses saves men from the trouble of thinking.

Ralph Barton Perry

Man does have motive power that is his own. He is not simply at the mercy of external agencies, strong and compelling as these obviously are. On the river of circumstance he still is borne along, but he moves there not inertly, like a log, but as a boat moves that contains within it power enough to give it steerage way at least, and sometimes even to carry it upstream against the current.

Edmund W. Sinnott

I never knew a man of merit neglected; it was generally his own fault that he failed of success.

Samuel Johnson

God does not decree that a man should be good or evil. It is only fools and ignoramuses among Gentiles and Jews who maintain this nonsense. Any man born is free to become as righteous as Moses, as wicked as Jeroboam, a student or an ignoramus, kind or cruel, generous or niggardly.

Moses Maimonides

We are our own devils; we drive ourselves out of our Edens.

Johann Wolfgang von Goethe

All successful men have agreed in being causationists; they believed that things were not by luck, but by law—that there was not a weak or cracked link in the chain that joins the first and last of things—the cause and effect.

Ralph Waldo Emerson

It is one of the deepest lessons of history that men do not need to be the slaves of their surroundings. They can master them. Every exodus in the history of mankind has been led by a Moses who was stronger than his environment.

Lynn Harold Hough

Life is not the creature of circumstance. Indeed, in the whole universe of everything that is, life alone, life by its very nature, is the antagonist of circumstance. Inanimate things all drift. Water flows to the sea by the path of least resistance. But life climbs the mountains and conquers the wilderness and mounts into the sky. If there is any one thing that is utterly clear about the nature of life, it is that it was meant to master circumstance. At the human level, it is meant to master even its own circumstances—the oppositions within as well as the barriers without. The

spirit conquers all things when the spirit wills it, and no excuse remains when we fail to live as we wish.

A. Powell Davies

The winds and waves are always on the side of the ablest navigators.

Edward Gibbon

Nothing splendid has ever been achieved except by those who dared believe that something inside them was superior to circumstance.

Bruce Barton

No life is so hard that you can't make it easier by the way you take it.

Ellen Glasgow

Nothing can stop a determined man. Cripple him and you have a Sir Walter Scott; put him in prison and you have a John Bunyan; bury him in snow at Valley Forge and you have a George Washington; have him born in abject poverty and you have an Abraham Lincoln; load him with bitter racial prejudice and you have a Disraeli; afflict him with asthma as a boy and you have a Theodore Roosevelt; stab him with rheumatic pains until he cannot sleep without opiate and you have a Charles Steinmetz; paralyze his legs and you have a Franklin Roosevelt. In short, it's one's character that determines one's destiny.

Author Unknown

We cannot tell what may happen to us in the strange medley of life. But we can decide what happens in us—how we take it, what we do with it—and that is what really counts in the end. How to take the raw stuff of life and make it a thing of worth and beauty— that is the test of living.

Joseph Fort Newton

In the fields of observation, chance favors only the prepared minds.

Louis Pasteur

Every one is responsible for his own acts.

Cervantes

The same wind that carries one vessel into port may blow another off shore.

C. N. Bovee

The common argument that crime is caused by poverty is a kind of slander on the poor.

H. L. Mencken

Man has the capacity of almost complete control of fate. If he fails it will be by the ignorance or folly of men.

E. L. Thorndike

It never occurs to fools that merit and good fortune are closely united.

Johann Wolfgang von Goethe

Free will and determinism, I was told, are like a game of cards. The hand that is dealt you represents determinism. The way you play your hand represents free will.

Norman Cousins

You cannot choose your battle-field,
The gods do that for you,
But you can plant a standard
Where a standard never flew.

Nathalia Crane

Shallow men believe in luck.

Ralph Waldo Emerson

Fate is something you believe in when things are not going well. When they are, you forget it.

Aubrey Menen

One need remain in hell no longer than he chooses to; and the moment he chooses not to remain longer, not all the powers in the universe can prevent his leaving it. One can rise to any heaven he himself chooses; and when he chooses so to rise, all the higher powers of the universe combine to help him heavenward.

Ralph W. Trine

The shaping of our own life is our own work. It is a thing of beauty, or a thing of shame, as we ourselves make it. We lay the corner and add joint to joint, we give the proportion, we set the finish. It may be a thing of beauty and of joy forever. God forgive us if we pervert our life from putting on its appointed glory!

William Ware

What we call Luck is simply Pluck,
And the doing things over and over;
Courage and will, perseverance and skill,
Are the four leaves of Luck's clover.

Author Unknown

When you have a lemon, make a lemonade.

Julius Rosenwald

Can a man control his future? Yes. Despite the system they live under, men everywhere have, I believe, more power over the future than ever before. The important thing is that we must choose to exercise it.

What we do today determines how the world shall go, for tomorrow is made up of the sum total of today's experiences. No one knows what the formula is, nor how slight a change may reshape the pattern to our heart's desire. Far from feeling hopeless or helpless, we must seize every opportunity, however small, to help the world around us toward peace, productivity and human brotherhood.

Boris Pasternak

We are what we accept ourselves as being. We can be what we convince ourselves we can be.

Elmer G. Leterman

I do not believe in that word Fate. It is the refuge of every self-confessed failure.

Andrew Soutar

It could be written, for most of us: due to circumstances within our control.

Marcelene Cox

Circumstances!—I make circumstances!

Napoleon

Our remedies oft in ourselves doth lie, which we ascribe to heaven.

William Shakespeare

Weak men wait for opportunities; strong men make them.

Anderson M. Baten

What lies behind us and what lies before us are tiny matters compared to what lies within us.

William Morrow

I endeavor to subdue circumstances to myself, and not myself to circumstances.

Horace

It often amuses me to hear men impute all their misfortunes to fate, luck or destiny, whilst their successes or good fortune they ascribe to their own sagacity, cleverness, or penetration.

Samuel Taylor Coleridge

Man must cease attributing his problems to his environment, and learn again to exercise his will— his personal responsibility in the realm of faith and morals.

Albert Schweitzer

Luck means the hardships and privations which you have not hesitated to endure; the long nights you have devoted to work. Luck means the appointments you have never failed to keep; the trains you have never failed to catch.

Max O'Rell

I do not believe in a fate that falls on men however they act, but I do believe in a fate that falls on them unless they act.

G. K. Chesterton

The best men are not those who have waited for chances but who have taken them; besieged the chance; conquered the chance; and made chance the servitor.

Edwin Hubbell Chapin

23. IN PRAISE OF HUMILITY

A man finds he has been wrong at every preceding stage of his career, only to deduce the astonishing conclusion that he is at last entirely right.

Robert Louis Stevenson

Modesty is a shining light; it prepares the mind to receive knowledge, and the heart for truth.

François Pierre Guizot

Haughtiness toward men is rebellion to God.

Nahmanides

To do much for me the author should make me think little of himself; to do more, he must make me think little of myself.

Ivan N. Panin

The great act of faith is when man decides that he is not God.

Oliver Wendell Holmes, Jr.

Conceited men often seem a harmless kind of men, who, by an overweening self-respect, relieve others from the duty of respecting them at all.

Henry Ward Beecher

Without humility you will not learn even the simplest lessons of life.

John Thompson

If ever man becomes proud, let him remember that a mosquito preceded him in the divine order of creation!

The Midrash

The true way to be humble is not to stoop till you are smaller than yourself, but to stand at your real height against some higher nature that shall show you what the real smallness of your greatest greatness is.

Phillips Brooks

How hard it is to confess that we have spoken without thinking, that we have talked nonsense. How many a man says a thing in haste and heat, without fully understanding or half meaning it, and then, because he has said it, holds fast to it, and tries to defend it as if it were true! But how much wiser, how much more admirable and attractive it is when a man has the grace to perceive and acknowledge his mistakes! It gives us assurance that he is capable of learning, of growing, of improving, so that his future will be better than his past.

Henry Van Dyke

A great man is always willing to be little.

Ralph Waldo Emerson

Humility, like darkness, reveals the heavenly lights.

Henry Thoreau

Conceit is God's gift to little men.

Bruce Barton

Success is too easy. In our country a young man can gain it with no more than a little industry. He can gain it so quickly and easily that he has not had time to learn the humility to handle it with, or even to discover, realize that he will need humility.

William Faulkner

If a little knowledge is dangerous, where is the man who has so much as to be out of danger?

Thomas Henry Huxley

The greatest of faults, I should say, is to be conscious of none.

Thomas Carlyle

The beginning of greatness is to be little, the increase of greatness is to be less, and the perfection of greatness is to be nothing.

Dwight Moody

Every man can be seen as a fraction, whose numerator is his actual qualities and its denominator his opinion of himself. The greater the denominator the less is the absolute quantity of the fraction.

Leo Tolstoy

We all make mistakes, but everyone makes different mistakes.

Ludwig van Beethoven

When he consults himself man knows that he is great. When he contemplates the universe around him he knows that he is little and his ultimate greatness consists in his knowledge of his littleness.

Blaise Pascal

Everybody makes mistakes; that's why they put erasers on pencils.

Author Unknown

He who thinks he can find in himself the means of doing without others is much mistaken; but he who thinks that others cannot do without him is still more mistaken.

François Rochefoucauld

Last week I saw a man who had not made a mistake in 4,000 years. He was a mummy in the British Museum.

H. L. Wayland

It is well that there is no one without a fault, for he would not have a friend in the world. He would seem to belong to a different species.

William Hazlitt

The doctrine of human equality reposes on this; that there is no man really clever who has not found that he is stupid. There is no big man who has not felt small. Some men never feel small; but these are the few men who are.

G. K. Chesterton

It is no great thing to be humble when you are brought low; but to be humble when you are praised is a great and rare attainment.

St. Bernard

God revealed Himself in a bush, to teach us that the loftiest may be found in the lowliest.

Eleazar ben Arak

Greatness is a two-faced coin— and its reverse is humility.

Marguerite Steen

I believe that the first test of a truly great man is his humility. I do not mean by humility, doubt of his own powers. But really great men have a curious feeling that the greatness is not in them, but through them. And they see something divine in every other man.

John Ruskin

A proud man is seldom a grateful man, for he never thinks he gets as much as he deserves.

Henry Ward Beecher

I have three precious things, which I hold fast and prize. The first is gentleness; the second is frugality; the third is humility, which keeps me from putting myself before others. Be gentle and you can be bold; be frugal, and you can be liberal; avoid putting yourself before others, and you can become a leader among men.

Lao-Tse

It is not so difficult to be humble in trouble, but it is exceedingly difficult to be humble in triumph.

Richard L. Evans

Vanity is the quicksand of reason.

George Sand

There is no king who has not had a slave among his ancestors, and no slave who has not had a king among his.

Helen Keller

God said: There's no room in the world for both the arrogant and Me.

The Talmud

Oh! Why should the spirit of mortal be proud?
Like a swift-fleeing meteor, a fast flying cloud,
A flash of the lightning, a break of the wave,
Man passes from life to his rest in the grave.

William Knox

Everybody is ignorant, only on different subjects.

Will Rogers

O habitants of homes of clay,
Why lift ye such a swelling eye,
Ye are but as the beasts that die,

What do ye boast of more than they?

Solomon Ibn Gabirol

There is a crack in everything God has made.

Ralph Waldo Emerson

I do not know, what I may appear to the world; but to myself I seem to have been only like a boy playing on the seashore of knowledge; and diverting myself in now and then finding a smoother pebble or a prettier shell than ordinary, whilst the great ocean of truth lay all undiscovered before me.

Isaac Newton

Humility is not a weak and timid quality; it must be carefully distinguished from a groveling spirit. There is such a thing as an honest pride and self-respect. Though we may be servants of all, we should be servile to none.

Edwin Hubbel Chapin

Whoever will be cured of ignorance, let him confess it.

Michel de Montaigne

Never be haughty to the humble; never be humble to the haughty.

Jefferson Davis

Everyone is a moon, and has a dark side which he never shows to anybody.

Mark Twain

Learn the great art of being small.

Joseph Brenner

Genuine humility does not arise from the sense of our pitiable kinship with the dust that is unworthy of us but from the realization of our awful nearness to a magnificence of which we are unworthy.

William L. Sullivan

Say not, "I have found the truth," but rather, "I have found a truth."

Kahlil Gibran

There is small chance of truth at the goal where there is not a child-like humility at the starting post.

Samuel Taylor Coleridge

He bids fair to grow wise who has discovered that he is not so.

Syrus

If wise men never erred, fools would have to despair.

Johann Wolfgang von Goethe

Humility is the wish to be great and the dread of being called great. It is the wish to help and the dread of thanks. It is the love of service and the distaste for rule. It is trying to be good and blushing when caught at it.

Frank Crane

Humility is strong—not bold; quiet—not speechless; sure—not arrogant.

Estelle Smith

We have an old saying in Japan that a woman cannot love a man who is truly vain, for there is no crevice in his heart for love to enter and fill up.

Okakura Kakuzo

---

24. THE POWER OF THE SPIRIT

Our faith comes in moments: our vice is habitual. Yet there is a depth in those brief moments which constrains us to ascribe more reality to them than to all other experiences.

Ralph Waldo Emerson

There is nothing quite so powerful in the world as an idea whose time has come.

Victor Hugo

I have discovered early that the hardest thing to overcome is not a physical disability but the mental condition which it induces. The world, I found, has a way of taking a man pretty much at his own rating. If he permits his loss to make him embarrassed and apologetic, he will draw embarrassment from others. But if he gains his own

respect, the respect of those around him comes easily.

Alexander de Seversky

The past is littered with the wreckage of nations which tried to meet the crises of their times by physical means alone.

Raymond B. Fosdick

When one subdues men by force, they do not submit to him in heart, but because they are not strong enough to resist. When one subdues men by virtue, they are pleased to the heart's core, and sincerely submit.

Mencius

I am more and more convinced that our happiness or unhappiness depends far more on the way we meet the events of life than on the

nature of those events themselves.
Wilhelm Von Humboldt

It is the spiritual always which determines the material.
Thomas Carlyle

To defy external forces, to rise above circumstances, is to proclaim the sovereignty of the human spirit.
Chaim Weizmann

Circumstances are beyond the control of man; but his conduct is in his own power.
Benjamin Disraeli

It is important for us to recognize that neither the atomic weapons nor any other form of power and force constitutes the true source of American strength. . . . That source is our ethical and moral standards of precepts, and our democratic faith in man. This faith is the chief armament of our democracy. It is the most potent weapon devised. Compared with it, the atomic bomb is a firecracker.
David E. Lilienthal

The more I study the world, the more I am convinced of the inability of brute force to create anything durable.
Napoleon I

Some things cannot be measured —we do not think of a ton of truth, a bushel of beauty or an inspiration a mile long.
Joseph Fort Newton

Spiritual force is stronger than material force; thoughts rule the world.
Ralph Waldo Emerson

The spirit cannot endure the body when overfed but, if under-fed, the body cannot endure the spirit.
St. Francis De Sales

The power of ideals is incalculable. We see no power in a drop of water. But let it get into a crack in the rock and be turned to ice, and it splits the rock; turned into steam, it drives the pistons of the most powerful engines. Something has happened to it which makes active and effective the power that is latent in it.
Albert Schweitzer

We are a people who have built upon a faith in the spirit of man.
David L. Lilienthal

Without faith a man can do nothing; with it all things are possible.
Sir William Osler

Each conception of spiritual beauty is a glimpse at God.
Moses Mendelssohn

Mightier than the atom, mightier than bacteriological warfare, mightier than all other terrible weapons of destruction is the power of the spirit—the power of the soul and conscience.
Benjamin A. Cohen

If we can harness the moral conscience of the world, we shall have a force greater than armies.
Woodrow Wilson

The basic difference between physical and spiritual power is that men use physical power but spiritual power uses men.
Justin Wrof Nixon

A week before Tchaikovsky created his superb "Symphony No. 6

in B Minor" (Pathetique), he had written to a friend, "My faith in myself is shattered and it seems my role is ended." He did not realize that the human spirit is capable of kindling firebrands out of the ashes of frustration and defeat.

Alexander A. Steinbach

One person with a belief is equal to a force of ninety-nine who have only interests.

John Stuart Mill

Nothing is impossible: there are ways which lead to every thing; and if we had sufficient will we should always have sufficient means.

François Rochefoucauld

---

25. THE ART OF SPEAKING GENTLY

Gossip is a sort of smoke that comes from the dirty tobacco-pipes of those who diffuse it; it proves nothing but the bad taste of the smoker.

George Eliot

In the case of scandal, as in that of robbery, the receiver is always thought as bad as the thief.

Lord Chesterfield

The only way to speak the truth is to speak lovingly.

Henry David Thoreau

How many men would be mute if they were forbidden to speak well of themselves and evil of others.

Mme. de Fontaine

The men who are lifting the world upward and onward are those who encourage more than criticize.

Elizabeth Harrison

Taunt not a penitent or a proselyte about his past.

The Talmud

If your lips would keep from slips
Five things observe with care:

To whom you speak, of whom you speak,
And how, and when, and where.

Author Unknown

Kind words are the music of the world. They have a power which seems to be beyond natural causes, as if they were some angel's song which had lost its way and come on earth.

W. F. Faber

A saintly colored woman who was greatly loved in her community was asked how she made and kept so many friends. She replied, "I stop and taste my words before I let them pass my teeth."

Claude A. Ries

A gentleman is a man who can disagree without being disagreeable.

Author Unknown

There are two good rules which ought to be written upon every heart. Never believe anything bad about anybody, unless you positively know that it is true. Never tell even that, unless you feel that it is absolutely necessary, and that God is listening while you tell it.

Henry Van Dyke

Kind words are the music of the world. They have a power which seems to be beyond natural causes, as if they were some angel's song which had lost its way and come on earth. It seems as if they could almost do what in reality God alone can do—soften the hard and angry hearts of men. No one was ever corrected by a sarcasm—crushed, perhaps, if the sarcasm was clever enough, but drawn nearer to God, never.

W. F. Faber

A way to weigh words is to keep them in the heart until they are gentle and until the lips will speak them softly.

Douglas Meador

Nothing is so strong as gentleness, Nothing is so gentle as real strength.

Francis De Sales

Rabban Gamaliel commanded his slave, Tobi, to buy the best edible in the market. The slave brought home a tongue. The next day Rabban Gamaliel commanded him to buy the worst thing in the market, and again Tobi brought home a tongue. When asked for an explanation, the wise slave replied: "There is nothing better than a good tongue, and nothing worse than an evil tongue."

The Midrash

Let no one be willing to speak ill of the absent.

Sextus Propertius

Raised voices lower esteem. Hot tempers cool friendships. Loose tongues stretch truth. Swelled heads shrink influence. Sharp words dull respect.

William Ward

If I thought that a word of mine
Perhaps unkind and untrue,
Would leave its trace on a loved
    one's face,
I'd never speak it—
    Would you?
If I thought that a smile of mine
Might linger the whole day through
And lighten some heart with a
    heavier part,
I'd not withhold it—
    Would you?

Author Unknown

Words of understanding and sympathy are wonderful instruments for unlocking the hearts and minds of men. They transcend all cultures, turning strangers into brothers, blotting out tolerance and discrimination.

Lucy R. Goodwin

Thy friend has a friend, and thy friend's friend has a friend; be discreet.

The Talmud

I hate the man who builds his name On ruins of another's fame.

John Gay

Believe nothing against another, but on good authority; nor report what may hurt another, unless it be a greater hurt to some other to conceal it.

William Penn

Gossip kills three: the speaker, the spoken of, and the listener.

The Midrash

The animals will one day remonstrate with the serpent and say,

"The lion treads upon his prey and devours it; and the wolf tears and eats it. What profit hast thou in biting?"

The serpent will reply, "I am no worse than a slanderer."

The Talmud

Conversation is the oldest form of instruction of the human race. It is still an indispensable one. Great books, scientific discoveries, works of art, great perceptions of truth and beauty in any form—all require great conversation to complete their meaning; without it they are abracadabra—color to the blind or music to the deaf. Conversation is the handmaid of learning, true religion and free government. It would be impossible to put too high a price on all we stand to lose by suffering its decay.

A. Whitney Griswold

Who steals my purse steals trash;
  'tis something, nothing;
'Twas mine, 'tis his, and has been
  slave to thousands;
But he that filches from me my
  good name
Robs me of that which not enriches him,
And makes me poor indeed.

William Shakespeare

The gossiper stands in Syria and kills in Rome.

The Jerusalem Talmud

26. THE ELOQUENT SILENCE

Better to remain silent and be thought a fool, than to speak out and remove all doubt.

Author Unknown

If a word spoken in its time is worth one piece of money, silence in its time is worth two.

The Talmud

How rare to find a soul still enough to hear God speak.

Francis de Fenelon

In the ordinary course of nature, the great beneficent changes come slowly and silently. The noisy changes, for the most part, mean violence and disruption. The roar of storms and tornadoes, the explosions of volcanoes, the crash of the thunder, are the result of a sudden break in the equipoise of the elements; from a condition of comparative repose and silence they become fearfully swift and audible. The still small voice is the voice of life and growth and perpetuity . . . In the history of a nation it is the same.

John Burroughs

The ability to speak several languages is an asset, but to be able to hold your tongue in one language is priceless.

Sydney Smith

Men were made more to listen than to talk, for Nature has given them two ears, but only one mouth.

Benjamin Disraeli

Blessed is the man who, having nothing to say, abstains from giving in words evidence of the fact.

George Eliot

He knew the precise psychological moment when to say nothing.
Oscar Wilde

A man who lives right, and is right, has more power in his silence than another has by his words.
Phillips Brooks

Silence is one great art of conversation. He is not a fool who knows when to hold his tongue; and a person may gain credit for sense, eloquence, wit, who merely says nothing to lessen the opinion which others have of these qualities in themselves.
William Hazlitt

He who, silent, loves to be with us, and loves us in our silence, has touched one of the keys that ravish hearts.
John Casper Lavater

Let us keep our silent sanctuaries for in them the eternal perspectives are preserved.
Etienne Senancour

Let us be silent that we may hear the whispers of the gods.
Ralph Waldo Emerson

The silence of the place was like a sleep, so full of rest it seemed.
Henry Wadsworth Longfellow

If silence be good for the wise, how much the better for fools.
The Talmud

Modern man seems to be afraid of silence. We are conditioned by radio and television on which every minute must be filled with talking, or some kind of sound. We are stimulated by the American philosophy of keeping on the move all the time—busy, busy, busy. This tends to make us shallow. A person's life can be deepened tremendously by periods of silence, used in the constructive ways of meditation and prayer. Great personalities have spent much time in the silences of life.
Robert E. Lyon

Speech may sometimes do harm; but so may silence, and a worse harm at that. No offered insult ever caused so deep a wound as a tenderness expected and withheld; and no spoken indiscretion was ever so bitterly regretted as the words one did not speak.
Jan Struther

Truth is not only violated by falsehood; it may be equally outraged by silence.
Henri Frederic Amiel

I think the first virtue is to restrain the tongue; he approaches nearest to the gods who knows how to be silent, even though he is in the right.
Cato

He who sleeps in continual noise is wakened by silence.
W. D. Howells

The child's entire life is influenced by his ability to listen. Good listening habits make it possible for him to broaden his knowledge, enjoy music, conversation, storytelling, drama; discriminating listening makes it possible for him to select radio and television programs for enjoyment. Critical listening helps him function intelligently in selection of governmental leaders. It is quite possible that the ability to listen effectively may be one of the most valuable tools he can use in his efforts to bring understanding and peace to the world.

Lucile Cypreansen

Animals when once they have gained our affection never lose it; they cannot talk.

Ivan N. Panin

Never speak unless you can improve on silence.

Author Unknown

A happy life must be to a great extent a quiet life, for it is only in an atmosphere of quiet that true joy can live.

Bertrand Russell

One of the fundamentals in learning to speak is knowing when not to. This is probably the most thoroughly ignored rule in civilized society today. We are all constantly being urged, exhorted, commanded to become facile speakers. We are tempted by correspondence courses, evening classes, articles that promise we can all become devastatingly interesting conversationalists. Our age, indeed, has seen the Flower of Babel.

And, pray tell, what good is all the conversation if nobody listens? What we need is a course in how not to speak—a brief refresher in how to listen to what somebody else is saying. Its graduates would be in tremendous demand.

Sylvia Strum Bremer

He had occasional flashes of silence, that made his conversation perfectly delightful.

Sydney Smith

It is more important to listen to questions than to answer them. To listen with full intent, with full openness, with a genuine desire to understand not the question only, but the question behind the question, and to be at one with the questioner—this is an engagement very difficult.

William B. J. Martin

Noise proves nothing. Often a hen who has merely laid an egg cackles as if she had laid an asteroid.

Mark Twain

They say to fruit-bearing trees: "Why do you not make any noise?" The trees reply: "Our fruits are sufficient advertisement for us."

The Midrash

What a strange power there is in silence! How many resolutions are formed, how many sublime conquests effected, during that pause when lips are closed, and the soul secretly feels the eye of her Maker upon her! They are the strong ones of earth who know how to keep silence when it is a pain and grief unto them, and who give time to their own souls to wax strong against temptation.

Ralph Waldo Emerson

Plainly this is not an age of the meditative man. It is a squinting, sprinting, shoving age. Substitutes for repose are a million dollar business. Silence, already a nation's most critical shortage, is almost a nasty word. Modern man may or may not be obsolete, but he is certainly wired for sound.

Norman Cousins

I need not shout my faith. Thrice eloquent
Are quiet trees and the green listening sod;

Hushed are the stars, whose power
   is never spent;
The hills are mute: yet how they
   speak of God!

   Charles Hanson Towne

It is a great misfortune neither
to have enough wit to talk well
nor enough judgment to be silent.

   La Bruyere

The pause—that impressive silence, that eloquent silence, that
geometrically progressive silence
which often achieves a desired af-
fect where no combination of words
howsoever felicitous could accomplish it.

   Mark Twain

---

27. THE GREATNESS OF LITTLE THINGS

It takes so little to make people
happy. Just a touch, if we know
how to give it, just a word fitly
spoken, a slight readjustment of
some bolt or pin or bearing in the
delicate machinery of a soul.

   Frank Crane

It was not the guns that broke
Napoleon on the Moscow road; it
was the might of the snow-flakes.

   James Reid

The true, strong, and sound mind
is the mind that can embrace
equally great things and small.

   Samuel Johnson

The creation of a thousand forests is in one acorn.

   Ralph Waldo Emerson

If I can not do great things, I
can do small things in a great way.

   J. F. Clarke

Anyone can carry his burden,
however hard, until nightfall. Anyone can do his work, however hard,
for one day. Anyone can live
sweetly, patiently, lovingly, purely,
till the sun goes down. And this is
all that life really means.

   Robert Louis Stevenson

Big doesn't necessarily mean better. Sunflowers aren't better than
violets.

   Edna Ferber

If you want to live more you
must master the art of appreciating
the little, everyday blessings of life.
This is not altogether a golden
world, but there are countless
gleams of gold to be discovered in
it if we give our minds to them.

   Henry Alford Porter

There is nothing too little for so
little a creature as man. It is by
studying little things that we attain
the great art of having as little
misery and as much happiness as
possible.

   Samuel Johnson

There is no great and no small
to the soul that maketh all.

   Ralph Waldo Emerson

The greatest things ever done on
earth have been done by little and
little—little agents, little persons,
little things, by every one doing
his own work, filling his own
sphere, holding his own post, and

saying, "Lord, what wilt thou have me to do?"

Thomas Guthrie

Little drops of water,
Little grains of sand,
Make the mighty ocean
And the pleasant land.

Little deeds of kindness,
Little words of love,
Make our world an Eden
Like the Heaven above.

Julia F. Carney

One of the most serious thoughts that life provokes is the reflection that we can never tell, at the time, whether a word, a look, a touch, an occurrence of any kind, is trivial or important.

E. V. Lucas

Little words are the sweetest to hear; little charities fly furthest and stay longest on the wing; little lakes are the stillest; little hearts are the fullest, and little farms are the best tilled. Little books are read the most and little songs the dearest loved. And when Nature would make anything especially rare and beautiful, she makes it little; little pearls, little diamonds, little dews. Life is made up of little things that count. Day is made up of little beams, and night is glorious with little stars.

Author Unknown

It is the greatest of all mistakes to do nothing because you can only do a little. Do what you can.

Sydney Smith

The man who removes a mountain begins by carrying away small stones.

Chinese Proverb

It is the little bits of things that fret and worry us; we can dodge an elephant, but we can't a fly.

Josh Billings

Many strokes, though with a little axe,
Hew down and fell the hardest-timber'd oak.

William Shakespeare

For want of a nail the shoe was lost,
For want of a shoe the horse was lost;
For want of a horse the rider was last, and all
For want of a horseshoe nail.

G. Herbert

Think naught a trifle, though it small appears; small sands make mountains, moments make the year, and trifles, life!

E. J. Young

A little hole will sink a large ship.

Ephraim Domoratzki

A man who does a little more work than he's asked to—who takes a little more care than he's expected to—who puts the small details on an equal footing with the more important ones—he's the man who is going to make a success of his job. Each little thing done better is the thin end of the wedge into something bigger.

Author Unknown

The tree which needs two arms to span its girth sprang from the tiniest shoot. Yon tower, nine stories high, rose from a little mound of earth. A journey of a thousand miles began with a single step.

Lao-Tse

Little self-denials, little honesties, little passing words of sympathy, little nameless acts of kindness, little silent victories over favorite temptations—these are the silent threads of gold which, when woven together, gleam out so brightly in the pattern of life that God approves.

Frederic W. Farrar

A speck cuts the value of a diamond in half—a race horse that can run a mile a few seconds faster than any other is worth twice as much. That little extra all through life proves to be the greatest value.

John D. Hess

Nobody ever stubs his toe against a mountain. It's the little temptations that bring a man down.

I. L. Peretz

Life is made up, not of great sacrifices or duties, but of little things, in which smiles and kindnesses and small obligations, given habitually, are what win and preserve the heart and secure comfort.

Sir Humphry Davy

Reverence the highest, have patience with the lowest. Are the stars too distant, pick up the pebble that lies at thy feet.

Margaret Fuller

Kindness means doing a lot of little things kindly and always; not just a big thing now and then.

Neville Hobson

"I cannot see where you have made any progress since the last time I was here," a visitor to the studio of Michelangelo said. "I have retouched this part," the master said, "polished that, softened this feature, brought out that muscle, given more expression to the lip and more energy to the limb." "But those things are all trifles," exclaimed the visitor. "That may be," said Michelangelo, "but trifles make perfection, and perfection is no trifle."

Walter Dudley Cavert

Men will talk about little things and great things, as if they knew which were little and which were great.

Robert Louis Stevenson

Men do not stumble over mountains, but over molehills.

Confucius

Little faithfulnesses are not only the preparation for great ones, but little faithfulnesses are in themselves the great ones. . . . The essential fidelity of the heart is the same whether it be exercised in two mites or in a regal treasury; the genuine faithfulness of the life is equally beautiful whether it be displayed in governing an empire or in writing an exercise. . . . It has been quaintly said that if God were to send two angels to earth, the one to occupy a throne, and the other to clean a road, they would each regard their employments as equally distinguished and equally happy.

F. W. Faber

It is little things in life that are the sublime things. It is the minor parts of the great drama which make up the whole. The handclasp, the smile, the words of confidence or encouragement; these are the strength and bulwark of society, business, religion—and home life.

Without them, there would be no trust; without trust, our world would collapse.

John Randolph Stidman

God has chosen little nations as the vessels by which He carries his choicest wines to the lips of humanity to rejoice their hearts, to exalt their vision, to strengthen their faith.

David Lloyd George

One step at a time, and that well
     placed,
We reach the grandest height;
One stroke at a time, earth's hidden
     stores
Will slowly come to light;
One seed at a time, and the forest
     grows;
One drop at a time, and the river
     flows
Into the boundless sea.

Author Unknown

Little things console us, because little things afflict us.

Blaise Pascal

Petty vexations may at times be petty, but still they are vexations. The smallest and most inconsiderable annoyances are the most piercing. As small letters weary the eyes most, so also the smallest affairs disturb us most.

Michael De Montaigne

The happiness of life is made up of minute fractions—the little soon-forgotten charities of a kiss or smile, a kind look, a heartfelt compliment, and the countless infinitesimals of pleasurable and genial feeling.

Samuel Taylor Coleridge

Who scorns the little was not born for the great.

Isaac Friedmann

The little and pure is much, the much and impure is little.

Bahya

Johnson well says, "He who waits to do a great deal of good at once will never do anything." Life is made up of little things. It is very rarely that an occasion is offered for doing a great deal at once. True greatness consists in being great in little things.

Charles Simmons

The everyday cares and duties, which men call drudgery, are the weights and counterpoises of the clock of time, giving its pendulum a true vibration, and its hands a regular motion; and when they cease to hang upon the wheels, the pendulum no longer swings, the hands no longer move, and the clock stands still.

Henry Wadsworth Longfellow

What sunshine is to the flowers, smiles are to humanity. They are but trifles, to be sure; but, scattered along life's pathway, the good they do is inconceivable.

Author Unknown

Small opportunities are often the beginning of great enterprises.

Demosthenes

To give high joy great things are needful; to give deep pain little things are enough.

Ivan N. Panin

We should mind little things—little courtesies in life, little matters of personal appearance, little minutes of wasted time, little details in our work. It seems that a thing cannot be too small to command our attention. The first hint Newton had leading to his important optical discoveries originated from a child's soap bubble. Goodyear neglected his skillet until it was red hot, and the accident led him to the making of vulcanized rubber.

Author Unknown

Many little leaks may sink a ship.

Thomas Fuller

The power of little things to give instruction and happiness should be the first lesson in life, and it should be inculcated deeply.

Russell H. Conwell

Every minute starts an hour.

Paul Gandola

---

28. THE ART OF PERFORMING OUR DUTY

Who does no more than his duty is not doing his duty.

Bahya

We live in a world which is full of misery and ignorance, and the plain duty of each and all of us is to try to make the little corner he can influence somewhat less ignorant that it was before he entered it.

Thomas Huxley

Duty, then, is the sublimest word in our language. Do your duty in all things. You cannot do more. You should never wish to do less.

Robert E. Lee

God requires a faithful fulfilment of the merest trifle given us to do, rather than the most ardent aspiration to things to which we are not called.

St. Francis De Sales

Our duty is to be useful, not according to our desires but according to our powers.

Henri Frederic Amiel

Duties are the tasks we look forward to with distaste, perform with reluctance, and brag about ever after.

Patsy Traflinger

Seek happiness for its own sake, and you will not find it; seek for duty, and happiness will follow as the shadow comes with the sunshine.

Tryon Edwards

What is to become of us when everything leaves us—health, joy, affections, the freshness of sensation, memory, capacity for work—when the sun seems to us to have lost its warmth, and life is stripped of all its charm? What is to become of us without hope? Must we either harden or forget? There is but one answer—keep close to duty. Never mind the future, if only you have peace of conscience, if you feel yourself reconciled, and in harmony with the order of things. Be what you ought to be; the rest is God's affair.

Henri Frederic Amiel

The consciousness of duty performed gives us music at midnight.

Author Unknown

The true source of rights is duty. If we all discharge our duties, rights will not be far to seek.

Mohandas K. Gandhi

I studied the lives of great men and famous women; and I found that the men and women who got to the top were those who did the jobs they had in hand, with everything they had of energy and enthusiasm and hard work.

Harry S. Truman

The highest holiness will not work miracles, but only do its duty.

Phillips Brooks

We must find our duties in what comes to us, not in what we imagine might have been.

George Eliot

The day returns and brings us the petty rounds of irritating concerns and duties. Help us to play the man, help us to perform them with laughter and kind faces, let cheerfulness abound with industry. Give us to go blithely on our business all the day, bring us to our resting beds weary and content and undishonored, and grant us in the end the gift of sleep. Amen.

Robert Louis Stevenson

A social organism is what it is because each member proceeds to his own duty with a trust that the other members will simultaneously do theirs. A government, an army, a commercial system, a ship, a college, an athletic team, all exist on this condition without which not only is nothing achieved, but nothing is even attempted.

William James

The two most beautiful things in the universe are the starry heavens above our heads, and the feeling of duty in our hearts.

Jacques B. Bossuet

Let us have faith that Right makes Might, and in that faith let us to the end dare to do our duty as we understand it.

Abraham Lincoln

Whatever our station in life may be, those of us who mean to fulfill our duty ought, first, to live on as little as we can; and, secondly, to do all the wholesome work for it we can, and to spend all we can spare in doing all the sure good we can.

John Ruskin

One's immediate duty is happily, as a rule, clear enough. "Do the next thing," says the old shrewd motto.

A. C. Benson

In his own life, then, a man is not to expect happiness, only to profit by it gladly when it shall arise; he is on duty here; he knows not how or why, and does not need to know; he knows not for what hire, and must not ask. Somehow or other, though he does not know what goodness is, he must try to be good; somehow or other, though he cannot tell what will do it, he must try to give happiness to others. . . .

Robert Louis Stevenson

Perhaps the most valuable result of all education is the ability to make yourself do the thing you have to do, when it ought to be done, whether you like it or not.

It is the first lesson that ought to be learned.

Thomas H. Huxley

My duty I myself must do. Not even God can do it for me.

Josiah Royce

However tempting it might be to some when much trouble lies ahead to step aside adroitly and put someone else up to take the blows, I do not intend to take that cowardly course, but, on the contrary, to stand to my post and persevere in accordance with my duty as I see it.

Winston Churchill

Do the duty which lies nearest to you. Every duty which is bidden to wait returns with seven fresh duties at its back.

Charles Kingsley

Let me do the thing that ought to be done, when it ought to be done, as it ought to be done, whether I like to do it or not.

Author Unknown

Dare to do your duty always; this is the height of true valor.

Charles Simmons

If any man is rich and powerful he comes under the law of God by which the higher branches must take the burnings of the sun, and shade those that are lower; by which the tall trees must protect the weak plants beneath them.

Henry Ward Beecher

A life regardful of duty is crowned with an object, directed by a purpose, inspired by an enthusiasm, till the very humblest routine, carried out conscientiously for the sake of God is elevated into moral grandeur; and the very obscurest office, filled conscientiously at the bidding of God, becomes an imperial stage on which all the virtues play. To one who lives thus the insignificant becomes important, the unpleasant delightful, the evanescent eternal.

F. W. Faber

Great things often come from where despair reigns. The performance of duty still determines man's destiny.

Ralph E. Lyne

He who eats the fruit should at least plant the seed.

Henry David Thoreau

Obedience to duty means resistance to self.

Henri Bergson

To feel that you have done what should be done raises you in your own eyes.

Eugene Delacroix

Fellowships we want, that will hold, not religion as a duty, but duty as a religion.

Felix Adler

So nigh is grandeur to our dust,
So near is God to man,
When Duty whispers low, Thou must,
The youth replies, I can.

Ralph Waldo Emerson

Our main business is not to see what lies dimly at a distance but to do what lies clearly at hand.

Thomas Carlyle

The best way to get rid of your duties is to discharge them.

Author Unknown

The reward of one duty is the power to fulfill another.

George Eliot

29. THE ART OF SEEING

If trees barked like dogs and flowers hooted like owls, their grace and elegance would be noticed by millions who now pass by unseeing.

Alexander A. Steinbach

Like a great poet, Nature produces the greatest results with the simplest means. These are simply a sun, flowers, water and love. Of course, if the spectator be without the last, the whole will present but a pitiful appearance; and, in that case, the sun is merely so many miles in diameter, the trees are good for fuel, the flowers are classified by stamens, and the water is simply wet.

Heinrich Heine

Two men look out through the same bars:
One sees the mud, and one the stars.

Frederick Langbridge

Reflect upon your present blessings, of which every man has many; not on your past misfortunes, of which all men have some.

Charles Dickens

Stand close to a mountain and you will see only a massive wall of earth and stone. Stand at a distance and you will see heights. Often we find fault with what we see, when the fault really lies in where we stand.

Alexander A. Steinbach

Citizenship papers are seeable, touchable and weighable, but patriotism is not. A marriage license is purchasable, but love is not. Birthday and anniversary gifts can be measured in terms of dollars and cents, but thoughtfulness and appreciation cannot.

Harold E. Kohn

The tree of life is always in bloom somewhere if we only know where to look.

Havelock Ellis

If spring came but once in a century instead of once a year, or burst forth with the sound of an earthquake and not in silence, what wonder and expectation there would be in all hearts, to behold the miraculous change.

Henry Wadsworth Longfellow

There are two types of realist. There is the one who offers a good deal of dirt with his potato to show that it is a real potato. And there is the one who is satisfied with the potato brushed clean.

Robert Frost

The whole cosmic order is one miracle. No room is left for single or exceptional miracles.

Kaufman Kohler

Intellectually all water is H_2O. From the viewpoint of "technical reason" not only is the mud puddle H_2O, but so also is the mountainous wave lashed up by a storm at sea. So also is awe-inspiring Niagara, Mirror Lake in Yosemite reflecting mountains and sky, or Lake Louise nestled in the Canadian Rockies. From a purely intellectual approach the dirty little mud puddle that plays havoc with your "shine" is on a par with all the rest of them. It too is H_2O. But is that the end of the matter? Intellectually it may be. But life contradicts such a verdict.

Harold Cooke Phillips

Regard as enormous the little wrong you did to others, and as trifling the great wrong done to you.

The Talmud

Poverty, like many other miseries of life, is often little more than an imaginary calamity. Men often call themselves poor, not because they want necessaries, but because they have not more than they want.

Samuel Johnson

A work of art is not completed on the canvas. It is completed in the mind of the man who looks at it.

Daniel Henry Kahnweiler

The prophet and the martyr do not see the hooting throng. Their eyes are fixed on the eternities.

Benjamin Cardozo

Some things have to be believed to be seen.

Ralph Hodgson

To see a world in a grain of sand,
And a heaven in a wild flower,
Hold infinity in the palm of your hand,
And eternity in an hour.

William Blake

I pity the man who can travel from Dan to Beersheba, and cry, 'tis all barren—and so it is, and so is all the world to him who will not cultivate the fruits it offers.

Laurence Sterne

There was a wise man in the East whose contant prayer was that he might see today with the eyes of tomorrow.

Alfred Mercier

I who am blind can give one hint to those who see—one admonition to those who would make full use of the gift of sight: Use your eyes as if tomorrow you would be stricken blind. And the same method can be applied to the other senses. Hear the music of voices, the song of a bird, the mighty strains of an orchestra, as if you would be stricken deaf tomorrow. Touch each object you want to touch as if tomorrow your tactile sense would fail. Smell the perfume of flowers, taste with relish each morsel, as if tomorrow you could never smell and taste again. Make the most of every sense; glory in all the facets of pleasure and beauty which the world reveals to you through the several means of contact which Nature provides. But of all the senses, sight must be the most delightful.

Helen Keller

That only which we have within, can we see without. If we meet no gods, it is because we harbor none. If there is grandeur in you, you will find grandeur in porters and sweeps.

Ralph Waldo Emerson

Give us clear vision that we may know where to stand and what to stand for, because unless we stand for something, we shall fall for anything.

Peter Marshall

Experience is not what happens to man. It is what man does with what happens to him.

Aldous Huxley

Four men climbed a mountain to see the view. The first wore new and expensive shoes which did not fit, and he complained constantly of his feet. The second had a greedy eye and kept wishing for this house or that farm. The third saw clouds and worried for fear it might rain. But the fourth really saw the marvelous view. His mountaintop experience was looking away from the valley out of which he had just climbed to higher things.

Howard D. Bare

Chico in the play SEVENTH HEAVEN, by Austin Strong, is an admirable person. He knows how to live heroically amidst adverse circumstances. He reveals the secret of his life in these words, "I work in the sewers, but I live near the stars. I never look down; I always look up. That's why I am such a remarkable fellow."

Thomas S. Kepler

One sees the past better than it was; one finds the present worse than it is; one hopes for a future happier than it will be.

Mme. d'Epinay

The situation of no one in the world is such that it could not be of peculiar use to his soul.

Rainer Maria Rilke

One of the hardest lessons we have to learn in this life, and one that many persons never learn, is to see the divine, the celestial, the pure in the common, the near at hand—to see that heaven lies about us here in this world.

John Burroughs

Every moment of this strange and lovely life from dawn to dusk is a miracle. Somewhere, always, a rose is opening its petals to the dawn. Somewhere, always, a flower is fading in the dusk. The incense that rises with the sun, and the scents that die in the dark, are all gathered, sooner or later, into the solitary fragrance that is God. Faintly, elusively that fragrance lingers over all of us.

Beverly Nichols

To me the greatest miracle is this that many a veritable miracle by use and want grows stale and commonplace.

G. E. Lessing

Better keep yourself clean and bright; you are the window through which you must see the world.

George Bernard Shaw

No life is so hard but you can't make it easier by the way you take it.

Ellen Glasgow

Some have eyes
That see not; but in every block of marble
I see a statue—see it as distinctly
As if it stood before me shaped and perfect
In attitude and action. I have only
To hew away the stone wall that imprisons

The lovely apparition, and reveal
it
To other eyes as mine already see
it.
Henry Wadsworth Longfellow

Envy has a thousand eyes, but
none with correct vision.
Isachar Hurwitz

If your everyday life seems poor
to you, do not accuse it; accuse
yourself, tell yourself you are not
poet enough to summon up its
riches; since for the Creator there
is no poverty and no poor or unimportant place.
Rainer Maria Rilke

The man who cannot wonder is
but a pair of spectacles behind
which there is no eye.
Thomas Carlyle

In the ideal sense nothing is un-
interesting; there are only unin-
terested people.
Brooks Atkinson

If the stars should appear one
night in a thousand years, how
would men believe and adore!
Ralph Waldo Emerson

If the matter is one that can be
settled by observation, make the
observation yourself. Aristotle
could have avoided the mistake of
thinking women have fewer teeth
than men by asking Mrs. Aristotle
to keep her mouth open while he
counted. He did not do so because
he thought he knew.
Bertrand Russell

A cynic is a man who knows the
price of everything, and the value
of nothing.
Oscar Wilde

I would sooner live in a cottage
and wonder at everything than live
in Warwick castle and wonder at
nothing.
John Ruskin

If we would be intelligent, we
must pamper curiosity and cultivate
the powers of observation, so that
we shall go through life with the
alertness of those few people born
blind and then given sight who
look upon everything with the attention and the enthusiasm of an
astronomer seeing a new world
swim into his ken.
Samuel L. Marsh

He who can no longer pause to
wonder and stand rapt in awe is as
good as dead; his eyes are closed.
Albert Einstein

We see things not as they are,
but as we are.
H. M. Tomlinson

Love blinds us to faults, hatred
to virtues.
Moses Ibn Ezra

If a man has lost the use of his
eyes, will the keen sight of his ancestors help him to see?
Philo

The atheist is a man who has
no invisible means of support.
Lord Tweedsmuir

Sight is a gift, but seeing is an
art. Seeing is the difference between the painter and the artist,
the laborer and the architect, the
happy and the unhappy.
William C. Kiessel, Jr.

The cynic is one who never sees
a good quality in a man, and never
fails to see a bad one. He is the

human owl, vigilant in darkness, and blind to light, mousing for vermin, and never seeing noble game.

Henry Ward Beecher

Cynics are only happy in making the world as barren for others as they have made it for themselves.

George Meredith

An optimist sees an opportunity in every calamity; a pessimist sees a calamity in every opportunity.

Author Unknown

If all the World looks drear, perhaps the meaning
Is that your Windows need a little cleaning.

Arthur Guiterman

What happens to a man is less significant than what happens within him.

Louis L. Mann

An adventure is only an inconvenience rightly considered. An inconvenience is only an adventure wrongly considered.

G. K. Chesterton

There's none so blind as they that won't see.

Jonathan Swift

As much of heaven is visible as we have eyes to see.

William Winter

The present is great with the future.

G. W. Leibnitz

Curiosity is one of the permanent and certain characteristics of a vigorous intellect.

Samuel Johnson

Familiarity is a magician that is cruel to beauty, but kind to ugliness.

Ouida

The world is full of wonders and miracles but man takes his little hand and covers his eyes and sees nothing.

Israel Baal Shem

To some people a tree is something so incredibly beautiful that it brings tears to the eyes. To others it is just a green thing that stands in the way.

William Blake

I have walked with people whose eyes are full of light but who see nothing in sea or sky, nothing in city streets, nothing in books. It were far better to sail forever in the night of blindness with sense, and feeling, and mind, than to be content with the mere act of seeing. The only lightless dark is the night of darkness in ignorance and insensibility.

Helen Keller

The lesson which life repeats and constantly enforces is "look under foot." You are always nearer the divine and the true sources of your power than you think. The lure of the distant and the difficult is deceptive. The great opportunity is where you are. Do not despise your own place and hour. Every place is under the stars, every place is the centre of the world.

John Burroughs

Vision looks inward and becomes duty. Vision looks outward and becomes aspiration. Vision looks upward and becomes faith.

Stephen S. Wise

30. THE HIGH COST OF WORRYING

When I consider how we fret
About a woman or a debt,
And strive and strain and cark and
    cuss,
And work and want and sweat and
    fuss,
And then observe the monkey
    swing
A casual tail at everything,
I am inclined to think that he
Evolved from apes like you and me.
                Samuel G. Hoffenstein

A doctor who had many patients
that were in the large income
brackets made a study of why they
worried so much. Here is what he
found: 40% of their worries were
about things that never happened.
30% were about matters entirely beyond their control. 12% were related
to the physical ills which were
caused or aggravated by their emotional attitudes. 10% were about
friends or relatives who were quite
able to look after themselves.

Only 8% were about matters that
really needed their attention—but
worry even in these cases was not
the remedy to apply.
                Author Unknown

It is better to employ our minds
in supporting the misfortunes
which actually happen, than in anticipating those which may happen
to us.
                François Rochefoucauld

It has been well said that no man
ever sank under the burden of the
day. It is when tomorrow's burden
is added to the burden of today
that the weight is more than a man
can bear. Never load yourselves, so,

my friends. If you find yourselves
so loaded, at least remember this:
it is your own doing, not God's. He
begs you to leave the future to
Him, and mind the present.
                George MacDonald

Man, like the bridge, was designed to carry the load of the
moment, not the combined weight
of a year at once.
                William A. Ward

Worry affects the circulation, the
heart, the glands, the whole nervous system, and profoundly affects
the health. I have never known a
man who died from overwork, but
many who died from doubt.
                Dr. Charles Mayo

Some there are that torment
themselves afresh with the memory
of what is past; others, again, afflict themselves with the apprehension of evils to come; and very ri-
diculously both—for the one does
not now concern us, and the other
not yet. . . .
                Seneca

Our fatigue is often caused not
by work, but by worry, frustration
and resentment.
                Dale Carnegie

A pessimist is one who feels bad
when he feels good for fear he'll
feel worse when he feels better.
                Author Unknown

Happy is the man who has
broken the chains which hurt the
mind, and has given up worrying
once and for all.
                Ovid

A Chicago physician specializing in research on ulcers told recently that his laboratories had been obliged to abandon the use of dogs in their experiments. The fool critters just wouldn't worry—and worry is the think that makes ulcers and keeps them active. You can inflict an ulcer upon a dog by artificial methods and he will sit down placidly and cure himself by refusing to be bothered about anything. It's just possible that there might be a lesson here for humans!

Lee Ragsdale

Worry distorts our thinking, disrupts our work, disquiets our soul, disturbs our body, disfigures our face, destroys our poise, depresses our friends, demoralizes our life, defeats our faith and debilitates our energy.

William A. Ward

For every evil under the sun,
There is a remedy or there is none.
If there is one, try to find it,
If there is none, never mind it.

Author Unknown

To worry is a sin. Only one sort of worry is permissible: to worry because one worries.

Noah Lekhivitzer

A large industrial concern discovered that nine out of ten cases of workers' inefficiency were caused by worry. A life insurance company found that four out of five nervous breakdowns began not in actual events but in worry. A medical clinic's analysis of its patients showed that thirty-five per cent of all illnesses on its records started with worry.

Charles M. Crowe

Worry, whatever its source, weakens, takes away courage, and shortens life.

John Lancaster Spalding

Some of your hurts you have cured
And the sharpest you still have survived
But what torments of grief you endured
From evils that never arrived.

Ralph Waldo Emerson

Worry often gives a small thing a big shadow.

Swedish Proverb

To carry care to bed, is to sleep with a pack on your back.

Thomas C. Haliburton

Worry is a thin stream of fear trickling through the mind. If encouraged, it cuts a channel into which all other thoughts are drained.

Arthur Somers Roche

Worry is an old man with bended head,
Carrying a load of feathers
Which he thinks are lead.

Author Unknown

Worry is a form of fear, and all forms of fear produce fatigue. A man who has learned not to feel fear will find the fatigue of daily life enormously diminished.

Bertrand Russell

Worry is interest paid on trouble before it becomes due.

Dean Inge

31. THE BLESSING OF WORK

It is the art of mankind to polish the world, and everyone who works is scrubbing in some part.

Henry David Thoreau

We have too many people who live without working, and we have altogether too many who work without living.

Charles R. Brown

The genius of the Hebrew language coined the term "malak" for angel, which is identical with "melaka" for work or labor, so that angel and working are identical.

Isaac M. Wise

This for the day of life I ask:
Some all-absorbing useful task;
And when 'tis wholly, truly done,
A tranquil rest at set of sun.

Author Unknown

Thank God every morning when you get up that you have something to do which must be done, whether you like it or not. Being forced to work, and forced to do your best, will breed in you temperance, self-control, diligence, strength of will, content, and a hundred other virtues which the idle never know.

Charles Kingsley

When men are rightly occupied their amusement grows out of their work as the color-petals out of a fruitful flower.

John Ruskin

No, work is not an ethical duty imposed upon us from without by a misguided and outmoded Puritan morality; it is a manifestation of man's deepest desire that the days of his life shall have significance.

Harold W. Dodds

No thoroughly occupied man was ever yet very miserable.

Letitia Elizabeth Landon

Genius is one per cent inspiration and ninety-nine per cent perspiration.

Thomas A. Edison

Every calling is great when greatly pursued.

Oliver Wendell Holmes, Jr.

Why do birds sing? Because the song is in them, and if they did not let it forth, they would split; it must come out. It is the spontaneity and the urgency of this feeling in them that impels their utterance. Why should men work? Because their hearts want some outlet to give expression to the feeling of earnest sympathy that is in them. Where a man has a strong and large benevolence, he will always be busy, and pleasantly busy.

Henry Ward Beecher

The test of a vocation is the love of the drudgery it involves.

Logan Pearsall Smith

There is nothing truly valuable which can be purchased without pains and labour.

Joseph Addison

It is only those who do not know how to work that do not love it. To those who do, it is better than play —it is religion.

J. H. Patterson

Work is the great anodyne. It brings us forgetfulness of sorrow, courage to face it.

Morris Joseph

Honest work bears a lovely face for it is the father of pleasure and the mother of good fortune. It is the keystone of prosperity and the sire of fame. And best of all, work is relief from sorrow and the hand-maiden of happiness.

Eugene P. Bertin

Common duties become religious acts when performed with fervor.

St. Francis De Sales

It is work which gives flavor to life.

Henri F. Amiel

We don't consider manual work as a curse, or a bitter necessity, not even as a means of making a living. We consider it as a high human function, as the basis of human life, the most dignified thing in the life of the human being, and which ought to be free, creative. Men ought to be proud of it.

David Ben Gurion

The reason a lot of people do not recognize an opportunity when they meet it is that it usually goes around wearing overalls and looking like hard work.

Author Unknown

To sow you need only to stand; to reap you must stoop.

Ivan N. Panin

A man's happiness is to do a man's true work.

Marcus Aurelius

The great composer does not set to work because he is inspired, but becomes inspired because he is working. Beethoven, Wagner, Bach and Mozart settled down day after day to the job in hand with as much regularity as an accountant settles down each day to his figures. They didn't waste time waiting for an inspiration.

Ernest Newman

No race can prosper till it learns that there is as much dignity in tilling a field as in writing a poem.

Booker T. Washington

Nothing worthwhile comes easily. Half effort does not produce half results. It produces no results. Work, continuous work and hard work, is the only way to accomplish results that last.

Hamilton Holt

Idleness is not a vice: it is a rust that destroys all virtues.

Duc de Nemours

Work is life and good work is good life.

James W. Elliott

The superstition that all our hours of work are a minus quantity in the happiness of life, and all the hours of idleness are plus ones, is a most ludicrous and pernicious doctrine, and its greatest support comes from our not taking sufficient trouble, not making a real effort, to make work as near pleasure as it can be.

Lord Balfour

The higher men climb the longer their working day. And any young man with a streak of idleness in him may better make up his mind at the beginning that mediocrity will be his lot. Without immense, sustained effort he will not climb high. And even though fortune or chance were to lift him high, he would not stay there. There are no office hours for leaders.

James Cardinal Gibbons

If you are poor, work. If you are rich, work. If you are burdened with seemingly unfair responsibilities, work.

If you are happy, continue to work; idleness gives room for doubts and fears. If sorrow overwhelms you, and loved ones seem not true, work. If disappointments come, work.

If faith falters and reason fails, just work. When dreams are shattered and hopes seem dead—work, work as if your life were in peril; it really is.

No matter what ails you, work. Work faithfully, and work with faith. Work is the greatest material remedy available. Work will cure both mental and physical afflictions.

Author Unknown

God gives every bird its food— but He does not throw it into the nest.

J. G. Holland

I never did anything worth doing by accident, nor did any of my inventions come by accident; they came by work.

Thomas A. Edison

Blessed is he who has found his work; let him ask no other blessedness. He has a work, a life-purpose; he has found it, and will follow it! Labor is life: from the inmost heart of the worker rises his God-given force, the sacred, celestial life-essence breathed into him by Almighty God.

Thomas Carlyle

When I was a young man I observed that nine out of every ten things I did were failures. I didn't want to be a failure. So I did ten times more work.

George Bernard Shaw

I never did a day's work in my life. It was all fun.

Thomas A. Edison

Work keeps at bay three great evils: boredom, vice and need.

Voltaire

When God wanted sponges and oysters, He made them, and put one on a rock, and the other in the mud. When He made man, He did not make him to be a sponge or an oyster; He made him with feet and hands, and head and heart, and vital blood, and a place to use them and said to him, "Go work!"

Henry Ward Beecher

With six days of hard labor we buy one day of happiness. But whoever does not know the six will never have the seventh.

Auguste Rodin

Work is what keeps all the faculties of the mind and all the organs of the body in trim, alert and ready for any emergency. Work pushes worry aside, alleviates sorrow, and banishes discouragement. Work disillusions the prophets of failure. Work and more work softens the edge of disappointment, gives comfort to the soul and brightens the vision. God furnishes the essential tools to those who would make their work in the world useful and important. No matter how apparently menial, all work carries with it an undenying dignity.

George Matthew Adams

The happy people are those who are producing something; the bored people are those who are consuming much and producing nothing. Boredom is a certain sign that we are allowing our faculties to rust in idleness. When people are bored, they generally look about for a new pleasure, or take a holiday. There is no greater mistake: what they want is some hard piece of work, some productive drudgery. Doctors are fond of sending their fashionable patients to take a rest cure. In nine cases out of ten a work cure would do them far more good.

Dean Inge

Nothing is really work unless you would rather be doing something else.

James Barrie

The gods sell us all good things for hard work.

Epicharmus

I am the foundation of all prosperity. Everything that is of value springs up from me. I am the sole support of the poor. The rich who think they do without me lead futile lives. I have made this nation. I have built her railroads, created her skyscrapers.

I am the friend of every worthy youth. If he makes my acquaintance when he is young and keeps me at his side, I can do more for him than the richest parent. I am the parent of genius itself. Who am I? My name is Work.

Charles B. Roth

When we do ill the devil is' tempting us; when we do nothing we are tempting him.

Author Unknown

Man must work. That is certain as the sun. But he may work grudgingly or he may work gratefully; he may work as a man, or he may work as a machine. There is no work so rude, that he may not exalt it; no work so impassive, that he may not breathe a soul into it; no work so dull that he may not enliven it.

Henry Giles

THE ART OF LIVING

WITH OURSELVES

32. THE GRANDEUR OF MAN

The imperishable thing in Hawthorne is not, as some have said, his prose. . . . His one deathless virtue is that rare thing in any literature, an utterly serious imagination. It was serious, and so it was loving; it was loving, and so it could laugh; it could laugh, and so it could endure the horror it saw in every human heart. But it saw the honor here along with the horror, the dignity by which in some eternity our pain is measured. Hawthorne was out of touch with his time, and he will be out of touch with any time. He thought man was immortal; a mistake made only by the greatest writers.

Mark Van Doren

He is of the earth, but his thoughts are with the stars. Mean and petty his wants and desires; yet they serve a soul exalted with grand, glorious aims,—with immortal longings, with thoughts which sweep the heavens and wander through eternity. A pigmy standing on the outward crest of this small planet, his far-reaching spirit stretches outward to the infinite, and there alone finds rest.

Thomas Carlyle

The significance of man is that he is that part of the universe that asks the question, What is the significance of Man? He alone can stand apart imaginatively and, regarding himself and the universe in their eternal aspects, pronounce a judgement: The significance of man is that he is insignificant and is aware of it.

Carl Becker

Man is very peculiar, so different from everything else that you can plausibly argue that he is not really an animal at all but a quite new sort of phenomenon in the world. The canyons of Manhattan may be trivial when compared with the Grand Canyon of the Colorado, but the canyons of Manhattan still are awe-inspiring, and they were built by the efforts of a quite puny animal in a very few years. They are the products of the human mind. A mind that seems very different from anything else we find in nature.

Marston Bates

Man and his littleness perish, erased like an error and cancelled; Man and his greatness survive, lost in the greatness of God.

William Watson

The heart of man is by turns a sanctuary and a cesspool.

Denis Diderot

If you are planning for a year, plant grain. If you are planting for a decade, plant trees. If you are planning for a century, plant men.

Chinese Proverb

He is to be educated not because he is to make shoes, nails, and pins, but because he is a man.

William Ellery Channing

One man means as much to me as a multitude and a multitude only as much as one man.

Democritus

Human life has beautiful mysteries, as it has sad secrets.

François P. Guizot

Every single man is a new thing in the world, and is called upon to fulfill his particularity in this world.

Yehiel Michael of Zlotchov

Every man, no matter how great or small, must be viewed not as a means to an end, but as an end in himself.

Hayim Greenberg

Man is but a reed, the feeblest of Nature's growths, but he is a thinking reed. There is no need for the whole universe to take up arms to crush him; a breath, a drop of water, may prove fatal. But were the universe to kill him, he would still be more noble than his slayer; for man knows that he is crushed, but the universe does not know that it crushes him.

Blaise Pascal

I have believed the best of every man, And find that to believe it is enough To make a bad man show him at his best, Or even a good man swing his lantern higher.

William Butler Yeats

The astonishing thing about the human being is not so much his intellect and bodily structure, profoundly mysterious as they are. The astonishing and least comprehensible thing about him is his range of vision; his gaze into the infinite distance; his lonely passion for ideas and ideals, far removed from his material surroundings and animal activities, and in no way suggested by them, yet for which, such is his affection, he is willing to endure toils and privations, to sacrifice pleasures, to disdain griefs and frustrations. The inner truth is that every man is himself a creator, by birth and nature, an artist, an architect and fashioner of worlds. If this be madness—and if the universe be the machine some think it, a very ecstasy of madness it most manifestly is—none the less it is the lunacy in which consists the romance of life, in which lies our chief glory and our only hope.

W. MacNeile Dixon

He who saves one life is considered as if he had preserved the whole world.

The Talmud

Adam was created single, to teach us that to destroy one person is to destroy a whole world, and to preserve one person is to preserve a whole world; that no man should say to another, "my father was superior to yours!" . . . that though no two men are exactly alike, God stamped us all with the same mould, the seal of Adam; that everyone must say, The world was created for my sake!

The Mishna

The world is a better place to live in because it contains human beings who will give up ease and security and stake their own lives in order to do what they themselves think worth doing. They do the useless, brave, noble, the divinely foolish and the very wisest things that are done by man. And what they prove to themselves and to others is that man is no mere automaton in his routine, but that in the dust of which he is made there is also fire, lighted now and then by great winds from the sky.

Walter Lippmann

Every individual has a place to fill in the world, and is important, in some respect, whether he chooses to be so or not.

Nathaniel Hawthorne

What a piece of work is a man! how noble in reason! how infinite in faculty! in form and moving how express and admirable! in action how like an angel! in apprehension how like a god.

William Shakespeare

There is something in human nature which makes an individual recognize and reward merit, no matter under what color of skin merit is found.

Booker T. Washington

Man is not the creature of circumstance—circumstances are the creatures of men.

Benjamin Disraeli

There is no such thing as an average man. Each one of us is a unique individual. Each one of us expresses his humanity and his divinity in some distinctly different way. The beauty and the bloom of each human soul is a thing apart— a separate holy miracle under God, never once repeated throughout all the millenniums of time.

Lane Weston

Despise not any man, and do not spurn anything; for there is no man that has not his hour, nor is there anything that has not its place.

Ben Azai

Be humble, for the worst thing in the world is of the same stuff as you; be confident, for the stars are of the same stuff as you.

Nicholai Velimirovic

We are still souls, even though we may have lost the definition of what souls are.

Shailer Mathews

The genes of the ant provide him at birth with all his tiny faculties fully usable and developed. There is no further growth of powers. Man, unlike the ant, is born helpless but with the potential steadily to extend his faculties and augment his grasp and reach. He has the built-in quality of growth, of life-enchantment and of reaching for the stars.

James R. Killian, Jr.

After the tragic sinking of the "Titanic" an American newspaper carried two pictures. One showed the ship's side torn open and about to sink—the symbol of fragility—and underneath the picture were these words, "The weakness of man; the supremacy of nature." The other illustration showed the passengers stepping back to give the one place in the lifeboat to a woman with her baby in her arms. Under this picture were the words, "The weakness of nature; the supremacy of man."

Luther Wesley Smith

Your body is the harp of your soul.

Kahlil Gibran

One machine can do the work of 50 ordinary men. No machine can do the work of one extraordinary man.

Elbert Hubbard

When someone asked a Dublin judge what remained in his mind, what had most deeply impressed him, during his fifty years in the criminal courts, his answer was, "The goodness of human nature."

Van Wyck Brooks

The sacred rights of mankind are not to be rummaged for among old parchments or musty records. They are written, as with a sunbeam, in the whole volume of human nature, by the hand of the Divinity itself, and can never be erased or obscured by mortal power.

Alexander Hamilton

A human being can go without food longer than he can go without human dignity.

Harry Golden

It is people that count. You must put yourself into people; they touch others; these, others, and so you go on working for others forever.

Alice Freeman Palmer

Man is the only animal whose desires increase as they are fed; the only animal that is never satisfied. The wants of every other living thing are uniform and fixed. The ox of today aspires to no more than did the ox when man first yoked him. The sea gull of the English Channel, who poises himself above the swift steamer, wants no better food or lodging than the gulls who circled round as the keels of Caesar's galleys first grated on a British beach. Of all that nature offers them, be it ever so abundant, all living things save man can take, and care for, only enough to supply wants which are definite and fixed.

Henry George

The body has its charms, the intellect its gifts: are we to say the heart has nothing but vices? and that man, who is capable of reason, is incapable of virtue?

Vauvenargues

I believe that man will not merely endure: we will prevail. He is immortal not because he alone among creatures has an inexhaustible voice, but because he has a soul, a spirit capable of compassion and sacrifice and endurance.

William Faulkner

The last and best lesson of history is that man is tough. He has survived a thousand catastrophes, and will survive these that encompass him now. Even when the sky falls upon him (as almost literally in modern war) he finds some way to protect himself, some hole in which to hide; and when the evil moment is past he lifts himself out of the debris of his home, his city, or his civilization, brushes off the dirt, wipes away the blood, and marches on. Somewhere, somehow, he will build again.

Will Durant

Not a day passes over the earth, but men and women of no note to do great deeds, speak great words and suffer noble sorrows.

Charles Reade

Take even a common man, the commonest, and beat and bruise him enough and you will see his soul rise God-like.

Frank Crane

Primitive man mistakenly treats things as if they were persons, but modern man treats persons as if they were things; and that is perhaps an even more dangerous superstition.

Lewis Mumford

Man is the miracle in nature. God is the One Miracle to Man.

Jean Ingelow

If man lives in slime—and there is slime always at the core of the soul—it is nevertheless this briefly animated dust that beholds stars, writes symphonies, and imagines God.

Irwin Edman

To me it seems as if when God conceived the world, that was poetry; He formed it, and that was sculpture; He varied and colored it, and that was painting;

and then, crowning all, He peopled it with living beings, and that was the grand divine, eternal drama.

Charlotte Cushman

Man is a piece of the universe made alive.

Ralph Waldo Emerson

God has put something noble and good into every heart which His hand created.

Mark Twain

I believe, with all my heart, that the Spirit of God is within every man, however mean, ugly, or diseased; and that when we visit indignities upon other men, we are affronting our Creator, and we are also harming ourselves.

Bartley C. Crum

It is a pleasant fact that you will know no man long, however low in the social scale, however poor, miserable, intemperate, and worthless he may appear to be, a mere burden to society, but you will find at last that there is something which he understands and can do better than any other.

Henry David Thoreau

Wherever there is lost the consciousness that every man is an object of concern for us just because he is a man, civilization and morals are shaken, and the advance to fully developed inhumanity is only a question of time.

Albert Schweitzer

Moral principles that exalt themselves by degrading human nature are in effect committing suicide.

John Dewey

It is difficult to make a man miserable while he feels he is worthy of himself and claims kindred to the great God who made him.

Abraham Lincoln

The fact that man possessed the capacity to rise from bestial savagery to civilization, at a time when it had never before been done, is the greatest fact in the history of the universe as known to us. For this amazing new capability, transcending merely physical development and the evolution of more efficient organs, disclosed a kind of buoyancy of the human spirit, never before displayed in the history of life on our planet. For the first time it demonstrated the ability of the creature man to rise. In so far then, as the career of life is known to terrestrial intelligence, the emergence of a creature capable of thus rising is, I repeat, the greatest fact in the universe.

James Henry Breasted

Man is an animal which alone among the animals refuses to be satisfied by the fulfillment of animal desires.

Alexander Graham Bell

There was a famous king in history who appointed a man to live in his royal presence and to say every day to him, "Philip, remember thou art mortal," lest he forget his kinship with the earth. But doesn't every person need another daily whisper in his ears, "Remember, thou art immortal," lest he forget his kinship with eternity?

J. Wallace Hamilton

The weakest among us has a gift, however seemingly trivial, which is peculiar to him, and which worthily used, will be a gift also to his race.

John Ruskin

Sin is twisting and distorting out of its proper shape a human personality which God designed to be a thing of beauty and a joy forever.

Walter L. Carson

So nigh is grandeur to our dust,
So near is God to man,
When Duty whispers low, Thou Must,
The youth replies, I can.

Ralph Waldo Emerson

We must never undervalue any person. The workman loves not to have his work despised in his presence. Now God is present everywhere, and every person is His work.

Saint Francis De Sales

We differ from the animals who live each day without a thought of the morrow. Only man stands off from himself and tries to explain and understand. He alone possesses the objective ability to evaluate himself and the result is anxiety and despair.

Gerald Francis Burrill

Persons are to be loved; things are to be used.

Reuel Howe

Every man of us has all the centuries in him.

John Morey

There is in every man something greater than he had begun to dream of. Men are nobler than they think themselves.

Phillips Brooks

How powerful is man! He is able to do all that God wishes him to do. He is able to accept all that God sends upon him.

Marcus Aurelius

We are blind until we see
That in the human plan
Nothing is worth the making
If it does not make the man.

Why build these cities glorious
If man unbuilded goes
In vain we build the world unless
The Builder also grows.

Edwin Markham

Men are children of this world,
Yet hath God set eternity in their hearts.

Moses ibn Ezra

Man was made to stand on the shore, to celebrate the sun and the sky, to use the wind and master the water, to care passionately for the children tumbling about the sand. He was made to grow in the image of his Father, to embrace his fellows everywhere, to open the doors, to feed the hungry, to return good for evil. Nothing is harder, but anything else is sure damnation.

Sydney J. Harris

There are seeds of kindness and justice in men's hearts. If self-interest rules there, I dare affirm this is not only natural, but just too, so long as no one suffers by that self-love, or as society loses less than it gains by it.

Vauvenargues

Whether or not the philosophers care to admit that we have a soul, it seems obvious that we are equipped with something or other which generates dreams and ideals, and which sets up values.

John Erskine

We are the miracle of miracles, the great inscrutable mystery of God.

Thomas Carlyle

Each person is a temporary focus of forces, vitalities, and values that carry back into an immemorial past and that reach forward into an unthinkable future.

Lewis Mumford

In the midst of winter, I finally learned that there was in me an invincible summer.

Albert Camus

Perhaps the only true dignity of man is his capacity to despise himself.

George Santayana

It is dangerous to show man too clearly that he is on a level with the beasts without showing him his greatness, and it is also dangerous to show him too plainly his greatness without showing him his baseness. It is more dangerous still to leave him in ignorance of both. But it is very desirable that the one and the other should be placed before him.

Blaise Pascal

Engineers are prone to talk of the efficiency of modern machines. But no machine has ever been constructed that is so efficient as man himself. Where can we find a pump as perfect as the human heart? If the boss treats it right, it stays on the job for more than 600,000 hours, making 430 strokes and pumping 15 gallons an hour. We have no telegraphic mechanism equal to our nervous system; no radio so efficient as the voice and the ear; no cameras as perfect as the human eye; no ventilating plant as wonderful as the nose, lungs, and skin, and no electrical switchboard can compare with the spinal cord. Isn't such a marvelous mechanism worthy of the highest respect and the best care?

Floyd Parsons

Every single man is a world which is born and which dies with him; beneath every gravestone lies a world's history.

Heinrich Heine

The Jews would not willingly tread upon the smallest piece of paper in their way, but took it up; for possibly, said they, the name of God may be on it. Though there was a little superstition in this, yet truly there is nothing but good religion in it, if we apply it to men. Trample not on any; there may be some work of grace there, that thou knowest not of. The name of God may be written upon that soul thou treadest on.

Samuel T. Coleridge

---

33. THE ART OF CHOOSING

It is perfectly possible for you and me to purchase intellectual peace at the price of intellectual death. The world is not without refuges of this description; nor is it wanting in persons who seek their shelter, and try to persuade others to do the same. The unstable and the weak have yielded and will yield to this persuasion, and they to whom repose is sweeter than the truth. But I would exhort you to refuse the offered shelter, and to scorn the base repose; to accept, if the choice be forced upon you, commotion before stagnation, the leap of the torrent before the stillness of the swamp.

John Tyndall

Choose the life that is most useful, and habit will make it the most agreeable.

Francis Bacon

Free will was granted to humanity. Man became conscious of good and evil, and his power of free choice. He acquired simultaneously Freedom and Responsibility. Henceforth he could help or he could hinder.

Sir Oliver Lodge

As human beings, we are endowed with freedom of choice, and we cannot shuffle off our responsibility upon the shoulders of God or nature. We must shoulder it ourselves. It is up to us.

Arnold J. Toynbee

Selection is the very keel on which our mental ship is built. And in the case of memory, its utility is obvious. If we remembered everything, we should on most occasions be as badly off as if we remembered nothing.

William James

It is a wretched taste to be gratified with mediocrity when the excellent lies before us.

Isaac D'Israeli

Morality may consist solely in the courage of making a choice.

Leon Blum

If we are not responsible for the thoughts that pass our doors, we, at least, are responsible for those which we admit and entertain.

Charles B. Newcomb

One summer a college friend who had some sort of muscle paralysis decided to sell books, and he began by visiting the home of the college president. The wife of the president informed him that they did not need any books. As he turned to leave, she saw the limp in his walk and said: "Oh, I am so sorry! I did not know you were lame." The young man, who was not seeking pity, bristled all over; and the woman, realizing that she had perhaps said the wrong thing, hastened to add, "I did not mean to imply anything except admiration, but doesn't being lame rather color your life?" "Yes," he replied, "but thank God I can choose the color."

Frank A. Court

As you and I march across the decades of time, we are going to meet a lot of unpleasant situations that are so. They cannot be otherwise. We have our choice. We can either accept them as inevitable and adjust ourselves to them, or we can ruin our lives with rebellion and maybe end up with a nervous breakdown.

Dale Carnegie

Temptation is a part of life. No one is immune.—at any age. For temptation is present wherever there is a choice to be made, not only between good and evil, but also between a higher and lower good. For some, it may be a temptation to sensual gratification; for others a temptation to misuse their gifts, to seek personal success at the cost of the general welfare, to seek a worthy aim by unworthy means, to lower their ideal to win favor with the electorate, or with their companions and associates.

Ernest Trice Thompson

Cultivate only the habits that you are willing should master you.

Elbert Hubbard

When you have to make a choice and don't make it, that is in itself a choice.

William James

All pleasure may be bought at the price of pain. The difference between false pleasure and true is just this; for the true, the price is paid before you enjoy it; for the false, after you enjoy it.

John Foster

A moral decision is the loneliest thing that exists. Knowledge is shed abroad everywhere. Anybody may dip his cup into that great sea and take out what he can. It is a public appropriation from a public store. But what the man himself must do as a moral being, what ordering he shall make of his life, what allegiance he shall choose, what cause he shall cleave to—this is decided in that solitude where his soul in authentic presence lives with no other companion than the Final

Authority which he recognizes as supreme.

William L. Sullivan

God asks no man whether he will accept life; that is not the choice. You must take it; the only choice is how.

Henry Ward Beecher

Intelligence is derived from two words—*inter* and *legere*—*inter* meaning "between" and *legere* meaning "to choose." An intelligent person, therefore, is one who has learned "to choose between." He knows that good is better than evil, that confidence should supersede fear, that love is superior to hate, that gentleness is better than cruelty, forbearance than intolerance, compassion than arrogance and that truth has more virtue than ignorance.

J. Martin Klotsche

God offers to every mind its choice between truth and repose. Take which you please,—you can never have both.

Ralph Waldo Emerson

Man has the unique capacity to choose between ends. Man is the creature who can say no to his appetites and often does so on the basis of moral considerations. The higher animals sometimes show genuine intelligence by the way they ask and answer the question, "How can I get it?" But man shows something beyond mere intelligence by his capacity to ask and answer the vastly different question, "Ought I to get it?" This is a difference so crucial that it must be termed a difference in kind rather than merely a difference in degree.

Elton Trueblood

---

34. THE ART OF LOOKING WITHIN

Men seek retreats for themselves, houses in the country, seashores and mountains; and thou too art wont to desire such things very much. But it is within thy power whenever thou shalt choose to retire into thyself. For nowhere, either with more quiet or more freedom from trouble, does a man retire than into his own soul, particularly when he has within him such thoughts that by looking into them he is immediately in perfect tranquillity is nothing else than the good ordering of the mind. Look within. Within is the fountain of good.

Marcus Aurelius

The fault, dear Brutus, is not in our stars,
But in ourselves, that we are underlings.

William Shakespeare

If you think you are beaten, you are;
If you think you dare not, you don't.
If you'd like to win, but think you can't,
It's almost a cinch you won't.
If you think you'll lose, you're lost,
For out in the world we find
Success begins with a fellow's will;
It's all in the state of mind.

Life's battles don't always go
   To the stronger or faster man;
But soon or late the man who wins
   Is the one who thinks he can.

Walter D. Wintle

Most of the shadows of this life are caused by standing in our own sunshine.

Ralph Waldo Emerson

The mind is its own place, and in
   itself
Can make a Heaven of Hell, a Hell
   of Heaven.

John Milton

If an Arab in the desert were suddenly to discover a spring in his tent, and so would always be able to have water in abundance, how fortunate he would consider himself—so too, when a man, who as a physical being is always turned toward the outside, thinking that his happiness lies outside him, finally turns inward and discovers that the source is within him; not to mention his discovery that the source is his relation to God.

Sören A. Kierkegaard

Happiness does certainly not depend immediately on external things at all, but upon our inward mode of dealing with them.

William E. Hocking

Not in the clamor of a crowded
   street
Not in the shouts and plaudits of
   the throng,
But in ourselves are triumph and
   defeat.

Henry W. Longfellow

Peace must be established by transforming man from the interior, and not by erecting external structure. The source of all wars, the source of all evil, lies in us. No outside protection will be efficient if the enemy cowering at the bottom of our hearts is authorized to live.

Lecomte Du Nuoy

Happiness is the greatest paradox in nature. It can grow in any soil, live under any condition. It defies environment. The reason for this is that it does not come from without but from within. Whenever you see a person seeking happiness outside himself, you can be sure he has never yet found it.

F. Lincicome

Whenever two people meet there are really six people present. There is each man as he sees himself, each man as the other person sees him, and each man as he really is.

William James

When we cannot find contentment in ourselves, it is useless to seek it elsewhere.

François Rochefoucauld

Solitary we must be in life's great hours of moral decisions; solitary in pain and sorrow; solitary in old age and in our going forth at death. Fortunate the man who has learned what to do in solitude and brought himself to see what companionship he may discover in it, what fortitude, what content.

William L. Sullivan

If a man harbors any sort of fear, it percolates through all his thinking, damages his personality, makes him landlord to a ghost.

Lloyd C. Douglas

You cannot find peace anywhere save in your own self.

Simha Bunam

Though we travel the world over to find the beautiful, we must carry it with us or we find it not.

Ralph Waldo Emerson

The most frequent impediment to men's turning the mind inward upon themselves is that they are afraid of what they shall find there. There is an aching hollowness in the bosom, a dark cold speck at the heart, an obscure and boding sense of something that must be kept out of sight of the conscience; some secret lodger, whom they can neither resolve to reject nor retain.

Samuel Coleridge

What is man's chief enemy? Each man is his own.

Anacharsis

Happiness is everywhere, and its spring is in our own heart.

John Ruskin

A man must be arched and buttressed from within, else the temple crumbles to the dust.

Marcus Aurelius

It's a gay old world when you're gay,
And a glad old world when you're glad;
But whether you play
Or go toiling away
It's a sad old world when you're sad.

It's a grand old world if you're great,
And a mean old world if you're small;

It's a world full of hate
For the foolish who prate
Of the uselessness of it all.

It's a beautiful world to see
Or it's dismal in every zone;
The thing it must be
In its gloom or its glee
Depends on yourself alone.

Author Unknown

A man's own self is his friend, a man's own self is his foe.

Bhagavad-Gita

Man must cease attributing his problems to his environment, and learn again to exercise his will— his personal responsibility in the realm of faith and morals.

Albert Schweitzer

I sent my soul through the invisible
Some letter of that after-life to spell:
And by and by my soul returned to me,
And answered, "I myself am heaven and hell."

The Rubaiyat of Omar Khayyam

I do not ask for any crown
But that which all may win;
Nor try to conquer any world
Except the one within.
Be thou my guide until I find,
Led by a tender hand,
The happy kingdom in myself
And dare to take command.

Louisa May Alcott

Everybody acts not only under external compulsion but also in accordance with inner necessity.

Albert Einstein

Every man's enemy is within himself.

Bahya

35. TO THINE OWN SELF BE TRUE

I do the very best I know how; the very best I can; and I mean to keep on doing it to the end. If the end brings me out all right, what is said against me will not amount to anything. If the end brings me out all wrong, then a legion of angels swearing I was right will make no difference.

Abraham Lincoln

Whoso would be a man, must be a nonconformist. He who would gather immortal palms must not be hindered by the name of goodness, but must explore if it be goodness. Nothing is at last sacred but the integrity of your own mind.

Ralph Waldo Emerson

Great tranquillity of heart is his who cares for neither praise nor blame.

Thomas à Kempis

Pride is a force that it were better to use than to conquer.

Comtesse Diane

Be whatever you want to be, but be it with all your heart.

David Wolffsohn

Use what talents you possess: the woods would be very silent if no birds sang there except those that sang best.

Henry Van Dyke

Nothing requires a rarer intellectual heroism than willingness to see one's equation written out.

George Santayana

Many people go throughout life committing partial suicide—destroying their talents, energies, creative qualities. Indeed, to learn how to be good to oneself is often more difficult than to learn how to be good to others.

Joshua Loth Liebman

Neither the clamor of the mob nor the voice of power will ever turn me by the breadth of a hair from the course I mark out for myself, guided by such knowledge as I can obtain, and controlled and directed by a solemn conviction of right and duty.

Robert M. LaFollette

Let everyone be himself, and not try to be someone else. Let us not torment each other because we are not all alike, but believe that God knew best what he was doing in making us so different. So will the best harmony come out of seeming discords, the best affection out of differences, the best life out of struggle, and the best work will be done when each does his own work, and lets everyone else do and be what God made him for.

James Freeman Clarke

I hope I shall always possess firmness and virtue enough to maintain what I consider the most enviable of all titles, the character of an Honest Man.

George Washington

True dignity abides with him only, who, in the silent hour of inward thought, can still suspect, and still revere himself, in lowliness of heart.

William Wordsworth

It makes a great difference in the force of a sentence whether a man be behind it or no.

Ralph Waldo Emerson

We would rather die on our feet than live on our knees.

Franklin D. Roosevelt

Our first duty to society is to be somebody; that is, be ourselves.

Abbé Dimnet

It may be embarrassing to be different if one is wrong—but it is an enviable distinction to be different if one is right.

Richard L. Evans

I desire so to conduct the affairs of this administration that if at the end, when I come to lay down the reins of power, I have lost every other friend on earth, I shall at least have one friend left, and that friend shall be down inside of me.

Abraham Lincoln

Most of us live too near the surface of our abilities, dreading to call upon our deeper resources. It is as if a strong man were to do his work with only one finger.

John Charles Wynn

To keep clear of concealment, to keep clear of the need of concealment, to do nothing which he might not do out on the middle of Boston Common at noonday,—I cannot say how more and more that seems to me to be the glory of a young man's life. It is an awful hour when the first necessity of hiding anything comes. The whole life is different thenceforth. When there are questions to be feared and eyes to be avoided and subjects which must not be touched, then the bloom of life is gone. Put off that day as long as possible. Put it off forever if you can.

Phillips Brooks

Every human being is intended to have a character of his own; to be what no other is, and to do what no other can do.

William Ellery Channing

What a great deal of ease that man gains who lets his neighbor's behavior alone and takes care that his own actions are honest.

Marcus Aurelius

Misfortunes one can endure, they come from outside, they are accidents. But to suffer for one's faults —ah! there is the sting of life.

Oscar Wilde

What a man is inwardly he will ultimately display outwardly. He may for a time, like the barren fig tree, make a great display of false profession, but the truth will come out, and he will be known for what he is.

Author Unknown

Confidence is that feeling by which the mind embarks in great and honorable courses with a sure hope and trust in itself.

Cicero

We have more power than will; and it is often by way of excuse to ourselves that we fancy things are impossible.

François Rochefoucauld

No man was ever great by imitation.

Samuel Johnson

What you think of yourself is much more important than what others think of you.

Seneca

Keeping up appearances is the most expensive thing in the world.

A. C. Benson

If you have anything really valuable to contribute to the world it will come through the expression of your own personality—that single spark of divinity that sets you off and makes you different from every other living creature.

Bruce Barton

A man has to live with himself, and he should see to it that he always has good company.

Charles Evans Hughes

That man is great, and he alone,
Who serves a greatness not his own,
For neither praise or pelf;
Content to know and be unknown;
Whole in himself.

Owen Meredith

If I could get the ear of every young man but for one word, it would be this; make the most and best of yourself. There is no tragedy like a wasted life—a life failing of its true end, and turned to a false end.

T. T. Munger

Resolve to be thyself; and know that he who finds himself loses his misery.

Matthew Arnold

No one can disgrace us but ourselves.

J. G. Holland

We are so much accustomed to disguise ourselves to others, that at length we disguise ourselves to ourselves.

François Rochefoucauld

A temporary compromise is a diplomatic act, but a permanent compromise is the abandonment of a goal.

Leo Stein

Never esteem anything as of advantage to thee that shall make thee break thy word or lose thy self-respect.

Marcus Aurelius

"Your task . . . to build a better world," God said. I answered "how? . . . This world is such a large, vast place, so complicated now, and I so small and useless am, there's nothing I can do." But God in all his wisdom said, "just build a better you."

Author Unknown

When a man is sure that all he wants is happiness, then most grievously he deceives himself. All men desire happiness, but they want something different, compared to which happiness is trivial, and in the absence of which happiness turns to dust and ashes in the mouth. There are many names for that which men need—the one thing needful—but the simplest is "whole-ness."

Middleton Murry

We try to be like others, to conform, so that we will be accepted. But only to the degree that one is different has he anything to offer. Every contribution is an evidence of difference, of uniqueness.

Don Robinson

The world is made better by every man improving his own conduct; and no reform is accomplished wholesale.

William Allen White

The only guide to a man is his conscience; the only shield to his memory is the rectitude and sincerity of his actions. It is very imprudent to walk through life without this shield, because we are often mocked by the failure of our hopes and the upsetting of our calculations; but with this shield, however the fates may play, we march always in the ranks of honour.

Winston Churchill

By despising himself too much a man comes to be worthy of his own contempt.

Henri Frederic Amiel

What another would have done as well as you, do not do it. What another would have said as well as you, do not say it. What another would have written as well, do not write it. Be faithful to that which exists nowhere but in yourself—and thus make yourself indispensable.

André Gide

It is necessary to the happiness of man that he be mentally faithful to himself.

Thomas Paine

The greatest want of the world is the want of men—men who will not be bought or sold; men who in their inmost souls are true and honest; men who do not fear to call sin by its right name; men whose conscience is as true to duty as the needle to the pole; men who will stand for the right though the heavens fall.

E. G. White

Be good yourself and the world will be good.

Hindu Proverb

We are never made as ridiculous through the qualities we have as through those we pretend to.

François Rochefoucauld

Let the truth and right by which you are apparently the loser be preferable to you to the falsehood and wrong by which you are apparently the gainer.

Moses Maimonides

Most of us are like snowflakes trying to be like each other, yet knowing full well that no two snowflakes are ever identical. If we were to devote the same amount of energy in trying to discover the true self that lies buried deep within our own nature, we would all work harmoniously *with* life instead of forever *fighting* it.

Walter E. Elliott

Insist on yourself; never imitate. Your own gift you can present every moment with the cumulative force of a whole life's cultivation; but of the adopted talent of another, you have only an extemporaneous half-possession. That which each can do best none but his Maker can teach him.

Ralph Waldo Emerson

What is wrong with difference is not difference, but man's reluctance to allow and encourage it, and to cultivate it creatively.

Milton Steinberg

We are inconsolable at being deceived by our enemies, and betrayed by our friends; and yet we are often content to be so by ourselves.

François Rochefoucauld

When I look back upon the more than sixty years that I have spent on this entrancing earth and when I am asked which of all the changes that I have witnessed appears to me to be the most significant, I am inclined to answer that it is the loss of a sense of shame.

Harold Nicolson

This above all: to thine own self be true;
And it must follow, as the night the day,
Thou canst not then be false to any man.

William Shakespeare

I never can hide myself from me;
I see what others may never see;
I know what others may never know,
I never can fool myself, and so
Whatever happens, I want to be
Self-respecting and conscience free.

Author Unknown

The greatest happiness is to be that which one is.

Theodore Herzl

There are two people I must please—God and Garfield. I must live with Garfield here, with God hereafter.

James A. Garfield

It is very easy to manage our neighbor's business, but our own sometimes bothers us.

Josh Billings

It is the chiefest point of happiness that a man is willing to be what he is.

Erasmus

The imitative faculty is very strong in human makeup, and it has its valuable points and its very weak points. It must be watched or it will make monkeys of us all.

J. B. Gambrell

Prosperity, obtained through truth and righteousness, is built on a sure rock. Happiness derived from falsehood, injustice and lust, is built on sand.

Moses Maimonides

Nothing is a greater impediment to being on good terms with others than being ill at ease with yourself.

Honore de Balzac

Most remarks that are worth making are commonplace remarks. The thing that makes them worth saying is that we really mean them.

Robert Lynd

No man can produce great things who is not thoroughly sincere in dealing with himself.

James Russell Lowell

If the devil ever laughs it must be at hypocrites, they serve him well and receive no wages.

Author Unknown

Honesty is something more than keeping out of jail, living within the law, avoiding trouble with the authorities. Honesty is the pure-gold bullion of integrity. The honest man determines to scrupulously keep the rules of the game. He stands upright, no matter how great the storm that breaks over him. He is fearlessly outspoken. He is courageously true in action and expression. Our country needs honest men today. The man of high integrity does not "have his price." He can never be bought.

Gordon Palmer

"Know thyself" is indeed a weighty admonition. But in this, as in any science, the difficulties are discovered only by those who set their hands to it. We must push against a door to find out whether it is bolted or not.

Michel de Montaigne

Great God, I ask thee for no meaner pelf
Than that I may not disappoint myself,
That in my action I may soar as high
As I can now discern with this clear eye.

Henry Thoreau

There is a deportment which suits the figure and talents of each person; it is always lost when we quit it to assume that of another.

Jean Jacques Rousseau

Do not wish you were like someone else. God made you as you are in order to use you as He planned.

J. C. Macaulay

Were we to take as much pains to be what we ought to be, as we do to disguise what we really are, we might appear like ourselves without being at the trouble of any disguise whatever.

Francois Rochefoucauld

There is a time in every man's education when he arrives at the conviction that envy is ignorance, that imitation is suicide; that he must take himself for better or for worse, as his portion; that though the wide universe is full of good, no kernel of nourishing corn can come to him but through his toil bestowed on that plot of ground which is given to him to till. The power which resides in him is new in nature, and none but he knows what that is which he can do, nor does he know until he has tried.

Ralph Waldo Emerson

Live truly, and thy life shall be
A great and noble creed.

Horatius Bonar

Give me heart, touch with all that live,
And strength to speak my word;
But if that is denied me, give
The strength to live unheard.

Edwin Markham

The most exhausting thing in life is being insincere.

Anne Morrow Lindbergh

Preoccupation with watching other people's blemishes would prevent me from investigating my own, a task more urgent.

Bahya

If you want to be original, be yourself. God never made two people exactly alike.

Author Unknown

The first and worst of all frauds is to cheat one's self.

Philip James Bailey

---

36. THE ART OF SELF-CONTROL

Drunkenness is temporary suicide: the happiness that it brings is merely negative, a momentary cessation of unhappiness.

Bertrand Russell

He who gains a victory over other men is strong; but he who gains a victory over himself is all powerful.

Lao-tse

Let not any one say that he cannot govern his passions, nor hinder them from breaking out and carrying him to action; for what he can do before a prince or a great man, he can do alone, or in the presence of God, if he will.

John Locke

Anger raises invention, but it overheats the oven.

Lord Halifax

Two things a man should not be angry at: what he can help, and what he cannot help.

Author Unknown

Of what avail are great machines, if the men who mind them are mean? Man's increased command of nature is paltry if it be not accompanied by an increased control of himself. That is the only sort of command relevant to the evolution of man into a higher being.

George Bernard Shaw

Most powerful is he who has himself in his power.

Seneca

Whatever liberates our spirit without giving us self-control is disastrous.

Johann Wolfgang von Goethe

According to the Book of Genesis, the Creator gave man dominion over the whole wide earth. A mighty big present. But I am not interested in any such super-royal prerogatives. All I desire is dominion over myself—dominion over my thoughts; dominion over my fears; dominion over my mind and over my spirit. And the wonderful thing is that I know that I can attain this dominion to an astonishing degree, any time I want to, by merely controlling my actions—which in turn control my reactions.

Dale Carnegie

The first and best victory is to conquer self; to be conquered by self is of all things the most shameful and vile.

Plato

He who reigns within himself and rules his passions, desires and fears is more than a king.

John Milton

Everybody thinks of changing humanity and nobody thinks of changing himself.

Leo Tolstoy

Whatever is begun in anger ends in shame.

Benjamin Franklin

Govern thyself, and you will be able to govern the world.

Chinese Proverb

If you would cure anger, do not feed it. Say to yourself: "I used to be angry every day; then every other day; now only every third or fourth day." When you reach 30 days, offer a sacrifice of thanksgiving to the gods.

Epictetus

A man should first direct himself in the way he should go. Only then should he instruct others.

Buddha

He is a fool who cannot be angry; but he is a wise man who will not.

English Proverb

Anger is an acid that can do more harm to the vessel in which it's stored than to anything on which it's poured.

Author Unknown

Remember that when you're in the right you can afford to keep your temper and that when you're in the wrong you can't afford to lose it.

J. Graham

The conquest of nature, not the imitation of nature, is the whole duty of man.

E. E. Slosson

What we do on some great occasion will probably depend on what we already are, and what we are will be the result of previous years of self-discipline.

Canon Liddon

Queen Elizabeth, who knew something about hot temper, once said to a courtier who had lost his head, "Ah, Sir Philip, anger often makes men witty but it always keep them poor."

Ralph W. Sockman

When a man's fight begins within himself, he is worth something.

Robert Browning

Man who man would be
Must rule the empire of himself.

Percy Bysshe Shelley

People who fly into a rage always make a bad landing.

Will Rogers

In managing human affairs, there is no better rule than self-restraint.

Lao-tse

We are discovering the right things in the wrong order, which is another way of saying that we are learning how to control nature before we have learned how to control ourselves.

Raymond Fosdick

It is not our business to murder the bounding animal in us, dreaming insanely over his ebbing blood, but to tame him and ride him, rejoicing in his swiftness and strength.

George Meredith

Anger is a wind which blows out the lamp of the mind.

Robert Ingersoll

I have had more trouble with myself than with any other man.

Dwight L. Moody

In vain do they talk of happiness who never subdued an impulse in obedience to a principle. He who never sacrificed a present to a future good, or a personal to a general one, can speak of happiness only as the blind do of colors.

Horace Mann

Self-reverence, self-knowledge, self-control,
These three alone lead life to sovereign power.

Alfred Lord Tennyson

Self-control is not worth a farthing unless we build up a great self worth controlling.

Morris R. Cohen

It is easier to suppress the first desire than to satisfy all that follow it.

Ben Franklin

The Chinese have a story based on three or four thousand years of civilization. Two Chinese coolies were arguing heatedly in the midst of a crowd. A stranger expressed surprise that no blows were being struck. His Chinese friend replied, "The man who strikes first admits that his ideas have given out."

Franklin Delano Roosevelt

What man's mind can create, man's character can control.

Thomas Edison

No man is free who is not master of himself.

Epictetus

Anybody can become angry—that is easy. But to be angry with the right person, and to the right degree, and at the right time, and for the right purpose, and in the right way—that is not within everybody's power and is not easy.

Aristotle

Man's conquest of nature has been astonishing. His failure to conquer human nature has been tragic.

Julius Mark

Can you walk on water? You have done no better than a straw. Can you fly in the air? You have done no better than a bluebottle. Conquer your heart; then you may become somebody.

Ansari of Herat

Every man is a tamer of wild beasts, and these wild beasts are his passions. To draw their teeth and claws, to muzzle and tame them, to turn them into servants and domestic animals, fuming, per-

haps, but submissive—in this consists personal education.

Henri F. Amiel

In a controversy the instant we feel anger we have already ceased striving for the truth, and have begun striving for ourselves.

Thomas Carlyle

The happiness of a man in this life does not consist in the absence but in the mastery of his passions.

Alfred North Tennyson

Anger is a thief that seizes control of man's faculties and uses them blindly and destructively. Usually a man who loses his temper also temporarily loses his ability to think logically.

Lowell Fillmore

For me, life can hold no higher adventure than to see man learn to control his own nature as he now controls the atoms.

Walter B. Pitkin

The pledge to myself which I have endeavored to keep through the greater part of my life is: I will not allow one prejudiced person or one million or one hundred million to blight my life. I will not let prejudice or any of its attendant humiliations and injustices bear me down to spiritual defeat. My inner life is mine, and I shall defend and maintain its integrity against all the powers of hell.

James Weldon Johnson

More people are killed by overeating and drinking than by the sword.

Sir William Osler

Every minute you are angry you lose sixty seconds of happiness.

Author Unknown

Anger begins with madness, and ends with regret.

Abraham Hasdai

---

37. THE ART OF JUDGING OURSELVES

To do everything he is asked to do, a man must overestimate himself.

Johann Wolfgang von Goethe

Observe thyself as thy greatest enemy would do, so shalt thou be thy greatest friend.

Jeremy Taylor

Man sees your actions, but God your motives.

Thomas à Kempis

Perhaps the only true dignity of man is his capacity to despise himself.

George Santayana

There is in every man something greater than he had begun to dream of. Men are nobler than they think themselves.

Phillips Brooks

We judge ourselves by what we are capable of doing; others judge us by what we have done.

Henry Wadsworth Longfellow

It is easy to look down on others; to look down on ourselves is the difficulty.

Lord Peterborough

How shall we expect charity toward others when we are uncharitable to ourselves? Charity begins at home, is the voice of the world. Yet is every man his greatest enemy, and, as it were, his own executioner.

Sir Thomas Browne

When you have closed your doors, and darkened your room, remember never to say that you are alone, for you are not alone; God is within, and your genius is within, —and what need have they of light to see what you are doing?

Epictetus

We keep on deceiving ourselves in regard to our faults, until we at last come to look upon them as virtues.

Heinrich Heine

If we wish to be just judges of all things, let us first persuade ourselves of this: that there is not one of us without fault; no man is found who can acquit himself; and he who calls himself innocent does so with reference to a witness, and not to his conscience.

Seneca

We judge others by their words and deeds, ourselves by our thoughts and our intentions.

Comtesse Diane

The only way to relieve the world's ills is not by understanding each other, but by each one understanding himself; for there can be no genuine rapport between persons who are ignorant of their own deepest motivations and needs.

Sydney J. Harris

Though not always called upon to condemn ourselves, it is always safe to suspect ourselves.

Whately

When you see a good man, think of emulating him; when you see a bad man, examine your own heart.

Chinese Proverb

To be granted the opportunity to know one's true self, a self much greater and finer than one has ever dared to suspect, such is indeed the gift of gifts.

Walter E. Eliott

If we had no faults ourselves, we should not take so much pleasure in remarking them in others.

Francois Rochefoucald

He is not laughed at by others, that laughs at himself first.

Author Unknown

It is equally a mistake to hold one's self too high, or to rate one's self too cheap.

Johann Wolfgang von Goethe

Before God can deliver us we must undeceive ourselves.

Saint Augustine

It seems that Nature, which has so wisely disposed our bodily organs with a view to our happiness, has also bestowed on us pride, to spare us the pain of being aware of our imperfections.

Francois Rochefoucauld

We have a bat's eyes for our own faults, and an eagle's for the faults of others.

J. L. Gordon

---

38. THE ART OF INDEPENDENCE

There's no sort of work that could ever be done well if you minded what fools say. You must have it inside you that your plan is right, and that plan you must follow.

George Eliot

When Jane Addams was once asked what she thought about the new style of women's bobbed hair, she answered, "I am not quite so concerned about the uniformity of women's heads on the outside, as I am by the uniformity of women's heads on the inside."

There are those who are fearful to be alone with themselves. They run with the crowd not out of love

for others but out of fear to remain alone with themselves, terrified lest they hear the voice of their own spirit, or fearful of remaining alone with their own void.

Morris Adler

It is not by a perpetual Amen to every utterance of a great authority that truth or literature gains anything.

Solomon Schechter

No man must surrender his private judgment. The eyes are directed forwards, not backwards.

Moses Maimonides

What I am, what I am not, in the eye of the world, is what I never cared for much.

Robert Browning

What forests of laurel we bring, and the tears of mankind, to those who stood firm against the opinion of their contemporaries!

Ralph Waldo Emerson

Had I to carve an inscription on my tombstone I would ask for none other than "The Individual."

Sören Kierkegaard

If a man does not keep pace with his companions, perhaps it is because he hears a different drummer. Let him keep step to music which he hears, however measured or far away.

Henry David Thoreau

They are slaves who wear to speak
For the fallen and the weak;
They are slaves who dare not be
In the right with two or three.

James Russell Lowell

Solitude is to the mind what fasting is to the body, fatal if it is too prolonged, and yet necessary.

Vauvenargues

When I find the road narrow, and can see no other way of teaching a well-established truth except by pleasing one intelligent man and displeasing ten thousand fools, I prefer to address myself to the one man, and to take no notice whatever of the contemplation of the multitude.

Moses Maimonides

He only is a great man who can neglect the applause of the multitude, and enjoy himself independent of its favour.

Richard Steele

Every custom was once an eccentricity; every idea was once an absurdity.

Holbrook Jackson

Nothing is at last sacred but the integrity of your own mind.

Ralph Waldo Emerson

The strongest man is the one who stands most alone.

Henrik Ibsen

Conversation enriches the understanding, but solitude is the school of genius.

Edward Gibbon

We must neither run with the crowd nor deride it, but seek sober counsel for it, and for ourselves.

Woodrow Wilson

Criticism has few terrors for a man with a great purpose.

Benjamin Disraeli

Do not consider it a proof just because it is written in books, for a liar who will deceive with his tongue will not hesitate to do the same with his pen.

Moses Maimonides

All great truths began as blasphemies.

George Bernard Shaw

In response to a survey, student editors expressed concern about the danger of conformity. One said, "People are too much alike and like it too much." That's not good: either for enduring freedom, or democracy.

Rae Noel

We settle things by a majority vote, and the psychological effect of doing that is to create the impression that the majority is probably right. Of course, on any fine issue the majority is sure to be wrong. Think of taking a majority vote on the best music. Jazz would win over Chopin. Or on the best novel. Many cheap scribblers would win over Tolstoy. And any day a prizefight will get a bigger crowd, larger gate receipts and wider newspaper publicity than any new revelation of goodness, truth or beauty could hope to achieve in a century. . . .

Harry Emerson Fosdick

I cannot give you the formula for success, but I can give you the formula for failure—which is: Try to please everybody.

Herbert B. Swope

Education in its deepest sense is the improvement of man so that he will be a thinking individual, not afraid of the validity of his conclusions even though they may deviate from what may be acceptable and safe at the moment.

Henry R. Heald

The man who has no refuge in himself, who lives, so to speak, in his front rooms, in the outer whirlwind of things and opinions, is not properly speaking a personality at all; he is not distinct, free, original, a cause—in a word, some one. He is one of the crowd, a taxpayer, an elector, an anonymity, but not a man.

Henri F. Amiel

The nurse of full-grown souls is solitude.

James Russell Lowell

It is easy in the world to live after the world's opinion; it is easy in solitude to live after our own; but the great man is he who in the midst of the crowd keeps with perfect sweetness the independence of solitude.

Ralph Waldo Emerson

An unlearned carpenter of my acquaintance once said in my hearing: "There is very little difference between one man and another; but what little there is, is very important."

William James

It is the minorities that hold the key to progress. It is always through those who are unafraid to be different that advance comes to human society.

Raymond B. Fosdick

I never found the companion that was so companionable as solitude.

Henry Thoreau

A perfect life is like that of a ship of war which has its own place in the fleet and can share in its strength and discipline, but can also go forth alone in the solitude of the infinite sea. We ought to belong to society, to have our place in it, and yet be capable of a complete individual existence outside of it.

Philip G. Hamerton

Great men stand like solitary towers in the city of God.

Henry Wadsworth Longfellow

Whoso would be a man must be a nonconformist.

Ralph Waldo Emerson

I had rather be hissed for a good verse than applauded for a bad one.

Victor Hugo

39. THE POWER OF TRUTH

The mind celebrates a little triumph every time it can formulate a truth.

George Santayana

In the long run, truth is aided by nothing so much as by opposition.

William Ellery Channing

A newspaperman once asked Sam Rayburn: "Mr. Speaker, you see probably a hundred people a day. You tell each one 'Yes,' or 'No,' or 'Maybe.' You never seem to make notes on what you have told them, but I never heard of your forgetting anything you have promised them. What is your secret?"

Rayburn's hot brown eyes flashed: "If you tell the truth the first time," he replied, "you don't have to remember."

D. B. Hardeman

Truth and sincerity have a certain distinguishing native lustre about them which cannot be perfectly counterfeited; they are like fire and flame, that cannot be painted.

Benjamin Franklin

The search for truth is in one way hard, and in another way easy. For it is evident that no one can master it fully, nor yet miss it wholly. But each adds a little to our knowledge of nature, and from all the facts assembled, there arises a certain grandeur.

Aristotle

Time, whose tooth gnaws away everything else, is powerless against truth.

Thomas H. Huxley

The passion for truth has underlying it a profound conviction that what is real is best; that when we get to the heart of things we shall find there what we most need.

G. S. Merriam

No face which we can give to a matter will stead us so well at last as the truth. This alone wears well.

Henry Thoreau

Peace without truth is a false peace.

Mendel of Kotzk

There is nothing so powerful as truth; and often nothing as strange.

Daniel Webster

Truth is incontrovertible. Panic may resent it; ignorance may deride it; malice may distort it; but there it is.

Winston Churchill

Truth never need fear the light. Sunlight falling on a dead log may hasten the process of decay, but sunlight falling on a living tree makes it grow and become luxuriant.

Joseph R. Sizoo

If you tell the truth, you don't have to remember anything.

Mark Twain

That truth is mighty and shall prevail, I have no doubt; but for the next race of men, if not for us. Truth can lose an argument, a nation, even a world—but it carries a creative core that is imperishable, invulnerable, and innocently growing in the very heart of corruption.

Sydney J. Harris

Defeat is a school in which truth always grows strong.

Henry Ward Beecher

If you are out to describe the truth, leave elegance to the tailor.

Albert Einstein

Men have to find truth; not because it is lost, but because they are lost.

Ivan N. Panin

Truth crushed to earth will rise again; the eternal years of God are hers; but error wounded writhes in pain, and dies amid her worshippers.

William Cullen Bryant

Truth is a jewel which should not be painted over; but it may be set to advantage and shown in a good light.

George Santayana

Truth is the disciple of the ascetic, the quest of the mystic, the faith of the simple, the ransom of the weak, the standard of the righteous, the doctrine of the meek, and the challenge of Nature. Together, all these constitute the Law of the Universe.

John Hay Allison

Truth possesses within herself a penetrating force, unknown alike to error and falsehood. I say "truth" and you understand my meaning. For the beautiful words truth and justice need not be defined in order to be understood in their true sense. They bear within them a shining beauty and a heavenly light. I firmly believe in the triumph of truth, that is what upholds me in times of trials.

Anatole France

To live in the presence of great truths, to be dealing with eternal laws, to be led by permanent ideals, —that is what keeps a man patient when the world ignores him, and calm and unspoiled when the world praises him.

Francis G. Peabody

Words which come from the heart enter the heart.

Moses Ibn Ezra

The ultimate test for us of what a truth means is the conduct it dictates or inspires.

William James

Truth is the most powerful thing in the world, since even Fiction itself must be governed by it, and can only please by its resemblance.

Anthony Shaftesbury

When the truth is in your way, you are on the wrong road.

Josh Billings

Every man who expresses an honest thought is a soldier in the army of intellectual liberty.

Ralph Ingersoll

Every violation of truth is a stab at the health of human society.

Ralph Waldo Emerson

One of the best ways to get rid of weeds is to plant something in their stead. The great need, therefore, is to encourage people with good ideas to go into the marketplace rather than to concentrate too much on driving out those with evil designs.

James Keller

Such is the irresistible nature of truth that all it asks, and all it wants is the liberty of appearing. The sun needs no inscription to distinguish him from darkness.

Thomas Paine

Truth gets well if she is run over by a locomotive, while error dies of lockjaw if she scratches her finger.

William Cullen Bryant

He who has truth in his heart need never fear the want of persuasion on his tongue.

John Ruskin

Things are never quite the same somehow after you have to lie to a person.

Christopher Morley

In any emergency in life there is nothing so strong and safe as the simple truth.

Charles Dickens

Life is short, and truth works far and lives long: let us speak the truth.

Arthur Schopenhauer

It is the same whether a man offers much or little, provided his heart is directed to Heaven.

The Mishnah

Truth is tough. It will not break like a bubble at a touch; nay, you will kick it about all day, like a football, and it will be round and full at evening.

Oliver Wendell Holmes

THE ART OF LIVING
WITH OUR FAMILIES

40. THE ART OF BUILDING A HOME

Where we love is home,
Home that our feet may leave, but
not our hearts.
Oliver Wendell Holmes

The one word above all others
that makes marriage successful is
"ours."
Robert Quillen

Anyone can build an altar; it requires a God to provide the flame.
*Anybody can build a house; we
need the Lord for the creation of a
home.* A house is an agglomeration
of brick and stones, with an as-
sorted collection of manufactured
goods; a home is the abiding-place
of ardent affection, of fervent hope,
of genial trust. There is many a
homeless man who lives in a richly
furnished house. There is many a
fifteen-pound house in the crowded
street which is an illuminated and
beautiful home. The sumptuously
furnished house may only be an ex-
quisitely sculptured tomb; the
scantily furnished house may be
the very hearthstone of the eternal
God.
John Henry Jowett

On the banks of the James River,
a husband erected a tombstone in
memory of his wife, one of those
100 maidens who had come to Virginia in 1619 to marry the lonely
settlers. The stone bore this legend:
"She touched the soil of Virginia
with her little foot and the wilderness became a home."
Eudora Ramsay Richardson

Two persons who have chosen
each other out of all the species,
with the design to be each other's
mutual comfort and entertainment,
have, in that action, bound themselves to be good-humored, affable,
discreet, forgiving, patient, and joyful, with respect to each other's
frailties and perfections, to the end
of their lives.
Joseph Addison

The home is the empire! There
is no peace more delightful than
one's own fireplace.
Cicero

Whatever woman may cast her
lot with mine, should any ever do
so, it is my intention to do all in

my power to make her happy and contented; and there is nothing I can imagine that would make me more unhappy than to fail in the effort.

Abraham Lincoln

The grandest of heroic deeds are those which are performed within four walls and in domestic privacy.

Jean Paul Richter

You can no more measure a home by inches, or weigh it by ounces, than you can set up the boundaries of a summer breeze, or calculate the fragrance of a rose. Home is the love which is in it.

Edward Whiting

Love is always building up. It puts some line of beauty on every life it touches. It gives new hope to discouraged ones, new strength to those who are weak, new joys to those who are sorrowing. It makes life seem more worth while to every one into whose eyes it looks.

Author Unknown

To Adam paradise was home. To the good among his descendants, home is paradise.

August W. Hare

During the last war, London parents shipped as many children as possible into the country where they would be physically safe from air bombardments. Studies made after the war showed that children who remained in London with their parents suffered less, physically and emotionally, than did the children sent to the country for safety. The true security was found to be family unity, not physical safety.

Henry C. Link

The home is a place where we can begin to remake our culture. If our culture has slipped into unsound habits of irresponsibility and egocentricity, the home is a place where we can begin to mitigate these habits. If our culture has slipped into carelessness regarding human values, the home is a place where these values can be cherished and made to grow in influence. If our culture has learned to put a disastrously high premium on competition, the home is a place where the cooperative arts can be a strength and a delight. Nowhere in our culture is there an institution that can, more variously and deeply, serve the needs of our maturing than can the home.

Harry A. Overstreet

If there be righteousness in the heart,
    There will be beauty in the character,
If there be beauty in the character,
    There will be harmony in the home.

If there be harmony in the home,
    There will be order in the nation.
If there be order in the nation,
    There will be peace in the world.

Chinese Proverb

Marriage is not and should not be an interminable conversation. The happy marriage allows for privileged silences.

Ashley Montague

I regard marriage as the holiest institution among men. Without the fireside there is no human advancement; without the family relation there is no life worth living.

Robert Ingersoll

Love does not consist in gazing at each other but in looking outward together in the same direction. *Antoine De Saint-Exupery*

The beauty of the house is order;
The blessing of the house is contentment;
The glory of the house is hospitality;
The crown of the house is godliness.
Author Unknown

He is happiest, be he king or peasant, who finds his peace in his home.
Johann Wolfgang von Goethe

The happiest moments of my life have been the few which I have passed at home in the bosom of my family.
Thomas Jefferson

It will be great to go to the moon. But earth never invented anything better than coming home —provided home is a center of affection where parents love each other and their children intelligently, and where children admire and respect their parents and want to grow up to be like them.
Erwin D. Canham

Where there is room in the heart there is always room in the house.
Thomas Moore

Come in the evening, or come in the morning,
Come when you're looked for, or come without warning,
Kisses and welcome you'll find here before you,
And the oftener you come here the more I'll adore you.
Thomas O. Davis

A family is not sufficient unto itself. Home ties are not safe unless the members of the family have larger interests in causes outside themselves.
Ralph W. Sockman

Good dates don't necessarily make good mates.
Barnett Brickner

Sweet is the smile of home; the mutual look,
When hearts are of each other sure.
John Keble

The family is like a book—
The children are the leaves,
The parents are the covers
That protecting beauty gives.

At first the pages of the book
Are blank and purely fair,
But Time soon writeth memories
And painteth pictures there.

Love is the little golden clasp
That bindeth up the trust;
Oh, break it not, lest all the leaves
Should scatter and be lost!
Author Unknown

The husband needs to be blind at times; the wife, deaf; both need much of the time to be dumb.
Ivan N. Panin

Marriage should combat without respite that monster which devours everything—habit.
Honoré de Balzac

The greatest, most formidable force in the life of a child, with no second competitor, is his home. A leading Eastern university spent a quarter of a million dollars to formally establish this fact. This is approximately how the child's waking time is divided: The public school has him 16% of his time. The church, 1% (if he is consistent in his attendance). The home has him 83% of his time.

Howard Hendricks

There is no synthetic replacement for a decent home life. Our high crime rate, particularly among juveniles, is directly traceable to a break down in moral fiber—to the disintegration of home and family life. Religion and home life are supplementary. Each strengthens the other. It is seldom that a solid and wholesome home life can be found in the absence of religious inspiration.

J. Edgar Hoover

Marriage is that relation between man and woman in which the independence is equal, the dependence mutual, and the obligation reciprocal.

Louis K. Anspacher

All that a husband or wife really wants is to be pitied a little, praised a little, appreciated a little; and for each to realize that the hard work is not all on one side.

Warren H. Goldsmith

The kindest and the happiest pair
Will find occasion to forbear;
And something, every day they live,
To pity, and perhaps forgive.

William Cowper

A dramatist named Alfred Sutro once wrote a fine, if forgotten, play called "A Maker of Men," in which a bank clerk returns home, after missing promotion, and says, "I see other men getting on; what have *I* done?"

His wife answers: "You have made a woman love you. You have given me respect for you, and admiration, and loyalty, and devotion —everything a man can give his wife, except luxury, and that I don't need. Still you call yourself a failure, who within these four walls are the greatest success?"

Isn't she right?

Channing Pollock

God oft hath a great share in a little house.

George Herbert

Whom God loves, his house is sweet to him.

Cervantes

A successful marriage is an edifice that must be rebuilt every day.

André Maurois

Home is where the great are small and the small are great.

Author Unknown

To be happy at home is the ultimate result of all ambition.

Samuel Johnson

The worst reconciliation is preferable to the best divorce.

Cervantes

A woman who runs her house well is both its queen and its subject. She is the one who makes work possible for her husband and children; she protects them from worries, feeds them and cares for them. She is Minister of Finance, and, thanks to her, the household budget is balanced. She is Minister of Fine Arts, and it is to her doing if the house or apartment has charm. She is Minister of Family Education and responsible for the boys' entry into school and college and the girls' cleverness and cultivation. A woman should be as proud of her success in making her house into a perfect little world as the greatest statesman of his in organizing a nation's affairs.

André Maurois

Hospitality consists in a little fire, a little food, and an immense quiet.

Ralph Waldo Emerson

A house becomes a home through love and respect among its residents, not from a stylish address or a motto on the wall.

Ralph E. Howland, Jr.

Home should be an oasis of peace and beauty in the arid desert of worldly affairs; a harbor safe from the storms of social and business life; an isle of rest from emotional encounters which upset one's poise. Home should be the spot where all cares are dropped when one enters the door, where the day's discordant thoughts and emotional reactions are left outside.

T. Wilcox Putnam

The most important thing a father can do for his children is to love their mother.

Theodore Hesburgh

Every home is a cell. It is a cell in the penological sense, or it is a cell in the biological sense. It is a prison, or it is a unit of growth. It is a jail, or it is a living body. A prison is a place where people are denied their freedom, and a jail an instrument of cramping and hurting. But when you speak of cells as plants and animals and human beings have them, then all the mystery of life is bound up in them. Cells like that have vigor and vitality. They have movement and development. They have freedom and hope.

Roy M. Pearson

The parent's life is the child's copy-book.

Author Unknown

The family is the spiritual atom of the atomic age.

Ralph W. Sockman

Home is not where you live but where they understand you.

Christian Morgenstern

We need to think of the home as the cradle into which the future is born, and the family as the nursery in which the new social order is being reared. The family is a covenant with posterity.

Sidney Goldstein

Love withers under constraint: its very essence is liberty: it is compatible neither with obedience, jealousy, nor fear: it is there most pure, perfect, and unlimited where its votaries live in confidence, equality, and unreserve.

Percy Bysshe Shelley

There is an emanation from the heart in genuine hospitality which cannot be described, but is immediately felt and puts the stranger at once at his ease.

Washington Irving

The highest happiness on earth is in marriage. Every man who is happily married is a successful man even if he has failed in everything else.

William Lyon Phelps

Six things are requisite to create a "happy home." Integrity must be the architect, and tidiness the up-holsterer. It must be warmed by affection, lighted up with cheer-fulness; and industry must be the ventilator, renewing the atmos-phere and bringing in fresh salu-brity day by day; while over all, as a protecting canopy and glory, nothing will suffice except the blessing of God.

Alexander Hamilton

The family is the miniature com-monwealth upon whose integrity the safety of the larger common-wealth depends.

Felix Adler

Marriage is an opportunity for happiness, not a gift. It is a step by which two imperfect individuals unite their forces in the struggle for happiness.

Henry C. Link

Affection can withstand very severe storms of vigor, but not a long polar frost of indifference.

Sir Walter Scott

There are realms in which arith-metic does not work. It has no place in the kingdom of love. For instance, we are not to count the number of times we forgive.

Charles E. Jefferson

Only so far as a man is happily married to himself, is he fit for married life to another, and for family life generally.

Friedrich von Hardenberg Novalis

I chose my wife, as she did her wedding gown, for qualities that would wear well.

Oliver Goldsmith

Certainly in the case of adults and to some lesser extent in the case of children there is another side to the truth: "Human beings should be loved." It is: "Human beings should be lovable."

Joseph Wood Krutch

It is as absurd to pretend that one cannot love the same woman always as to pretend that a good artist needs several violins to exe-cute a piece of music.

Honoré de Balzac

The magic of marriage is that it creates meaningful goals to work for, struggle for, sacrifice for. It is the joint struggle that gives the relationship its meaning, and keeps people alive.

Henry Gregor Felsen

During a depression we lose our houses; during prosperity we lose our homes.

Sterling Price

One father is more than a hun-dred schoolmasters.

George Herbert

Some truths between husband and wife must be spoken, but let them be spoken with sweetness. Wounded vanity is fatal to love. It makes one hate the person who inflicted the wound. In married conversation, as in surgery, the knife must be used with care.

André Maurois

I never by chance hear the rat-tling of dice that it doesn't sound to me like the funeral bell of a whole family.

Douglas William Jerrold

My home may be made beautiful by wealth of the world, but if it has not love, it is an empty shell. My home may be the rendezvous of the witty; and the meeting place of the wise, but if it has not love, it is only a noisy home.

My home may distribute its welcome to men of every estate; my home may toil for the betterment of mankind, but if it has not love, its influence will soon vanish.

Robert W. Burns

A happy marriage is a long conversation that always seems too short.

André Maurois

The secret of happy marriage is simple: Just keep on being as polite to one another as you are to your best friends.

Robert Quillen

Home should be a place where we have the benefit of the world's greatest freedom, and at the same time, in that freedom, we should be ever on guard to set the right kind of example for those who will come after us.

Marvin L. Gray

The great capacity of the Jews and the Chinese, above all other peoples, to survive the cancerous attacks of dehumanized power has derived from their sense of the family; their loyalty to the generations behind them and those yet to come. *Lewis Mumford*

All happy families are alike, but every unhappy one is unhappy in its own way.

Leo Tolstoy

Marriage is a job. Happiness or unhappiness has nothing to do with it. There was never a marriage that could not be made a success, nor a marriage that could not have ended in bitterness and failure.

Kathleen Norris

When men enter into the state of marriage, they stand nearest to God.

Henry Ward Beecher

A house is built of logs and stone,
Of tiles and posts and piers;
A home is built of loving deeds
That stand a thousand years.

Victor Hugo

Keep thy eyes wide open before marriage; and half shut afterward.

Thomas Fuller

Architecture has much to teach about the art of staying married, for the basic laws of building are, likewise, the basic laws of the home. A good foundation and balanced proportion are essential. Honest materials are needed, for you cannot build a noble building out of cheap, unworthy materials and you cannot build a home to stand against the stormy winds or worries unless you build it with the simple virtues of faithfulness and loyalty to one another.

Robert W. Burns

A good laugh is sunshine in a house.

William M. Thackeray

No nation can be destroyed while it possesses a good home life.

John G. Holland

The family is still the one social relationship which can give the human person a sense of the complete life in the presence of today's fragmented experience: it alone can endeavor to sift out of new conflict values a set of norms and principles that can be reliable guideposts on our human journey.

Lawrence J. McGinley

Success in marriage does not come merely through finding the right mate, but through being the right mate.

Barnett Brickner

A palace without affection is a poor hovel, and the meanest hut with love in it is a palace for the soul.

Robert G. Ingersoll

Let there be spaces in your togetherness.

Kahlil Gibran

I will be so polite to my wife as though she were a perfect stranger.

R. J. Burdette

A house is not home unless it contains food and fire for the mind as well as the body.

Margaret Fuller

---

41. THE GIFTS OF LOVE

Bitterness imprisons life; love releases it. Bitterness paralyzes life; love empowers it. Bitterness sours life; love sweetens it. Bitterness sickens life; love heals it. Bitterness blinds life; love anoints its eyes.

Harry Emerson Fosdick

There is nothing enduring in life for a woman except what she builds in a man's heart.

Judith Anderson

In the man whose childhood has known caresses and kindness, there is always a fibre of memory that can be touched to gentle issues.

George Eliot

Work done for love's sake seems short and seems sweet.

Claude G. Montefiore

At the touch of love every one becomes poet.

Plato

In all the crowded universe
There is but one stupendous word:
Love.
There is no tree that rears its crest,
No fern or flower that cleaves the sod
Nor bird that sings above its nest,
But tries to speak this word of God.

Josiah Gilbert Holland

He who loves brings God and the World together.

Martin Buber

I love you for what you are, but I love you yet more for what you are going to be.

I love you not so much for your realities as for your ideals. I pray for your desires that they may be great, rather than for your satisfactions, which may be so hazardously little.

A satisfied flower is one whose petals are about to fall. The most beautiful rose is one hardly more than a bud wherein the pangs and ecstacies of desire are working for larger and finer growth.

Not always shall you be what you are now.

You are going forward toward something great. I am on the way with you and therefore I love you.

Carl Sandburg

A bit of fragrance always clings to the hand that gives you roses.

Chinese Proverb

The hoarding of things cannot produce joy. Love is of no value in producing happiness unless it is used or passed on to make others happy.

Lowell Filmore

When death has dropped the curtain we shall hear no more applause, and, although we fondly dream that it will continue after we have left the stage, we do not realize how quickly it will die away in silence while the audience turns to look at the new actor and the next scene. Our position in society will be filled as soon as it is vacated, and our name remembered only for a moment, except, please God, by a few who have learned to love us not because of fame, but because we have helped them and done them some good.

Henry Van Dyke

A man loved by a beautiful and virtuous woman carries with him a talisman that renders him invulnerable; everyone feels that such a one's life has a higher value than that of others.

George Sand

We receive love—from our children as well as others—not in proportion to our demands or sacrifices or needs, but roughly in proportion to our own capacity to love. And our capacity to love depends, in turn, upon our prior capacity to be persons in our own right. To love means, essentially, to give; and to give requires a maturity of self-feeling. Love is shown in the statement of Spinoza's . . . that truly loving God does not involve a demand for love in return. It is the attitude referred to by the artist Joseph Bender: "To produce art requires that the artist be able to love—that is to give without thought of being rewarded."

Rollo May

Love that is hoarded moulds at last
Until we know some day
The only thing we ever have
Is what we gave away.

Louis Ginsberg

Love is always building up. It puts some line of beauty on every life it touches. It gives new hope to discouraged ones, new strength to those who are weak. It helps the despairing to rise and start again. It makes life seem more worth while to everyone into whose eyes it looks. Its words are benedictions. Its every breath is full of inspiration.

Aurthor Unknown

Love consists in this that two solitudes protect and touch and greet each other.

Rainer Maria Rilke

Love without criticism is not love.

The Midrash

While faith makes all things possible, it is love that makes all things easy.

Evan H. Hopkins

Love is the beginning, the middle, and the end of everything.

Locordaire

If you would be loved, love and be lovable.

Benjamin Franklin

Involuntary obedience corrupts the soul.

Ludwig Lewisohn

Love and you shall be loved. All love is mathematically just, as much as the two sides of an algebraic equation.

Ralph Waldo Emerson

When the one man loves the one woman and the one woman loves the one man, the very angels leave heaven and come and sit in that house and sing for joy.

Brahma

Ah, how skillful grows the hand
That obeyeth Love's command!
It is the heart, and not the brain,
That to the highest doth attain,
And he who followeth Love's behest
Far excelleth all the rest!

Henry Wadsworth Longfellow

For every beauty there is an eye somewhere to see it; for every truth there is an ear somewhere to hear it; for every love there is a heart somewhere to receive it. But though my beauty meet no eye it still doth glow; though my truth meet no ear, it still doth shine; but when my love meets no heart, it can only break.

Ivan N. Panin

A man may be a miser of his wealth; he may tie up his talent in a napkin; he may hug himself in his reputation; but he is always generous in his love. Love cannot stay at home; a man cannot keep it to himself. Like light, it is constantly traveling. A man must spend it, must give it away.

Alexander Macleod

Love is the doorway thru which the human soul passes from selfishness to service and from solitude to kinship with all mankind.

Author Unknown

Man is like a child in a family. He can tolerate much deprivation, much sickness, even much pain, if only he be securely at home, sure of belonging, confident of being loved. But if these central assurances are lacking, then food and shelter and toys in abundance can leave him empty and insecure in the center of his life. So it is with man in his world.

Angus Dun

True affection is a body of enigmas, mysteries and riddles, wherein two so become one that they both become two.

Thomas Browne

Never a lip is curved with pain
That can't be kissed into smiles again.

Bret Harte

Like the water in the boiler, the depth of our spiritual existence is impossible to measure without a gauge. Outward appearances are not always accurate. But there is one truthful measure and that measure is love.

Juanita A. Morrison

I would give up all my genius, and all my books, if there were only some woman, somewhere, who cared whether or not I came home late for dinner.

Ivan Turgenev

Life is a flower of which love is the honey.

Victor Hugo

There is no progress without love.

Frederick Mayer

Love covers a multitude of sins. When a scar cannot be taken away, the next kind office is to hide it. Love is never so blind as when it is to spy faults. It is like the painter, who, beginning to draw the picture of a friend having a blemish in one eye, would picture only the other side of his face.

Robert South

Giving and receiving love clears the nervous system of its muck and mire. You feel strong when you give love and worthy when you receive it. You can't be distressed, confused or unhappy in an atmosphere of love.

Dr. David Goodman

A man that is deeply in love with himself will probably succeed in his suit owing to lack of rivals.

Austin O'Malley

Joys divided are increased.

John G. Holland

Rabbi Joshua ben Ilem dreamed that his neighbor in Paradise would be Nanas, the butcher. He visited this Nanas to inquire what good deeds he was performing to deserve a high place in Paradise. The butcher replied: "I know not, but I have an aged father and mother who are helpless, and I give them food and drink, and wash and dress them daily."

The Rabbi said: "I will be happy to have thee as my neighbor in Paradise."

The Midrash

It is astonishing how little one feels poverty when he loves.

Bulwer Lytton

Time is
Too slow for those who Wait,
Too swift for those who Fear,
Too long for those who Grieve,
Too short for those who Rejoice;
But for those who Love,
    Time is
    Eternity.

Jones Very

The medical profession tells us that there are four conditions which must be met if we are to have any chance of leading a happy life: physical security, social recognition, adventure, emotional security. In today's highly technical and scientific life, these four considerations become increasingly important, but we should add one vital ingredient: love. Love of our fellow man, love for our work, and the conviction that this love insures the future for all of us.

A. Quincy Jones

What Is Love? I have met in the streets a very poor young man who was in love. His hat was old, his coat worn, the water passed through his shoes and the stars through his soul.

Victor Hugo

There are many kinds of love, as many kinds of light,

And every kind of love makes a
glory in the night.
There is love that stirs the heart,
and love that gives it rest,
But the love that leads life upward
is the noblest and the best.
Henry Van Dyke

It is strange that men will talk
of miracles, revelations, inspira-
tions, and the like, as things past,
while love remains.
Henry David Thoreau

Each of us has to learn that it's
no true gift to have another say:
"Beside you, nobody else matters—" since the only tribute to be
trusted in life is, in the end, the
one that means: "Because of you,
all others in some way matter
more."
Doris Peel

I have seen almost all the beautiful things God has made; I have
enjoyed almost every pleasure that
He has planned for man; and yet
as I look back I see standing out
above all the life that has gone
about four or five short experiences
when the love of God reflected
itself in some poor imitation, some
small act of love of mine, and these
seem to be the things which alone
of all one's life abide. Everything
else in all our lives is transitory.
Every other good is visionary. But
the acts of love which no man
knows about, or can ever know
about—they never fail.
Henry Drummond

We are shaped and fashioned by
what we love.
Johann Wolfgang von Goethe

Up to a certain point it is good
for us to know that there are people in the world who will give us
love and unquestioned loyalty to
the limit of their ability. I doubt,
however, if it is good for us to feel
assured of this without the accompanying obligation of having to
justify this devotion by our behavior.
Eleanor Roosevelt

To love very much is to love
inadequately; we love—that is all.
Love cannot be modified without
being nullified. Love is a short
word but it contains everything.
Love means the body, the soul,
the life, the entire being. We feel
love as we feel the warmth of our
blood, we breathe love as we
breathe the air, we hold it in ourselves as we hold our thoughts.
Nothing more exists for us. Love is
not a word; it is a wordless state
indicated by four letters. . . .
Guy De Maupassant

Riches take wings, comforts vanish, hope withers away, but love
stays with us. Love is God.
Lew Wallace

No cord or cable can draw so
forcibly, or bind so fast, as love
can do with only a single thread.
Henry Burton

I wonder if ever you change
human beings with arguments
alone: either by peppering them
with little sharp facts or by blowing them up with great guns of
truth. You scare them, but do you
change them? I wonder if ever you
make any real difference in human
beings without understanding them
and loving them. For when you

argue with a man, you are some-how trying to pull him down and make him less; but when you try to understand him, when you like him, how eager is he then to know the truth you have; and you add to him in some strange way, you make him more than he was be-fore; and at the same time, you yourself become more.

David Grayson

The heart does not need much space for its heaven nor many stars therein if only the star of love has arisen.

Jean Paul Richter

To love is to place our happiness in the happiness of another.

Gottfried Wilhelm Von Leibnitz

Not where I breathe but where I love, I live.

Robert Southwell

I never knew a night so black
Light failed to follow on its track.
I never knew a storm so gray
It failed to have its clearing day.
I never knew such bleak despair
That there was not a rift, some-where.
I never knew an hour so drear
Love could not fill it full of cheer!

John Kendrick Bangs

I've seen much bread that was cast upon the waters, and that returned, buttered, covered with jam, wrapped in paraffin paper, and marked, "with love."

Channing Pollock

What we can do for another is the test of powers; what we can suffer for is the test of love.

Bishop Westcott

Love is the master key that opens the gates of happiness.

Holmes

A needle's eye is not too narrow for two lovers, but the whole world is not wide enough for two enemies.

Ibn Gabirol

He who comes to do good knocks at the gate; he who loves finds the door open.

Rabindranath Tagore

Love is never lost. If not recipro-cated it will flow back and soften and purify the heart.

Washington Irving

People with love in their hearts go through life untouched by pov-erty regardless of the amount of monetary wealth they may acquire.

Douglas Meador

Love is not blind—it sees more, not less. But because it sees more, it is willing to see less.

Julius Gordon

So long as we love we serve; so long as we are loved by others, I would almost say we are indispen-sable; and no man is useless while he has a friend. The true services of life are inestimable in money, and are never paid. Kind words and caresses, high and wise thoughts, humane designs, tender behaviour to the weak and suffering, and all the charities of man's existence, are neither bought nor sold.

Robert Louis Stevenson

To love is to admire with the heart; to admire is to love with the mind.

T. Gautier

The more one loves the nearer he approaches to God, for God is the spirit of infinite love.

Ralph W. Trine

Liking people is one of the important ingredients for getting the most out of life. If you like people, you have a zest, an enthusiasm for working and for living—you give of yourself to others and, in return, you find yourself getting a great deal from them. Once it becomes a part of you it will pay dividends not only in your work but in sheer enjoyment of living. Try it and see for yourself!

Samuel Goldwyn

If there are no books in this world, then nothing need be said, but since there are books, they must be read; if there is no wine, then nothing need be said, but since there is wine, it must be drunk; if there are no famous hills, then nothing need be said, but since there are, they must be visited; if there are no flowers and no moon, then nothing need be said, but since there are, they must be enjoyed; if there are no talented men and beautiful women, then nothing need be said, but since there are, they must be loved and protected.

Chang Ch'ao

We like someone because. We love someone although.

Henri De Montherlant

I was taught when I was young that if people would only love one another, all would be well with the world. This seemed simple and very nice; but I found when I tried to put it in practice not only that other people were seldom loveable, but that I was not very loveable myself.

George Bernard Shaw

To renounce your individuality, to see with another's eyes, to hear with another's ears, to be two and yet but one, to so melt and mingle that you no longer know you are you or another, to constantly absorb and constantly radiate, to reduce earth, sea and sky and all that in them is to a single being so wholly that nothing whatever is withheld, to be prepared at any moment for sacrifice, to double your personality in bestowing it—that is love.

Theophile Gautier

I hold it true, whate'er befall
I feel it, when I sorrow most
'Tis better to have loved and lost
Than never to have loved at all.

Alfred Lord Tennyson

The reduction of the universe to a single being, the dilation of a single being as far as God, such is love.

Victor Hugo

The World is a great mirror. It reflects back to you what you are. If you are loving, if you are friendly, if you are helpful, the world will prove loving and friendly and helpful to you. The world is what you are.

Thomas Dreier

The way to love anything is to realize it might be lost.

G. K. Chesterton

Those who love deeply never grow old; they may die of old age, but they die young.

Arthur Wing Pinero

Love is more than a sentiment; it is a need, a hunger, a thirst which is perfectly natural. Anyone who thinks he can live and be happy without it does not really know what he is talking about— psychologically, emotionally, physiologically, or spiritually. Love is the beginning and end, the one sentiment in nature that will not be denied.

Ernest Holmes

Fathers and teachers, I ponder "What is hell?" I maintain that it is the suffering of being unable to love.

Feodor Dostoevski

42. THE ART OF BEING PARENTS

Great ideas and fine principles do not live from generation to generation just because they are good, nor because they have been carefully legislated. Ideals and principles continue from generation to generation only when they are built into the hearts of children as they grow up.

George Benson

The little child is the only true democrat.

Harriet Beecher Stowe

Children have more need of models than of critics.

Joseph Joubert

A parent must respect the spiritual person of his child, and approach it with reverence.

George MacDonald

A child is as sensitive to outside influences and forces as a seismograph is sensitive to an earthquake which is ten thousand miles away, indicating its direction, its position, its center and its force.

Luther Burbank

What a father says to his children is not heard by the world, but it will be heard by posterity.

Jean Paul Richter

Children need love, especially when they don't deserve it.

Harold S. Hulbert

The stamp of a parent's life on a child's is indelible in every phase of living. What a parent passes on to his child is, essentially, all that he himself is. And the essentials of life are found in the attitudes of heart and mind.

Elsie Landon Buck

When we are out of sympathy with the young, then I think our work in this world is over.

George MacDonald

From one's table manners to his manner of looking at life, from his humor to his health, his swearing to his praying, his grammar to his accent, his truthfulness to his trustworthiness, the home will get its way. What happens to him later in life, from the crime he commits to the emotional illness to which he falls heir can be traced directly or indirectly to those indelible years when he was in the palm of the hands of parents.

David A. Redding

The most difficult job teenagers have today is learning good conduct without seeing any.

H. G. Hutcheson

I was present when an old mother, who had brought up a large family of children with eminent success, was asked by a young one what she would recommend in the case of some children who were too anxiously educated, and her reply was—"I think, my dear, a little wholesome neglect."

Sir Henry Taylor

Wise parents spend less time searching, examining, and pruning the branches of their family trees, and more time planting the right seeds in the lives of their children.

William A. Ward

If you want to see what children can do, you must stop giving them things.

Norman Douglas

God intends that parents, not the children, shall direct the household.

Arthur S. Maxwell

Children need discipline, but discipline without love means over-severity. Love without discipline means over-indulgence.

Author Unknown

We commit the blotted manuscript of our lives more willingly to the flames when we find the immortal text half engrossed in a fairer copy.

George Santayana

Parents should live for their children, but not through them; the parents whose satisfactions are wholly reflections of their children's achievements are as much monsters as the parents who neglect their offspring. Nothing can deform a personality so much as the burden of a love that is utterly self-sacrificing.

Sydney J. Harris

Parents owe it to the children they bring into the world to put the tools of living in their hands—hands which we have made as strong and capable as we can. But, having given them the hands and the tools, we owe it to them *not* to do their digging for them.

Lenora Mattingly Weber

A happy family is but an earlier heaven.

Sir John Bowring

Perhaps parents would enjoy their children more if they stopped to realize that the film of childhood can never be run through for a second showing.

Evelyn Nown

I remember with gratitude that our parents seldom or never punished us, and never, unless we went too far in our domestic dissentions or tricks, even chided us. This, I am convinced, is the right attitude for parents to observe, modestly to admit that nature is wiser than they are, and to let their little ones follow, as far as possible, the bent of their own minds, or whatever it is they have in place of minds.

W. H. Hudson

Train children in their youth, and they won't train you in your old age.

Yiddish Proverb

A child who has a good home; who can grow up in an atmosphere of confidence and harmony; who is surrounded by people who have a sound sense of what is worthwhile in life; who sees religion lived as well as hears it talked about; who finds outside his home in school and church allies that support the best things for which his home stands—such a child has a better chance of developing a stable personality and a stalwart character than does the child who never knows security or faith in his own home.

Morgan Phelps Noyes

Respect the child. Be not too much his parent. Trespass not on his solitude.

Ralph Waldo Emerson

Of all nature's gifts to the human race, what is sweeter to a man than his children?

Cicero

The real object of education is to give children resources that will endure as long as life endures; habits that time will ameliorate, not destroy; occupations that will render sickness tolerable, solitude pleasant, age venerable, life more dignified and useful, and death less terrible.

Sydney Smith

To spoil children is to deceive them concerning life; life herself does not spoil us.

Comtesse Diane

The best way to make children good is to make them happy.

Oscar Wilde

The child will get a conception of goodness because you are good to him and to other people; of love, because you and your husband increasingly love each other as well as him; of truth, because you are unfailingly truthful; of kindliness of speech, because your words and tones of speech are never harsh; of constancy, because you have kept your promise; of consideration for others, because he sees these things in you.

Rev. A. Fox

A visitor to Coleridge argued strongly against the religious instruction of the young and declared his own determination not to "prejudice" his children in favor of any form of religion, but to allow them at maturity to choose for themselves. The answer of Coleridge was pertinent and sound: "Why not let the clods choose for themselves between cockleberries and strawberries?"

Author Unknown

Among the greatest gifts a parent can give a child—even greater than a hovering, solicitous protection—are the wisdom, the character, the standards that will help him safely to make his own decisions and provide his own protection.

Richard L. Evans

Never tell a young person that something cannot be done. God may have been waiting for centuries for somebody ignorant enough of the impossible to do that very thing.

J. A. Holmes

You cannot teach a child to take care of himself unless you will let him take care of himself. He will make mistakes, and out of these mistakes will come his wisdom.

Henry Ward Beecher

We have no power to fashion our
  children as suits our fancy;
As they are given by God, we so
  must have them and love them;
Teach them as best we can, and
  let each of them follow his nature.
One will have talents of one sort,
  and different talents another.
Every one uses his own, in his
  own individual fashion.

Johann Wolfgang von Goethe

Parents who expect gratitude from their children (there are even some who insist on it) are like usurers who gladly risk their capital if only they receive interest.

Franz Kafka

Age needs a critic; youth only a model.

Ivan N. Panin

A happy childhood is one of the best gifts that parents have it in their power to bestow.

Mary Cholmondeley

A child educated only at school is an uneducated child.

George Santayana

One laugh of a child will make the holiest day more sacred still.

Robert G. Ingersoll

One must not promise to give something to a child, and not give it to him, because thereby he is taught to lie.

The Talmud

The world does not owe every child a living but it does owe it access to the things by which life can be lived.

Author Unknown

Perhaps some day we'll leave our children alone and spend our time on ourselves. The home's not so much insufficient as oversufficient. It is cloying; it tries too hard.

F. Scott Fitzgerald

Whatever is great and good in the institutions and usages of mankind is an application of sentiments that have drawn their first nourishment from the soil of the family.

Felix Adler

A man cannot leave a better legacy to the world than a well-educated family.

Thomas Scott

Children don't want to be told; they want to be shown. It takes years of telling to undo one unwise showing.

Eileen M. Haase

To be a good child he needs but little of the man in him; to be a good man he needs much of the child in him.

Ivan N. Panin

Train up a child in the way he should go—and walk there yourself once in a while.

Josh Billings

Before you beat a child, be sure you yourself are not the cause of the offense.

Austin O'Malley

There is a mistaken notion prevailing among some parents that discipline is the same thing as punishment. It is not. Discipline comes from a Latin word meaning "to teach." The best discipline is that which teaches, not the kind that hurts.

J. C. Wynn

We owe our children a set of good habits; for habit is to be either their best friend or their worst enemy, not only during childhood, but through all the years. We shall therefore need to repeat every now and then nature's irrevocable law: that back of every habit lies a series of acts; that ahead of every act lies a habit; that habit is nine-tenths of conduct; that conduct is but character in the making; and that character ends in destiny.

George Herbert Betts

An infallible way to make your child miserable, is to satisfy all his demands. Passion swells by gratification; and the impossibility of satisfying every one of his wishes will oblige you to stop short at last after he has become headstrong.

Henry Home

Little children are still the symbol of the eternal marriage between love and duty.

George Eliot

Call not that man wretched, who whatever else he suffers as to pain inflicted or pleasure denied, has a child for whom he hopes and on whom he dotes.

Samuel Taylor Coleridge

The training of our children is the one most important thing the Almighty lets us live for. When we fail at this, all of our spectacular successes in other lines crumble up like paper in our hands.

John Holland

One of the most difficult lessons parents have to learn is this one: Children are only loaned for a brief term of infancy and childhood. Soon they become people, strangers in the home, and instead of children to be directed they are grown-ups to be studied, understood and accepted. The acceptance is never quite complete on either side, but affection will bridge the gap if it is permitted to do so.

Angelo Patri

Never teach your child to be cunning, for you may be certain you will be one of the very first victims of his shrewdness.

Josh Billings

There is no sure way to guarantee that your child will grow up to be the kind of person you would like him to be. The most likely way is for you to be the kind of person you would like him to be.

Author Unknown

An 11th commandment has been suggested: "Fathers and Mothers, honor your children."

John D. Hill

There is never much trouble in any family where the children hope some day to resemble their parents.

William Lyon Phelps

Feel the dignity of a child. Do not feel superior to him, for you are not.

Robert Henri

No school is more necessary to children than patience, because either the will must be broken in childhood or the heart in old age.

Jean Paul Richter

Who does not teach his son a trade teaches him to steal.

Judah bar Ilai

It is better to bind your children to you by respect and gentleness, than by fear.

Terence

The best chaperone a child can have is the one that has been built into his character.

Marcelene Cox

I am the king of a tiny kingdom of three sons. I desire above all things on earth that they may grow up fair and fine and free. Not seldom am I filled with fear of my responsibilities. And because of the knowledge which that fear brings, every day of my life I pray, "God save the king."

Studdert Kennedy

America's future will be determined by the home and the school. The child becomes largely what it is taught, hence we must watch what we teach it, and how we live before it.

Jane Addams

If I could get to the highest place in Athens, I would lift up my voice and say: "What mean ye, fellow citizens, that ye turn every stone to scrape wealth together, and take so little care of your children, to whom ye must one day relinquish all?"

Socrates

The child in man is not dead, but sleeps; it awakens at the call of other children.

Comtesse Diane

Parents are of course expected to be warm and sympathetic to-ward their children, and there are times when they should relax and be informal with their sons and daughters. But children should never come to look upon their parents as they would their school chums; they should always look to their parents with respect and reverence. Parents are in many ways like teachers, perhaps even more so, for they are the teachers of a lifetime.

Simon Glustrom

Some parents bring up their children on thunder and lightning, but thunder and lightning never yet made anything grow. Rain or sunshine cause growth—quiet penetrating forces that develop life.

Author Unknown

The parent who patiently disciplines his child will be rewarded by the achievements of the child. As a rule this is so but there are exceptions. Proper discipline produces dependable men and women who can behave wisely in a crisis and who can stand in the storm. This brings happiness to them and to the one who trained them.

Dennis M. Dodson

Every child comes with the message that God is not yet discouraged of man.

Rabindranath Tagore

Life is a flame that is always burning itself out, but it catches fire again and again every time a child is born. *Author Unknown*

In order to reap the full possibilities of youth we must not tie them too rigidly to the theories of an older generation. Their value lies in being a voice; not an echo.

Willett L. Hardin

We must bow reverently before all children: they are our masters, we work for them.

Ludwig Boerne

Youth is a world in miniature: bounded on the north by a thin substance called the skull bone; on the south by twin bits of shoe leather, and on the east and west by the outstretched fingertips of expectation and hope.

Henry W. Prentiss

Successful parenthood is built on three great principles which, like shafts thrust deep into the foundations of a structure, support and stimulate the right formation of habit in the building of life. They are love, discipline, and security. Without all these, a child's life is stunted from the very beginning.

Elsie Landon Buck

Perhaps the most important contribution parents can make in preparing their young people to be more marriageable is that of making the home a place where emotional needs are met.

Dorothy E. Pitman

Parental delinquency begets youthful delinquency, and the economic and social standing of a family has nothing to do with it. Neither money nor social prestige is a substitute for right values, nor do the social graces do more than veneer a life devoid of spiritual perception.   *L. Nelson Bell*

If you can give your children a trust in God they will have one sure way of meeting all the uncertainties of existence.

Eleanor Roosevelt

Honi ha-Ma'aggel once saw on his travels an old man planting a carob tree. He asked him when he thought the tree would bear fruit. "After seventy years," was the reply.

"Dost thou expect to live seventy years and eat the fruit of thy labor?"

"I did not find the world desolate when I entered it," said the old man, "and as my fathers planted for me before I was born, so do I plant for those who will come after me."

The Talmud

---

43. MOTHERS OF MEN

A mother is a mother still, the holiest thing alive.

Samuel Coleridge

A father may turn his back on his child; brothers and sisters may become inveterate enemies; husbands may desert their wives, and wives their husbands. But a moth-

er's love endures through all; in good repute, in bad repute, in the face of the world's condemnation, a mother still loves on, and still hopes that her child may turn from his evil ways, and repent; still she remembers the infant smiles that once filled her bosom with rapture, the merry laugh, the joyful shout of his childhood, the opening promise of his youth; and she can never be brought to think him all unworthy.

Washington Irving

"What is wanting," said Napoleon one day to Madame Campan, "in order that the youth of France be well educated?" "Good mothers," was the reply. The Emperor was most forcibly struck with this answer. "Here," said he, "is a system in one word."

John S. C. Abbott

An ounce of mother is worth a pound of clergy.

Spanish Proverb

My mother's influence in molding my character was conspicuous. She forced me to learn daily long chapters of the Bible by heart. To that discipline and patient, accurate resolve I owe not only much of my general power of taking pains, but the best part of my taste for literature.

John Ruskin

Many of the strongest influences for nobility in living come to us through the precepts our mothers taught us, or through the examples they set for us as they moved about as the queens of their homes and the inspirers of our deepest love.

Leo Bennett

Blessed are the Mothers of the earth, for they have combined the practical and the spiritual into the workable way of human life. They have darned little stockings, mended little dresses, washed little faces, and have pointed little eyes to the stars, and little souls to eternal things.

William L. Stinger

They say that man is mighty,
He governs land and sea,
He wields a mighty scepter
O'er lesser powers that be;
But a mightier power and stronger
Man from his throne has hurled,
For the hand that rocks the cradle
Is the hand that rules the world.

William Ross Wallace

What is taken in with the milk, only goes out with the soul.

Author Unknown

Next to God we are indebted to woman, first for life itself, and then for making it worth living.

C. N. Bovee

Mighty is the force of motherhood! It transforms all things by its vital heat.

George Eliot

It is the general rule, that all superior men inherit the elements of superiority from their mothers.

Jules Michelet

To be a mother of men, a woman must make men of her boys. She demands their best, not because it belongs to her, but because it is due them. For that which is due children is not ease and luxury but hardening of muscles, the habit of work, a sense of honor, and a self-respect born of integrity.

Adeline Bullock

The bravest battle that ever was fought;
Shall I tell you where and when?
On the maps of the world you will find it not;

It was fought by the mothers of men.

Joaquin Miller

God has placed the genius of women in their hearts; because the works of this genius are always works of love.

Alphonse de Lamartine

The mother's heart is the child's schoolroom.

Henry Ward Beecher

Mother is the name for God in the lips and hearts of little children.

William Makepeace Thackeray

Most of all the other beautiful things in life come by twos and threes, by dozens and hundreds. Plenty of roses, stars, sunsets, rainbows, brothers and sisters, aunts and cousins, but only one mother in the whole world.

Kate Douglas Wiggin

The future destiny of a child is always the work of the mother.

Napoleon Bonaparte

A mother is not a person to lean on, but a person to make leaning unnecessary.

Dorothy Canfield Fisher

I think it must somewhere be written, that the virtues of mothers shall be visited on their children, as well as the sins of the fathers.

Charles Dickens

God could not be everywhere and therefore he made mothers.

Author Unknown

THE ART OF LIVING WITH

OUR FELLOW MAN

44. THE ART OF LIVING TOGETHER

"When will I bless the world?" said
    God.
"When every sorry human clod
Stops hating every alien sod,
Then will I bless the world," said
    God.
"Let men together earn my nod.
I'll bless them none or all," said
    God.

William Hard

There is a destiny that makes us
    brothers:
    None goes his way alone;
All that we send into the lives of
    others
    Comes back into our own.

Author Unknown

Ten Commandments of Good Will:

1. I will respect all men and
women regardless of race and religion.

2. I will protect and defend my
neighbor and my neighbor's children against the ravages of racial
or religious bigotry.

3. I will exemplify in my own
life the spirit of good will and understanding.

4. I will challenge the philosophy of racial superiority by whom-
soever it may be proclaimed,
whether they be kings, dictators, or
demagogues.

5. I will not be misled by the
lying propaganda of those who
seek to set race against race or nation against nation.

6. I will refuse to support any
organization that has for its purpose
the spreading of anti-Semitism,
anti-Catholicism, or anti-Protestant-
ism.

7. I will establish comradeship
with those who seek to exalt the
spirit of love and reconciliation
throughout the world.

8. I will attribute to those who
differ from me the same degree of
sincerity that I claim for myself.

9. I will uphold the civil rights
and religious liberties of all citizens and groups whether I agree
with them or not.

10. I will do more than live and let live—I will live and help live.
Walter W. Van Kirk

A man's kind deeds are used as seed in the Garden of Eden; thus every man creates his own Paradise.
Dov Ber

Man never fastened one end of a chain around the neck of his brother, that God did not fasten the other end round the neck of the oppressor.
Alphonse de Lamartine

The brotherhood of man is not a dream; it is a fact. And if mankind is to survive as a species, this fact must be recognized. This curious point where biology and religion meet must be our new point of departure, the only basis for a brave new world—its alternative being war and chaos.
Stuart Cloete

We must learn to live together as brothers or we will perish together like fools.
Martin Luther King

On the way to the highest goal I must take my fellow-beings with me.
Felix Adler

Science points the way to survival and happiness for all mankind through love and cooperation. Do what we will, our drives toward goodness are as biologically determined as are our drives toward breathing. Our highly endowed potentialities for social life have been used to pervert and deny their very nature, and this has led us close to the brink of disaster. We cannot continue to deny these potentialities without destroying ourselves.
Ashley Montague

Kindness is the golden chain by which society is bound together.
Johann Wolfgang von Goethe

A single enemy is one too many.
Asher ben Yehiel

If we do not go out into the world and call every man our brother, there are those who will go out and call him "comrade."
E. Paul Hovey

The King of Denmark, when he was urged by the Nazis to institute anti-Jewish legislation, is said to have replied: "But you see, there isn't any Jewish problem here. We do not consider ourselves inferior to them."
Ernest Fremont Tittle

It does not seem as if nature had made men to be independent.
Vauvenargues

When we understand each other, we find it difficult to cut one another's throats.
Van Wyck Brooks

We may safely say that mutual aid is as much a law of animal life as mutual struggle; but that as a factor of evolution, it most probably has a far greater importance, inasmuch as it favors the development of such habits and characters as insure the maintenance and further development of the species, together with the greatest amount of welfare and enjoyment of life for the individual, with the least waste of energy.
Peter A. Kropotkin

How much suffering must humanity endure before it finally learns to put the whole before the part, to understand that only in the safety of a community of nations can any nation find its own safety?

Sumner Welles

The days of the rugged individualist are over and the days of the cooperative individual are here. The pioneer on his homestead was independent and could go it alone. His descendants, whether at the plow, or loom or desk, whether in village or city, are interdependent. The pioneer forged a free world on his own; his children's children must find their way with all other peoples to a free world.

Paul G. Hoffman

No man is an island entire; every man is part of the main. If a clod be washed away by the sea, Europe is the less, as well as if a promontory were, as well as if a manor of thy friends or thine own were. Any man's death diminishes me because I am involved in mankind, and therefore never send to know for whom the bell tolls; it tolls for thee.

John Donne

I don't set up to be no judge of
  right and wrong in men,
I've lost the trail sometimes myself
  an' may get lost again;
An' when I see a chap who looks as
  though he'd gone astray,
I want to shove my hand in his an'
  help him find the way.

J. A. Foley

Prejudice cuts at the very roots of emotional health—our self-respect. It is as harmful emotionally to the excluders as to the excluded.

An integrated society would be a healthier society.

Robert M. Metcalfe

We make our friends; we make our enemies, but God makes our next-door neighbor.

That is why the old religions and the old Scriptural language showed so sharp a wisdom when they spoke, not of one's duty toward humanity, but of one's duty toward one's neighbor. Duty toward humanity may take the form of some choice which is personal or even pleasurable. But we have to love our neighbor because he is there— he is the sample of humanity that is actually given us.

G. K. Chesterton

To have courage without pugnacity,
To have conviction without bigotry,
To have charity without condescension,
To have faith without credulity,
To have love of humanity without
  mere sentimentality
To have meekness with power
And emotion with sanity—
That is brotherhood.

Charles E. Hughes

The best way to uncolor the negro is to give the white man a white heart.

Ivan N. Panin

To do unto others as you would have them do unto you is well; but to do unto them as they would themselves be done by is better.

Comtesse Diane

We do not want the men of another color for our brothers-in-law, but we do want them for our brothers.

Booker T. Washington

It is a terrible, an inexorable, law that one cannot deny the humanity of another without diminishing one's own; in the face of the victim one sees oneself.

James Baldwin

We ask the leaf, "Are you complete in yourself?" And the leaf answers, "No, my life is in the branches." We ask the branch, and the branch answers, "No my life is in the root." We ask the root, and it answers, "No my life is in the trunk and the branches and the leaves. Keep the branches stripped of leaves, and I shall die." So it is with the great tree of being. Nothing is completely and merely individual.

Harry Emerson Fosdick

Here lies a miser who lived for himself,
And cared for nothing but gathering pelf,
Now, where he is or how he fares,
Nobody knows and nobody cares.

Tombstone Inscription

The race of mankind would perish from the earth did they cease to aid each other.

Sir Walter Scott

Twenty thousand years ago the family was the social unit. Now the social unit has become the world in which it may truly be said that each person's welfare affects that of every other.

Arthur H. Compton

There is a destiny that makes us brothers;
None goes his way alone:
All that we send into the lives of others
Comes back into our own.

Edwin Markham

A split atom and a split mankind cannot co-exist indefinitely on the same planet.

Liston Pope

'Tis the human touch in this world that counts,
The touch of your hand and mine,
Which means far more to the fainting heart
Than shelter and bread and wine;
For shelter is gone when the night is o'er,
And bread lasts only a day,
But the touch of the hand and the sound of the voice
Sing on in the soul alway.

Spencer Michael Free

Man is a special being, and if left to himself, in an isolated condition, would be one of the weakest creatures; but associated with his kind, he works wonders.

Daniel Webster

There is more power in the open hand than in the clenched fist.

Herbert N. Casson

The true civilization is where every man gives to every other every right that he claims for himself.

Robert G. Ingersoll

No one could tell me where my soul might be;
I searched for God, and He eluded me;
I sought my brother out, and found all three.

Ernest Crosby

Thomas Carlyle tells of an Irish widow who, for the support of her three children, appealed to charitable establishments in Edinburgh, where her husband died. Continually rebuffed, she fell exhausted, contracted typhus fever, died, and infected her street. Seventeen others perished as a consequence. Am I my brother's keeper? Carlyle concludes, "Had human creature ever to go lower for proof?"

Eldon L. Johnson

Much of the world has never been free, and a large part of mankind has always been hungry. Once this was inevitable, but now hunger is not necessary, and freedom is possible. Men who have never known freedom are today willing to die for it. Men who have seldom known what they would eat tomorrow have learned the truth, that there can be enough for all. These men will not rest until they have emerged into the light, and the world will know no peace until their just demands have been met.

Author Unknown

Because we live within a stone's throw of each other is no reason why we should throw stones at each other.

Stephen S. Wise

The cry of the age is more for fraternity than for charity. If one exists the other will follow, or better still, will not be needed.

Edwin H. Chapin

In a community in which there is involuntary starvation every well-fed person is a thief.

Holbrook Jackson

One day when famine had wrought great misery in Russia, a beggar, weak, emaciated, all but starved to death, asked for alms. Tolstoy searched his pockets for a coin but discovered that he was without as much as a copper piece. Taking the beggar's worn hands between his own, he said: "Do not be angry with me, my brother; I have nothing with me." The thin, lined face of the beggar became illumined as from some inner light, and he whispered in reply: "But you called me brother—that was a great gift."

Wesley Boyd

We talk about building bridges of brotherhood around the world in answer to the communist pretensions, and that's a splendid vision. But brotherhood begins on a man-to-man basis at home and not on a man-to-man basis across the oceans. Without that footing it is idle talk and an empty vision.

Eric Johnston

Independence? That's middle class blasphemy. We are all dependent on one another, every soul of us on earth.

George Bernard Shaw

The world is now too dangerous for anything but the truth, too small for anything but brotherhood.

A. Powell Davies

So many gods, so many creeds—
So many paths that wind and wind,
While just the art of being kind
Is all the sad world needs.

Ella Wheeler Wilcox

If err we must, let us err on the side of tolerance.

Felix Frankfurter

Brotherhood, according to the dictionary is the relationship of two male persons having the same parents—or the members of a fraternity or organization.

I don't think the dictionary goes far enough. To me brotherhood isn't just something you're born with or something you join. It's something deep inside you, like love or loyalty, that reaches out to all the world and everybody in it—men, women, children.

Just the thought of brotherhood has a sobering effect on me, for it reminds me that I am only a transitory member of a very large family called Humanity.

Bellamy Partridge

When we have learned to honor and respect each other's faults, and have ceased to feel that we must make everyone like ourselves and are morally compelled to make everyone believe like ourselves, we shall be far along the road towards a rich and enduring brotherhood of man.

Donald Harrington

Anything, God, but hate;
I have known it in my day,
And the best it does is scar your
    soul
And eat your heart away.
Man must know more than hate,
As the years go rolling on;
For the stars survive and the spring
    survives,
Only man denies the dawn.
God, if I have but one prayer
Before the cloud-wrapped end,
I'm sick of hate and the waste it
    makes.
Let me be my brother's friend.

Author Unknown

Freud, in blasting the idea of human aloneness, has revived the intuitive wisdom of the prophets of Israel who sang the song of man's relatedness to man.

Joshua Loth Liebman

Man is a social animal. . . .
Men can provide for their wants much more easily by mutual help, and only by uniting their forces can they escape from the dangers that beset them.

Benedict Spinoza

You cannot do a kindness too soon, because you never know how soon it will be too late.

Author Unknown

If we are to have peace, we must serve each other. Only through service can man find himself. It is not that others need you, but that you need others.

Madame Rajkumair Amrit Kaur

A man is like a letter of the alphabet: to produce a word, it must combine with another.

Benjamin Mandelstamm

Your own safety is at stake when your neighbor's house is in flames.

Horace

I believe with all my heart that civilization has produced nothing finer than a man or woman who thinks and practices true tolerance.

Frank Knox

Brotherhood is not just a Bible word. Out of comradeship can come and will come the happy life of all.

Heywood Broun

We have committed the Golden Rule to memory; let us now commit it to life.

Edwin Markham

To be of true service I must know two things: his need, my capacity.

Ivan N. Panin

If our brothers are oppressed, then we are oppressed. If they hunger, we hunger. If their freedom is taken away our freedom is not secure.

Stephen V. Benet

God divided man into men, that they might help each other.

Seneca

Hell is where no one has anything in common with anybody else except the fact that they all hate one another and cannot get away from one another and from themselves.

Thomas Merton

"Men work together," I told him from the heart,
"Whether they work together or apart."

Robert Frost

The crest and crowning of all good,
Life's final star, is Brotherhood.

Edwin Markham

The idea that only a limited number of people can live in a country is a profound illusion. It all depends on their cooperative and inventive power. There is no limit to the ingenuity of man if it is properly and vigorously applied under conditions of peace and justice.

Winston S. Churchill

45. THE ART OF GIVING

Even a poor man, who receives charity, should give charity.

The Talmud

There are ten strong things. Iron is strong, but fire melts it. Fire is strong, but water quenches it. Water is strong, but the clouds evaporate it. Clouds are strong, but wind drives them away. Man is strong, but fears cast him down. Fear is strong, but wine allays it. Wine is strong, but sleep overcomes it. Sleep is strong, but death is stronger, but loving kindness survives death.

The Talmud

All progress is made by men of faith who believe in what is right and, what is more important, actu-

ally do what is right in their own private affairs. You cannot add to the peace and goodwill of the world if you fail to create an atmosphere of harmony and love right where you live and work.

Thomas Dreier

Behold, I do not give lectures or a little charity,
When I give I give myself.

Walt Whitman

Those who think they have nothing to give should remember that they can always give themselves, and that they can always render some kind of service even if it be nothing more than a few words of cheer.

Lowell Fillmore

What you save from frivolity, add to your charity.

Elijah ben Raphael

He gives only the worthless gold who gives from a sense of duty.

James Russell Lowell

Charity is injurious unless it helps the recipient to become independent of it.

John D. Rockefeller, Jr.

If thou doest aught good, do it quickly. For what is done quickly will be acceptable. Favors slowly granted are unfavorably received.

Ausonius

If, instead of a gem or even a flower, we would cast the gift of a lovely thought into the heart of a friend, that would be giving as the angels give.

George MacDonald

The best cure for worry, depression, melancholy, brooding, is to go deliberately forth and try to lift with one's sympathy the gloom of somebody else.

Arnold Bennett

In helping others, we shall help ourselves, for whatever mood we give out completes the circle and comes back to us.

Flora Edwards

The heart hath its own memory, like the mind,
And in it are enshrined
The precious keepsakes, into which is wrought
The giver's loving thought.

Henry W. Longfellow

There are three ways in which a man can go about performing a good deed. If he says: "I shall do it soon," the way is poor. If he says: "I am ready to do it now," the way is of average quality. If he says: "I am doing it," the way is praiseworthy.

The Kotzker Rebbe

The best means of benefitting the community is to place within its reach the ladders upon which the aspiring can rise.

Andrew Carnegie

I could almost dislike the man who refuses to plant walnut-trees, because they do not bear fruit till the second generation; and so— many thanks to our ancestors, and much joy to our successors.

Sir Walter Scott

Every good act is charity. Your smiling in your brother's face, is charity; an exhortation of your fellow-man to virtuous deeds, is equal to alms-giving; your putting a wanderer in the right road, is charity; your assisting the blind, is charity; your removing stones, and thorns, and other obstructions from the road, is charity; your giving water to the thirsty, is charity. A man's true wealth hereafter, is the good he does in this world to his fellow-man. When he dies, people will say, "What property has he left behind him?" but the angels will ask, "What good deeds has he sent before him?"

Mohammed Mahomet

There are some things we would like to give, but cannot afford. But all of us can give friendship to those who need it; loyalty to those who depend upon us; courtesy to all those with whom we come in contact; kindness to those whose paths may cross ours; understanding to those whose views may not be exactly in accord with your own opinions.

Carl E. Holmes

Give what you have. To some one it may be better than you dare to think.   *Henry W. Longfellow*

Self-interest is but the survival of the animal in us. Humanity only begins for a man with self-surrender.

Henri F. Amiel

It is not written, blessed is he that feedeth the poor, but he that considereth the poor. A little thought and a little kindness are often worth more than a great deal of money.

John Ruskin

To boast of the help you gave a needy brother is to cancel the good of your deed.

Samuel HaNagid

Whatever your deed—
    If you do it from Duty,
For the one who receives it,
    It loses its beauty.
If there isn't a bit
    Of your heart right behind it,
Nor the thrill of good will—
    And you find that you mind it.
What good is your deed—
    Or your gift—without backing?
It's a cold, lifeless thing
    When the heart's warmth is lacking!

Lillian Berdow

We should eat and drink below our means; dress according to our means, give beyond our means.

Ivan N. Panin

Nobody is ever impoverished through the giving of charity.

Moses Maimonides

We enjoy thoroughly only the pleasures that we give.

Alexandre Dumas

It was a rainy afternoon and a kindly old gentleman noticed a newsboy shivering in a doorway, trying to protect his papers from the rain. As he bought a paper, the old gentleman said, "My boy, aren't you terribly cold standing here?"

The boy looked up with a smile and replied, "I was, sir, before you came."

Raymond C. Otto

Love all God's creation, the whole and every grain of sand in it. Love every leaf, every ray of God's light. Love the animals, love the plants, love everything. If you love everything, you will perceive the divine mystery in things. Once you perceive it, you will begin to comprehend it better every day. And you will come at last to love the whole world with an all-embracing love.

Feodor Dostoevski

The same people who can deny others everything are famous for refusing themselves nothing.

Leigh Hunt

During the war an artillery shell had gone through the top of a church, just missing some of Bellini's famous murals. The church was ruined, but the murals weren't touched, and the people thought this was a miracle. They started to raise money to rebuild the church. I saw people who didn't even have shoes come up and put money in the box. It was cold, and I knew most of them didn't have enough to eat. I asked one man, "Why do you do this?" He hesitated a moment and then said, "Signor, what I give is only a little, but in giving I become a part of something beautiful."

Stanley Andrews

He who sees a need and waits to be asked for help is as unkind as if he had refused it.

Dante Purgatorio

A hundred times a day I remind myself that my inner and outer life depend on the labors of other men, living and dead, and that I must exert myself in order to give in the same measure as I have received and am receiving.

Albert Einstein

The manner of giving shows the character of the giver more than the gift itself.

Johann Kaspar Lavater

You must give some time to your fellow men. Even if it's a little thing, do something for others—something for which you get no pay but the privilege of doing it.

Albert Schweitzer

It is not so much our friends' help that helps us as the confidence of their help.

Epicurus

Faith has to do with the basis, the ground on which we stand. Hope is reaching out for something to come. Love is just being there and acting.

Emil Brunner

No one can live without being a debtor; no one should live without being a creditor.

Ivan N. Panin

The best thing to give to your enemy is forgiveness; to an opponent, tolerance; to a friend, your heart; to your child, a good example; to a father, deference; to your mother, conduct that will make her proud of you; to yourself, respect; to all men, charity.

Arthur James Balfour

A rabbi saw a man give a penny to a beggar publicly. He said to him: Better had you given him nothing than put him thus to shame.

The Talmud

A man ought to carry himself in the world as an orange tree would if it could walk up and down in the garden, swinging perfume from every little censer it holds up to the air.

Henry Ward Beecher

We like to give in the sunlight, and to receive in the dark.

J. Petit-Senn

There is a gift that is almost a blow, and there is a kind word that is munificence; so much is there in the way of doing things.

Sir Arthur Helps

Shall we call ourselves benevolent, when the gifts we bestow do not cost us a single privation?

Degerando

It is boorish to give with a bad grace. If the act of giving entails an effort, what matters the additional cost of a smile?

La Bruyere

I have always been deeply impressed by an old Jewish proverb which says, "What you give for the cause of charity in health is gold; what you give in sickness is silver; what you give after death is lead."

Nathan Straus

A bone to the dog is not charity. Charity is the bone shared with the dog, when you are just as hungry as the dog.

Jack London

We cannot save life by hoarding it. When a person tries to be a miser with his health, he usually makes himself miserable. We develop our physical and mental powers by spending them. Whoever tries to save his muscle or his memory by not using them is sure to weaken them. The power of love or sympathy is never exhausted by use. But these do shrivel by self-protection.

Ralph W. Sockman

The word "alms" has no singular, as if to teach us that a solitary act of charity scarcely deserves the name. *Author Unknown*

This only is charity, to do all, all that we can.

John Donne

If you would know a man, first learn to love him.

Austin O'Malley

You give but little when you give of your possessions. It is when you give of yourself that you truly give.

Kahlil Gibran

He only confers favors generously who appears, when they are once conferred, to remember them no more.

Samuel Johnson

If you really want to help your fellow-man, you must not merely have in you what would do them good if they should take it from you, but you must be such a man that they can take it from you. The snow must melt upon the mountain and come down in a spring torrent, before its richness can make the valley rich.

Phillips Brooks

Nothing is so dull as to be encased in self, nothing so exhilarating as to have attention and energy directed outward.

Bertrand Russell

An opal lay in the case, cold and lusterless. It was held a few moments in a warm hand, when it gleamed and glowed with all the beauty of the rainbow. All about us are human lives of children or of older persons, which seem cold and unbeautiful, without spiritual radiance or gleams of indwelling light which tell of immortality. Yet they need only the touch of a warm human hand, the pressure of love, to bring out in them the brightness of the spiritual beauty that is hidden in them.

J. R. Miller

We should give as we would receive, cheerfully, quickly, and without hesitation, for there is no grace in a benefit that sticks to the fingers.

Seneca

Liberality consists less in giving much than in giving at the right moment.

La Bruyere

In giving of thine alms inquire not so much into the person, as his necessity.—God looks not so much on the merits of him that requires, as to the manner of him that relieves.—If the man deserve not, thou has given to humanity.

Francis Quarles

As the purse is emptied the heart is filled.

Victor Hugo

Blessed are those who can give without remembering, and take without forgetting.

Elizabeth Bibesco

It is well to give when asked, but it is better to give unasked, through understanding.

Kahlil Gibran

Today we are continuously being asked for financial contributions, some are voluntary, some compulsory. Often forgotten is the fact that the greatest contribution of human value one person can make to others is by example.

Ralph E. Lyne

He who wishes to secure the good of others has already secured his own.

Confucius

As nothing great has ever been achieved without enthusiasm, so happiness or peace of mind cannot be achieved without sharing oneself with others, serving those in need, whether materially or spiritually.

Martha Pingel

And there are those who give and know not pain in giving,
Nor do they seek joy, nor give with mindfulness of virtue;

They give as in yonder valley the myrtle breathes its fragrance into space.
Through the hands of such as these God speaks, and from behind their eyes He smiles upon the earth.

Kahlil Gibran

And a thousand million lives are his Who carries the world in his sympathies.

James Russell Lowell

When you dig another out of his trouble, you find a place to bury your own.

Author Unknown

The whole worth of a benevolent deed lies in the love that inspires it.

The Talmud

To feed men and not to love them is to treat them as if they were barnyard cattle. To love them and not to respect them is to treat them as if they were household pets.

Mencius

A certain gentleman was being conducted on a tour of the other world. On reaching the nether regions he was greatly surprised to find the people all seated at a banquet table loaded with appetizing food. On the wall was the one law of the place—strictly enforced. Everyone must use the knives and forks provided by the management, but the tools of service had such long handles that no one could get a morsel of food near his mouth. They were all starving to death. And that was hell!

In the celestial city our visiting friend also found the people seated at banquet tables loaded with the same food and holding the same long-handled forks. But they were having a delightful time. They were feeding each other. And that was heaven!

Lewis L. Dunningham

Whoever gives a small coin to a poor man has six blessings bestowed upon him, but he who speaks a kind word to him obtains eleven blessings.

The Talmud

A wise lover values not so much the gift of the lover as the love of the giver.

Thomas à Kempis

A man there was and they called him mad; the more he gave the more he had.

John Bunyan

He gives twice who gives quickly.

Leon of Modena

In the end it may well be that Britain will be honored by the historians more for the way she disposed of an empire than for the way in which she acquired it.

Sir David Ormsby Gore

He who is not liberal with what he has, deceives himself when he thinks he would be liberal if he had more.

W. S. Plumer

He who is too much afraid of being duped has lost the power of being magnanimous.

Henri F. Amiel

Those who love not their fellow beings live unfruitful lives.

Percy Bysshe Shelley

There is an element of time in all human wants. When a man is cold,

he needs warmth now—not after spring thaws him out.

Richard L. Evans

No person was ever honored for what he received. Honor has been the reward for what he gave.

Calvin Coolidge

He profits most who serves best.

Arthur F. Sheldon

Not what we give, but what we share,
For the gift without the giver is bare:
Who gives himself with his alms feeds three,
Himself, his hungering neighbor, and Me.

James Russell Lowell

To complain that life has no joys while there is a single creature whom we can relieve by our bounty, assist by our counsels, or enliven by our presence, is to lament the loss of that which we possess, and is just as rational as to die of thirst with the cup in our hands.

William Melmoth Fitzosborne

We must take care to indulge only in such generosity as will help our friends and hurt no one; for nothing is generous, if it is not at the same time just.

Cicero

The whole universe obeys the law of giving and receiving. We see it at work in the seasons of the year, in the ebb and flow of the tide, in countless ways. We cannot evade the law; if we do not give voluntarily, then we have to give anyway, involuntarily.

Catherine Thrower Ponder

The miser deprives himself of everything for fear that some day he may be deprived of something.

Comtesse Diane

To make oneself beloved, says an old French proverb, this is, after all, the best way to be useful.

The truth is that most of us who have any ambitions at all, do not start in life with a hope of being useful, but rather with an intention of being ornamental. We think, like Joseph in his childish dreams, that the sun and the moon and the eleven stars, to say nothing of the heavens, are going to make obeisance to us. We want to be impressive, rich, beautiful, influential, admired, envied; and then, as we move forward, the visions fade. We have to be content if, in a quiet corner, a single sheaf gives us a nod of recognition; and as for the eleven stars, they seem unaware of our very existence! And then we make further discoveries; that influence comes mostly to people who do not pursue it, and that the best kind of influence belongs to those who do not even know that they possess it.

Arthur Christopher Benson

---

46. A TOUCH OF KINDNESS

He who has a claim for money upon his neighbor and knows that the latter is unable to pay, must not keep crossing his path.

The Talmud

Loving-kindness is the better part of goodness. It lends grace to the sterner qualities of which this consists and makes it a little less difficult to practice those minor virtues of self-control and self-restraint, patience, discipline and tolerance, which are the passive and not very exhilarating elements of goodness. Goodness is the only value that seems in this world of appearances to have any claim to be an end in itself. Virtue is its own reward. I am ashamed to have reached so commonplace a conclusion. With my instinct for effect I should have liked to end my book with some startling and paradoxical announcement or with a cynicism that my readers would have recognized with a chuckle as characteristic. It seems I have little more to say than can be read in any copybook or heard from any pulpit. I have gone a long way round to discover what everyone knew already.

W. Somerset Maugham

He who receives a good turn should never forget it; he who does one should never remember it.

Pierre Charron

One kind word can warm three winter months.

Japanese Proverb

Wisdom is knowing what to do next, skill is knowing how to do it, and virtue is doing it.

David Starr Jordan

Destiny commands a fleet of vessels on the wide sea of human service, but the flagship is compassion.

Douglas Meador

Life is short and we have not too much time for gladdening the hearts of those who are traveling the dark way with us. Oh, be swift to love! Make haste to be kind!

Henri F. Amiel

Help thy brother's boat across, and lo! thine own has reached the shore.

Hindu Proverb

Our gifts and attainments are not only to be light and warmth in our own dwellings, but are to shine through the window, into the dark night, to guide and cheer bewildered travellers on the road.

Henry Ward Beecher

People once felt that ignorance was the only bar to social happiness. Now, having seen mass murder in the age of culture, we know that human happiness is barred by active evil in human character, callousness and active cruelty. There is so much man-made misery in the world that one begins to hunger for a little considerateness and a little patience. Whether or not this change of taste reveals a basic change in my personal motivation, I know that I have come to prefer a different type of person. I once liked clever people. Now I like good people.

Solomon B. Freehof

Kindness is the inability to remain at ease in the presence of another person who is ill at ease, the inability to remain comfortable in the presence of another who is uncomfortable, the inability to have peace of mind when one's neighbor is troubled.

Samuel H. Holdenson

Die when we may, I want it said of me, by those who knew me best, that I always plucked a thistle and planted a flower, when I thought a flower would grow.

Abraham Lincoln

No one is useless in the world who lightens the burden of it for anyone else.

Charles Dickens

Make a rule, and pray to God to help you to keep it, never, if possible, to lie down at night without being able to say: "I have made one human being at least a little wiser, or a little happier, or at least a little better this day."

Charles Kingsley

Sympathy is two hearts tugging at one load.

Charles Henry Parkhurst

To make a sunrise in a place
  Where darkness reigned alone;
To light new gladness in a face
  That joy has never known;
To plant a little happiness
  In plots where weeds run riot—
Takes very little time, and oh,
  It isn't hard—just try it!

Mary Carolyn Davies

Unless we cultivate tenderness, what will become of a human world that is now as red as nature in tooth and claw? *Van Wyck Brooks*

In this world, one must be a little too kind to be kind enough.

Marivaux

Little acts of kindness are stowed away in the heart like bags of lavendar in a drawer to sweeten every object around them.

Author Unknown

Kindness in ourselves is the honey that blunts the sting of unkindness in another.

Walter Savage Landor

Kindness is the sunshine in which virtue grows.

Robert G. Ingersoll

"You have no tenderness, you have only justice, and therefore you are unjust," says Dostoevsky. Tenderness is total love, whereas justice is only a part of love, though it believes itself, mistakenly, to be the whole.

C. F. Ramuz

Stop complaining about the management of the universe. Look around for a place to sow a few seeds of happiness.

Henry Van Dyke

Guard within yourself that treasure kindness. Know how to give without hesitation, how to lose without regret, how to acquire without meanness.

George Sand

What do we live for, if it is not to make life less difficult to each other?

George Eliot

"What is real Good?"
I asked in musing mood.

Order, said the law court;
Knowledge, said the school;
Truth, said the wise man;
Pleasure, said the fool;
Love, said a maiden;
Beauty, said the page;
Freedom, said the dreamer;
Home, said the sage;
Fame, said the soldier;
Equity, the seer;—
Spake my heart full sadly,

"The answer is not here."
Then within my bosom
Softly this I heard:
"Each heart holds the secret;
Kindness is the word."

John Boyle O'Reilly

Live every day as if it were your last. Do every job as if you were the boss. Drive as if all other vehicles were police cars. Treat everybody else as if he were you.

Author Unknown

Do not do unto others as you would that they should do unto you. Their tastes may not be the same.

George Bernard Shaw

We should render a service to a friend to bind him closer to us, and to an enemy to make a friend of him.

Cleobulus

There will always be a frontier where there is an open mind and a willing hand.

Charles F. Kettering

Ninety per cent of all mental illness that comes before me could have been prevented, or cured by ordinary kindness.

Dr. William McGrath

Three-fourths of the people you will meet tomorrow are hungering and thirsting for sympathy. Give it to them, and they will love you.

Dale Carnegie

Kind hearts are the gardens;
Kind thoughts are the roots;
Kind words are the flowers;
Kind deeds are the fruits.

Author Unknown

Be ever soft and pliable like a reed, not hard and unbending like a cedar.

The Talmud

All ordinary violence produces its own limitations, for it calls forth an answering violence which sooner or later becomes its equal or its superior. But kindness works simply and perseveringly; it produces no strained relations which prejudice its working; strained relations which already exist it relaxes. Mistrust and misunderstanding it puts to flight, and it strengthens itself by calling forth answering kindness. Hence it is the furthest reaching and the most effective of all forces.

All the kindness which a man puts out into the world works on the heart and thoughts of mankind, but we are so foolishly indifferent that we are never in earnest in the matter of kindness. We want to topple a great load over, and yet will not avail ourselves of a lever which would multiply our power a hundredfold.

Albert Schweitzer

How beautiful a day can be
When kindness touches it!

Elliston

Kindness—a language which the dumb can speak, and the deaf can understand.

C. N. Bovee

When you rise in the morning, say that you will make the day blessed to a fellow creature. It is easily done: a left-off garment to the man who needs it: a kind word to the sorrowful; an encouraging expression to the struggling—trifles in themselves as light as air—will do at least for the twenty-four hours. And if you are young, depend upon it, it will tell when you are old; and if you are old, rest assured it will send you gently down the stream of time to eternity. By the most simple arithmetical sum, look into the result. If you send one person away happy through the day, there are 365 in the course of a year. And suppose you live forty years only. After you commence that course of medicine, you have made 14,600 persons happy, at all events for a time.

Author Unknown

If there was a hanging in his family, don't tell him, "Hang this up for me."

The Talmud

Thou must live for thy neighbor if thou wouldst live for thyself.

Seneca

---

47. THE QUALITY OF MERCY

Grant us brotherhood, not only for this day but for all our years— a brotherhood not of words but of acts and deeds.

Stephen V. Benet

With malice toward none, with charity for all, with firmness in the right, as God gives us to see the right, let us strive on to finish the work we are in, to bind up the nation's wounds, to care for him who shall have borne the battle, and for his widow, and his orphans—to do all which may achieve and cherish a just and lasting peace among ourselves and with all nations.

Abraham Lincoln

A man's feet must be planted in his country, but his eyes should survey the world.

George Santayana

Be noble! And the nobleness that lies
In other men, sleeping, but never dead,
Will rise in majesty to meet thine own.

James Russell Lowell

It is through pity that we remain truly a man.

Anatole France

None of us has solid ground under his feet; each of us is only held up by the neighborly hands grasping him by the scruff, with the result that we are each held up by the next man, and often, indeed most of the time, hold each other up mutually.

Franz Rosenzweig

The greatest object in the universe says a certain philosopher, is a good man struggling with adversity; yet there is still greater, which is the good man that comes to relieve it.

Oliver Goldsmith

A heart without affection is like a purse without money.

Benjamin Mandelstamm

Let every man pray that he may in some true sense be a soldier of fortune; that he may have the good fortune to spend his energies and his life in the service of his fellowmen in order that he may die to be recorded upon the rolls of those who have not thought of themselves but have thought of those whom they served.

Woodrow Wilson

God has placed the genius of women in their hearts; because the works of this genius are always works of love.

Alphonse de Lamartine

There is no better exercise
For the heart
Than reaching down
And lifting someone up.

John Andrew Holmes

Understanding is the cement which can make "one world" out of fragmentary groups. Now that the emotions of group prejudice—fear, hate, and spite—have atomic weapons at their disposal, understanding has become the sine qua non of survival. The verb to love, which is the first commandment of every religion, must be interpreted as meaning also to understand.

Everett R. Clinchy

In whatever direction the future moves, whether the earthquake is long in coming or not, we must from now onward learn to live and act in the knowledge that we are all responsible to and for one another, because we have one common eternal destiny and because we are dependent on the one Father, who make brothers of us all.

Pierre Van Paassen

When the heart is full, the eyes overflow.

Sholom Aleichem

Pity is already half piety.
Ivan N. Panin

I have not willingly planted a thorn in any man's bosom.
Abraham Lincoln

Far from being a handicap to command, compassion is the measure of it. For unless one values the lives of his soldiers and is tormented by their ordeals, he is unfit to command.
Omar N. Bradley

Shaming another in public is like shedding blood.
The Talmud

An inferior race is always hated most by those members of a superior race who are not very sure of their superiority.
Author Unknown

The man who lives by himself and for himself is apt to be corrupted by the company he keeps.
C. H. Parkhurst

The mind of the bigot is like the pupil of the eye; the more light you pour upon it, the more it will contract.
Oliver Wendell Holmes, Jr.

The vocation of every man and woman is to serve other people.
Leo Tolstoy

Great thoughts come from the heart.
Vauvenargues

Once I found a friend. "Dear me," I said, "he was made for me." But now I find more and more friends who seem to have been made for me, and more and yet more made for me. Is it possible we

were all made for each other all over the world?
G. K. Chesterton

A book or poem which has no pity in it had better not be written.
Oscar Wilde

We didn't all come over on the same ship, but we're all in the same boat.
Bernard M. Baruch

All men are responsible for one another.
The Talmud

Nature comes to the succor of the deserted; when all is lacking she gives back her whole self. She flourishes and grows green amid ruins; she has ivy for the stones and love for man.
Victor Hugo

Teach me to feel another's woe,
To hide the fault I see;
That mercy I to others show,
That mercy show to me.
Alexander Pope

Save us, O Lord, from the hardness of righteousness without mercy, and from the mushiness of mercy without righteousness.
Walter L. Moore

No matter how widely you have traveled, you haven't seen the world if you have failed to look into the human hearts that inhabit it.
Donald Culross Peattie

About racial prejudices we should all be taught to believe that the difference between peoples of any two countries is much smaller than that between the gentlemen and the gangsters of any particular country.

Author Unknown

God grant that you neither shame nor be shamed.

The Talmud

More helpful than all wisdom is one draught of simple human pity that will not forsake us.

George Eliot

When you feel pity, you don't ask other people first whether you ought to.

G. C. Lichtenberg

What is the noblest pedigree? Loving-kindness to men.

Solomon Ibn Gabirol

We marvel at the silence that divides the living and the dead.
Yet more apart
Are they who all life long live side by side
Yet never heart by heart.

Author Unknown

To live in mankind is far more than to live in a name.

Vachel Lindsay

Rabbi Baroka was walking one day through the crowded marketplace of his town, and met Elijah. "Who of all this multitude has the best claim to Heaven?" asked the Rabbi. The prophet pointed to a disreputable, weird-looking creature, a turnkey. "That man yonder, because he is considerate to his prisoners."

Victor Gollancz

To pity distress is but human; to relieve it is Godlike.

Horace Mann

The most powerful language in the world today is food. It is clearly understood. It builds bridges mightier by far than radio broadcasts or published material, especially when people have no radios or cannot read.

Norman Cousins

The quality of mercy is not strained;
It droppeth, as the gentle rain from heaven
Upon the place beneath: it is twice blessed;
It blesseth him that gives, and him that takes.

William Shakespeare

Among the attributes of God, although they are all equal, mercy shines with even more brilliancy than justice.

Cervantes

By using our hands we become strong; by using our brains, wise; but by using our hearts, merciful.

Nicholai Velimirovic

Heaven arms with pity those whom it would not see destroyed.

Lao-Tse

The old idea of a good bargain was a transaction in which one man got the better of another. The new idea of a good contract is a transaction which is good for both parties to it.

Louis D. Brandeis

Social problems can no longer be solved by class warfare any more than international problems can be solved by wars between nations. Warfare is negative and will sooner or later lead to destruction, while good will and cooperation are positive and supply the only safe basis for building a better future.

William Lyon Phelps

Your education has been a failure, no matter how much it has done for your mind, if it has failed to open your heart.

Author Unknown

The Day of Atonement atones for sins against God, not for sins against man, unless the injured man has been appeased.

The Mishnah

"Give me a theme," the little poet cried,
"And I will do my part;"
" 'Tis not a theme you need," the world replied;
"You need a heart."

R. W. Gilder

Our earth is but a small star in the great universe. Yet of it we can make, if we choose, a planet unvexed by war, untroubled by hunger or fear, undivided by senseless distinctions of race color or theory.

Stephen V. Benet

Sympathy is a thing to be encouraged, because it supplies us with materials for wisdom. It is probably more instructive to entertain a sneaking kindness for any unpopular person than to give way to perfect raptures of moral indignation against his abstract vices.

Robert Louis Stevenson

It is better for a man to cast himself into a flaming oven than to shame his comrade in public.

The Talmud

If you your ears would save from jeers,
These things keep meekly hid;
Myself and I, and mine and my,
And how I do and did.

Author Unknown

Man, like a generous vine, supported lives;
The strength he gains is from the embrace he gives.

Alexander Pope

Our aim should be, not one civilization, supreme at the cost of others, but as many types flourishing on this earth as possible.

Felix Adler

---

48. THE ART OF CARING

Strengthen me by sympathizing with my strength not my weakness.

Amos Bronson Alcott

Hang yourself, brave Crillon.
We fought at Arques, and you were not there.

Henry IV, to Crillon after a great victory.

He who does not live in some degree for others, hardly lives for himself.

Michel de Montaigne

In making our decisions, we must use the brains that God has given us. But we must also use our hearts which He also gave us.

Fulton Oursler

"Someone ought to do it, but why
should I?

Someone ought to do it, so why
not I?"

Between these two sentences lie
whole centuries of moral evolution.

Annie Besant

Justice will be achieved only
when those who are not injured feel
as indignant as those who are.

Solon

I met a little maid
A rosy burden bearing;
"Is he not heavy?" I said
As past me she was hurrying.
She looked at me with grave, sweet
eyes,
This fragile little mother,
And answered in swift surprise:
"Oh, no Sir. He's my brother."

Author Unknown

When von Hugel, that great
philosopher, mystic, and saint, was
dying, his niece bent over her
uncle because she could see his lips
moving and could not catch what
he said. She put her ear close
against his mouth and heard this,
the last words that great saint ever
uttered: "Caring is everything;
nothing matters but caring."

Leslie D. Weatherhead

Years ago I recognized my kinship with all human beings, and I
made up my mind I was not one
whit better than the meanest on
earth. I said then and I say now
that while there is a lower class,
I am of it; while there is a criminal
class, I am of it; while there is a
soul in prison, I am not free.

Eugene V. Debs

The real evil in the world is not
the spectacular, the occasional, the
vividly catastrophic. The real evil
lies in our neglect of causes, our
indifference to conditions, our un-
willingness to give the time, the
money and the effort to stop pre-
ventable disaster.

Sydney J. Harris

If I were a godfather wishing a
gift on a child, it would be that
he should always be more interested in other people than in himself. That's a *real* gift.

Sir Compton Mackenzie

If man had not been troubled
millions of years ago he would still
be living in caves. If he is not
troubled now, and does not remain
troubled, he will soon be back in
the caves.

Thomas Surgrue

The least pain in our little finger
gives us more concern and uneasiness, than the destruction of millions of our fellow-beings.

William Hazlitt

All that is necessary for the triumph of evil is that good men do
nothing.

Edmund Burke

A man should share the action
and passion of his time at peril
of being judged not to have lived.

Oliver Wendell Holmes

A generous heart feels other's ills
as if it were responsible for them.

Vauvenargues

It may well be that the greatest
tragedy of this period of social
transition is not the glaring noisi-
ness of the so-called bad people,
but the appalling silence of the
so-called good people. It may be
that our generation will have to

repent not only for the diabolical actions and vitriolic words of the children of darkness, but also for the crippling fears and tragic apathy of the children of light.

Martin Luther King

I never ask the wounded person how he feels; I myself become the wounded person.

Walt Whitman

Take care of your own soul and of another man's body, not of your own body and of another man's soul.

The Kotzker Rebbe

Civilization has nearly in these days suffered shipwreck, not because of the power of its enemies, but because of the slackness of its defenders.

Clement Attlee

There is an evil which most of us condone and are even guilty of: indifference to evil. We remain neutral, impartial, and not easily moved by the wrongs done unto other people. Indifference to evil is more insidious than evil itself; it is more universal, more contagious, more dangerous.

Abraham J. Heschel

In every matter of right and wrong we can't be neutral.

Theodore Roosevelt

Where there is no concern in the heart, there comes no music from the soul.

Roger Imhoff

The worst sin against our fellow creatures is not to hate them but to be indifferent to them.

George Bernard Shaw

We cannot shut our windows and draw our curtains and be careless of what is happening next door or on the other side of the street. No nation can close its frontiers and hope to live secure. We cannot have prosperity in one country and misery in its neighbor; peace in one hemisphere and war in another.

Anthony Eden

There is not a person we employ who does not, like ourselves, desire recognition, praise, gentleness, forbearance, patience.

Henry Ward Beecher

The penalty good men pay for indifference to public affairs is to be ruled by evil men.

Plato

Who is thy neighbor? He whom thou
Hast power to aid or bless;
Whose aching heart or burning brow
Thy soothing hand may press.

Thy neighbor? Pass no mourner by;
Perhaps thou canst redeem
A breaking heart from misery;
Go share thy lot with him.

Author Unknown

No one is so accursed by fate,
No one so utterly desolate,
But some heart, though unknown,
Responds unto his own.

Henry Wadsworth Longfellow

I care more for that long age which I shall never see than for my own small share of time.

Cicero

49. THE ART OF FORGIVING

There are realms in which arithmetic does not work. It has no place in the kingdom of love. For instance, we are not to count the number of times we forgive.

Charles E. Jefferson

Forgive and forget if you can; but forgive anyway; and pray heartily and kindly for all men, for thus only shall we be the children of our Father who maketh His sun to rise on the evil and on the good, and sendeth rain on the just and on the unjust.

Henry Van Dyke

Since I myself stand in need of God's pity, I have granted an amnesty to all my enemies.

Heinrich Heine

God forgives sins committed against Him, but offenses against man must first be forgiven by the injured person.

The Talmud

He who cannot forgive himself with regard to you will never forgive you.

Francis Bradley

He who cannot forgive breaks the bridge over which he himself must pass.

George Herbert

The sweetest revenge is to forgive.

Isaac Friedmann

A man who values a good night's rest will not lie down with enmity in his heart, if he can help it.

Laurence Sterne

To forgive our enemies their virtues—that is a greater miracle.

Voltaire

An apology
Is a friendship preserver
Is often a debt of honor,
Is never a sign of weakness,
Is an antidote for hatred,
Costs nothing but one's pride,
Always saves more than it costs,
Is a device needed in every home.

Author Unknown

Who avenges subdues one, who forgives rules over two.

Isachar Hurwitz

If you use the heart with which you reprove others to reprove yourself, there will be fewer faults: if you use the heart with which you forgive yourself to forgive others, there will be perfect friendship.

S. C. Shampion

It is much safer to reconcile an enemy than to conquer him; victory may deprive him of his position, but reconciliation of his will.

Owen Feltham

Forgive and forget. The first helps your soul. The second, your liver.

Author Unknown

We win by tenderness; we conquer by forgiveness.

Frederick William Robertson

The most complete revenge is not to imitate the aggressor.

Marcus Aurelius

The grave buries every error, covers every defect, extinguishes every resentment. From its peaceful bosom spring none but fond regrets and tender recollections. Who can look down upon the grave of a enemy, and not feel a compunctious throb that he should have warred with the poor handful of dust that lies moldering before him.

Washington Irving

They who forgive most, shall be most forgiven.

Josiah W. Bailey

Humanity is never so beautiful as when praying for forgiveness, or else forgiving another.

Jean Paul Richter

The most beautiful thing man can do is to forgive.

Eleazar ben Judah

Nothing is more costly, nothing is more sterile, than vengeance.

Winston S. Churchill

To forgive is the quickest way to end trouble and to have peace and unity. For a forgiving spirit is by its very nature a unifying force. It can remove the barriers of separation between peoples and nations and weld them together in peace and goodwill, something that legislation with the help of armies can never accomplish. To hate is to die physically and spiritually, but to forgive is to live.

Charles R. Loss

Every man should keep a fair-sized cemetery in which to bury the faults of his friends.

Henry Ward Beecher

When two quarrel, he who yields first displays the nobler nature.

The Talmud

The Norwegian writer tells of a man whose little child was killed by a neighbor's dog. Revenge would not long satisfy this man, so he found a better way to relieve the agony of his heart. When a famine had plagued the people and the neighbor's fields lay bare and he had no corn to plant for next year's harvest, the troubled father went out one night and sowed the neighbor's field, explaining: "I went and sowed seed in my enemy's field that God might exist."

Johan Bojer

Only the brave know how to forgive; it is the most refined and generous pitch of virtue that human nature can arrive at.

Laurence Sterne

In the very depths of yourself dig a grave. Let it be like some forgotten spot to which no path leads; and there, in the eternal silence, bury the wrongs that you have suffered. Your heart will feel as if a weight had fallen from it, and a divine peace come to abide with you.

Charles Wagner

If I owe Smith $10.00 and God forgives me, that doesn't pay Smith.

Robert G. Ingersoll

To err is human, to forgive divine.

Alexander Pope

No sin is too big for God to pardon, and none is too small for habit to magnify.

Bahya

Who takes vengeance or bears a grudge acts like one who, having cut one hand while handling a knife, avenges himself by stabbing the other hand.

The Jerusalem Talmud

If we could read the secret history of our enemies we should find in each man's life sorrow and suffering enough to disarm all hostility.

Henry Wadsworth Longfellow

The highest and most difficult of all moral lessons, to forgive those we have injured.

Joseph Jacobs

---

50. A TOUCH OF COURTESY

Life is not so short but that there is always room for courtesy.

Ralph Waldo Emerson

Self-respect is at the bottom of all good manners. They are the expression of discipline, of good-will, of respect for other people's rights and comfort and feelings.

Edward Sandford Martin

If we treat people too long with that pretended liking called politeness, we shall find it hard not to like them in the end.

Logan Pearsall Smith

There is great force hidden in a sweet command.

George Herbert

Politeness is to human nature what warmth is to wax.

Arthur Schopenhauer

The small courtesies sweeten life; the greater, ennoble it.

Christian Nestell Bovee

Politeness costs nothing, and gains everything.

Lady Mary Wortley Montagu

Manners, the final and perfect flower of noble character.

William Winter

Politeness is the art of choosing among one's real thoughts.

Abel Stevens

Polished brass will pass upon more people than rough gold.

Lord Chesterfield

In our disturbed and uncertain age, not knowing where we are going, how and if we shall get there, the least we can do in our common predicament is to treat one another with a certain amount of respect. It is more important and more urgent today to teach our children this humble form of tolerance—courtesy and good manners are nothing else but that—than to try to convince them that capitalism is better than communism, or vice versa. If history has proved something, it is that means and ways are more important than the distant ends.

Romain Gary

Of Courtesy, it is much less
Than Courage of Heart or Holiness,
Yet in my Walks it seems to me
That the Grace of God is in Courtesy.

Hilaire Belloc

It takes no personal development nor stature to be tactless or inconsiderate. Such behavior is nothing more than immaturity seeking expression. It is an unconscious effort to conceal or cover up our sense of inferiority and of inadequacy. The mature person, on the other hand, lives on the level of human equation. He need not belittle in order to make himself an equal. He has the sense of adequacy within himself. He needs no false props to bolster his sense of importance.

Tom D. Eilers

Politeness is not always the sign of wisdom, but the want of it always leaves room for the suspicion of folly.

Walter Savage Landor

A gentleman never heard a story before.

Austin O'Malley

Good manners and soft words have brought many a difficult thing to pass.

Sir John Vanbrugh

Rudeness is the weak man's imitation of strength.

Eric Hoffer

Good manners are made up of small sacrifices.

Ralph Waldo Emerson

Manners are of more importance than laws. Upon them, in a great measure, the laws depend. The law touches us but here and there, and now and then. Manners are what vex or soothe, corrupt or purify, exalt or debase, barbarize or refine us, by a constant, steady, uniform, insensible operation, like that of the air we breathe in.

Edmund Burke

Politeness is like an air cushion; there may be nothing in it, but it eases our jolts wonderfully.

Samuel Johnson

A man's own good-breeding is his best security against other people's ill manners.

Lord Chesterfield

Politeness has been well defined as benevolence in small things.

Thomas Babington Macaulay

Etiquette means behaving yourself a little better than is absolutely essential.

Will Cuppy

A polite man is one who listens with interest to things he knows about, when they are told to him by a person who knows nothing about them.

Phillipe de Mornay

We cannot always oblige, but we can always speak obligingly.

Voltaire

The test of good manners: to bear patiently with bad ones.

Solomon Ibn Gabirol

Tact is the knack of making a point without making an enemy.

Howard W. Newton

In all the affairs of life, social as well as political, courtesies of a small and trivial character are the ones which strike deepest to the grateful and appreciating heart.

Henry Clay

There is a great difference between the politeness that comes from strength and the politeness that comes from weakness; the former is a virtue, while the latter is only a strategy.

Sydney J. Harris

Americans can never be called ill-mannered people. It has been estimated that we pay more than ten million dollars every year in toll charges in order to add the polite word "please" to our telegrams.

Author Unknown

Good manners may in Seven
  Words be found:
Forget Yourself and think of
  Those Around.

Arthur Guiterman

A man has no more right to say an uncivil thing than to act one— no more right to say a rude thing to another man than to knock him down.

Samuel Johnson

Nothing is ever lost by courtesy. It is the cheapest of the pleasures; costs nothing and conveys much. It pleases him who gives and him who receives, and thus, like mercy, is twice blessed.

Erastus Wiman

Never claim as a right what you can ask as a favor.

John Churton Collins

All doors open to courtesy.

Thomas Fuller

Manners are the happy ways of doing things. If they are superficial, so are the dewdrops which give such a depth to the morning meadows.

Ralph Waldo Emerson

Politeness is to goodness what words are to thought. It tells not only on the manners, but on the mind and the heart; it renders the feelings, the opinions, the words, moderate and gentle.

Joseph Joubert

51. THE ART OF JUDGING OTHERS

If we had no faults, we should take less pleasure in noticing those of others.

François Rochefoucauld

One must be fond of people and trust them if one is not to make a mess of life.

E. M. Forster

Suspicion is far more apt to be wrong than right; oftener unjust than just. It is no friend to virtue, and always an enemy to happiness.

Hosea Ballou

How can we venture to judge others when we know so well how ill-equipped they are for judging us?

Comtesse Diane

Believe me, every man has his secret sorrows, which the world knows not; and oftentimes we call a man cold when he is only sad.

Henry Wadsworth Longfellow

He who mistrusts most should be trusted least.

Theognis

It is literally true that in judging others we trumpet abroad our secret faults. Allow any man to give free vent to his feelings about others, and then you may with perfect safety turn and say, Thou art the man.

J. A. Hadfield

We discover in ourselves what others hide from us, and we recognize in others what we hide from ourselves.

Vauvenargues

Rare is the person who can weigh the faults of others without putting his thumb on the scales.

Byron J. Langenfeld

The envious praise only that which they can surpass; that which surpasses them, they censure.

Caleb C. Colton

It is hard to believe that a man is telling the truth when you know that you would lie if you were in his place.

H. L. Mencken

If it be an evil to judge rashly or untruly of any single man, how much a greater sin it is to condemn a whole people.

William Penn

There is so much good in the worst of us,
And so much bad in the best of us,
That it ill behooves any of us.

Author Unknown

We must be as courteous to a man as we are to a picture, which we are willing to give the advantage of a good light.

Ralph Waldo Emerson

Good and bad men are each less so than they seem.

Samuel Taylor Coleridge

I always seek the good that is in people and leave the bad to Him who made mankind and knows how to round off the corners.

Goethe's Mother

Every man gauges us by himself. A rogue believes all men are rascals; and moral weakness excuses mankind on the same ground. But a Parsival sees no rascality in any one, for the pure see all things purely.

Author Unknown

Men do not suspect faults which they do not commit.

Samuel Johnson

He is incapable of truly a good action who finds not a pleasure in contemplating the good actions of others.

Johann Kasper Lavater

A judge must bear in mind that when he tries a case he is himself on trial.

Philo

No rewards are offered for finding fault.

Author Unknown

Search thy own heart; what paineth thee in others in thyself may be.

John Greenleaf Whittier

The cynic is one who never sees a good quality in a man, and never fails to see a bad one. He is the human owl, vigilant in darkness and blind to light, mousing for vermin, and never seeing noble game. The cynic puts all human actions into two classes—openly bad and secretly bad.

Henry Ward Beecher

The sorrow of knowing that there is evil in the best is far out-balanced by the joy of discovering that there is good in the worst.

Austen Fox Riggs

Oh, great Father, never let me judge another man until I have walked in his moccasins for two weeks.

Indian Prayer

All men have their frailties, and whosoever looks for a friend without imperfection will never find what he seeks. We love ourselves notwithstanding our faults, and we ought to love our friends in like manner.

Cyrus

Never does a man portray his own character more vividly than in his manner of portraying another's.

Ralph Waldo Emerson

To better understand one another, we should all swap places for a while with each other. Every doctor should have an operation, every policeman and minister spend a number of months in jail and every industrialist become a labor-union member.

Edwin T. Kahlberg

What we love and what we hate in others is ourselves, always ourselves.

Comtesse Diane

Endeavor to be always patient of the faults and imperfections of others; for thou hast many faults and imperfections of thine own that require forbearance. If thou art not able to make thyself that which thou wishest, how canst thou expect to mold another in conformity to thy will.

Thomas à Kempis

God himself, sir, does not propose to judge man until the end of his days.

Samuel Johnson

A man should never be assumed foolish till he has proved himself foolish—this we owe to him. A man should never be assumed wise till he has proved himself wise—this we owe to ourselves.

Ivan N. Panin

If a prince wear a Bohemian glass stone on his finger, it will be taken for a diamond; should a beggar wear a genuine diamond ring, everyone will feel convinced it is only glass.

Heinrich Heine

In men whom men condemn as ill
I find so much of goodness still,
In men whom men pronounce divine
I find so much of sin and blot
I do not dare to draw a line
Between the two, where God has not.

Joaquin Miller

If you see a fault in others, think of two of your own, and do not add a third one by your hasty judgment.

Flammer

And in self-judgment if you find
Your deeds to others are superior,
To you has Providence been kind,
As you should be to those inferior.
Example sheds a genial ray

Of light, which men are apt to borrow,
So, first, improve yourself today
And then improve your friends tomorrow.

Author Unknown

Nice distinctions are so troublesome. It is so much easier to say that a thing is black than to discriminate the particular shade of brown, blue, or green, to which it really belongs. It is so much easier to make up your mind that your neighbor is good for nothing than to enter into all the circumstances that would oblige you to modify that opinion.

George Eliot

It is more disgraceful to distrust one's friends than to be deceived by them.

François Rochefoucauld

Only the thinnest line divides the righteous from the self-righteous; the pure from the priggish; the holy from the holier-than-thou; the virtuous from the repressed—and only God knows where the line is drawn.

Sydney J. Harris

Keep searching for the other fellow's good points. Remember, he has to hunt for yours and maybe he'll be harder put than you are.

Author Unknown

There is an old story of a woman who made artificial fruits so perfectly that people could not tell them from the real fruit. But she had some critics who would find fault with the shape of the fruit, the color and other things. One day as the critics stood before a table on which she had placed several pieces of fruit, they criticized particularly one apple. When they had finished, the woman picked up the apple, cut it in half, and began to eat it, for it was a real apple.

Homer H. Elliott

52. THE BLESSING OF FRIENDSHIP

I have three chairs in my house: one for solitude, two for friendship, three for company.

Henry Thoreau

Friendship is to be purchased only by friendship. A man may have authority over others, but he can never have their heart but by giving his own.

Thomas Wilson

What man is there whom contact with a great soul will not exalt? A drop of water upon the petal of a lotus glistens with the splendors of the pearl.

Author Unknown

Honest men esteem and value nothing so much in this world as a real friend. Such a one is as it were another self, to whom we impart our most secret thoughts, who partakes of our joy, and comforts us in our affliction; add to this, that his company is an everlasting pleasure to us.

Pilpay

Tell me what company thou keepest, and I'll tell thee what thou art.

Cervantes

A friend is a present you give yourself.

Robert Louis Stevenson

The test of friendship is its fidelity when every charm of fortune and environment has been spent away, and the bare, undraped character alone remains; if love still holds steadfast, and the joy of companionship survives in such an hour, the fellowship becomes a beautiful prophecy of immortality.

Hamilton W. Mabie

Go often to the house of thy friend, for weeds choke the unused path.

Ralph Waldo Emerson

The greatest effort of friendship is not to show our own faults to a friend, but to make him see his own.

Francois Rochefoucauld

Half the pleasure of solitude comes from having with us some friend to whom we can say how sweet solitude is.

William Jay

A true friend is one soul in two bodies.

Aristotle

What a great blessing is a friend with a heart so trusty you may safely bury all your secrets in it, whose conscience you may fear less than your own, who can relieve your cares by his conversation, your doubts by his counsels, your sadness by his good humor,

and whose very looks give you comfort.

Seneca

Friendship is like a treasury: you cannot take from it more than you put into it.

Benjamin Mandelstamm

No man can be provident of his time that is not prudent in the choice of his company.

Jeremy Taylor

As widowers proverbially marry again, so a man with the habit of friendship always finds new friends. My old age judges more charitably and thinks better of mankind than my youth ever did. I discount idealization, I forgive one-sidedness, I see that it is essential to perfection of any kind. And in each person I catch the fleeting suggestion of something beautiful, and swear eternal friendship with that.

George Santayana

A friend is a person with whom I may be sincere.

Ralph Waldo Emerson

Nothing makes the earth seem so spacious as to have friends at a distance; they make the latitudes and longitudes.

Henry Thoreau

There is no better way to become well-mannered than to associate with people who have good manners; there is no better way to learn a language than to live with people who speak it; there is no better way to become honest than to live with honest people; there is no better way to attain dignity, poise, moral excellence, self-control than to live with people who have these qualities. He who walks with wise men shall be wise.

Henry Colestock

A true friend unbosoms freely, advises justly, assists readily, adventures boldly, takes all patiently, defends courageously, and continues a friend unchangeable.

William Penn

Friendship—one heart in two bodies.

Joseph Zabara

If you have a friend worth loving,
Love him! Yes, and let him know
That you love him, ere life's evening
Tinge his brow with sunset glow.
Why should good words ne'er be said
Of a friend—till he is dead?

Scatter thus your seeds of kindness
All enriching as you go—
Leave them! Trust the Harvest-Giver;
He will make each seed to grow.
And until the happy end,
Your life shall never lack a friend.

Author Unknown

"What is the secret of your life?" asked Mrs. Browning of Charles Kingsley. "Tell me, that I may make mine beautiful, too." He replied: "I had a friend."

William Channing Gannett

It is my joy in life to find
At every turning of the road
The strong arm of a comrade kind
To help me onward with my load.

And since I have no gold to give,
And love alone must make amends,
My only prayer is, while I live—
God make me worthy of my friends.

Frank Dempster Sherman

Fame is the scentless sunflower,
with gaudy crown of gold;
But friendship is the breathing
rose, with sweets in every fold.

Oliver Wendell Holmes

The glory of Friendship is not the outstretched hand, nor the kindly smile, nor the joy of companionship; it is the spiritual inspiration that comes to one when he discovers that someone else believes in him and is willing to trust him with his friendship.

Ralph Waldo Emerson

A real friend is one who walks in when the rest of the world walks out.

Walter Winchell

In love one has need of being believed, in friendship of being understood.

Abel Bonnard

Friends are needed both for joy and for sorrow.

Yiddish Proverb

One's friends are that part of the human race with which one can be human.

George Santayana

A friend is not so much one to whom you can go for help when you are in trouble. That has its value. But a friend is one to whom you can go when he is in trouble.

L. O. Dawson

Friendliness is contagious. The trouble is, many of us wait to catch it from someone else, when we might better be giving them a chance to catch it from us.

Donald A. Laird

Make new friends, but keep the old;

Those are silver, these are gold.
New-made friendships, like new
wine,
Age will mellow and refine.
Friendships that have stood the
test—
Time and change—are surely best;
Brow may wrinkle, hair grow gray;
Friendship never knows decay.
For 'mid old friends, tried and true,
Once more we our youth renew.
But old friends, alas! may die;
New friends must their place sup-
ply.
Cherish friendship in your breast—
New is good, but old is best;
Make new friends, but keep the
old;
Those are silver, these are gold.

Joseph Parry

Blessed are they who have the
gift of making friends, for it is
one of God's best gifts. It involves
many things, but above all, the
power of going out of one's self,
and appreciating whatever is noble
and loving in another.

Thomas Hughes

It is one of the severest tests of
friendship to tell your friend his
faults. So to love a man that you
cannot bear to see a stain upon
him, and to speak painful truth
through loving words, that is
friendship.

Henry Ward Beecher

He is a happy man that has a
true friend at his need, but he is
more truly happy that has no
need of his friend.

A. Warwick

My friend is he who will tell me
my fault in private.

Solomon Ibn Gabirol

To have known true friends is
to have warmed one's hands at the
central fire of life . . . As I look
back I would not ask for wealth or
power; I would ask only for the
supreme gift of friends. That I have
had in full measure. It has given
me a sense of fellowship that has
given to life and happiness beyond the power of sorrow to destroy.

Harold J. Laski

Geese keep together by nature,
the fellowship of souls must be
cultivated.

Ivan N. Panin

Develop the art of friendliness.
One can experience a variety of
emotions staying home and reading
or watching television; one will be
alive but hardly living. Most of
the meaningful aspects of life are
closely associated with people.
Even the dictionary definition of
life involves people.

William L. Abbott

He who has a thousand friends has
not a friend to spare,
And he who has one enemy will
meet him everywhere.

Ralph Waldo Emerson

Friendship is the only cement
that will hold the world together.

Woodrow Wilson

Oh, the comfort—the inexpressible
comfort of feeling safe with a
person,
Having neither to weigh thoughts,
Nor measure words—but pouring
them
All right out—just as they are—
Chaff and grain together—
Certain that a faithful hand will
Take and sift them—

Keep what is worth keeping—
And with the breath of kindness
Blow the rest away.

Dinah Maria Mulock Craik

We are all travellers in the wilderness of this world, and the best that we find in our travels is an honest friend.

Robert Louis Stevenson

To let friendship die away by negligence and silence is certainly not wise. It is voluntarily to throw away one of the greatest comforts of this weary pilgrimage.

Samuel Johnson

There is no man that imparteth his joys to his friends, but he joyeth the more; and no man that imparteth his griefs to his friend, but he grieveth the less.

Francis Bacon

Friendship is the allay of our sorrows, the ease of our passions, the discharge of our oppressions, the sanctuary to our calamities, the counselor of our doubts, the clarity of our minds, the emission of our thoughts, the exercise and improvement of what we meditate.

Jeremy Taylor

Do not keep the alabaster boxes of your love and tenderness sealed up until your friends are dead. Fill their lives with sweetness. Speak approving, cheering words while their ears can hear them and while their hearts can be thrilled by them.

Henry Ward Beecher

The ornaments of our house are the friends that frequent it.

Ralph Waldo Emerson

The best way to keep your friends is not to give them away.

Wilson Mizner

Three Men Are My Friends:

He that loves me, he that hates me, he that is indifferent to me. Who loves me, teaches me tenderness. Who hates me, teaches me caution. Who is indifferent to me, teaches me self-reliance.

Ivan Panin

All men have their frailties; and whoever looks for a friend without imperfections, will never find what he seeks. We love ourselves notwithstanding our faults, and we ought to love our friends in like manner.

Cyrus

You could read Kant by yourself, if you wanted; but you must share a joke with someone else.

Robert Louis Stevenson

---

53. JUSTICE, JUSTICE SHALT THOU PURSUE

Justice is symbolized on courthouses and elsewhere by the figure of a blindfolded woman with scales in her hand, the implication being that the essence of justice is the weighing of the facts in hand with an impartiality which might be lost if we could see the parties involved. But such a portrayal is hardly adequate. To put it graphically though crudely, the blindfold should be removed and spectacles should be substituted. If we would weigh a situation justly, we must see not only the persons involved but also their backgrounds.

Ralph W. Sockman

All knowledge that is divorced from justice must be called cunning rather than wisdom.

Plato

If we are to keep our democracy there must be one commandment: "Thou shalt not ration justice."

Judge Learned Hand

When it is our duty to do an act of justice it should be done promptly. To delay is injustice.

La Bruyere

There is hope that law, rather than private force, may come to govern the relations of nations within the present century. If this hope is not realized we face utter disaster; if it is realized, the world will be far better than at any previous period in the history of man.

Bertrand Russell

Justice has nothing to do with expediency. It has nothing to do with any temporary standard whatever. It is rooted and grounded in the fundamental instincts of humanity.

Woodrow Wilson

It has always seemed to me a sad incongruity the way we represent the figure of Justice. We put a sword in one hand, a pair of scales in the other; then we tie a bandage tightly over her eyes. Blindfolded, she cannot see where to strike; cannot read her own scales, and never knows when they balance. That, ironically enough, is the trouble, with our kind of justice. Neither the love nor the justice of God is blindfolded.

Paul Scherer

If there is no justice, there is no peace.

Bahya ben Asher

Under a government which imprisons any unjustly, the true place for a just man is also a prison.

Henry Thoreau

Justice is the ligament which holds civilized beings and civilized nations together.

Daniel Webster

That some should be rich shows that others may become rich, and hence is just encouragement to industry and enterprise. Let not him who hath no house tear down the house of his neighbor; but rather let him strive diligently to build one for himself, thus, for example, showing confidence that when his own is built, it will stand undisturbed.

Abraham Lincoln

If we do justice to our brother, even though we may not like him, we will come to love him; but if we do injustice to him because we do not love him we shall come to hate him.

John Ruskin

Justice is truth in action.

Benjamin Disraeli

Man's capacity for justice makes democracy possible; but man's inclination to injustice makes democracy necessary.

Reinhold Niebuhr

Justice and power must be brought together, so that whatever is just may be powerful, and whatever is powerful may be just.

Blaise Pascal

We cannot break God's laws—but we can break ourselves against them.

Al Maude Royden

The firm basis of government is justice, not pity.

Woodrow Wilson

---

54. IN PRAISE OF PRAISE

Words of praise, indeed, are almost as necessary to warm a child into a congenial life as acts of kindness and affection. Judicious praise is to children what the sun is to flowers.

Christian Nestell Bovee

Flattery is friendship diseased.

Philo

I like to praise and reward loudly, to blame quietly.

Catherine of Russia

I can live for two months on a good compliment.

Mark Twain

We can help raise our standard by praising the good whenever and wherever we find it. As we praise the good at hand we grow in our ability to find more good.

Lowell Fillmore

Few people are wise enough to prefer useful reproof to treacherous praise.

François Rochefoucauld

If your friend is a help, a joy, an inspiration to you, tell him so.

There are discouraged hearts everywhere just hungry for appreciation and sympathy.

Author Unknown

The deepest principle of human nature is the craving to be appreciated.

William James

Praise makes good men better and bad men worse.

Thomas Fuller

I have yet to find the man, however exalted his station, who did not do better work and put forth greater effort under a spirit of approval than under a spirit of criticism.

Charles Schwab

If you want to praise, praise God; if you want to blame, blame yourself.

Bahya

It is a great mistake for men to give up paying compliments, for when they give up saying what is charming, they give up thinking what is charming.

Oscar Wilde

The mischief of flattery is, not that it persuades any man that he is what he is not, but that it suppresses the influence of honest ambition by raising an opinion that honor may be gained without the toil of merit.

Samuel Johnson

The praise that comes of love does not make us vain, but humble rather.

James M. Barrie

Some of a man's praise may be sung in his presence, all of it in his absence.

Eleazar ben Azariah

Those who are greedy of praise prove that they are poor in merit.

Plutarch

Just as we can dig a channel to control the direction of a stream, we can control the direction of our children's activities through praise and recognition.

Natalie Cole

A habit for all of us to develop would be to look for something to appreciate in everyone we meet. We can all be generous with appreciation. Everyone is grateful for it. It improves every human relationship, it brings new courage to people facing difficulties, and it brings out the best in everyone. So, give appreciation generously whenever you can. You will never regret it.

Carl Holmes

Try praising your wife, even if it does frighten her at first.

Billy Sunday

If you would reap praise you must sow the seeds; gentle words and useful deeds.

Author Unknown

There is an old Jewish legend as to the origin of praise. After God had created mankind, says the legend, He asked the angels what they thought of the world He had made. "Only one thing is lacking," they said. "It is the sound of praise to the Creator." So, the story continues, "God created music, the voice of birds, the whispering wind, the murmuring ocean, and planted melody in the hearts of men."

William T. McElroy

Correction does much, but encouragement does more. Encouragement after censure is as the sun after a shower.

Johann Wolfgang von Goethe

Adverse criticism of one who knows is more flattering than praise of one who is ignorant.

Alfred Stevens

The sweetest of all sounds is praise.

Xenophon

James Stewart tells somewhere of how Napoleon, when an artillery officer at the siege of Toulon, built a battery in such an exposed position that he was told he would never find men to man it. But he had a surer instinct. He set by the side of it a placard: "The Battery of Men without Fear." And it was always manned.

Paul Scherer

There is not a person we employ who does not, like ourselves, desire recognition, praise, gentleness, forbearance, patience.

Henry Ward Beecher

I like not only to be loved, but to be told that I am loved; the realm of silence is large enough beyond the grave.

George Eliot

---

55. THE CURSE OF WAR

To delight in war is a merit in the soldier, a dangerous quality in the captain, and a positive crime in the statesman.

George Santayana

No human precaution can protect a nation from the sacrifices which war levies upon future talent—the undiscovered scientists, the gifted minds, the intellectual and spiritual leaders upon whom each generation must build the hope and promise of the generation to come.

Raymond B. Fosdick

War has proved to have been the proximate cause of the breakdown of every civilization.

Arnold J. Toynbee

For as long a time as we can see into the future, we shall be living between war and peace, between a war that cannot be fought and a peace that cannot be achieved. The great issues which divide the world cannot be decided by a war that could be won, and they cannot be settled by a treaty that can be negotiated. There . . . is the root of the frustration which our people feel. Our world is divided as it has not been since the religious wars of the 17th century and a large part of the globe is in a great upheaval, the like of which has not been known since the end of the Middle Ages. But the power which used to deal with the divisions and conflicts of the past namely, organized war, has become an impossible instrument to use.

Walter Lippmann

Yes; quaint and curious a war is! You shoot a fellow down you'd treat if met where any bar is, or help to half a crown.

Thomas Hardy

A great war leaves the country with three armies—an army of cripples, an army of mourners, and an army of thieves.

German Proverb

I have seen war. I have seen war on land and sea. I have seen blood running from the wounded. I have seen the dead in the mud. I have seen cities destroyed. I have seen two hundred limping, exhausted men come out of the line—the survivors of a regiment of one thousand that went forward forty-eight hours before. I have seen children starving. I have seen the agony of mothers and wives. I hate war.

Franklin D. Roosevelt

One nation cannot defeat another today. That concept died with Hiroshima. War is like fire: you can prevent a fire, or you can try to put it out, but you can't "win" a fire.

General H. H. Arnold

War is no more inevitable than the plague is inevitable. War is no more a part of human nature than the burning of witches is a human act.

Meyer London

The tragedy of war is that it uses man's best to do man's worst.

Harry Emerson Fosdick

Give me the money that has been spent in war and I will clothe every man, woman, and child in an attire of which kings and queens will be proud. I will build a schoolhouse in every valley over the whole earth. I will crown every hillside with a place of worship consecrated to peace.

Charles Sumner

War is dirty business. It plumbs the depths of degradation, yet demands the best that one can give. In the last war, what I did and what I saw do not rest easily on my memory. But in all the filth and stupidities of that experience, I saw courage, fortitude, sacrifice, self-abnegation, generosity—yes, and tenderness, compassion and idealism of a quality that I have not seen since. It is because these qualities become diluted in peacetime that wars return.

Samuel T. Williamson

War, with its tidal waves of destruction, slaughter and grief, is the answer to no human problem, and it is an insult to the intelligence that God gave us that we cannot find other answers.

Francis Pendleton Gaines

Now, in the atomic age, victory has become almost indistinguishable from defeat.

James P. Warburg

I had come to despise and be revolted by war, out of any logical proportion. I couldn't find the Four Freedoms among the dead men.

Ernie Pyle

No society is sound or vigorous enough to sustain death on the staggering scale that wars make inevitable. No one can win a war. There are survivors, but no victors.

Brooks Atkinson

War determines not who is right but who is left.

Sidney Greenberg

War as a useful extension of diplomacy is obsolete. No aggressor can hope to come out a winner, as was made clear in a recent report by a member organization of the Fund for the Republic. "In any future war," the report declares, "the consolation prizes can only be surrender, stalemate, or death." . . . If people can face these facts of life—or death—and still expect to survive, then, says the report, "a broad and significant new habit pattern will have been introduced and accepted, one grotesquely different from any we have known for thousands of years—that of adjusting ourselves to the idea of living in holes. From that time onward it will be simple to adjust ourselves to living in *deeper* holes." And, of course, civilization will cease to have any meaning.

Murray D. Lincoln

War is the concentration of all human crimes. It turns man into a beast of prey.

William Ellery Channing

I have made a pilgrimage to Hiroshima. In the center of the city they have kept the ghostly, twisted ruins of the former exhibition hall and have made it a permanent exhibition of death, idiocy and shame. A wire fence has been erected around the ruin. As it stands, it is to be the central memorial. On a standard outside, designating the mass of horror, is one word only, inscribed in large, bold letters. The word is Peace.

Charles T. Leber

More than an end to war, we want an end to the beginnings of all wars.

Franklin D. Roosevelt

Violence and war never solve problems; they only make them more acute. They create new dilemmas and new paradoxes. Thus World War I was fought by some to make the world safe for democracy; in our time democracy is less safe than ever. Every major war has resulted in more dictatorships and more totalitarianism and has created new seeds of conflict.

Frederick Mayer

Nothing in history has turned out to be more impermanent than military victory.

Harry Emerson Fosdick

Throughout history there has never been an evitable war. The greatest danger of war always lies in the widespread acceptance of its inevitability.

James P. Warburg

The belief in the possibility of a short decisive war appears to be one of the most ancient and dangerous of human illusions.

Robert Lynd

War some day will be abolished by the will of man. This assertion does not in any way invalidate the truth that war is fundamentally caused by impersonal, political, economic and social forces. But it is the destiny of man to master and control such force, even as it is his destiny to harness rivers, chain the lightning and ride the storm. It is human will, operating under social forces, that has abolished slavery, infanticide, duelling, and a score of other social enormities. Why should it not do the same for war?

John Haynes Holmes

The Duke of Wellington knew what war was, and after the battle of Waterloo he wrote that his heart was broken for the loss of his beloved comrades, and that, except a battle lost, there is nothing in the world so melancholy as a battle won.

F. W. Farrar

Enough treasure was spent in the two world wars and will continue to be spent in their aftermath, to bridge every river in the world, to drain every swamp, to irrigate every desert, to fertilize every field, to teach every man his alphabet, and to do all those things in our day which would redeem the world from its terrors and fears of war.

Jonah B. Wise

Since barbarism has its pleasures, it naturally has its apologists. There are panegyrists of war who say that without a periodical bleeding a race decays and loses its manhood. Experience is directly opposed to this shameless assertion. It is war that wastes a nation's wealth, chokes its industries, kills its flower, narrows its sympathies, condemns it to be governed by adventurers, and leaves the puny, deformed and unmanly to breed the next generation.

George Santayana

The victor belongs to the spoils.
F. Scott Fitzgerald

I am sick and tired of war. Its glory is all moonshine. It is only those who have never fired a shot, nor heard the shrieks and cries of the wounded, who cry aloud for blood, more vengeance, more desolation.

William T. Sherman

---

56. PATHWAYS TO PEACE

Peace will never be entirely secure until men everywhere have learned to conquer poverty without sacrificing liberty to security.
Norman Thomas

It is perhaps more difficult to wage peace than war, but it is also eminently more profitable.
Ralph Bunche

The currency with which you pay for peace is made up of manly courage, fearless virility, readiness to serve justice and honor at any cost, and a mind and a heart attuned to sacrifice.
Frank Knox

Genuine peace is not a negative thing. It is not merely the absence of open warfare. Rather it is a positive program having four component parts, no one of which can be ignored. The components are economic cooperation, controlled power to enforce peace, and genuine understanding among peoples.
Milton S. Eisenhower

A fact does not become a truth until people are willing to act upon it; the fact that war is now a losing proposition for everybody will not flower into an effective truth until we are prepared to make as many sacrifices for our children's future peace as for their present comforts.
Sydney J. Harris

Feeding the people of the world is no longer a philanthropic project for the missionaries. There will be no peace in this world, until the worst imbalances around the world are eliminated.
Hans-Bröder Krohn

What mankind wants is not merely the absence of war but real peace. The mere possibility of another world war is a haunting nightmare. You cannot stand indefinitely on the brink of a precipice and pray that the sense of balance will never forsake you or that you may never be pushed unawares into the chasm. It is an ordeal which may of itself produce the fatal loss of equilibrium.
Moshe Sharett

A scientist had a conversation with a cannibal and tried to explain how superior his society was because it had no cannibalism. The cannibal, on the other hand, who had heard a lot about the white man's wars, accepted the fact that cannibalism was bad but wanted to know, "What does the white man do with so much human meat that is being made available in each war?" When the scientist tried to explain to him that they killed people without eating them afterwards, the cannibal was confounded by the absurdity and stupidity of such behavior.

Ernest Dichter

What we now need to discover in the social realm is the moral equivalent of war: something heroic that will speak to men as universally as war does, and yet will be as compatible with their spiritual selves as war has proved itself to be incompatible.

William James

A secure and stable peace is not a goal we can reach all at once and for all time. It is a dynamic state produced by effort and faith, with justice and courage. The struggle is continuous and hard. The prize is never irrevocably ours.

Dean Acheson

If there is righteousness in the heart, there is beauty in the character. If there is beauty in the character, there will be harmony in the home. If there is harmony in the home, there will be order in the nation. When there is order in the nation, there will be peace in the world.

Chinese Proverb

Dr. Robert Oppenheimer, who supervised the creation of the first atomic bomb, appeared before a Congressional Committee. They inquired of him if there was any defense against the weapon.
"Certainly," the great physicist replied.
"And that is—"
Dr. Oppenheimer looked over the hushed, expectant audience and said softly, "Peace."

Author Unknown

The world will never have lasting peace so long as men reserve for war the finest human qualities. Peace, no less than war, requires idealism and self-sacrifice and a righteous and dynamic faith.

John Foster Dulles

Peace is a value which man has always sought: Peace among nations, peace among men, but most of all peace of mind. While man has sought peace external to himself, he may have overlooked the fact that the peace that will influence all living things will be the peace that is first discovered within himself.

Cecil A. Poole

Peace is the soft and holy shadow that virtue casts.

Josh Billings

Peace is not absence of war, it is a virtue, a state of mind, a disposition for benevolence, confidence, justice.

Benedict Spinoza

The "price of peace" can never reach such dimensions as to equal the smallest fraction of war's deadly cost.

Ambassador Abba Eban

Peace is the healing and elevating influence of the world.

Woodrow Wilson

It is when we all play safe that we create a world of utmost insecurity.

Dag Hammarskjold

The struggle for peace has become in this nuclear age the struggle for human survival.

G. L. Mehta

Men must be able to find in peacetime pursuits the same satisfaction, the same opportunity for sacrifice, the same outlet for idealistic emotion as, till now, only war has been able to provide them.

James Bryan

Peace cannot be kept by force. It can only be achieved by understanding.

Albert Einstein

Peace is the evening star of the soul, as virtue is its sun; and the two are never far apart.

Caleb C. Colton

A Chinese sage was asked by a farmer when will the world truly know peace. The sage said, follow me. And he brought the man to the side of a brook and the Chinese sage put his hand on the head of the farmer and pressed it into the water until finally the farmer came up gasping for air, for life itself. And the sage said: there is your answer—when man wants peace, when he wants peace as much as you have just wanted air, when he comes up gasping for peace, when he wants to give everything in himself to have peace, as you have

given everything to have air, he will have peace.

Author Unknown

Nothing can bring you peace but yourself; nothing can bring you peace but the triumph of principles.

Ralph Waldo Emerson

Peace is positive, and it has to be waged with all our thought, energy, and courage and with the conviction that war is not inevitable.

Dean Acheson

The grim fact is that we prepare for war like precocious giants and for peace like retarded pygmies.

Lester B. Pearson

Peace is not the absence of conflict from life, but the ability to cope with it.

Author Unknown

It is safe to say that no farmer ever got a corn crop by simply reassuring himself periodically, "I'm not going to let my land grow up to weeds!" Similarly, the people of the world can never hope to reap the benefits of permanent peace by reassuring themselves daily, "We will have no more war." Just as there is no corn crop without planting and cultivation, so there will be no growth toward peace without the planting and cultivation of attitudes that breed peace.

Helen L. Toner

Monopoly is as injurious to religions as to trades; they are only strong and energetic by free competition.

Heinrich Heine

War is an invention of the human mind. The human mind can invent peace.

Norman Cousins

The real problem is in the hearts and minds of men. It is not a problem of physics but of ethics. It is easier to denature plutonium than to denature the evil spirit of man.

Albert Einstein

Who lifts a hand against another, even if he does not strike him, is called a wicked man.

The Talmud

THE ART OF LIVING WITH

OUR HERITAGE

57. ART AND BEAUTY

In every man's heart there is a secret nerve that answers to the vibrations of beauty.

Christopher Morley

Beauty and grace command the world.

Park Benjamin

Fine art is that in which the hand, the head and the heart go together.

John Ruskin

The Beautiful is as useful as the useful.

Victor Hugo

The crystal-like beauty of a newly opened rose bathed in early morning dew can inspire a song; a lovely countryside at sunset can suggest a sonnet. The creative work of others, a painting, a poem, a piece of sculpture, can fill the mind with the glow of inspiration and imagination. There are many sources of inspiration and each is a virtual storehouse of ideas. But nature with an infinite beauty of forms, color and textures is one of the greatest sources.

Mary E. Thompson

There is beauty in the forest
When the trees are green and fair,
There is beauty in the meadow
When wild flowers scent the air.

There is beauty in the sunlight
And the soft blue beams above.
Oh, the world is full of beauty
When the heart is full of love.

Author Unknown

Never lose an opportunity of seeing anything that is beautiful; for beauty is God's handwriting—a wayside sacrament. Welcome it in every fair face, in every fair sky, in every fair flower, and thank God for it as a cup of blessing.

Ralph Waldo Emerson

Art is nothing less than a way of making joys perpetual.

Rebecca West

If I were called upon to choose between beauty and truth, I should not hesitate; I should hold to beauty, being confident that it bears within it a truth both higher and deeper than truth itself. I will go so far as to say there is nothing true in the world save beauty.

Anatole France

Art, if it is to be reckoned as one of the great values of life, must teach men humility, tolerance, wisdom and magnanimity. The value of art is not beauty, but right action.

W. Somerset Maugham

There is only one kind of beauty that can transcend time, and many women possess it. It is, of course, beauty of the spirit that lights the eyes and transforms even a plain woman into a beautiful one. Women with wit, charm and warmth, who are interested in others and forget themselves, and who accept each stage of life gracefully are the lasting beauties of this world—and the happiest.

Deirdre Budge

Art is a veritable "fountain of youth." The ancients had a saying, "Those whom the gods love, die young." I would interpret that saying to mean not that those favored by the gods die young in years, but that by the grace of the gods they remain young to their dying day, however long that be deferred. I venture to question whether there is any tonic as stimulating, any gland-transplantation as rejuvenating, as is the quickening of the blood, the stirring of the inner, deeper self, which the powerful medicine of art can bring about. Those who love art and are truly susceptible to its spell, do die young

in the sense that they remain young to their dying day.

Otto H. Kahn

The universe is to be valued because there is truth in it and beauty in it; and we live to discover the truth and the beauty no less than to do what is right. Indeed, we cannot attain to that state of mind in which we shall naturally do what is right unless we are aware of the truth and the beauty of the universe.

A. Clutton-Brock

Beauty is power; a smile is its sword.

Charles Reade

Every April God rewrites the Book of Genesis.

Austin O'Malley

Beautiful young people are accidents of nature. But beautiful old people are works of art.

Marjorie Barstow Breenbie

Religion without art has no fruit, and art without religion has no roots.

Trilochan Singh

Nature is a revelation of God; Art a revelation of man.

Henry Wadsworth Longfellow

Beauty is a form of genius—is higher, indeed, than genius, as it needs no explanation.

Oscar Wilde

A work of art is an experience, a soul message if you like. It is educational, if you insist, but it educates only the psyche which is ripe and ready to submit to its spell. It is never explicit; it preaches, but only in symbolic terms.

Lawrence Durrell

When, at 16, I was vain because someone praised me, my father said: "They are only praising your youth. You can take no credit for beauty at 16. But if you are beautiful at 60, it will be your own soul's doing. Then you may be proud of it and be loved for it."

Marie Stopes

Every artist dips his brush in his own soul, and paints his own nature into his pictures.

Henry Ward Beecher

Beauty is the first present Nature gives to women, and the first it takes away.

George B. Mere

Let us not judge life by the number of its breaths taken, but by the number of times the breath is held, or lost, either under a deep emotion, caused by love, or when we stand before an object of interest and beauty.

W. H. Davies

We are living in a world of beauty but how few of us open our eyes to see it! What a different place this would be if our senses were trained to see and hear! We are the heirs of wonderful treasures from the past: treasures of literature and of the arts. They are ours for the asking—all our own to have and to enjoy, if only we desire them enough.

Lorado Taft

Art is man added to nature.

Francis Bacon

All that is good in art is the expression of one soul talking to another, and is precious according to the greatness of the soul that utters it.

John Ruskin

Beauty is something wonderful and strange that the artist fashions out of the chaos of the world in the torment of his soul.

W. Somerset Maugham

Next to beauty is the power of appreciating it.

Margaret Fuller

A thing of beauty is a joy forever:
Its loveliness increases; it will never
Pass into nothingness; but still will keep
A bower quiet for us, and a sleep
Full of sweet dreams, and health, and quiet breathing.

John Keats

In all ranks of life the human heart yearns for the beautiful; and the beautiful things that God makes are his gift to all alike.

Harriet Beecher Stowe

Art, as far as it has the ability, follows nature, as a pupil imitates his master, so that art must be, as it were, a descendant of God.

Dante Alighieri

Beauty raises our spirits, temporarily takes us out of ourselves, so to speak, and makes us feel closer to God.

Edith Wilkinson

Science, at the very most, can only give to our existence comfort, convenience, and longevity, but music, literature, and art, at the very least, give life its charm, romance and immortality.

Ely Slotkin

There is no cosmetic for beauty like happiness.

Countess of Blessington

Beauty does not lie in the face. It lies in the harmony between man and his industry. Beauty is expression. When I paint a mother I try to render her beautiful by the mere look she gives her child.

Millet

---

58. MUSIC HATH CHARMS

Music was a thing of the soul—a rose-lipped shell that murmured of the eternal sea—a strange bird singing the songs of another shore.

J. C. Holland

Music raises in the mind of the hearer great conceptions: it strengthens and advances praise into rapture.

Joseph Addison

Music is well said to be the speech of angels.

Thomas Carlyle

After silence that which comes nearest to expressing the inexpressible is music.

Aldous Huxley

There's music in the sighing of a reed;
There's music in the gushing of a rill;
There's music in all things, if men had ears:
Their earth is but an echo of the spheres.

Lord Byron

We love music for the buried hopes, the garnered memories, the tender feelings it can summon at a touch.

Letitia Elizabeth Landon

Great music is a flame that lights the tapers of man's noblest thoughts and drives shadows from the corridors of his soul.

Douglas Meador

Music is the only language in which you cannot say a mean or sarcastic thing.

John Erskine

Music is the heartbeat of the universe. It reaches into the outer ramparts of eternity where time and space are nonexistent; it touches the stars and is reflected in the beauty of the galaxy. It is exemplified in the mathematical precision found in the largest star and the tiniest molecule. Music is emotional. It touches the heart and creates a response within the listener without his being aware of the technique.

John Rossel

Serious nations, all nations, that can still listen to the mandate of nature have prized song and music as the highest; as a vehicle for worship, prophecy, and for whatsoever within them was divine.

Thomas Carlyle

God sent his singers on earth
With songs of gladness and mirth

That they might touch the hearts of men
And bring them back to Heaven again.
Henry Wadsworth Longfellow

There is something marvelous in music. I might say it is, in itself a marvel. Its position is somewhat between the region of thought and that of phenomena; a glimmering medium between mind and matter, related to both and yet differing from either. Spiritual, and yet requiring rhythm; material, and yet independent of space.
Heinrich Heine

How many of us ever stop to think
Of music as a wondrous magic link
   with God; taking sometimes the place of prayer,
When words have failed us 'neath the weight of care.
Music, that knows no country, race or creed,
But gives to each according to his need.
Author Unknown

Music has been called the speech of angels; I will go further, and call it the speech of God Himself.
Charles Kingsley

When people hear good music, it makes them homesick for something they never had, and never will have.
E. W. Howe

Music is the medicine of the breaking heart.
Alfred William Hunt

Music is a prophecy of what life is to be; the rainbow of promise translated out of seeing into hearing.
Lydia M. Child

It can be said without qualification that music expresses all the various shadings of life's moods and the greatest portion of life's experiences. There is perhaps no more adequate tool than music to relate mankind to life.
Jeannette Kirk

If I were to begin life again, I would devote it to music. It is the only cheap and unpunished rapture upon earth.
Sidney Smith

Good music has no politics. It is always exportable and crosses borders with the greatest ease. It is a passport which secures a warm welcome for the composer and for the performer. It brushes away the artificial hostility created by false propaganda, and presents people directly, one to another, in one of the most essential of human activities.
J. F. Leddy

Music is for the betterment and enrichment of the individual, just as education and reading are. When people come together to play music as they do to play bridge, civilization will have taken its longest stride forward since the beginning of time. Music is something to live with always, and children should be taught to regard it as a close and inalienable friend.
Jascha Heifetz

Where words fail, music speaks.
Hans Andersen

There are halls in the heavens above that open but to the voice of song.
The Zohar

Music is the shorthand of emotion. Emotions which let themselves be described in words with such difficulty, are directly conveyed to man in music, and in that is its power and significance.

Leo Tolstoy

The best music should be played as the best men and women should be dressed—neither so well nor so ill as to attract attention to itself.

Samuel Butler

Singing is the highest expression of music because it is the most direct expression of the emotions of the soul.

Clara Kathleen Rogers

Music moves us, and we know not why; we feel the tears, but cannot trace their source. Is it the language of some other state, born of its memory? For what can wake the soul's strong instinct of another world like music?

Letitia Elizabeth Landon

Yea, music is the prophet's art; among the gifts that God hath sent, one of the most magnificent.

Henry Wadsworth Longfellow

59. TREASURES IN BOOKS

There are books which take rank in our life with parents and lovers and passionate experience.

Ralph Waldo Emerson

When we are collecting books, we are collecting happiness.

Vincent Starrett

Good books are good friends, the wisest and wittiest nearly all of us can hope to meet, and I never put one down without a feeling of quiet exultation that I have been lifted out of myself because of it: more informed, more perceptive and understanding, more articulate, and thus able to contribute more to my family, friends and society.

George Waller

Be as careful of the books you read as the company you keep. Your habits and character will be as much influenced by the former as by the latter.

Paxton Hood

Books are no substitute for living, but they can add immeasurably to its richness. When life is absorbing, books can enhance our sense of its significance. When life is difficult, they can give us momentary release from trouble or a new insight into our problems, or provide the hours of refreshment we need.

May Hill Arbuthnot

Make your books your companions; let your cases and shelves be your pleasure-grounds and orchards. Bask in their paradise, gather their fruit, pluck their roses, take their spices.

Judah Ibn Tibbon

A great library contains the diary of the human race.

George Dawson

Without books, God is silent, justice dormant, natural science at a standstill, philosophy lame, letters dumb, and all things in Cimerian darkness.

Thomas Bartholin

Reading is a habit. Once you've got the habit you never lose it. But you must somehow be exposed to reading early enough in life to have it become part of your daily routine, like washing your face or breathing.

Richard L. Tobin

Books are masters who instruct us without rods, without words or anger, without bread or money. If you approach them, they are not asleep; if you seek them, they do not hide; if you blunder, they do not scold; if you are ignorant, they do not laugh at you.

Richard de Bury

For books are more than books, they are the life,
The very heart and core of ages past.
The reason why men lived, and worked, and died,
The essence and quintessence of their lives.

Amy Lowell

Who gives a good book gives more than cloth, paper, and ink . . . more than leather, parchment and words. He reveals a foreword of his thoughts, a dedication of his friendship, a page of his presence, a chapter of himself, and an index of his love.

William A. Ward

A book may be as great a thing as a battle.

Benjamin Disraeli

It is doubtful whether a writer can give anything to a reader that is not already there in some measure. All he can do is to make him conscious or more deeply conscious of what he already possesses by stimulating apprehension, by smoothing or ruffling the surface of consciousness, and, in rare instances, by striking below the surface and opening the way to vision or revelation. Books at their best and in their most favorable moments of reception revitalize. The end of reading is not more books but more life.

Holbrook Jackson

Books are lighthouses erected in the great sea of time.

Edwin Percy Whipple

When the father of a good friend of mine was told that he would have to live on one floor of the house because of a heart condition, he said, "If the library is on the floor where I am supposed to live, life won't close in on me. I'll have books."

Laura Zirbes

Books are a series of windows opening on the strangeness of the world—the physical world, which we are finding more intricate than we ever dreamed; the world of the emotions, which the novelist knows is of equal intricacy; and the world of the spirit, where all of us need as much light as we can get.

Marchette Chute

Culture is knowing the best that has been thought and said in the world; in other words, culture means reading, not idle and casual reading, but reading that is controlled and directed by a definite purpose.

Albert Jay Nock

An empty mind is little different from an empty house. It, too, soon decays. Just as muscles die when not used, so the brain is weakened through idleness. It needs relaxation and entertainment. But it also needs exercise. It needs and must have work, or it will wither. It must be lived in.

Alden C. Palmer

Without the love of books the richest man is poor; but endowed with this treasure of treasures, the poorest man is rich. He has wealth which no power can diminish; riches which are always increasing; possessions which the more he scatters the more they accumulate; friends which never desert him and pleasures which never die.

Leon Gutterman

We live in an era when books have become the beginning and the end of our ability to compete successfully for national and personal fulfillment. We need to compare, not only the number of miles our missiles can cover compared to Russia's, but also the number of book stores and libraries that exist in Moscow and New York and, most important of all, the number of people who read books in both cities.

Ernest Dichter

The books that help you most, are those which make you think the most.—The hardest way of learning is that of easy reading; but a great book that comes from a great thinker is a ship of thought, deep freighted with truth and beauty.

Theodore Parker

The world of books is the most remarkable creation of man. Nothing else that he builds ever lasts. Monuments fall; nations perish; civilizations grow old and die out; and, after an era of darkness, new races build on others. But in the world of books are volumes that have seen this happen again and again, and yet live on, still young, still as fresh as the day they were written, still telling men's hearts of the hearts of men centuries dead.

Clarence Day

Without good reading, human growth is slow at best. Without human growth, no civilization can long survive.

Roderick L. Haig-Brown

In a world divided between those forced to live under Communism and those who live in freedom, the value of reading for us becomes all the more urgent. Reading is another "freedom"—a freedom which people living under Communism cannot enjoy. This is because the freedom to read carries with it the freedom to discover new ideas and to question old ones. No totalitarian dictator is safe in such a climate.

Derick D. Schermerhorn

Never read any book that is not a year old.

Ralph Waldo Emerson

Every man who knows how to read has it in his power to magnify himself, to multiply the ways in which he exists, to make his life full, significant and interesting.

Aldous Huxley

Books are a finer world within the world.

Alexander Smith

You open doors when you open books. Doors that swing wide to unlimited horizons of knowledge, wisdom, and inspiration that will enlarge the dimensions of life.

Wilferd A. Peterson

The thoughtful reader enters into the community of learners around the world who have discovered and cherished the ideas behind human endeavor through the centuries. He has moments of conversation with the good and the great of this hour; he becomes a citizen of the country of the mind. He enters the long vistas of the past and here joins the fellowship of the saints.

Paul & Mary Bechtel

It is in the home that roots go deep, nurtured by understanding and love; by sharing pleasures and responsibilities. It is here that common backgrounds are built, common experiences shared. Wings grow there, too, and one of the surest ways for children to possess them is to discover early, children and parents together, the deep and lasting satisfactions that books and reading give.

Ruth Gagliardo

A truly good book teaches me better than to read it. I must soon lay it down and commence living on its hint . . . What I began by reading I must finish by acting.

Henry Thoreau

Of all the inanimate objects, of all men's creations, books are the nearest to us, for they contain our very thoughts, our ambitions, our indignations, our illusions, our fidelity to truth, and our persistent leaning toward error. But most of all they resemble us in their precarious hold on life.

Joseph Conrad

All good books are alike in that they are truer than if they really happened and after you are finished reading one you will feel that all that happened to you and afterwards it all belongs to you: the good and the bad, the ecstasy, the remorse and sorrow, the people and the places and how the weather was.

Ernest Hemingway

Books are the key to man's culture. If they vanished overnight and could not be replaced, our culture and civilization would disappear within two generations. The most significant thing man has ever learned to do with his hands, since he stopped walking on all fours or swinging from trees, is to use them to write books and to open their pages in order to read them.

Richard Powell

A house without books is like a room without windows. No man has a right to bring up his children without surrounding them with books, if he has the means to buy them. It is a wrong to his family. Children learn to read by being in the presence of books. The love of knowledge comes with reading and grows upon it. And the love of knowledge in a young mind is almost a warrant against the inferior excitement of passions and vices.

Horace Mann

Best reading for a man is the life of a good man; next best is the life of a bad one.

A. J. Whitehead

We all know that books burn—yet we have the greater knowledge that books cannot be killed by fire. People die, but books never die. No man and no force can abolish memory. In this war, we know, books are weapons.

Franklin D. Roosevelt

Reading books in one's youth is like looking at the moon through a crevice; reading books in middle age is like looking at the moon in one's courtyard; and reading books in old age is like looking at the moon on an open terrace. This is because the depth of benefits of reading varies in proportion to the depth of one's own experience.

Chang Ch'ao

Books are the treasured wealth of the world, the fit inheritance of generations and nations.

Henry David Thoreau

Reading should be for children an integral part of life, like eating and loving and playing. An early familiarity with books unconsciously introduces the child to a fundamental, liberating truth: that the largest part of the universe of space and time can never be apprehended by direct firsthand experience.

The child who has never really understood this truth remains, in the most literal sense, mentally unbalanced.

Clifton Fadiman

A book can give greater riches than any other form of recreation but it cannot provide the last answers. They must be found in the loneliness of a man's own mind. Books can help a man be ready for those moments. But neither books nor teachers can provide the answers.

Carl Sandburg

If all the crowns of Europe were placed at my disposal on condition that I should abandon my books and studies, I should spurn the crowns away and stand by the books.

Francis de S. Fenelon

Ancient books of wisdom are to the unripe mind that which the mother's milk is to the nurseling.

Russell Maguire

Balzac, a French writer, after spending an evening with friends who talked about everything in general and nothing of significance, went to his study when he got home, took off his coat, rubbed his hands, and regarding the books of the masters on the shelves, cried, "Now for some real people!"

Harold A. Bosley

Truly each new book is as a ship that bears us away from the fixity of our limitations into the movement and splendor of life's infinite ocean.

Helen Keller

Books are the food of youth, the delight of old age; the ornament of prosperity, the refuge and comfort of adversity; a delight at home, and no hindrance abroad; companions by night, in traveling, in the country.

Cicero

Nothing in this life, after health and virtue, is more estimable than knowledge, nor is there anything so easily attained, or so cheaply purchased, the labor, only sitting still, and the expense but time, which, if we do not spend, we cannot save.

Lawrence Sterne

When others fail him, the wise man looks
To the sure companionship of books.

Andrew Lang

When we are collecting books, we are collecting happiness.

Vincent Starrett

To destroy the Western tradition of independent thought it is not necessary to burn the books. All we have to do is to leave them unread for a couple of generations.

Robert M. Hutchins

Book love, my friends, is your pass to the greatest, the purest, and the most perfect pleasure that God has prepared for His creatures. It lasts when all other pleasures fade. It will support you when all other recreations are gone. It will last you until your death. It will make your hours pleasant to you as long as you live.

Anthony Trollope

When a book raises your spirit, and inspires you with noble and manly thoughts, seek for no other test of its excellence. It is good and made by a good workman.

La Bruyere

The greatest tribute that a writer can earn is not that we keep our eye fast upon his page, forgetting all else, but that sometimes, without knowing that we have ceased to read, we allow his book to rest, and look out over and beyond it with newly opened eyes.

Charles Morgan

Who without books, essays to learn,
Draws water in a leaky urn.

Austin Dobson

The art of reading is not a virtue or a duty, but a faculty which at no time has won the indulgence of more than a small if satisfied following; but it has the virtue of being one of the few entirely disinterested occupations. When we read solely to please, or in other words to express ourselves, we rob no one, hurt no one, compete with no one, and expect nothing in return but the pleasure of the experience.

Holbrook Jackson

Reading good books is like having a conversation with the highly worthy persons of the past who wrote them; indeed, it is like having a prepared conversation in which those persons disclose to us only their best thinking.

René Descartes

We should accustom the mind to keep the best company by introducing it only to the best books.

Sydney Smith

The proper study of mankind is books.

Aldous Huxley

There are four kinds of readers. The first is like the hourglass; their readings being as the sand, it runs in and runs out, and leaves not a vestige behind. The second is like a sponge, which imbibes everything and returns it in nearly the same state, only a little dirtier. The third is like a jellybag, allowing all that is pure to pass away, and retaining only the refuse and the dregs. And the fourth is like the slaves in the diamond mines of

Golconda who, casting aside all that is worthless, retain only the pure gems.

Samuel Taylor Coleridge

I am in every sense of that abused word, a reader. And by "every sense" I mean you to understand that I read, not with the eyes alone, but with the imagination, the heart, the nerves, the blood stream.

Ellen Glasgow

The best teacher is not life, but the crystallized and distilled experience of the most sensitive, and most observant of our human beings, and this experience you will find preserved in our great books and nowhere else.

Nathan M. Pusey

Our civilization is the sum of the knowledge and memories accumulated by the generations that have gone before us. We can only partake of it if we are able to make contact with ideas of these past generations. The only way to do this—and so become a "cultured" person—is by reading.

André Maurois

The wise man reads both books and life itself.

Lin Yutang

There is no reader so parochial as the one who reads none but this morning's books. Books are not rolls, to be devoured only when hot and fresh. A good book retains its interior heat and will warm a generation yet unborn.

Clifton Fadiman

The man who does not read good books has no advantage over the man who can't read them.

Mark Twain

Books are read by people who read to find themselves—and who find in books not something bigger than life but something that makes their own lives bigger.

John Nazzaro

It is those books which a man possesses but does not read which constitutes the most suspicious evidence against him.

Victor Hugo

In an age of the inconsequential and frivolous, reading fills our minds with the consequential. Reading involves stewardship of a mind, that was created in the divine image, to think great thoughts as well as to notice the small sparrow. Reading stretches the mind.

Joe Bayly

Printers' ink has been running a race against gunpowder these many, many years. Ink is handicapped, in a way, because you can blow up a man with gunpowder in half a second, while it may take twenty years to blow him up with a book. But the gunpowder destroys itself along with its victim, while a book can keep on exploding for centuries.

Christopher Morley

We should be as careful of the books we read, as of the company we keep. The dead very often have more power than the living.

Tryon Edwards

Literature is my Utopia. Here I am not disfranchised. No barrier of the senses shuts me out from the sweet, gracious discourse of my book-friends. They talk to me without embarrassment or awkwardness.

Helen Keller

'Tis the good reader that makes the good book; in every book he finds passages which seem confidences or asides hidden from all else and unmistakably meant for his ear; the profit of books is according to the sensibility of the reader; the profoundest thought or passion sleeps as in a mind until it is discovered by an equal mind and heart.

Ralph Waldo Emerson

A room without books is a body without a soul.

Cicero

The first time I read an excellent book, it is to me just as if I had gained a new friend. When I read over a book I have perused before, it resembles the meeting with an old one.

Oliver Goldsmith

Reading affords the opportunity to everyone—the poor, the rich, the humble, the great—to spend as many hours as he wishes in the company of the noblest men and women that the world has ever known.

David O. McKay

Read the best books first, or you may not have a chance to read them at all.

Henry David Thoreau

The best test of a nation's culture remains what it has always been since the days of Gutenberg: Its attitude towards books.

Allen Nevins

Except a living man there is nothing more wonderful than a book! a message to us from the dead—from human souls we never saw, who lived, perhaps thousands of miles away. And yet these, in those little sheets of paper, speak to us, arouse us, terrify us, teach us, comfort us, open their hearts to us as brothers.

Charles Kingsley

The best books are those which best teach men how to live.

Israel Abrahams

The true equalizers in the world are books; the only treasure house open to all comers is a library; the only wealth which will not decay is knowledge. To live in this equality, to share in these treasures, to possess this wealth, and to secure this jewel may be the happy lot of everyone. All that is needed for the acquisition of these inestimable treasures is—the love of books.

Leon Gutterman

---

60. THE BOOK OF BOOKS

Unless we form the habit of going to the Bible in bright moments as well as in trouble, we cannot fully respond to its consolations, because we lack equilibrium between light and darkness.

Helen Keller

The Bible has been the Magna Charta of the poor and oppressed. The human race is not in a position to dispense with it.

Thomas Henry Huxley

The Sword and the Book came from Heaven wrapped together, and the Holy One said: "Keep what is written in this Book, or be delivered to the sword."

The Midrash

We must not forget that the Sun of Homer, to use Schiller's well-known phrase, smiles only upon the fortunate few who enjoy life's eternal graces, whereas the Sun of the Bible penetrates into the proudest palaces and the humblest shanties; that the Sun of Homer smiles, spreading a bewitchingly beautiful glimmer over the surface of life, whereas the Sun of the Bible radiates warmth and strength, and has called into being a system of morality, which has become the cornerstone of human civilization.

Israel Friedlander

Set the Bible beside any of the truly great books produced by the genius of man, and see how they are diminished in stature. The Bible shows no concern with literary form, with verbal beauty, yet its absolute sublimity rings through all its pages. Its lines are so monumental and at the same time so simple that whoever tries to compete with them produces either a commentary or a caricature. It is a work we do not know how to assess. The plummet line of scholarship cannot probe its depth nor will critical analysis ever grasp its essence. Other books you can estimate, you can measure, compare; the Bible you can only extol. Its insights surpass our standards. There is nothing greater.

Abraham J. Heschel

If there is anything in my thoughts or style to commend, the credit is due to my parents for instilling in me an early love of the Scriptures. If we abide by the principles taught in the Bible, our country will go on prospering; but if we and our posterity neglect its instructions and authority, no man can tell how sudden a catastrophe may overwhelm us and bury all our glory in profound obscurity.

Daniel Webster

To my early knowledge of the Bible I owe the best part of my taste in literature, and the most precious, and on the whole, the one essential part of my education.

John Ruskin

The Bible is the sheet-anchor of our liberties.

Ulysses S. Grant

In all my perplexities and distresses, the Bible has never failed to give me light and strength.

Robert E. Lee

We search the world for truth. We cull
The good, the true, the beautiful,
From graven stone and written scroll,
And all old flower-fields of the soul;
And, weary seekers of the best,
We come back laden from our quest,
To find that all the sages said
Is in the Book our mothers read.

John Greenleaf Whittier

I know the Bible is inspired because it finds me at a greater depth of my being than any other book.

Samuel Taylor Coleridge

Nobody ever outgrows Scripture; the book widens and deepens with our years.

Charles Haddon Spurgeon

It is a plain old Book, modest as nature itself, and as simple, too; a book of an unpretending workday appearance, like the sun that warms or the bread that nourishes us. And the name of this book is simply—the Bible.

Heinrich Heine

So great is my veneration for the Bible that the earlier my children begin to read it the more confident will be my hope that they will prove useful citizens of their country and respectable members of society. I have for many years made it a practice to read through the Bible once every year.

John Quincy Adams

Most people are bothered by those passages of Scripture they do not understand, but. . . . the passages that bother me are those I do understand.

Mark Twain

The Bible is a book of faith, and a book of doctrine, and a book of morals, and a book of religion, of special revelation from God; but it is also a book which teaches man his own individual responsibility, his own dignity, and his equality with his fellow man.

Daniel Webster

Scholars may quote Plato in their studies, but the hearts of millions will quote the Bible at their daily toil, and draw strength from its inspiration, as the meadows draw it from the brook.

Moncure Daniel Conway

You will find the eternal verities in the eternal Book—and only there. The Bible is the record of God's dealings with men, humble men for the most part, men with problems that kept them awake nights, men with doubts that ate into their hearts. The Bible shows what happens when God touches a man, a single individual.

Daniel A. Poling

That book, sir, is the rock on which our republic rests.

Andrew Jackson

The Book of Psalms contains the whole music of the heart of man, swept by the hand of his Maker. In it are gathered the lyrical burst of his tenderness, the moan of his penitence, the pathos of his sorrow, the triumph of his victory, the despair of his defeat, the firmness of his confidence, the rapture of his assured hope.

Rowland E. Prothero

The Bible is worth all other books which have ever been printed.

Patrick Henry

I thoroughly believe in a university education for both men and women; but I believe a knowledge of the Bible without a college course is more valuable than a college course without the Bible. For in the Bible we have profound thought beautifully expressed; we have the nature of boys and girls, of men and women, more accurately charted than in the works of any modern novelist or playwright. You can learn more about human nature by reading the Bible than by living in New York City.

William Lyon Phelps

Born in the East and clothed in Oriental form and imagery, the Bible walks the ways of all the world with familiar feet and enters land after land to find its own everywhere. It has learned to speak in hundreds of languages to the heart of man. Children listen to its stories with wonder and delight, and wise men ponder them as parables of life.

Henry Van Dyke

The Bible, the great medicine chest of humanity.

Heinrich Heine

The Bible is the truest utterance that ever came by alphabetic letters from the soul of man, through which, as through a window divinely opened, all men can look into the stillness of eternity, and discern in glimpses their far-distant, long-forgotten home.

Thomas Carlyle

A people's entry into universal history is marked by the moment at which it makes the Bible its own in a translation.

Franz Rosenzweig

It is impossible to enslave mentally or socially a Bible-reading people. The principles of the Bible are the ground-work of human freedom.

Horace Greeley

From century to century, even unto this day, through the fairest regions of civilization, the Bible dominates existence. Its vision of life moulds states and societies. Its Psalms are more popular in every country than the poems of the nation's own poets. Besides this one book with its infinite editions, all other literatures seem "trifles light as air."

Israel Zangwill

England has two books: one which she made; the other which made her—Shakespeare and the Bible.

Victor Hugo

More people praise the Bible than read it, more read it than understand it, and more understand it than follow it.

Samuel Sandmel

---

61. THE LIGHT OF LEARNING

Education is the knowledge of how to use the whole of oneself. Many men use but one or two faculties out of the score with which they are endowed. A man is educated who knows how to make a tool of every faculty— how to open it, how to keep it sharp, and how to apply it to all practical purposes.

Henry Ward Beecher

An educated man is one who loves knowledge and will accept no substitutes and whose life is made meaningful through the never-ending process of the cultivation of his total intellectual resources.

Sterling M. McMurrin

Education is the leading of human souls to what is best, and making what is best out of them; and these two objects are always attainable together and by the same means; the training which makes men happiest in themselves also makes them most servicable to others.

John Ruskin

To be self-sustaining, a people has to attend to its economy. To be self-renewing it has to attend to the education of its youth.

Mordecai M. Kaplan

The old stereotype of schooling that assumed that you "mastered a subject" is now obsolete. You can, hypothetically, learn all of physics up until yesterday and will be lagging behind by tomorrow. Today we must conceive of the educated person, almost exclusively, as the one who comes out of school eager and able to go on teaching himself.

M. L. Story

Education is both a personal interest and a national asset. For education enlarges life—not only for each of us as a person, but for all of us as a nation.

Marion B. Folsom

Say not, when I have leisure I will study; you may not have leisure.

The Mishnah

Education makes a people easy to lead, but difficult to drive; easy to govern, but impossible to enslave.

Lord Brougham

Old age, to the unlearned, is winter; to the learned, it is harvest time.

Yiddish Folk Saying

In true education, anything that comes to our hand is as good as a book: the prank of a page-boy, the blunder of a servant, a bit of table-talk—they are all part of the curriculum.

Michel de Montaigne

The result of the educative process is capacity for further education.

John Dewey

Reading serves for delight, for ornament, for ability. The crafty condemn it; the simple admire it; the wise use it.

Francis Bacon

The great difficulty in education is to get experience out of ideas.

George Santayana

Learning is an ornament in prosperity, a refuge in adversity, and a provision in old age.

Aristotle

If, almost on the day of their landings, our ancestors founded schools and endowed colleges, what obligations do not rest upon us, living under circumstances so much favorable, both for providing and for using the means of education?

Daniel Webster

Education consists in being afraid at the right time.

Angelo Patri

It is hard for an empty sack to stand upright.

Benjamin Franklin

Virtue is an angel, but she is a blind one, and must ask of Knowledge to show her the pathway that leads to her goal.

Horace Mann

All who have meditated on the art of governing mankind have been convinced that the fate of empires depends on the education of youth.

Aristotle

A little learning is a dangerous thing;
Drink deep or taste not the Pierian spring;
There shallow draughts intoxicate the brain,
And drinking largely sobers us again.

Alexander Pope

We now provide free tuition, board and laundry for feeble-minded and delinquent young people. Would it not be wise to extend a similar opportunity to young people with first-rate minds?

Goodwin Watson

Wear your learning like your watch, in a private pocket; and do not pull it out, and strike it, merely to show that you have one.

Lord Chesterfield

Without the humanities science is merely a conglomerate of deadly cold facts; and without God the humanities are merely an assemblage of arid and cultural information. It is God, or the recognition of an everlasting ethical principle, that can give education a face, and give this face the view of a better tomorrow.

Dagobert D. Runes

Learning is the heart of life— the mystical power that turns a word into a sign, a look into a smile, a house into a home, and a people into a civilization.

Eugene P. Bertin

Education is that which remains, when one has forgotten everything he learned in school.

Albert Einstein

'Tis education forms the common mind;
Just as the twig is bent the tree's inclined.

Alexander Pope

Culture is the power which makes a man capable of appreciating the life around him, and the power of making that life worth appreciating.

Douglas Malloch

Education is leading human souls to what is best, and no crime can destroy, no enemy can alienate, no despotism can enslave. At home a friend, abroad an introduction, in solitude a solace, and in society an ornament. It chastens vice, it guides virtue, it gives at once grace and government to genius. Without it, what is man? A splendid slave, a reasoning savage.

Joseph Addison

To destroy the Western tradition of independent thought it is not necessary to burn the books. All we have to do is leave them unread for a couple of generations.

Robert M. Hutchins

At the Portieres of that silent Faubourg St. Germain, there is but brief question, "Do you deserve to enter? Pass. Do you ask to be the companion of nobles? Make yourself noble, and you shall be. Do you long for the conversation of the wise? Learn to understand it, and you shall hear it. But on other terms?—no. If you will not rise to us, we cannot stoop to you."

John Ruskin

It is in knowledge as in swimming; he who flounders and splashes on the surface, makes more noise, and attracts more attention than the pearl-diver who quietly dives in quest of treasures to the bottom.

Washington Irving

As some insects are said to derive their colour from the leaf upon which they feed, so do the minds of men assume their hue from the studies which they select for it.

Lady Marguerite Blessington

I learned much from my teachers, more from my colleagues, and most from my pupils.

Judah HaNasi

An educated man is one who can entertain a new idea, entertain another person and entertain himself.

Sydney Herbert Wood

If you do not want to bear the light burden of education, you will have to bear the heavy burden of ignorance.

Moses Ibn Ezra

Instruction increases inborn worth, and right discipline strengthens the heart.

Horace

The Creation is a museum, all full, and crowded with wonders and beauties and glories. One door, and one only, is open, by which you can enter this magnificent temple. It is the door of Knowledge. The learned laborer, the learned peasant, or slave, is ever made welcome at this door, while the ignorant, though kings, are shut out.

Horace Mann

Instruction ends in the schoolroom, but education ends only with life.

F. W. Robertson

If you were graduated yesterday, and have learned nothing today, you will be uneducated tomorrow.

Author Unknown

What we need more than anything else is not text-books but text-people.

Abraham J. Heschel

The two most engaging powers of an author are to make new things familiar, and familiar things new.

Samuel Johnson

Never regard study as a duty, but as the enviable opportunity to learn to know the liberating influence of beauty in the realm of the spirit for your own personal joy and to the profit of the community to which your later work belongs.

Albert Einstein

People sometimes refer to higher education as the higher learning, but colleges and universities are much more than knowledge factories; they are testaments to man's perennial stuggle to make a better world for himself, his children, and his children's children. This, indeed, is their sovereign purpose. They are great fortifications against ignorance and irrationality; but they are more than places of higher learning—they are centers and symbols of man's higher yearning.

W. H. Cowley

Education is not a process that continues for some years and then ends. Education has only one sovereign purpose: to prepare one for more education. All else is subsidiary to this. Education should create hungers—spiritual, moral, and aesthetic hungers for value.

There is a beautiful saying that comes to us from Hasidic lore: "There is only one thing that is whole in the entire world, and that is a broken heart." Reflect for a moment: here is a world that has not yet been redeemed, a world in which there is tragedy at the root of things. How could a moral and sensitive man walk about with a heart that is not broken? The broken-hearted—paradoxically and profoundly—are the whole-hearted. And the task of education, especially of Jewish education, should be to break your heart. Unless it breaks your heart it is a false education, a pseudo-education. The gift of education will be a heart that is whole.

Israel Knox

You should have education enough so that you won't have to look up to people; and then more education so that you will be wise enough not to look down on people.

M. L. Boren

If a man empties his purse into his head, no man can take it away from him. An investment in knowledge always pays the best interest.

Benjamin Franklin

Culture is not just an ornament; it is the expression of a native character, and at the same time, it is a powerful instrument to mould character. The end of culture is right living.

W. Somerset Maugham

If these distracted times prove anything, they prove that the greatest illusion is reliance upon the security and permanence of material possessions. We must search for some other coin. And we will discover that the treasure house of education has stood intact and unshaken in the storm. The man of cultivated life has founded his house upon a rock. You can never take away the magnificent mansion of his mind.

John Cudahy

Education is a debt due from the present to the future generations.

George Peabody

Every addition to true knowledge is an addition to human power.

Horace Mann

Learning is ever in the freshness of its youth, even for the old.

Aeschylus

Most Americans do value education as a business asset, but not as the entrance into the joy of intellectual experience or acquaintance with the best that has been said and done in the past. They value it not as an experience, but as a tool.

W. H. P. Faunce

We learn to do neither by thinking nor by doing; we learn to do by thinking about what we are doing.

George D. Stoddard

He who has imagination without learning, has wings and no feet.

Joseph Joubert

No idea, be it good or bad, is ever more than one generation from complete extinction.

I. Lynd Esch

You can take from a man his worldly belongings, you can take his home, his books, his pictures; you can separate him from his friends, from his family—but there is something no conqueror can take from him: that is his mind. Motorized divisions can crush fortifications; bombs can destroy towns, but as long as you are alive, there is in that frail little skull of yours a fortress no blitzkrieg can storm. Decorate and furnish with love and care that inner sanctuary of yours. We take a lot of trouble buying the right armchairs, tables, pictures; certainly we should take even more trouble to adorn the invisible walls of our minds.

André Maurois

Americans spend $20 billion a year on gambling, $5 billion on public education. Isn't this gambling with the future of the nation's youth?

Author Unknown

If you have acquired knowledge, what do you lack? If you lack knowledge, what have you acquired?

The Midrash

The real use of all knowledge is this: that we should dedicate that reason which was given us by God for the use and advantage of man.

Francis Bacon

A learned man has always riches within himself.

Philaedrus

There are obviously two educations. One should teach us how to make a living, and the other how to live.

James Truslow Adams

Learning is not picked up only within four walls. The ability to read books is not in itself of a higher order than the ability to read nature: to detect, for instance, a bird by its song, or to name a tree by its leaf. In times of threatened famine, would it still be a greater achievement for a boy or man to be able to write his name and address on straight and successive lines than to plough a field in straight and parallel ones? It would certainly not be so practically useful.

C. J. Woolen

As a field, however fertile, cannot be fruitful without cultivation, neither can a mind without learning.

Cicero

A man's mind is known by the company it keeps.

James Russell Lowell

Nations have recently been led to borrow billions for war; no nation has ever borrowed largely for education. Probably no nation is rich enough to pay for both war and civilization. We must make the choice; we can not have both.

Abraham Flexner

Most men believe that it would benefit them if they could get a little from those who have more. How much more would it benefit them if they would learn a little from those who know more.

William J. H. Boetcker

---

62. THE ART OF USING THE PAST

It is not I that belong to the past, but the past that belongs to me.

Mary Antin

And let us not clutter up today with the leavings of other days.

Oliver Wendell Holmes

The farther backward you can look, the farther forward you are likely to see.

Winston Churchill

The lesson of life is to believe what the years and the centuries say against the hours.

Ralph Waldo Emerson

All our ancestors are in us. Who can feel himself alone?

Richard Beer-Hoffmann

Every man is an omnibus in which all of his ancestors are seated.

Oliver Wendell Holmes

We do not honor the fathers by going back to the place where they stopped but by going on toward the things their vision foresaw.

Justin Wroe Nixon

We can pay our debt to the past by putting the future in debt to ourselves.

John Buchan

What you have inherited from your fathers you must earn for yourself before you can really call it yours.

Johann Wolfgang von Goethe

The more extensive a man's knowledge of what has been done, the greater will be his power of knowing what to do.

Benjamin Disraeli

He must support himself on tradition, for tradition is the expression of the inevitable idiosyncrasies of a nation's literature, but he must do everything he can to encourage its development in its natural direction. Tradition is a guide and not a jailer.

W. Somerset Maugham

The heritage of the past is the seed that brings forth the harvest of the future.

Inscription on the Archives Building in Washington

We live in the present, we dream of the future, but we learn eternal truths from the past.

Mme. Chiang Kai-Shek

Our past is our heritage, our present is our responsibility, and our future is our destiny.

Anna L. Rose Hawkes

The men who have gone before us have taught us how to live and how to die. We are the heirs of the ages.

Sidney Dark

Tradition is the extension of the franchise. Tradition means giving votes to the most obscure of all classes, the dead. It is the democracy of the dead. Tradition refuses to submit to the small and arrogant oligarchy of those who merely happen to be walking about. All democrats object to men being disqualified by the accident of birth, tradition objects to their being disqualified by the accident of their death. Democracy tells us not to neglect a good man's opinion even if he is our groom, tradition asks us not to neglect a good man's opinion even if he is our father.

Harry E. Fosdick

The scholar who accumulates in himself the human past has something of that wisdom which goes, in individual life, with a long memory.

G. E. Woodberry

Tradition does not mean that the living are dead but that the dead are alive.

G. K. Chesterton

We wish to preserve the fire of the past, not the ashes.

William James

We cannot say the past is past without surrendering the future.

Winston S. Churchill

The past is our cradle, not our prison, and there is danger as well as appeal in its glamor. The past is for inspiration, not imitation, for continuation, not repetition.

Israel Zangwill

The past must push us—never pull us.

Clarence F. Scharer

The past lives in us, not we in the past.

David Ben Gurion

Those who have nothing to look back to have nothing to look forward to.

A people without a tradition is a people without hope.

Mordecai M. Kaplan

Those who cannot remember the past are condemned to repeat it.

George Santayana

People who take no pride in the noble achievements of remote ancestors will never achieve anything worthy to be remembered with pride by remote descendants.

Lord Macaulay

The man who has not anything to boast of but his illustrious ancestors is like a potato, the only good belonging to him is underground.

Sir Thomas Overbury

When a man looks back from any position of difficulty and stress in which his service lands him, he always sees behind him men who bore more of the same burden, suffered more of the same ill, overcame more of the same obstacle. He is unpayably indebted for his blessings to sacrifices greater than any he can make.

Harry E. Fosdick

We are the heirs of our fathers, not their coffins.

Micah Joseph Berdichewski

When mankind desires to create something big it must reach down deep into the reservoir of its past.

Wilhelm Stekel

There is no point in our ancestors speaking to us unless we know how to listen.

Mortimer J. Adler

63. THE ART OF TEACHING

To educate a man in mind and not in morals is to educate a menace to society.

Theodore Roosevelt

I put the relation of a fine teacher to a student just below the relation of a mother to a son, and I don't think I could say more than this.

Thomas Wolfe

When we teach a child to read, our primary aim is not to enable it to decipher a waybill or receipt, but to kindle its imagination, enlarge its vision, and open for it the avenues of knowledge.

Charles W. Eliot

It is better to inspire the heart with a noble sentiment than to teach the mind a truth of science.

Phillips Brooks

Education is not to teach men facts, theories or laws, not to reform or amuse them or make them expert technicians. It is to unsettle their minds, widen their horizons, inflame their intellect, teach them to think straight, if possible, but to think nevertheless.

Robert Maynard Hutchins

No assembly of people, whether scientists, spacemen, or statesmen could be more impressive or important than the members of America's teaching profession, for no group wields greater power and influence over the future than you. Every pupil you have carries in his mind or heart or conscience a bit of you. Your influence, your example, your ideas and values keep marching on —how far into the future and into what realms of our spacious universe you will never know.

Margaret E. Jenkins

A youth expects to be recognized as a person. From his viewpoint he is growing, achieving, experiencing, pressing on, becoming an adult. From the viewpoint of teacher and parent, he is doing these things, but he needs guidance, assistance, direction so that the product will be satisfactory to the parent and teacher. Youth pushes ahead; those of us directing youth pull, and restrain, and hold, and turn him. Both the youth and the guide are right, although the youth must be considered increasingly, for the object of our experience with him is to make ourselves unnecessary and to make him self-sufficient.

Paul D. Safer

Education is neither pouring a culture into a child nor drawing out his powers. It's both.

Earl H. Hanson

Good teaching must be slow enough so that it is not confusing, and fast enough so that it is not boring; like all arts, teaching is as much a matter of *timing* as of form or content; and masters of timing are rare in any art.

Sydney J. Harris

I took a piece of living clay,
And gently formed it day by day;
And molded it with power and art,
A young boy's soft and yielding
  heart.
I came again when years were
  gone,
It was a man I looked upon;
He still the early impress wore,
And I could change him never
  more.

Author Unknown

The teacher is often the first to discover the talented and unusual scholar. How he handles and encourages, or discourages, such a child may make all the difference in the world to that child's future —and to the world.

Loren Eiseley

Few sinners are saved after the first twenty minutes of a sermon.

Mark Twain

The aim of education should be to teach the child to think, not what to think.

John Dewey

Education does not mean teaching people what they do not know. It means teaching them to behave as they do not behave. It is not teaching the youth the shapes of letters and the tricks of numbers, and then leaving them to turn their arithmetic to roguery, and their literature to lust. It means, on the contrary, training them into the perfect exercise and kingly continence of their bodies and souls. It is a painful, continual and difficult work, to be done by kindness, by watching, by warning, by precept and by praise, but above all— by example.

John Ruskin

Education fails unless the three R's at one end of the school spectrum lead ultimately to the four P's at the other—Preparation for Earning, Preparation for Living, Preparation for Understanding, and Preparation for Participation in the problems involved in the making of a better world.

Norman Cousins

A teacher who can arouse a feeling for one single good action, for one single good poem, accomplishes more than he who fills our memory with rows and rows of natural objects, classified with name and form.

Johann Wolfgang von Goethe

There are five tests of the evidences of education—correctness and precision in the use of the mother tongue; refined and gentle manners, the result of fixed habits of thought and action; sound standards of appreciation of beauty and of worth, and a character based on these standards; power and habit of reflection; efficiency or the power to do.

Nicholas Murray Butler

A man who reforms himself has contributed his full share towards the reformation of his neighbor.

Norman Douglas

Real education belongs to the future; most of our education is a form of tribal conditioning, a pilgrimage in routine and premature adjustment. When education stirs our innermost feelings and loyalties, when it awakens us from the slumber of lethargy, when it brings individuals together through understanding and compassion, it becomes our foremost hope for lasting greatness.

Frederick Mayer

If I had a child who wanted to be a teacher I would bid him Godspeed as if he were going to war. For indeed the war against prejudice, greed and ignorance is eternal, and those who dedicate themselves to it give their lives no less because they may live to see some faction of the battle won.

James Hilton

The classroom should be an entrance to the world, not an escape from it.

John Ciardi

Education worthy of its name is not merely an intellectual process. It is no less a spiritual process. Its purpose is not only to pile up knowledge and skills but to ennoble man's soul. Rarely in the past has there been such an urgent need for the kind of insight and understanding that we call spiritual.

David Sarnoff

Advice is like snow; the softer it falls, the longer it dwells upon, and the deeper it sinks into, the mind.

Samuel Taylor Coleridge

It is the supreme art of the teacher to awaken joy in creative expression and knowledge.

Albert Einstein

The fine art of teaching is so to guide the growth of the learner that after each experience he is one step closer to maturity.

Ovid F. Parody

The teacher is a sculptor of the intangible future. There is no more dangerous occupation on the planet, for what we conceive as our masterpiece may appear out of time to mock us—a horrible caricature of ourselves . . . Ours is an ill-paid profession and we have our share of fools. We, too, like the generation before us, are the cracked, the battered, the malformed products of remoter chisels shaping the most obstinate substance in the universe; the substance of man.

Loren Eiseley

No one can give faith, unless he has faith; the persuaded persuade.

Matthew Arnold

The aim of education should be to convert the mind into a living fountain, and not a reservoir. That which is filled by merely pumping in, will be emptied by pumping out.

John M. Mason

The best teacher is not necessarily the one who possesses the most knowledge but the one who most effectively enables his students to believe in their ability to learn.

Norman Cousins

That we should practice what we preach is generally admitted; but anyone who preaches what he and his hearers practice must incur the gravest moral disapprobation.

Logan Pearsall Smith

A teacher who is attempting to teach without inspiring the pupil with a desire to learn is hammering on cold iron.

Horace Mann

The true aim of every one who aspires to be a teacher should be, not to impart his own opinions, but to kindle minds.

Frederick William Robertson

You cannot antagonize and influence at the same time.

J. S. Knox

This learned I from the shadow of a tree,
    Which, to and fro, did sway
    against a wall:
Our shadow-selves, our influence,
    may fall
Where we can never be.

A. E. Hamilton

The essence of all education is self-discovery and self-control. When education helps an individual to discover his own powers and limitations and shows him how to get out of his heredity its largest and best possibilities, it will fulfil its real function; when children are taught not merely to know things but particularly to know themselves, not merely how to do things but especially how to compel themselves to do things, they may be said to be really educated. For this sort of education there is demanded rigorous discipline of the powers of observation, of the reason, and especially of the will.

Edwin Grant Conklin

An honored teacher in a boys' school, who had taught for almost fifty years, when asked what he taught, replied, "Oh, almost anything. My real job has been that of a traffic officer. Usually it is the job of a traffic officer to prevent collisions. My job has been to arrange them. I have tried to arrange productive collisions between boys and ideas."

Author Unknown

The teacher who can give his pupils pleasure in their work shall be crowned with laurels.

Elbert Hubbard

The central purpose of American education is to prepare man to think and the major challenge facing us today is to keep man thinking.

Milo Bail

All true educators since the time of Socrates and Plato have agreed that the primary object of education is the attainment of inner harmony, or, to put it into more up-to-date language, the integration of the personality. Without such an integration learning is not more than a collection of scraps, and the accumulation of knowledge becomes a danger to mental health.

Sir Alfred Zimmerin

An education isn't how much you have committed to memory, or even how much you know. It's being able to differentiate between what you do know and what you don't. It's knowing where to go to find out what you need to know; and it's knowing how to use the information once you get it.

William Feather

A teacher affects eternity; he can never tell where his influence stops.

Henry Adams

It is because modern education is so seldom inspired by a great hope that it so seldom achieves a great result. The wish to preserve the past rather than the hope of creating the future dominates the minds of those who control the teaching of the young.

Bertrand Russell

Teaching a child good manners is a day-to-day practice. He doesn't stay taught anymore than an apple stays polished.

Marcelene Cox

The object of teaching a child is to enable him to get along without his teacher.

Elbert Hubbard

The teacher largely governs the moral and spiritual atmosphere of the classroom. After all, the self of the teacher is taught along with the regular materials of study. The right kind of person teaching history, literature, or chemistry will do far more good than will the wrong kind of person trying to teach a course in Bible!

Rodney Cline

The only rational way of educating is to be an example—if one can't help it, a warning example.

Albert Einstein

Our responsibility as educators is to teach youth to have respect for those who differ from the customary ways as well as for those who conform. In simpler words, we have a profound obligation both to education and to society itself to support and strengthen the right to be different, and to create a sound respect for intellectual superiority.

Robert C. Pooley

Knowledge begins with wondering. Set a child to wondering and you have put him on the road to understanding.

Samuel Langley

Teachers of today must have the ability to bring personal meaning to ideas as they investigate, interpret and integrate their thoughts. They must possess their own unique conceptual frameworks on which to hang ideas. They should be able to select, and build upon, significant ideas, observe relationships, and distinguish essential matters from irrelevant and incidental ones.

Dean C. Corrigan

The best sermon is preached by the minister who has a sermon to preach and not by the man who has to preach a sermon.

William Feather

To know how to suggest is the art of teaching.

Henri F. Amiel

What we want is to see the child in pursuit of knowledge and not knowledge in pursuit of the child, cane in hand.

George Bernard Shaw

It is almost the definition of a good teacher that she widens the gap of accomplishment between the most able and the least able children in her class; the definition of a great teacher that she widens this gap while greatly increasing the accomplishments of the least able.

Martin Mayer

The Art of Teaching does not consist only of instruction in the three R's. There is more to teaching than conveying information. Teaching is the continuous process of building character, establishing moral attitudes, creating respect for the good way of life and distaste for the lightheaded and irresponsible mode of existence.

Samuel Belkin

Education is the process by which the individual relates himself to the universe, gives himself citizenship in the changing world, shares the race's mind and enfranchises his own soul.

John H. Finley

Carlyle once received a letter from a young man which read like this: "Mr. Carlyle, I wish to be a teacher. Will you tell me the secret of successful teaching?" Carlyle immediately wrote back: "Be what you would have your pupils be. All other teaching is unblessed mockery and apery."

F. Russell Purdy

The word "teaching" is basically misleading. Schools cannot really teach; they can only instill a desire for learning.

Byron J. Nichols

Education is the biggest business in the country—largest number of owners, most extensive plants, and most valuable product. This enterprise called education is a growing concern—never passed a dividend, or watered its stock, or sold nonvoting stock. Never had a boom or a depression. It has always paid a profit and never turned away an intellectual beggar. All the people are its stock-holders, school-boards its directors, teachers its technicians, students its "raw materials" and the community its laboratory. And its product has had the greatest influence on both America and the world.

Eugene P. Bertin

If you have knowledge, let others light their candles at it.

Margaret Fuller

Nothing is so infectious as example, and we never do great good or evil without producing the like.

François Rochefoucauld

He who would teach junior high-school youth must possess other unique qualities, but suffice it to say that a vital element in the enterprise to insure a square deal for this "awkward-age" pupil is a worthy model for emulation. One frustrated lad was heard to remark, "Two things in life I've had are ample—good advice and bad example." Unfortunately, our youth do get good advice in ladles and good examples in teaspoons.

M. Dale Baughman

Harvard University pays me for doing what I would gladly pay for the privilege of doing it if I could only afford it.

Josiah Royce

64. WHAT IS WISDOM?

The doorstep to the temple of wisdom is the knowledge of our own ignorance.

Charles Haddon Spurgeon

The mintage of wisdom is to know that rest is rust, and that real life is in love, laughter, and work.

Elbert Hubbard

Common sense in an uncommon degree is what the world calls wisdom.

Samuel T. Coleridge

Every man is a damn fool for at least five minutes every day; wisdom consists in not exceeding the limit.

Elbert Hubbard

To finish the moment, to find the journey's end in every step of the road, to live the greatest number of good hours, is wisdom.

Ralph Waldo Emerson

The great danger in public education today is that we have failed to see the difference between knowledge and wisdom. We train the head and let the heart run hogwild. We allow culture and character to walk miles apart, stuffing the head with mathematics and languages—leaving manners and morals out of the picture.

Theodore H. Palmquists

In goodness there are all kinds of wisdom.

Euripides

Wisdom is knowing what to do next; virtue is doing it.

David Starr Jordan

Fortunately or otherwise, we live at a time when the average individual has to know several times as much in order to keep informed as he did only thirty or forty years ago. Being "educated" today, requires not only more than a superficial knowledge of the arts and sciences, but a sense of interrelationship such as is taught in few schools. Finally, being "educated" today, in terms of the larger needs, means preparation for world citizenship; in short, education for survival.

Norman Cousins

Knowledge may belong to the brain of the scholar; but wisdom is the breath of the people.

G. E. Woodberry

A wise man gets more use from his enemies than a fool from his friends.

Baltasar Gracian

The foundation of all foundations, the pillar supporting all wisdoms, is the recognition of the reality of God.

Moses Maimonides

From the experience of others, do thou learn wisdom: and from their failings, correct thine own faults.

Lord Chesterfield

It takes a clever man to turn cynic and a wise man clever enough not to.

Fannie Hurst

The art of being wise is the art of knowing what to overlook.

William James

To want to be the cleverest of all is the biggest folly.

Sholom Aleichem

An American clergyman once asked Ghandi what caused him most concern. "The hardness of heart of the educated," Gandhi replied.

Louis Fischer

That which the fool does in the end the wise man does in the beginning.

R. C. Trench

To profit from good advice requires more wisdom than to give it.

John Churton Collins

The understanding of human nature is above all wisdom.

Arnold H. Glasow

Who is a wise man? He who learns of all men.

The Talmud

Wisdom is not to be obtained from textbooks, but must be coined out of human experience in the flame of life.

Morris Raphael Cohen

The differences in human life depend, for the most part, not on what men do, but upon the meaning and purpose of their acts. All are born, all die, all lose their loved ones, nearly all marry and nearly all work, but the significance of these acts may vary enormously. The same physical act may be in one situation vulgar and in another holy. The same work may be elevating or degrading. The major question is not, "What act do I perform?" but "In what frame do I put it?" Wisdom about life consists in taking the inevitable ventures which are the very stuff of common existence, and glorifying them.

Elton Trueblood

It is better to sit with a wise man in prison, than with a fool in paradise.

Author Unknown

Those who come after us will know more than we, it may be, and will think themselves cleverer accordingly; but will they be happier or wiser? Are we ourselves, who know many things, better than our fathers, who knew so little?

Vauvenargues

He is a wise man who does not grieve for the things which he has not, but rejoices for those which he has.

Epictetus

Nine-tenths of wisdom is being wise in time.

Theodore Roosevelt

Our grandfathers could wait for a twice-a-week stagecoach without running a temperature; modern man gets mad if he misses one section of a revolving door. Life is gulped down, not savored. The only new vice of the past three hundred years is the breathless blasphemy of speed. Pascal's profound word is considered mere gibberish: "The unhappiness of mankind is due to one thing, we have not the wisdom to remain in tranquility at home."

James W. Clarke

Men who know themselves are no longer fools; they stand on the threshold of the Door of Wisdom.
Havelock Ellis

A wise man is never less alone than when he is alone.
Jonathan Swift

An educated person is one who can live harmoniously and happily with his fellow men.
Charles Hardaway

Cleverness is serviceable for everything, sufficient for nothing.
Henri F. Amiel

To be ready is very much, to be able to wait is still more, to take advantage of the right moment is all.
Arthur Schnitzler

The height of human wisdom is to bring our tempers down to our circumstances and to make a calm within, under the weight of the greatest storm without.
Daniel Defoe

It is not strength, but art, obtains the prize,
And to be swift is less than to be wise.
Homer

Wisdom is the right use of knowledge. To know is not to be wise. Many men know a great deal, and are all the greater fools for it. There is no fool so great a fool as a knowing fool. But to know how to use knowledge is to have wisdom.
Charles H. Spurgeon

Knowledge is proud that he has learned so much; wisdom is humble that he knows no more.
William Cowper

The invariable mark of wisdom is to see the miraculous in the common.
Ralph Waldo Emerson

---

65. THE ART OF PROGRESS

The art of progress is to preserve order amid change, and to preserve change amid order. Life refuses to be embalmed alive.
Alfred North Whitehead

Progress is the effect of an ever more rigorous subjugation of the beast in man, of an ever tenser self-restraint, an ever keener sense of duty and responsibility.
Max Nordau

Humanity cannot go forward, civilization cannot advance, except as the philosophy of force is replaced by that of human brotherhood.
F. B. Sayre

A fanatic is one who can't change his mind and won't change the subject.
Winston S. Churchill

The history of civilization is the history of the slow and painful enfranchisement of the human race.
Robert G. Ingersoll

Every great scientific truth goes thru three stages. First people say it conflicts with the Bible. Next they say it has been discovered before. Lastly they say they have always believed it.

Louis Agassiz

What the world needs is a fusion of the sciences and the humanities. The humanities express the symbolic, poetic, and prophetic qualities of the human spirit. Without them we would not be conscious of our history; we would lose our aspirations and the graces of expression that move men's hearts. The sciences express the creative urge in man to construct a universe which is comprehensible in terms of the human intellect. Without them, mankind would find itself bewildered in a world of natural forces beyond comprehension, victims of ignorance, superstition and fear.

Isidor I. Rabi

Progress—the onward stride of God.

Victor Hugo

It would do the world good if every man in it would compel himself occasionally to be absolutely alone. Most of the world's progress has come out of such loneliness.

Bruce Barton

The foolish and the dead alone never change their opinion.

James Russell Lowell

The fruit we wish to pick tomorrow lies hidden in the seed of today. The goals we are to reach and the problems we are to solve tomorrow depend upon today's diligence, hope, and faith, today's conviction of the almightiness of good.

Ralph E. Johnson

If we moderns had more curiosity we could get along with considerably less formal education. Progress depends upon curiosity. Curiosity is the only intelligence test which tells what one may become as well as what one is.

Saturday Review of Literature

The man who never alters his opinion is like standing water, and breeds reptiles of the mind.

William Blake

There is no greater disloyalty to the great pioneers of human progress than to refuse to budge an inch from where they stood.

William R. Inge

It is provided in the essence of things that from any fruition of success, no matter what, shall come forth something to make greater struggle necessary.

Walt Whitman

The tiger in his cage strides prodigiously forward but his path is a vicious circle.

Ludwig Lewisohn

Every great advance in science has issued from a new audacity of imagination.

John Dewey

The "silly question" is the first intimation of some totally new development.

Alfred North Whitehead

The world hates change, yet it is the only thing that has brought progress.

Charles F. Kettering

All progress is initiated by challenging current conceptions, and executed by supplanting existing institutions.

George Bernard Shaw

The advance of scientific knowledge as it really happens is not a steady resolute march to the stars. It goes something like this: One step forward, two steps sideways, fall flat on your face. Get up facing backwards, and try to see which way you were going; then repeat *da capo*.

Daniel Luzon Morris

We must not overlook the important role that extremists play. They are the gadflies that keep society from being too complacent or self-satisfied; they are, if sound, the spearhead of progress.

Abraham Flexner

Religion will not regain its old power until it can face change in the same spirit as does science.

Alfred North Whitehead

For centuries and centuries the world has been struggling to divide up economic scarcity, and for the first time we have the tools of abundance with which to meet mankind's basic economic and material needs. If we will use these tools intelligently, with a sense of social and moral responsibility, they will enable us to solve mankind's basic material needs. Then we can devote greater time and energy and effort to the facilitation of man's growth as a social and cultural and spiritual being, which is the real meaning of life on this earth.

Walter P. Reuther

We should so live and labor in our time that what came to us as seed may go to the next generation as blossom, and what came to us as blossom may go to them as fruit. This is what we mean by progress.

Henry Ward Beecher

True progress consists not so much in increasing our needs as in diminishing our wants.

Ivan N. Panin

The whole history of civilization is strewn with creeds and institutions which were invaluable at first, and deadly afterwards.

Walter Bagehot

A social system that cannot be changed cannot be maintained.

Holbrook Jackson

Static religions are the death of thought.

Alfred North Whitehead

Behold the turtle: He makes progress only when he sticks his neck out.

James Bryant Conant

There is no law of progress. Our future is in our own hands, to make or to mar. It will be an uphill fight to the end, and would we have it otherwise? Let no one suppose that evolution will ever exempt us from struggles. "You forget," said the Devil, with a chuckle, "that I have been evolving too."

William R. Inge

Every step of progress the world has made has been from scaffold to scaffold and from stake to stake.

Wendell Phillips

Real human progress depends not so much on inventive ingenuity as on conscience.

Albert Einstein

Whoever would change men must change the conditions of their lives.

Theodore Herzl

Whoever preaches absence of discipline is an enemy of progress.

Max Nordau

The test of our progress is not whether we add more to the abundance of those who have much; it is whether we provide enough for those who have too little.

Franklin D. Roosevelt

"Necessity is the mother of invention" is a silly proverb. "Necessity is the mother of futile dodges" is much nearer to the truth. The basis of the growth of modern invention is science, and science is almost wholly the outgrowth of pleasurable intellectual curiosity.

Alfred North Whitehead

Civilization is just a slow process of learning to be kind.

Charles L. Lucas

The final test of science is not whether it adds to our comfort, knowledge and power, but whether it adds to our dignity as men, our sense of truth.

David Sarnoff

Progress is the activity of today and the assurance of tomorrow.

Ralph Waldo Emerson

The real solution of every problem can be found by those people who are hurt by it, if they will take hold of life where it hurts, and find out, not how they themselves can escape from that hurt, but how they can prevent that hurt from becoming a permanent factor in the lives of their brothers and sisters.

A. Maude Royden

The moral law of the universe is progress. Every generation that passes idly over the earth without adding to that progress remains uninscribed upon the register of humanity, and the succeeding generation tramples its ashes as dust.

Giuseppe Mazzini

To be as good as our fathers we must be better.

Wendell Phillips

We must always change, renew, rejuvenate ourselves; otherwise we harden.

Johann Wolfgang von Goethe

Behind every advance of the human race is a germ of creation growing in the mind of some lone individual. An individual whose dreams waken him in the night while others lie contentedly asleep.

Crawford H. Greenewalt

The longer I live the more keenly I feel that whatever was good enough for our fathers is not good enough for us.

Oscar Wilde

THE ART OF LIVING

WITH DEMOCRACY

66. MY COUNTRY 'TIS OF THEE

To be an American is of itself almost a moral condition, an education, and a career.

George Santayana

A healthy loyalty is not passive and complacent, but active and critical.

Harold J. Laski

It is by the goodness of God that in our country we have those three unspeakably precious things; freedom of speech, freedom of conscience, and the prudence never to practise either of them.

Mark Twain

Most Americans are born drunk. They have a sort of permanent intoxication from within, a sort of invisible champagne. Americans do not need to drink to inspire them to do anything.

G. K. Chesterton

I believe in America because in it we are free—free to choose our government, to speak our minds, to observe our different religions;

Because we are generous with our freedom—we share our rights with those who disagree with us;

Because we hate no people and covet no people's land;

Because we are blessed with a natural and varied abundance;

Because we set no limit to a man's achievement: in mine, factory, field, or service in business or the arts, an able man, regardless of class or creed, can realize his ambition;

Because we have great dreams—and because we have the opportunity to make those dreams come true.

Wendell Willkie

What we want is an active class who will insist in season and out of season that we shall have a country whose greatness is measured not only by its square miles, its number of yards woven, of hogs packed, or bushels of wheat raised, not only by its skill to feed and clothe the body, but also by its power to feed and clothe the soul; a country which shall be as great morally as it is materially; a country whose very name shall call out all that is best within us.

James Russell Lowell

Our country right or wrong. When right to be kept right. When wrong to be put right.

Carl Schultz

We must make of our country not an idol, but a stepping-stone toward God.

Simone Weil

We are a people with a faith in reason, and when we lose that faith and substitute for it faith in weapons we become weak and are lost, even with our superatomic weapons.

David E. Lilienthal

Let our object be our country, our whole country, and nothing but our country. And, by the blessing of God, may that country itself become a vast and splendid monument, not of oppression and terror, but of wisdom, of peace and of liberty, upon which the world may gaze with admiration forever.

Daniel Webster

Bad officials are elected by good citizens who do not vote.

George Jean Nathan

Our country hath a gospel of her own
To preach and practice before all the world—
The freedom and divinity of man,
The glorious claims of human brotherhood,
And the soul's fealty to none but God.

James Russell Lowell

God gives all men all earth to love,
But since man's heart is small,
Ordains for each one spot should prove
Beloved over all.

Rudyard Kipling

What constitutes an American? Not color nor race nor religion. Not the pedigree of his family nor the place of his birth. Not the coincidence of his citizenship. Not his social status nor his bank account. Not his trade nor his profession. An American is one who loves justice and believes in the dignity of man. An American is one who will fight for his freedom and that of his neighbor. An American is one who will sacrifice property, ease and security in order that he and his children may retain the rights of free men. An American is one in whose heart is engraved the immortal second sentence of the Declaration of Independence. . . .

Harold L. Ickes

In America's history, change has not been thought subversive; on the contrary a man's devotion has been measurable by the zeal with which he sought to improve that which he already loved.

Walter Gelhern

He loves his country best who strives to make it best.

Robert G. Ingersoll

A man's feet should be planted in his country, but his eyes should survey the world.

George Santayana

Patriotism is the last refuge of a scoundrel.

Samuel Johnson

We have a long way to go before we end racial discrimination once and for all, but the progress made strengthens my faith, even in moments of depression, that an appeal to the American conscience and intelligence is by no means wasted effort.

Norman Thomas

Territory is but the body of a nation. The people who inhabit its hills and valleys are its soul, its spirit, its life.

James A. Garfield

America has been called a melting pot, but it seems better to call it a mosaic, for in it each nation, people or race which has come to its shores has been privileged to keep its individuality, contributing at the same time its share to the unified pattern of a new nation.

King Baudouin I of Belgium

The honor of a country depends much more on removing its faults than on boasting of its qualities.

Giuseppe Mazzini

Whatever America hopes to bring to pass in the world must first come to pass in the heart of America.

Dwight D. Eisenhower

We should behave toward our country as women do toward men they love. A loving wife will do anything for her husband except stop criticizing and trying to improve him. We should cast the same affectionate but sharp glance at our country. We should love it, but also insist upon telling all its faults. The noisy empty "patriot" not the critic is the dangerous citizen.

J. B. Priestly

America has believed that in differentiation, not in uniformity, lies the path of progress.

Louis D. Brandeis

Our system has its problems; and it is not exactly perfect; and yet—on balance, admitting all its bad points and assessing all the good, there is a vigor and a vitality that nothing can quite overcome. There is in this system the enormous vitality of free men, running their own government in their own way. If they are weak at times, it is because they have freedom to be weak; if they are strong, upon occasion, it is because they have the freedom to be strong—thanks to all men and women over the centuries who by their dreaming and their striving and their dying made it possible for their heirs to take with them into the future so great and powerful a gift.

Allen Drury

In the view of the Constitution, in the eyes of the law, there is in this country no superior, dominant, ruling class of citizens. There is no caste system here. The Constitution is color blind, and neither knows nor tolerates classes among citizens.

John Marshall Harlan

In no other country in the world is aspiration so definite a part of life as it is in America. The most precious gift God has given to this land is not its great riches of soil and forest and mine but the divine discontent planted deeply in the hearts of the American people.

William Allen White

It is worth saying once again that no nation has ever come into the possession of such powers for good or ill, for freedom or tyranny, for friendship or enmity among the peoples of the world, and that no nation in history has used those powers, by and large, with greater vision, restraint, responsibility and courage.

The London Times, March 1954

Love of country is like love of woman—he loves her best who seeks to bestow on her the highest good.

Felix Adler

I realize that patriotism is not enough. I must have no hatred toward any one.

Edith Cavell

America means opportunity, freedom, power.

Ralph Waldo Emerson

We are on the threshold of another great decisive era. History's headlong course has brought us, I devoutly believe, to the threshold of a new America of the great ideals and noble visions which are the stuff our future must be made of.

I mean a New America where poverty is abolished and our abundance is used to enrich the lives of every family.

I mean a New America where freedom is made real for all without regard to race or belief or economic condition.

I mean a New America which everlastingly attacks the ancient idea that men can solve their differences by killing each other.

These are the things I believe in and will work for with every resource I possess.

Adlai E. Stevenson

Patriotism consists not in waving the flag, but in striving that our country shall be righteous as well as strong.

James Bryce

I would not hesitate to say that the United States is the finest society on a grand scale that the world has thus far produced.

Alfred North Whitehead

We are an imperfect mixture of immigrants; the only common national factor among us is that almost none of us can claim to be an indigenous native or even descended from one. The nearest most of us come to that claim is to say, as Will Rogers is supposed to have replied to a dowager who boasted that her ancestors had come over on the Mayflower, "Mine met the boat."

T. S. Matthews

I believe in the United States of America as a government of the people, by the people, for the people; whose just powers are derived from the consent of the governed; a democracy in a republic; a sovereign nation of many sovereign states; a perfect union, one and inseparable; established upon those principles of freedom, equality, justice and humanity for which American patriots sacrificed their lives and fortunes. I therefore believe it is my duty to my country to love it, to support its constitution, to obey its laws, to respect its flag, and to defend it against all enemies.

William Tyler Page

Have you not learned that no stocks or bonds or products of mill or field are our country? It is the splendid thought that is in our minds.

Benjamin Harrison

It is a fabulous country, the only fabulous country; it is the only place where miracles not only happen, but where they happen all the time.

Thomas Wolfe

"My country, right or wrong," may have a glorious ring in war-time, but how hollow it sounds in a civilized society, and what an invitation to chaos it would constitute if adopted universally.

Arthur Sweetser

America is not a mere body of traders; it is a body of free men. Our greatness is built upon our freedom—is moral, not material. We have a great ardor for gain; but we have a deep passion for the rights of man.

Woodrow Wilson

---

67. THE IDEA OF DEMOCRACY

In a democracy, the opposition is not only tolerated as constitutional, but must be maintained because it is indispensable.

Walter Lippmann

What democracy really means is a determination on the part of everyone who possesses the ballot to exercise his right intelligently, an intent to participate personally in the government to the extent that his ability and circumstances warrant and make possible, and the endeavor always to inform himself and to keep informed in respect of every detail of the matter or matters being dealt with.

Marc T. Greene

No attack on democracy can hide the fact that it can be replaced only by a system that substitutes coercion for persuasion; one that replaces the individual's choice with the choice of some ruler.

William O. Douglas

The problem of democracy is not the problem of getting rid of kings. It is the problem of clothing the whole people with the elements of kingship. To make kings and queens out of a hundred million people! That is the problem of American democracy.

F. C. Morehouse

Two cheers for democracy: one because it admits variety and two because it permits criticism.

E. M. Forster

If the equality of individuals and the dignity of man be myths, they are myths to which the republic is committed.

Howard Mumford Jones

Man's capacity for justice makes democracy possible; but man's inclination to injustice makes democracy necessary.

Reinhold Niebuhr

President Lincoln defined democracy to be "the government of the people, by the people, for the people." This is a sufficiently compact statement of it as a political arrangement. Theodore Parker said that "Democracy meant not 'I'm as good as you are,' but 'You're as good as I am.'" And this is the ethical conception of it, necessary as a complement of the other.

James Russell Lowell

The fundamental truth of democracy is that the real pleasures of life are increased by sharing them.

Henry Dwight

Democracy does not mean the silly belief that the majority of the people are right in any given decision; but it does mean the passionate belief that the people have a right to be wrong, and that they have the capacity to correct their mistakes and amend their excesses, in a free and generous spirit which no other form of government can afford.

Sydney J. Harris

I think the true discovery of America is before us. I think the true fulfillment of our spirit, of our people, of our mighty and immortal land, is yet to come. I think the true discovery of our own democracy is still before us. And I think that all these things are certain as the morning, as inevitable as noon. I think I speak for most men living when I say that our America is Here, is Now, and beckons on before us, and that this glorious assurance is not only our living hope, but our dream to be accomplished.

Thomas Wolfe

The essential ingredient of democracy is not doctrine but intelligence, not authority but reason, not cynicism but faith in man, faith in God. Our strength lies in the fear-less pursuit of truth by the minds of men who are free.

David Lilienthal

Ultimately there can be no freedom for self unless it is vouchsafed for others; there can be no security where there is fear, and a democratic society presupposes confidence and ardor in the relations of men with one another and eager collaboration for the larger ends of life instead of the pursuit of petty, selfish or vain-glorious aims.

Felix Frankfurter

The real democratic American idea is not that every man shall be on a level with every other, but that everyone shall have liberty, without hindrance, to be what God made him.

Henry Ward Beecher

I protest against the counterfeit logic which concludes that, because I do not want a black woman for a slave I must necessarily want her for a wife. I need not have her for either. I can just leave her alone. In some respects she certainly is not my equal; but in her natural right to eat the bread she earns with her own hands without asking leave of any one else, she is my equal, and the equal of all others.

Abraham Lincoln

It is not tolerance that one is entitled to in America. It is the right of every citizen in America to be treated by other citizens as an equal.

Wendell L. Willkie

Sometimes it is said that man cannot be trusted with the government of himself. Can he, then, be trusted with the government of others?

Thomas Jefferson

The unpardonable sin for every human being is to have more knowledge than understanding, more power than love; to know more about the earth than about the people who live in it; to invent quick means of travel to faraway places when one cannot grope one's way within one's own heart. For freedom is a dreadful thing unless it goes hand in hand with responsibility. Democracy among men is a specter except when the hearts of men are mature.

Lillian Smith

There is no king who has not had a slave among his ancestors, and no slave who has not had a king among his.

Helen Keller

Of Equality—as if it harm'd me, giving others the same chances and rights as myself—as if it were not indispensable to my own rights that others possess the same.

Walt Whitman

We in the United States are amazingly rich in the elements from which to weave a culture; we have the best of man's past on which to draw, brought to us by our native folk from all parts of the world. In binding these elements into a national fabric of beauty and strength, let us keep the original fibers so intact that the fineness of each will show in the completed handiwork.

Franklin D. Roosevelt

I am not the flag; not at all. I am but its shadow. I am whatever you make me, nothing more. I am your belief in yourself, your dream of what a People may become. I am the day's work of the weakest man, and the largest dream of the most daring. I am no more than you believe me to be and I am all that you believe I can be. I am whatever you make me, nothing more.

Franklin K. Lane

U.S. means United States, not Uniform States. We have in-groups, out-groups, marginal men; ethnic, class, linguistic, regional variations; an incredibly divine culture. Look closely, and you can find in America every conceivable type of man—and some inconceivable ones —the chief characteristic of the American pattern is a lack of pattern.

Marshall Fishwick

We hold these truths to be self-evident,—that all men are created equal; that they are endowed by their Creator with certain unalienable rights; that among these are Life, Liberty, and the Pursuit of Happiness.

Declaration of Independence

The beauty of a Democracy is that you never can tell when a youngster is born what he is going to do with you, and that, no matter how humbly he is born he has got a chance to master the minds and lead the imaginations of the whole country.

Woodrow Wilson

The test of democracy is freedom of criticism.

David Ben-Gurion

I am the creature of God, and so is my fellow-man; I go early to my work and he to his; he does not boast of his labor nor I of mine, and if thou wouldst say "I accomplish great things and he little things." We have learnt that whether a man accomplish great things or small, his reward is the same if only his heart is set upon heaven.

The Talmud

Democracy means not "I am as good as you are," but "You are as good as I am."

Theodore Parker

Democracy, unlike refrigerators and steel mills, is not an exportable commodity. It is a way of life, contagious among those who have come to see its potentials for the spirit and mind of men. It takes root slowly in new lands. It may take a long, long time for full flowering.

William O. Douglas

All the ills of democracy can be cured by more democracy.

Alfred E. Smith

Democracy does not mean perfection. It means a chance to fight for improvement.

Meyer London

We must never lose sight of the fact that ours is a country that has grown because of our belief in ideas, not because of our belief in things. As things become more available, as they become more pleasant, ideas tend to fade away a little. We've got to be sure that we always remember that it is the idea —the big, clean idea and not the thing—that makes us and our country bigger.

Frank Pace, Jr.

Men are born unequal. The great benefit of society is to diminish this inequality as much as possible by procuring for everybody security, the necessary property, education, and succcor.

Joseph Joubert

Democracy is that form of society, no matter what its political classification, in which every man has a chance and knows that he has it.

James Russell Lowell

The test of democracy is not whether the majority prevails, but whether the minority is tolerated.

William Temple

Democracy is the only form of government which harmonizes fully with the religious principles of the Bible—the only form of government which can carry out the supremely religious function of binding free men together.

Henry A. Wallace

We are in danger of developing a cult of the common man—which means a cult of mediocrity. I have never been able to find out who this common man is. Most Americans get mad and insulted if you try calling them common. Let us remember that the great human advances have not been brought about by mediocre men and women. We believe in equal opportunity to rise to leadership—in other words, to be uncommon.

Herbert Hoover

Democracy means that the aggregate of mankind shall be so organized as to create for each man the maximum opportunity of growth in accordance with the dictates of his own genius and aspiration.

R. B. Perry

The doctrine of Democracy, like any other of the living faiths of men, is so essentially mystical that it continually demands new formulation. To fail to recognize it in a new form, to call it hard names, to refuse to receive it, may mean to reject that which our fathers cherished and handed on as an inheritance not only to be preserved but also to be developed.

Jane Addams

The equal right of all men to the use of land is as clear as their equal right to breathe the air—it is a right proclaimed by the fact of their existence. For we cannot suppose that some men have a right to be in this world, and others no right.

Henry George

Democracy is a cause that is never won, but I believe it will never be lost.

Charles A. Beard

Democracy is the recurrent suspicion that more than half of the people are right more than half of the time.

E. B. White

But this august dignity I treat of, is not the dignity of kings and robes, but that abounding dignity which has no robed investiture. Thou shalt see it shining in the arm that wields a pick or drives a spike; that democratic dignity which, on all hands, radiates without end from God; Himself! The great God absolute! The centre and circumference of all democracy! His omnipresence, our divine equality!

Herman Melville

It would be folly to argue that the people cannot make political mistakes. They can and do make grave mistakes. They know it, they pay the penalty, but compared with the mistakes which have been made by every kind of autocracy they are unimportant.

Calvin Coolidge

Democracy arose from men's thinking that if they are equal in any respect, they are equal absolutely.

Aristotle

It is in education more than anywhere else that we have sincerely striven to carry into execution "the Great American Dream": the vision of a longer and fuller life for the ordinary man, a life of widened freedom, of equal opportunity for each to make of himself all that he is capable of becoming.

John Dewey

The things that the flag stands for were created by the experience of a great people. Everything that it stands for was written by their lives.

Woodrow Wilson

The essence of totalitarianism is control of the whole man, especially of his higher faculties and gifts. The essence of democracy is to establish conditions under which individual choice of decision, the fullness of personality, can be achieved.

Eugene J. McCarthy

While democracy must have its organization and controls, its vital breath is individual liberty.

Charles Evans Hughes

Minds broken in two. Hearts broken. Conscience torn from acts. A culture split in a thousand pieces. That is segregation.

Lillian Smith

Democracy is the only form of government that is founded on the dignity of man, not the dignity of some men, of rich men, of educated men or of white men, but of all men. Its sanction is not the sanction of force, but the sanction of human nature. Equality and justice, the two great distinguishing characteristics of democracy follow inevitably from the conception of men, as rational and spiritual beings.

In this light freedom takes on meaning. It is not freedom to do as we please but freedom to achieve that autonomy which we approach in proportion as we develop our rational and spiritual nature. It is not mere freedom to live that concerns us most, but freedom to live human lives. Men must be free to exercise those powers which make them men.

Robert M. Hutchins

We are a nation of many nationalities, many races, many religions —bound together by a single unity, the unity of freedom and equality. Whoever seeks to set one race against another seeks to enslave all races. Whoever seeks to set one religion against another seeks to destroy all religion. I am fighting for a free America—for a country in which all men and women have equal rights to liberty and justice. I am fighting, as I always have fought, for the rights of the little man as well as the big man—for the weak as well as the strong, for those who are helpless as well as for those who can help themselves.

Franklin D. Roosevelt

If all mankind minus one were of one opinion, and only one person were of the contrary opinion, mankind would be no more justified in silencing that one person, than he if he had the power, would be justified in silencing mankind.

John Stuart Mill

Religion may be the concern of a people, but it must never become a concern of the state.

Leo Baeck

Democracy is the only system of government that trusts in its own persuasiveness, so that all the winds of doctrine have way within it. Democracy is the only system that has faith in the free mind. Democracy is the only system that does not make education the servant of power.

William Salter

Democracy is based upon the conviction that there are extraordinary possibilities in ordinary people.

Harry Emerson Fosdick

Why should there not be a patient confidence in the ultimate justice of the people? Is there any better or equal hope in the world?

Abraham Lincoln

The spirit of liberty is the spirit which is not too sure that it is right; the spirit of liberty is the spirit which seeks to understand the minds of other men and women; the spirit of liberty is the spirit which weighs their interests alongside its own without bias.

Learned Hand

The white man cannot keep the Negro in the ditch without sitting down there with him.

Booker T. Washington

What are the American ideals? They are the development of the individual through liberty and the attainment of the common good through democracy and social justice.

Louis D. Brandeis

We came to America, either ourselves or in the persons of our ancestors, to better the ideals of men, to make them see finer things than they had seen before, to get rid of the things that divide and to make sure of the things that unite. It was but an historical accident no doubt that this great country was called the "United States"; yet, I am very thankful that it has that word "United" in its title, and the man who seeks to divide man from man, group from group, interest from interest in this great Union is striking at its very heart.

Woodrow Wilson

The whole story of America—a story worth the telling and worth the understanding—began with an idea. This idea is actually the political expression of a basic law of nature—that there is strength in diversity. According to this idea, America is a place where people can be themselves. It is a human experience rather than a purely national or cultural experience. It is built upon fabulous differences—

religion, race, culture, customs, political thinking. These differences, or pluralism, as the sociologists call it, are actually the mortar that hold the nation together.

Norman Cousins

One of the astutest men I know has achieved a large measure of his prosperity and general contentment by behaving always as though all men were alike. Because, although of course they are not alike, the differences are too trifling to matter.

E. V. Lucas

Democracy is always a beckoning goal, not a safe harbor. For freedom is an unremitting endeavor, never a final achievement. That is why no office in the land is more important than that of being a citizen.

Felix Frankfurter

When I think of the flag, I see alternate strips of parchment upon which are written the rights of liberty and justice, and stripes of blood to vindicate those rights, and then, in the corner, a prediction of the blue serene into which every nation may swim which stands for these great things.

Woodrow Wilson

We here in America have the vitalizing idea and the promising hope for which men live. The idea is not fully planted in fertile ground. Our conception of democracy is a democracy that puts its trust in the people. It is based on the worth of the human personality against deadly invasions of power. It stresses human dignity and individual diversity. It holds that a free society must not tolerate differences but blend them in an inner strength. It knows that national unity cannot come from an imposed conformity. Its faith has a universal appeal, deeply rooted in human necessities and in human aspiration. It is predicated on the age-old principle that no prison can confine the human spirit. A freedom-thirsty world cannot be kept permanently in chains. Ultimately for all tyranny comes the final death knock on the door. Sooner or later the resurgent forces of the human spirit break through the barriers.

Raymond B. Fosdick

Too many people expect wonders from democracy. When the most wonderful thing of all is just having it.

Walter Winchell

68. FREEDOM'S HOLY LIGHT

What constitutes the bulwark of our own liberty and independence? It is not our frowning battlements, our bristling sea coasts, our army and our navy. These are not our reliance against tyranny. All of those may be turned against us without making us weaker for the struggle. Our reliance is in the love of liberty which God has planted in us. Our defense is in the spirit which prized liberty as the heritage of all men, in all lands everywhere. Destroy this spirit and you have planted the seeds of despotism at your own doors. Familiarize yourselves with the chains of bondage and you prepare your own limbs to wear them. Accustomed to trample on the rights of others, you have lost the genius of your own independence and become the fit subjects of the first cunning tyrant who rises among you.

Abraham Lincoln

The basic test of freedom is perhaps less in what we are free to do than in what we are free not to do.

Eric Hoffer

American liberty is a religion. It is a thing of the spirit. It is an aspiration on the part of people for not alone a free life but a better life.

Wendell L. Willkie

The danger of the past was that men became slaves. The danger of the future is that men may become robots.

Eric Fromm

It is better for a man to go wrong in freedom than to go right in chains.

Thomas Huxley

They set the slave free, striking off his chains.
Then he was as much of a slave as ever.
He was still chained to servility.
He was still manacled to indolence and sloth,

He was still bound by fear and
 superstition,
By ignorance, suspicion and sav-
 agery.
His slavery was not in the chains,
But in himself.
They can only set free men free.
And there is no need of that.
Free men set themselves free.

James Oppenheim

I have on my table a violin
string. It is free to move in any
direction I like. If I twist one end,
it responds; it is free. But it is
not free to sing. So I take it and
fix it into my violin. I bind it, and
when it is bound, it is free for the
first time to sing.

Rabindranath Tagore

Liberty is more than an ever-
burning torch held mightily aloft
by a heroic statue overlooking
New York harbor. It is a weight of
responsibility each American must
forever bear aloft for every other.
Only when freedom is so conceived
and so borne, with pride and with
the dignity of social conscience,
does it lend significance to the
bronze goddess gracing the gate-
way to our world.

Eugene Gay-Tifft

The American who cares about
freedom will have to discipline his
mind to a new way of thinking. He
will have to pass beyond his easy,
confident localism and learn to
think in world terms. This will be
a much harder way for him to
think, for the world patterns are
still unformed. But if he cares about
making freedom grow in strength
and grandeur, he will have to accustom himself to think in this
broader way. The day for provin-
cial Americanism is past. To save
the freedom of America, we shall
have somehow to help achieve the
freedom of the peoples of the
world.

Harry A. Overstreet

If there is any principle of the
Constitution that more imperatively
calls for attachment than any other
it is the principle of free thought—
not free thought for those who
agree with us but freedom for the
thought that we hate.

Oliver Wendell Holmes, Jr.

Liberty is a "natural right" only
for those who are willing to bear
its "natural" responsibility.

Wheeler McMillen

Freedom is an indivisible word.
If we want to enjoy it, we must
be prepared to extend it to everyone.

Wendell L. Willkie

The escape from the Ten Commandments through violating them
has never kept its promise of giving
a new freedom. The experience is
like the attempt to escape from the
law of gravitation by defying it.
The result is likely to be at least
a bad fall. The philosophy of license is really a network of clever
lies. The apostles of license are all
the while promising that which
they cannot give. You cannot become free physically by defying
the laws of nature. And you cannot
become free morally by defying
the laws of ethics.

Lynn Harold Hough

Civil liberties mean liberties for
those we like and those we don't
like, or even detest.

Felix Frankfurter

The right to think is the real difference between us and the enemy; it is likely to give us ultimate victory in the cold war—or in a hot war, if that should break out.

Elmer Davis

He that would make his own liberty secure must guard even his enemy from oppression.

Thomas Paine

The preservation of liberty is a contest, but it is not a spectator sport. We cannot remain on the sidelines while professionals play the game for us.

Willard M. Wilson

There is a higher concept of freedom than something that can be conferred or withdrawn, something that is an accident of birth. Freedom is an endowment of every human soul.

Peter Marshall

Freedom means mastery of our world. Fear and greed are common sources of bondage. We are afraid, beset by anxiety. We do not know what tomorrow will bring. We seem so helpless over against the forces that move on without apparent thought for men. And our inner freedom is destroyed by greed. We think that if we only had enough goods we should be free, happy, without care. And so there comes the lust for money, and slavery to the world of things. The world can enslave; it can never make us free.

H. F. Rall

The general spread of the light of science has already laid open to every view the palpable truth that the mass of mankind has not been born with saddles on their backs, nor a favored few booted and spurred, ready to ride them legitimately by the grace of God.

Thomas Jefferson

What a fool a man would be who took a sailing ship out on to the great ocean and said: "I am not going to be a bond slave to a pilot or a compass or a chart. I am free to sail the seas." I think the ocean would laugh at such folly, and the end of that voyage would be at the bottom of the sea, and it would be a short voyage. When he is enslaved by the compass, and the chart, and the stars, and the pilot who stands at his side and tells him when to change direction, when to drop anchor, when to let sail down, and when to pull sail up, then he finds he is free.

Leslie D. Weatherhead

Only in fetters is liberty:
Without its banks could a river be?

Louis Ginsberg

Free will is not the liberty to do whatever one likes, but the power of doing whatever one sees ought to be done, even in the very face of otherwise overwhelming impulse. There lies freedom, indeed.

George MacDonald

There is no man who does not love liberty; but the just demands it for all, the unjust only for himself.

Ludwig Boerne

There is a vast difference between toleration and liberty. Toleration is a concession; liberty is a right; toleration is a matter of expediency; liberty is a matter of principle; toleration is a grant of man; liberty is a gift of God.

George W. Truett

Real freedom is positive. It is not mere freedom from something —from interference or restraint or fear. It is freedom for something— freedom to be and to do what we judge to be best.

Luther A. Weigle

Freedom is more precious than any gifts for which you may be tempted to give it up.

Baltasar Gracian

The greatest glory of a freeborn people is to transmit that freedom to their children.

William Harvard

Freedom is like a bag of sand. If there is a hole anywhere in the bag, all the sand will run out. If any group of our people are denied their rights, sooner or later all groups stand to lose their rights. All the freedom will run out.

Robert P. Patterson

Liberty is the only thing you cannot have unless you are willing to give it to others.

William Allen White

Dictators are anti-Semitic because they know or sense that liberty is Semitic in origin and character.

Abba Hillel Silver

All theory is against freedom of the will; all experience for it.

Samuel Johnson

If a nation values anything more than freedom, it will lose its freedom; and the irony of it is that, if it is comfort or money that it values more, it will lose that too.

W. Somerset Maugham

There are two freedoms—the false, where a man is free to do what he likes; the true, where a man is free to do what he ought.

Charles Kingsley

God grants liberty only to those who love it, and are always ready to guard and defend it.

Daniel Webster

Originally freedom to speak was deemed a gift from heaven. A century later Judge Holmes and Judge Brandeis gave the concept a new connotation. No longer was it the right to speak—rather it was the right to hear. For only by the free flow of ideas does society become enriched.

Morris L. Ernst

We must never forget that it is by our faiths as well as by our weapons that we can keep this experiment in freedom from perishing at the hands of our enemies.

David E. Lilienthal

Freedom and responsibility are like Siamese twins: they die if they are parted.

Lillian Smith

Man seeks freedom as the magnet seeks the pole or water its level, and society can have no peace until every member is really free.

Josiah Warren

Freedom is the coin of the realm in the kingdom of human worth and dignity, and the coin has two sides. On one side are inscribed the rights and privileges of free men. On the other side are the responsibilities. Unless both sides are genuine and deeply cut, the coin is counterfeit.

P. E. Kay

Those who expect to reap the blessings of freedom, must, like men, undergo the fatigue of supporting it.

Thomas Paine

We want a state of things which allows every man the largest liberty compatible with the liberty of every other man.

Ralph Waldo Emerson

A horse that is hitched with others to a wagon is not free not to walk in front of the wagon; and if it will not draw, the wagon will strike its legs, and it will go whither the wagon goes and will pull it involuntarily. But, in spite of this limited freedom, it is free itself to pull the wagon, or be dragged along by it. The same is true of man.

Leo Tolstoy

God grant that not only the love of liberty but a thorough knowledge of the rights of man may pervade all the nations of the earth, so that a philosopher may set his foot anywhere on its surface and say: "This is my country!"

Benjamin Franklin

So long as there is any subject which men may not freely discuss, they are timid upon all subjects. They wear an iron crown and talk in whispers.

John Jay Chapman

In giving freedom to the slave we assure freedom to the free,—

honorable alike in what we give and what we preserve.

Abraham Lincoln

I desire not the liberty to myself which I would not freely and impartially weight out to all the consciences of the world beside.

Roger Williams

If you put a chain around the neck of a slave, the other end fastens itself around your own.

Ralph Waldo Emerson

Who, then, is free? The wise who can command his passions, who fears not want, not death, nor chains, firmly resisting his appetites and despising the honors of the world, who relies wholly on himself, whose angular points of character have all been rounded off and polished.

Horace

In the future days, which we seek to make secure, we look forward to a world founded upon four essential human freedoms.

The first is freedom of speech and expression—everywhere in the world.

The second is freedom of every person to worship God in his own way—everywhere in the world.

The third is freedom from want —which, translated into world terms, means economic understandings which will secure to every nation a healthy peacetime life for its inhabitants—everywhere in the world.

The fourth is freedom from fear —which, translated into world terms, means a world-wide reduction of armaments to such a point and in such a thorough fashion that no nation will be in a position to commit an act of physical aggression against any neighbor—anywhere in the world.

Franklin D. Roosevelt

We must keep in the forefront of our minds the fact that whenever we take away the liberties of those whom we hate, we are opening the way to loss of liberty for those we love.

Wendell L. Willkie

The burden of our history is unmistakable: the enemy of the Jew is the enemy of freedom. Those who organize the pogrom of today will attack tomorrow the general foundation of freedom. That is why the moral stature of the nation is set by its recognition that the claim of the Jew to freedom is the claim of its own people to strike off its chains. When it is silent before the agony of the Jew, it collaborates in the organization of its future servitude.

Harold Laski

Those who would give up essential liberty to purchase temporary safety deserve neither liberty nor safety.

Benjamin Franklin

You tell me that law is above freedom of utterance. And I reply that you can have no wise laws nor free enforcement of wise laws unless there is free expression of the wisdom of the people—and alas, their folly with it. But if there is freedom folly will die of its own poison, and the wisdom will survive. That is the history of the race.

William Allen White

What makes Western civilization worth saving is the freedom of the mind, now under heavy attack from the primitives who have persisted among us. If we have not the courage to defend that faith, it won't matter much whether we are saved or not.

This republic was not established by cowards; and cowards will not preserve it.

Elmer Davis

Freedom springs from within, whether in a man or in a people. To remove disabilities and confer the franchise is not enough. Men must be enabled to grow if they are to exercise their rights with dignity and effect. For this reason the widening of the franchise in democratic countries has always been accompanied or followed by the development of popular education.

Basil A. Yeaxlee

Not like the brazen giant of Greek fame,
With conquering limbs astride from land to land;
Here at our sea-washed, sunset gates shall stand
A mighty woman with a torch, whose flame
Is the imprisoned lightning, and her name
Mother of Exiles. From her beacon hand
Glows world-wide welcome; her mild eyes command
The air-bridged harbor that twin cities frame.
"Keep, ancient lands, your storied pomp" cries she
With silent lips. "Give me your tired, your poor,
Your huddled masses yearning to breathe free,

The wretched refuse of your teeming shore,
Send these, the homeless, tempest-
tost to me,
I lift my lamp beside the golden
door."

Emma Lazarus
Inscribed on the Statue of Liberty,
Bedloe Island, New York harbor

The fight for freedom is an endless battle. Its victories are never
final, its defeats are never permanent. Each generation must defend
its heritage, for each seeming conquest gives rise to new forces that
will attempt to substitute fresh
means of oppression for the old.
There can be no peace in a world
of life and growth—every battle
the fathers thought finished will
have to be fought anew by their
children if they wish to preserve
and extend their freedom.

Philip Van Doren Stern

Social progress does not have to
be bought at the price of individual
freedom.

John Foster Dulles

We must be willing to pay a
price for freedom, for no price
that is ever asked for it is half the
cost of doing without it.

H. L. Mencken

Freedom cannot exist in isola-
tion. Freedom cannot exist in
prison. We in the United States,
who have demonstrated our ability
to be free, cannot keep freedom
all to ourselves. To remain free we
must share freedom with others.
Of course, to hold this position we
must have faith; we must have
faith that men and women like ourselves in other lands are fit to be

free. We must have faith that, if
they are to be helped to this freedom, they will be able to govern
themselves wisely and well.

Wendell Willkie

The world is hungry for what
we have, not only for wealth like
ours, but also for the freedom
and enterprise that produced our
wealth. God has sown that hunger
for freedom in every human heart
—and then He planted the wheat
of freedom here in America and
gave us hands to reap it, and make
it bread for all mankind. And our
work is not done, nor may we take
our rest, as long as anywhere in
the world a human being hungers
for liberty and is not fed.

Cecil B. de Mille

Personal freedom, a wide range
of individual expression, a complete respect for a human mind
and the human personality—this
is the ideal of the democratic system. In all the documents of democracy, you find this respect, this
hope, this attitude of reverence
toward the fullest possible flowering of each human personality.
President Lincoln enjoyed quoting
the Irishman who said: "In this
country every man is as good as
the next one and for the matter of
that a little better." We are men,
not angels—that is sure. Also we
hope we are men and not mice.
And sometimes we feel like worms
of the dust, doing the best we can,
moving a little soil of the earth
from where it was to where it will
be.

Carl Sandburg

Freedom rests, and always will,
on individual responsibility, indi-

vidual integrity, individual effort, individual courage, and individual religious faith. It does not rest in

Washington. It rests with you and me.

Ed Lipscomb

---

69. IN PRAISE OF TOLERANCE

Some agitators hate the yellow race, and some hate the white race, and most of them appear to hate the human race.

Baltimore Evening Sun

Treat the other man's faith gently; it is all he has to believe with. His mind was created for his own thoughts, not yours or mine.

Henry S. Haskins

So many stars in the infinite space—
So many worlds in the light of God's face.

So many storms ere the thunders shall cease—
So many paths to the portals of Peace.

So many years, so many tears—
Sighs and sorrows and pangs and prayers.

So many ships in the desolate night—
So many harbors, and only one Light.

So many creeds like the weeds in the sod—
So many temples, and only one God.

Frank L. Stanton

The devil loves nothing better than the intolerance of reformers, and dreads nothing so much as their charity and patience.

James Russell Lowell

This duty of toleration has been summed up in the words, "Let both grow together until the harvest."

Alfred North Whitehead

Where is the Jim Crow section
On this merry-go-round
Mister, cause I want to ride?
Down South where I come from
White and colored
Can't sit side by side.
Down South on the train
There's a Jim Crow car.

On the bus we're put in the back—
But there ain't no back
To a merry-go-round;
Where's the horse
for a kid that's black?

Langston Hughes

Bigotry has no head and cannot think, no heart and cannot feel. When she moves it is in wrath; when she pauses it is amid ruin. Her prayers are curses, her god is a demon, her communion is death, her vengeance is eternity, her decalogue is written in the blood of her victims, and if she stops for a moment in her infernal flight it is upon a kindred rock to whet her vulture fang for a more sanguinary desolation.

Daniel O'Conner

The best creed we can have is charity toward the creeds of others.

Josh Billings

The chief value of history, if it is critically studied, is to break down the illusion that peoples are very different.

Leo Stein

When you hear a man say, "I hate," adding the name of some race, nation, religion, or social class, you are dealing with a belated mind. That man may dress like a modern, ride in an automobile, listen over the radio, but his mind is properly dated about 1000 B.C.

Harry Emerson Fosdick

Freedom of judgment can be attained only when we learn to estimate an individual according to his own ability and character. Then we shall find, if we were to select the best of mankind, that all races and all nationalities would be represented. Then we shall treasure and cultivate the variety of forms that human thought and activity has taken, and abhor, as leading to complete stagnation, all attempts to impress one pattern of thought upon whole nations or even upon the whole world.

Franz Boas

I will not permit any man to narrow and degrade my soul by making me hate him.

Booker T. Washington

He who holds convictions, respects convictions.

Leo Baeck

The alternative to peace is not war. It is annihilation.

Raymond Gram Swing

Tolerance is the positive and cordial effort to understand another's beliefs, practices and habits, without necessarily sharing or accepting them.

Joshua Loth Liebman

The only hope of preserving what is best, lies in the practice of an immense charity, a wide tolerance, a sincere respect for opinions that are not ours.

Philip G. Hamerton

The fact that racial and religious prejudice should, in any form, exist in a great democracy, is an incredible mockery of the very word democracy. It should be considered in the light of a personal disgrace to every citizen of that same democracy. A disgrace as shocking and as tragic as that of the discovery that a near and dear member of one's family has become a hardened criminal. For prejudice *is* a crime. It is a crime against the democratic ideal, a crime against the teachings of Christianity, Judaism and the other great religions, a crime against human decency and a crime against just plain common sense.

Cornelia Otis Skinner

Hatred toward any human being cannot exist in the same heart as love to God.

Dean Inge

In a republic, we must learn to combine intensity of conviction with a broad tolerance of difference of conviction.

Theodore Roosevelt

A prejudice is a vagrant opinion without visible means of support.

Ambrose Bierce

One has only to grow older to become more tolerant. I see no fault that I might not have committed myself.

Johann Wolfgang von Goethe

Hate ruins the very savor of food, the peace of sleep, all reverence in the soul.

Eleazar ben Judah

There is no more evil thing in this present world than race prejudice, none at all! I write deliberately—it is the worst single thing in life now. It justifies and holds together more obscene cruelty and abomination than any other sort of error in the world.

H. G. Wells

To admit of brotherhood as a fact, to live brotherhood as a practice, and to accept the responsibilities that such a course entails, is to participate in the very life that the U.S.A. has made possible, and for which it exists.

James P. Mitchell

We have just enough religion to make us hate, but not enough to make us love one another.

Jonathan Swift

A clash of doctrines is not a disaster—it is an opportunity.

Alfred North Whitehead

Every man has his follies—and often they are the most interesting things he has got.

Josh Billings

The prejudiced and obstinate man does not so much hold opinions, as his opinions hold him.

Tryon Edwards

American fair play would guarantee to every man the right to worship God according to his own convictions and not according to the persuasions or prejudices of his neighbor.

Stephen S. Wise

A rattlesnake, if cornered, will become so angry it will bite itself. That is exactly what the harboring of hate and resentment against others is—a biting of oneself. We think we are harming others in holding these spites and hates, but the deeper harm is to ourselves.

E. Stanley Jones

The tight skirts of prejudice impede the steps of progress.

Karl K. Quimby

Infidel: In New York, one who does not believe in the Christian religion; in Constantinople, one who does.

Ambrose Bierce

If we knew as much about mental health as we do about physical health, an epidemic of hate would be considered as dangerous as an epidemic of typhoid.

David M. Levy

I call heaven and earth to witness that whether it be Jew or heathen, man or woman, free or bondman—only according to their acts does the divine spirit rest upon them.

The Midrash

Fanaticism consists in redoubling your effort when you have forgotten your aim.

George Santayana

Until man places on tolerance and open-mindedness a value equal to the value that he places on material possessions, he will continue to be stranded on an island surrounded by his own prejudices, ideas, preconceived opinions, and knowledge that is limited by the horizon of his own ignorance.

Cecil A. Poole

A man who lives not by what he loves but what he hates is a sick man.

Archibald MacLeish

Prejudice is not held against people because they have evil qualities. Evil qualities are imputed to people because prejudices are held against them.

Marshall Wingfield

Every man, conducting himself as a good citizen, and being accountable to GOD alone for his religious opinions, ought to be protected in worshipping the Deity according to the dictates of his own conscience.

George Washington

In the sight of an anti-Semite, Jews can do nothing right. If they are rich, they are birds of prey. If they are poor, they are vermin. If they are in favor of war, they are exploiters of bloody feuds for their own profit. If they are anxious for peace, they are either instinctive cowards or traitors. If they give generously, they are doing it for some selfish purpose of their own. If they don't give, then what would one expect from a Jew.

Lloyd George

Love makes everything lovely; hate concentrates itself on the one thing hated.

George MacDonald

Differing from a man in doctrine is no reason why you should pull his house about his ears.

Samuel Johnson

Whenever someone speaks with prejudice against a group—Catholics, Jews, Italians, Negroes—someone else usually comes up with a classic line of defense: "Look at Einstein!" "Look at Carver!" "Look at Toscanini!" So, of course, Catholic (or Jews, or Italians or Negroes) must be all right.

They mean well, these defenders. But their approach is wrong. It is even bad. What a minority group wants is not the right to have geniuses among them but the right to have fools and scoundrels without being condemned as a group.

Agnes Elizabeth Benedict

Our institutions were not devised to bring about uniformity of opinion; if they had been, we might well abandon hope. It is important to remember that the essential characteristic of true liberty is that under its shelter, many different types of life and character and opinion and belief can develop unmolested and unobstructed.

Charles Evans Hughes

The test of courage comes when we are in the minority; the test of tolerance comes when we are in the majority.

Ralph W. Sockman

Every man must get to heaven his own way.

Frederick the Great

Make a faith or a dogma absolute, and persecution becomes a logical consequence.

William Makepeace Thackeray

A young Negro student said: "If you discriminate against me because I am uncouth, I can become mannerly. If you ostracize me because I am unclean, I can cleanse myself. If you segregate me because I am ignorant, I can become educated. But if you discriminate against me because of my color, I can do nothing. God gave me my color. I have no possible protection against race prejudice but to take refuge in cynicism, bitterness, hatred, and despair."

Harry Emerson Fosdick

This country will not be a good place for any of us to live in unless we make it a good place for all of us to live in.

Theodore Roosevelt

Tolerance is the lowest form of human co-operation. It is the drab, uncomfortable halfway house between hate and charity.

Robert I. Gannon

A man said to Stanley Jones, "My church is the Church." Replied the tolerant and noted leader, "Go fill your bathtub, put some salt in it, and call it the ocean."

Clinton C. Cox

In my life of professional teaching, I have never endeavoured to make young men more efficient; I have tried to make them more interesting. If one is interested, one is usually interesting. The business of the teacher is not to supply information, it is to raise a thirst. I like to hang pictures on the walls of the mind, I like to make it possible for a man to live with himself, so that he will not be bored with himself. For my own part, I live every day as if this were the first day I had ever seen and the last I were going to see.

William Lyon Phelps

Man is a creature who loves to draw lines, but God is the Power that ignores lines and man-made barriers. The more able we are to see some good in everyone and some truth in all beliefs, the closer we shall come to the mind of God.

Theodore Tiemeyer

It is a small thing to accept people for what they are: if we really love them we must want them to be what they are.

Alain

Tolerance is bigger than race, greater than creed, mightier than color. It is not a breaking down of all barriers between ourselves and the other fellow; it is the realization that, in reality, there are no barriers to break down.

Author Unknown

The word "tolerance" has of late lost much of its original meaning and value. Just to *tolerate* somebody or something is not enough. We can tolerate while being narrow, smug and even bigoted. In our pride we can look down upon that which we tolerate. All too much of our practice of brotherhood is founded upon this negative aspect of being tolerant. True tolerance . . . has a basis of equality, understanding and love. It does not condemn, but lifts up. It behaves toward others with respect and helpfulness. It never tries to get the better of those a little more unfortunate. It is even willing to sacrifice that others may rise to higher levels.

Stanley I. Stuber

Hate is a dead thing. Who of us would be a tomb?

Kahlil Gibran

In the midst of all triumphs of Christianity, it is well that the stately synagogue should lift its walls by the side of the aspiring cathedral, a perpetual reminder that there are many mansions in the Father's earthly house as well as in the heavenly one; that civilized humanity, longer in time and broader in space than any historical form of belief, is mightier than any one institution or organization it includes.

Oliver Wendell Holmes

As one can ascend to the top of a house by means of a ladder or a bamboo or a staircase or a rope, so diverse are the ways and means to approach God, and every religion in the world shows one of these ways.

Ramakrishna

Prejudice is the child of ignorance.

William Hazlitt

Hating is a precious liquor, a poison dearer than that of the Borgias, because it is made of our blood, our health, our sleep and two-thirds of our love.

Charles Baudelaire

Whoever kindles the flames of intolerance in America is lighting a fire underneath his own home.

Harold E. Stassen

Be not angry that you cannot make others as you wish them to be since you cannot make yourself as you wish to be.

Thomas à Kempis

The man who is consumed by hate is not only a misery to himself, but a source of misery to all around him, not because of the menace he offers to our interests but because he defiles the atmosphere we breathe and debases the currency of our kind.

A. G. Gardiner

He drew a circle that shut me out—
Heretic, rebel, a thing to flout.
But Love and I had the wit to win:
We drew a circle that took him in!

Edwin Markham

Minds are like parachutes. They only function when open.

Lord Dewar

Hate never builds anything; it can only blast.

Joseph Fort Newton

The fire you kindle for your enemy often burns yourself more than him.

Chinese Proverb

My definition of a free society is a society where it is safe to be unpopular.

Adlai Stevenson

An hour spent in hate is an eternity withdrawn from love.

Ludwig Boerne

You can never make your own religion look so well as when you show mercy to the religion of others.

Charles Dibdin

THE ART OF LIVING

WHEN LIFE IS DIFFICULT

---

70. THE USES OF ADVERSITY

Rembrandt's domestic troubles served only to heighten and deepen his art, and perhaps his best canvases were painted under stress of circumstances and in sadness of heart. His life is another proof, if needed, that the greatest truths and beauties are to be seen only through tears. Too bad for the man! But the world—the same ungrateful, selfish world that has always lighted its torch at the funeral pyres of genius—is the gainer.

John C. Van Dyke

As the flint contains the spark, unknown to itself, which the steel alone can awaken to life, so adversity often reveals to us hidden gems, which prosperity or negligence would forever have hidden.

Josh Billings

There is nothing the body suffers that the soul may not profit by.

George Meredith

To a brave man, good and bad luck are like his right and left hand. He uses both.

St. Catherine of Siena

The block of granite which is an obstacle in the pathway of the weak, becomes a stepping-stone in the pathway of the strong.

Thomas Carlyle

He who has been delivered from pain must not think he is now free again, and at liberty to take life up as it was before, entirely forgetful of the past. He is now a man whose eyes are open with regard to pain and anguish, and he must help to overcome these two enemies and bring to others the deliverance which he has himself enjoyed.

Albert Schweitzer

The gem cannot be polished without friction, nor man perfected without trials.

Confucius

Great trials seem to be necessary preparation for great duties.

E. Thompson

A little boy was leading his sister up a mountain path. "Why," she complained, "it's not a path at all. It's all rocky and bumpy." "Sure," he said, "the bumps are what you climb on."

J. Wallace Hamilton

Adversity introduces a man to himself.

Author Unknown

Character is the sum of all we struggle against.

Booker T. Washington

The art of living lies not in eliminating but in growing with troubles.

Bernard Baruch

Not to have had pain is not to have been human.

Yiddish Proverb

Who has never tasted what is bitter does not know what is sweet.

German Proverb

The curious thing about the tendency of Americans to cling to the notion that life ought to be "easy" and "secure," that suffering is to be avoided whenever possible and grief denied rather than transcended, is that it really doesn't correspond with our experience. Many a man who wants a clear road to success for his son looks back upon his own early struggles with relish and satisfaction. The times of our lives which hold the deepest meaning for us, from which we learn the most, are very often those when we are face to face with problems which seem too great for our strength, with illness, and with death.

Janet Harrison

Many men owe the grandeur of their lives to their tremendous difficulties.

Charles H. Spurgeon

Prosperity tries the fortunate, adversity the great.

Pliny the Younger

The owl is therefore the bird of wisdom, because even a fool can see when it is light; it is the wise man that can see when it is dark.

Ivan N. Panin

It has done me good to be somewhat parched by the heat and drenched by the rain of life.

Henry Wadsworth Longfellow

There is in every true woman's heart a spark of heavenly fire, which lies dormant in the broad daylight of prosperity; but which kindles up, and beams and blazes in the dark hour of adversity.

Washington Irving

Did we think victory great? So it is—but now it seems to me, when it cannot be helped, that defeat is great and that death and dismay are great.

Walt Whitman

As a rule, the game of life is worth playing, but the struggle is the prize.

William Ralph Inge

Any one can hold the helm when the sea is calm.

Publius Syrus

There is a story of a German baron who made a great Aeolian harp by stretching the wires from tower to tower of his castle. When the harp was ready he listened for the music. But it was in the still air; the wires hung silent. Autumn came with its gentle breezes and there were faint whispers of song. At length the winter winds swept over the castle, and now the harp answered in majestic music.

Such a harp is the human heart. It does not yield its noblest music in the summer days of joy, but in the winter of trial. The sweetest songs on earth have been sung in sorrow. The richest things in character have been reached in pain.

Dean Stanley

You never know what you can do without until you try.

Franklin P. Adams

I thank God for my handicaps, for, through them, I have found myself, my work, and my God.

Helen Keller

The man of character finds an especial attractiveness in difficulty, since it is only by coming to grips with difficulty that he can realize his potentialities.

Charles de Gaulle

Adversity is like the period of the former and of the latter rain, —cold, comfortless, unfriendly to man and to animal; yet from that season have their birth the flower and the fruit, the date, the rose, and the pomegranate.

Walter Scott

Our strength grows out of our weakness. Not until we are pricked and stung and sorely shot at, awakens the indignation which arms itself with secret forces. A great man is always willing to be little. Whilst he sits on the cushion of advantages, he goes to sleep. When he is pushed, tormented, defeated, he has a chance to learn something; he has been put on his wits, on his manhood; he has gained facts; learns his ignorance; is cured

of the insanity of conceit; has got moderation and real skill.

Ralph Waldo Emerson

Then, welcome each rebuff
That turns earth's smoothness rough,
Each sting that bids nor sit nor stand but go!
Be our joys three parts pain!
Strive and hold cheap the strain;
Learn, nor account the pang; dare, never grudge the throe!

Robert Browning

When fate is adverse, a wise man can always strive for happiness and sail against the wind to attain it.

Jean Jaques Rousseau

You don't know what things are real in art until you come to them in pain. Sorrow is the touchstone.

Romain Rolland

Prosperity is a great teacher; adversity is a greater. Possession pampers the mind; privation trains and strengthens it.

William Hazlitt

What is difficulty? Only a word indicating the degree of strength requisite for accomplishing particular objects; a mere notice of the necessity for exertion; a bug-bear to children and fools; only a mere stimulus to men.

Samuel Warren

Rome remained great as long as she had enemies who forced her to unity, vision and heroism. When she had overcome them all she flourished for a moment and then began to die.

Will Durant

As I look back on my life tuberculosis looms up as an ever-present and relentless foe. It robbed me of my dear ones and brought me my first great sorrows. It shattered my health when I was young and strong, and relegated me to this remote region (in the Adirondacks) where ever since I have seen its withering blight laid on those about me. And yet the struggle with tuberculosis has brought me experiences and left me recollections which I would not exchange for the wealth of the Indies.

Edward Livingston Trudeau

Rebellion against your handicaps gets you nowhere. Self-pity gets you nowhere. One must have the adventurous daring to accept oneself as a bundle of possibilities and undertake the most interesting game in the world—making the most of one's best.

Harry Emerson Fosdick

I was the son of an immigrant. I experienced bigotry, intolerance and prejudice, even as so many of you have. Instead of allowing these things to embitter me, I took them as spurs to more strenuous effort.

Bernard Baruch

Your pain is the breaking of the shell that encloses your understanding.

Kahlil Gibran

Difficulties are the things that show what men are.

Epictetus

The history of the world is in reality the story of tears transformed into triumphs.

Joseph R. Sizoo

Present suffering is not enjoyable, but life would be worth little without it. The difference between iron and steel is fire, but steel is worth all it costs.

Maltbie Babcock

God sometimes puts us on our back so that we may look upward.

Author Unknown

Why do we dread ordeal? Every good thing the human race has experienced was trouble for somebody. Our birth was trouble for our mothers. To support us was trouble for our fathers. Books, paintings, music, great buildings, good food, ideas, the nameless joys and excitements which add up to what we call "a good life" came out of the travail of countless hearts and minds.

Lillian Smith

A problem is an opportunity in work clothes.

Henry J. Kaiser, Jr.

Trouble makes us one with every human being in the world.

Oliver Wendell Holmes

Life is a school in which every sorrow, every pain, every heartbreak brings a precious lesson.

Swami Sivananda

Light that makes some things seen, makes some things invisible. Were it not for darkness and the shadow of the earth, the noblest part of the Creation would remain unseen, and the stars in heaven invisible.

Sir Thomas Browne

Dead wood carried—heavy rot became;

Dead wood burned—a brilliant
flame.
Misfortune carried—the very heart
grew lame;
Misfortune used—a new horizon
came.

Myrtle Dean Clark

There is a legend of a comfort
loving man who died and was borne
to the other world where every wish
was gratified. No effort, no struggle
was required of him. He became
bored and said, "I can't stand this
everlasting bliss any longer. I want
to feel there are things I cannot
have. I want to go to hell." The
attendant replied: "And where do
you think you are sir?"

Harry O. Ritter

Troubles are often the tools by
which God fashions us for better
things.

Henry Ward Beecher

Ugly facts are a challenge to
beautify them.

Henry S. Haskins

Adversity has the same effect on
a man that severe training has on
the pugilist—it reduces him to his
fighting weight.

Josh Billings

If you have the idea that physi-
cal perfection is necessary to suc-
cess in your chosen field, take a
look at this even dozen of famous
men and the handicaps that failed
to slow them; Lord Byron had a
clubfoot; Robert Louis Stevenson
and John Keats had tuberculosis;
Charles Steinmetz and Alexander
Pope were hunchbacks; Admiral
Nelson had only one eye; Edgar
Allan Poe was a psycho-neurotic;
Charles Darwin was an invalid;
Julius Caesar was an epileptic;
Thomas Edison and Ludwig von
Beethoven were deaf, and Peter
Stuyvesant had a wooden leg.

Wilfred Funk

It is by those who have suffered
that the world has been advanced.

Leo Tolstoy

Where there is no anguish in the
heart there will be no great music
on the lips.

Karl Barth

Misfortunes are needles with
which God sews our souls to the
eternal truths.

Author Unknown

What on earth would a man do
with himself if something did not
stand in his way?

H. G. Wells

We shall draw from the heart of
suffering itself the means of inspiration and survival.

Winston S. Churchill

Sweet are the uses of adversity;
Which, like the toad, ugly and venomous,
Wears yet a precious jewel in his
head.

Shakespeare

The tests of life are to make, not
break us. Trouble may demolish a
man's business but build up his
character. The blow at the outer
man may be the greatest blessing
to the inner man. If God, then, puts
or permits anything hard in our
lives, be sure that the real peril,
the real trouble, is that we shall
lose if we flinch or rebel.

Maltbie D. Babcock

Crises refine life. In them you discover what you are.

Allan Knight Chalmers

I called upon a minister who had recently passed through a most trying experience. To my amazement, he said it was almost a relief! "Why?" I asked incredulously. "Well," he said, "for thirty years I have visited people in their times of suffering, and I have wondered why I was exempt. I had never suffered any physical or mental pain, and I knew I did not deserve such immunity. My present suffering has eased that situation considerably."

Leslie D. Weatherhead

It is not what nature does with a man that matters but what he does with nature.

Ray S. Baker

---

71. THE ART OF FACING SORROW

It is dangerous to abandon one's self to the luxury of grief; it deprives one of courage, and even of the wish for recovery.

Henri F. Amiel

Build a little fence of trust
Around today;
Fill the space with loving works,
And therein stay;
Look not through the sheltering bars
Upon tomorrow,
God will help thee bear what comes
Of joy or sorrow.

Mary Frances Butts

To be mindful of my folly is already part of wisdom; to reckon with my weakness is already part of strength; to be content with my poverty is already part of riches. Only to accept my sorrow is not yet part of joy.

Ivan N. Panin

We deem those happy who from the experience of life have learned to bear its ills, without being overcome by them.

Juvenal

Hope and patience are two sovereign remedies for all, the surest reposals, the softest cushions to lean on in adversity.

Robert Burton

Whenever evil befalls us, we ought to ask ourselves, after the first suffering, how we can turn it into good. So shall we take occasion, from one bitter root, to raise perhaps many flowers.

Leigh Hunt

I love the man that can smile in trouble, that can gather strength from distress, and grow brave by reflection.

Thomas Paine

You cannot prevent the birds of sorrow from flying over your head, but you can prevent them from building nests in your hair.

Chinese Proverb

Be willing to have it so. Acceptance of what has happened is the first step to overcoming the consequences of any misfortune.

William James

If you face squarely into the sunlight, and gaze squarely toward the future, you will find that both your shadow and your failures have fallen behind you.

Vitali Negri

Darkness makes us aware of the stars,
And so when dark hours arise,
They may hold a bright and lovely thing,
We might never have known otherwise.

Peter A. Lea

There are times when God asks nothing of his children except silence, patience, and tears.

C. S. Robinson

Have courage for the great sorrows of life and patience for the small ones; and when you have laboriously accomplished your daily task, go to sleep in peace. God is awake.

Victor Hugo

Obedience and resignation are our personal offerings on the altar of duty.

Hosea Ballou

Man, born to die, can no more be exempt from pain than from death. To prevent an organized substance endowed with feeling from ever experiencing pain, it would be necessary that all the laws of nature should be changed; that matter should no longer be divisible; that it should neither have weight, action, nor force; that a rock might fall on an animal without crushing it; and that water should have no power to suffocate, or fire to burn it.

Voltaire

Oriental rugs which are found in many homes are all woven by hand. Usually, there will be a group of people weaving a single rug together under the directions of an artist who issues instructions to the rest. He determines the choice of colors and the nature of the pattern.

It often happens that one of the weavers inserts the wrong color thread. The artist may have called for blue and instead black was used. If you examine an oriental rug carefully, you may be able to detect such irregularities. What is significant about them is that they were not removed. The skillful artist just proceeded to weave them into the pattern.

Here is a wise procedure that we can follow in life. We should like the pattern of our lives to be woven exclusively of bright-colored threads. But every now and then a dark thread steals into the fabric. If we are true artists of life we can weave even this thread into the pattern and make it contribute its share to the beauty of the whole.

Sidney Greenberg

Over every mountain there is a path, although it may not be seen from the valley.

James D. Rogers

When Victor Hugo was being persecuted by his beloved France, his heart almost broken, in enforced exile, he would climb a cliff overlooking the harbor at sunset, select a pebble, and stand in deep meditation before throwing it down into the water. He seemed to derive great satisfaction in performing this simple ritual, each evening. Some children watched him throw these pebbles into the water, and one of the children grew bold enough to ask, "Why do you come here to throw these stones?"

Victor Hugo smiled gravely. He was silent a moment, and then answered quietly, "Not stones, my child, I am throwing self-pity into the sea."

Richard C. Hertz

Concealed griefs are the most consuming, as secret maladies are the most fatal.

Lady Marguerite Blessington

The only way to meet affliction is to pass through it solemnly, slowly, with humility and faith, as the Israelites passed through the sea. Then its very waves of misery will divide, and become to us a wall, on the right side and on the left, until the gulf narrows before our eyes, and we land safe on the opposite shore.

Dinah Maria Mulock

When Anaxagoras was told of the death of his son, he only said— "I knew he was mortal." So we in all casualties of life should say, I knew my riches were uncertain; that my friend was but a man. Such considerations would soon pacify us, because all our troubles proceed from their being unexpected.

Plutarch

On occasion I hear someone cry in anguish of soul, "What terrible thing have I done that God should punish me so?" The answer is— nothing! Suffering, except through the universal law of cause and effect, does not come as punishment. Once and for all, we should

rid ourselves of the thought that the Creator of Life sends pain as punishment. This is the basic point in the Bible's Book of Job. He wanted to demonstrate that the idea is unsound theologically and philosophically. Yet a rich harvest can ripen from the dark seeds of pain. Not as punishment, but in order that we may grow in faith and in character, God has placed us in a world where there is the presence of suffering.

Kenneth Hildebrand

There is no easy formula for a happy living. Anyone who says he has one is either joking or lying. Even if I could, I have no intention or desire of putting forth any patented, neatly packaged recipe of my own. But there is one simple thought I should like to pass on, if I may. It is no sure-fire prescription for happiness; it is not guaranteed to bring any bluebirds singing in your back yard. I offer it merely because I found it can help prevent much vain regret and self-defeat. *It is not what you have lost, but what you have left that counts.* Too many of us squander precious energy, time, and courage dreaming of things that were and never can be again, instead of dedicating ourselves to realities and the heavy tasks of today.

Harold Russell

That is best which God sends; it was his will; it is mine.

Owen Meredith

When in great misfortune, think of the past; you might have suffered it ten years before.

Comtesse Diane

The best way out is always through.

Robert Frost

God hath not promised
Skies always blue,
Flower-strewn pathways
All our lives through;
God hath not promised
Sun without rain,
Joy without sorrow,
Peace without pain.
But God hath promised
Strength for the day,
Rest for the labor,
Light for the way,
Grace for the trials,
Help from above,
Unfailing sympathy,
Undying love.

Annie Johnson Flint

Beware of desperate steps; the darkest day,
Lived till tomorrow, will have passed away.

William Cowper

For two decades the life of the great French artist Renoir was one of pain and misery. Rheumatism racked his body and distorted his fingers. Often when he held his brush between thumb and forefinger, and slowly and painfully applied his paints to the canvas, great beads of perspiration broke out upon his brow, because of his suffering.

Renoir could not stand at his work, but had to be placed in a chair, which was moved up and down to give him access to the various parts of his canvas. At intervals a physician administered sedatives, but the suffering was seldom allayed.

Yet the artist nobly persisted, painting in pain his masterpieces, of beauty and enchantment.

"Master," his disciple Matisse pleaded one day, "why do you do more? Why torture yourself?"

Gazing at one of his favorite canvases, Renoir replied, "The pain passes, but the beauty remains."

Adrian Anderson

These things are beautiful beyond belief:
The pleasant weakness that comes after pain,
The radiant greenness that comes after rain,
The deepened faith that follows after grief,
And the awakening to love again.

Author Unknown

I pray not for the joy that knows
No saving benison of tears;
The placid life of ease that flows
Untroubled through the changing years.

Grant me, O God, the mind to see
The blessings which my sorrows bring;
And give me, in adversity,
The heart that still can trust and sing.

Marion Franklin Ham

To dare is great. To bear is greater. Bravery we share with brutes. Fortitude with saints.

C. F. Deems

How hard for unaccustomed feet
Which only knew the meadow
Is this bleak road they now must tread
Through valleys dark with shadow.
Until they learn how sure Thy love
That girds each day, each morrow,
O Father, gently lead all hearts
That newly come to sorrow!

Leslie Savage Clark

72. THE BLESSING OF HOPE

If you have occasional spells of despondency and self-pity, if once in a while you begin to feel sorry for yourself, don't despair! The sun has a sinking spell every night, but it rises again all right the next morning.

Richard C. Hertz

If it were not for hope the heart would break.

Author Unknown

I hold the unconquerable belief that science and peace will triumph over ignorance and war, that nations will come together not to destroy but to construct, and that the future belongs to those who accomplish most for humanity.

Louis Pasteur

I avow my faith that we are marching towards better days. Humanity will not be cast down. We are going on—swinging bravely forwards along the grand high road —and already behind the distant mountains is the promise of the sun.

Winston Churchill

There are no hopeless situations; there are only men who have grown hopeless about them.

Clare Boothe Luce

Hope is the better half of courage. Hope! has it not sustained the work, and given the fainting heart time and patience to outwit the chances and changes of life.

Honoré de Balzac

The word which God has written on the brow of every man is Hope.

Victor Hugo

In his heart of hearts the cynic knows that he is a defeated man and that his cynicism is merely an expression of the fact that he has lost courage and is beaten.

George E. Vincent

To the being fully alive, the future is not ominous but a promise; it surrounds the present like a halo.

John Dewey

Dupery for dupery, what proof is there that dupery through hope is so much worse than dupery through fear?

William James

Never despair; but if you do, work on in despair.

Edmund Burke

Hope is a stubborn fellow: none but he knows how to wait.

Comtesse Diane

The march of Providence is so slow and our desires so impatient; the work of progress is so immense and our means of aiding it so feeble; the life of humanity is so long, that of the individual so brief, that we often see only the ebb of the advancing ways, and are thus discouraged. It is history that teaches us to hope.

Robert E. Lee

Hope, like the taper's gleaming light,

Adorns the wretches' way;
And still, as darker grows the
night,
Emits a brighter ray.
Oliver Goldsmith

Grow old along with me!
The best is yet to be,
The last of life, for which the first
was made;
Our times are in his hand
Who saith, "A whole I planned,
Youth shows but half; trust God;
see all, nor be afraid!"
Robert Browning

I am not afraid of tomorrow, for
I have seen yesterday and I love
today.
William Allen White

Hope is the gay, skylarking pa-
jamas we wear over yesterday's
bruises.
B. De Casseres

When God shuts a door, he
opens a window.
John Ruskin

The natural flights of the human
mind are not from pleasure to
pleasure, but from hope to hope.
Samuel Johnson

Judge not the Lord by feeble sense,
But trust Him for His grace;
Behind a frowning Providence
He hides a smiling face.
William Cowper

On the whole, I think we shall
survive. The outlook is as bad as it
has ever been, but thinking people
realize that—and therein lies the
hope of its getting better.
Jawaharlal Nehru

Ere now I would have ended my
miseries in death, but fond Hope
keeps the spark alive, whispering
ever that tomorrow will be better
than today.
Tibullus

Let us be of good cheer, remembering that the misfortunes hardest
to bear are those which never happen.
James Russell Lowell

These things are beautiful beyond
belief—
The pleasant weakness that comes
after pain;
The radiant greenness that comes
after rain;
The deepened faith that follows
after grief;
And the awakening to love again.
Author Unknown

Hell is the place where one has
ceased to hope.
A. J. Cronin

Hope is itself a species of happiness, and, perhaps, the chief happiness which this world affords.
Samuel Johnson

In my youth hope hired
In my heart a tent;
Promised me a fortune,
Never paid her rent.

Bankrupt is my tenant—
This I know at length—
Why then to expel her
Do I lack the strength?
Philip Raskin

Tomorrow comes to us untar-
nished by human living. No human
eyes have seen it and no one can
tell what it is going to be. The
Chinese word for tomorrow (ming-
tien) means "bright day." There is
the wisdom of sages and the
rapture of poets in that image.
Brooks Atkinson

Take from me the hope that I can change the future and you will drive me mad.

Israel Zangwill

Two travelers, one a veteran and the other a novice, were climbing in the Pyrenees. At night they were caught on one of the peaks and had to sleep upon a ledge. Toward morning a storm came up, and the howling wind wailed fiercely among the heights. The frightened novice awakened his friend and said, "I think it is the end of the world!" "Oh, no," said the veteran, "this is how the dawn comes in the Pyrenees!"

Hilaire Belloc

Hope is like the sun which, as we journey towards it, casts the shadow of our burden behind us.

Samuel Smiles

Hope is the promissory note of life on which the principal never matures but which pays compound interest to those who render their best services each day.

Author Unknown

I live on hope and that I think do all
Who come into this world.

Robert Bridges

At fifty, I take great comfort in God. I think He is considerably amused with us some times, but that He likes us, on the whole, and would not let us get at the match box so carelessly as He does, unless He knew that the frame of His universe was fireproof.

James Russell Lowell

Hope is life and life is hope.

Adele Shreve

---

73. THE MEANING OF COURAGE

Timidity is mistrust of self, and proceeds not from modesty but from conceit. A man is timid because he is afraid of not appearing to his best advantage.

Comtesse Diane

The probability that we may fail in the struggle ought not to deter us from the support of a cause we believe to be just.

Abraham Lincoln

Someone once asked James J. Corbett what was the most important thing a man must do to become a champion. He replied, "Fight one more round."
The Duke of Wellington said

that the British soldiers at the Battle of Waterloo were not braver than Napoleon's soldiers, but they were only braver five minutes longer. That made the difference between victory and defeat.

Author Unknown

Life is mostly froth and bubble,
Two things stand like stone—
Kindness in another's trouble,
Courage in your own.

Adam Lindsay Gordon

Nothing will ever be attempted if all possible objections must be first overcome.

Samuel Johnson

The most sublime courage I have ever witnessed has been among that class too poor to know they possessed it, and too humble for the world to discover it.

Josh Billings

The blackest days of Thomas Carlyle's life began when his friend, John Stuart Mill, came into his study one morning and said, "I don't know how to tell you this, but that manuscript you gave me to read? Well, the maid used it to start the fire."

Carlyle says that at first he alternated between rage and grief, but finally settled into deep despair. Then one day "I looked out my window and saw bricklayers at work. It came to me that as they lay brick on brick, so could I still lay word on word, sentence on sentence."

With that he began to rewrite "The French Revolution." The work he persevered in endures to this day as a classic in its field and a monument to the kind of courage that alone can conquer despair.

Margaret Blair Johnstone

You cannot run away from a weakness; you must sometime fight it out or perish. And if that be so, why not now, and where you stand?

Robert Louis Stevenson

Spend your brief moment according to nature's law, and serenely greet the journey's end as an olive falls when it is ripe, blessing the branch that bare it, and giving thanks to the tree that gave it life.

Marcus Aurelius

When the going gets tough, the tough get going.

Knute Rockne

He that raises a large family does, indeed, while he lives to observe them, *stand*, as Watts says, *a broader mark for sorrow;* but then he stands a broader mark for pleasure too. When we launch our little fleet of barks into the ocean, bound to different ports, we hope for each a prosperous voyage; but contrary winds, hidden shoals, storms, and enemies, come in for a share in the disposition of events; and though these occasion a mixture of disappointment, yet, considering the risk where we can make no insurance, we should think ourselves happy if some return with success.

Benjamin Franklin

Out of the earth, the rose,
    Out of the night, the dawn:
Out of my heart, with all its woes,
    High courage to press on.

Laura Lee Randall

Heroism is the brilliant triumph of the soul over the flesh, that is to say over fear: fear of poverty, of suffering, of calumny, of illness, of loneliness and of death. There is no real piety without heroism. It is the glorious concentration of courage.

Henri F. Amiel

We have more respect for a man who robs boldly on a highway than for a fellow who jumps out of a ditch and knocks you down behind your back. Courage is a quality so necessary for maintaining virtue, that it is always respected, even when it is associated with vice.

Samuel Johnson

He who fears he will suffer, already suffers because of his fear.
Michel de Montaigne

The courage we desire and prize is not the courage to die decently, but to live manfully.
Thomas Carlyle

Don't play for safety. It's the most dangerous thing in the world.
Hugh Walpole

Act as if it were impossible to fail.
Dorothea Brande

God give me the courage to face a fact, though it slay me.
Thomas Huxley

Who is the bravest hero? He who turns his enemy into a friend.
The Midrash

Spiritual life and secure life do not go together. To save oneself one must struggle and take risks.
Ignazio Silone

The best way out of a difficulty is through it.
Author Unknown

When you get into a tight place and everything goes against you, till it seems as though you could not hold on a minute longer, never give up then, for that is just the place and time that the tide will turn.
Harriet Beecher Stowe

Courage is the human virtue that counts most—courage to act on limited knowledge and insufficient evidence. That's all any of us have, so we must have the courage to go ahead and act on a hunch. It's the best we can do.
Robert Frost

If we take the generally accepted definition of bravery as a quality which knows not fear, I have never seen a brave man. All men are frightened. The more intelligent they are, the more they are frightened. The courageous man is the man who forces himself, in spite of his fear, to carry on. Discipline, pride, self-respect, self-confidence, and the love of glory are attributes which will make a man courageous even when he is afraid.
George S. Patton, Jr.

You should never wear your best trousers when you go out to fight for freedom and truth.
Henrik Ibsen

Wealth lost, something lost; honor lost, much lost; courage lost, all lost.
Johann Wolfgang von Goethe

He who will not reason, is a bigot; he who cannot is a fool; and he who dares not, is a slave.
William Drummond

Fear of life in one form or another is the great thing to exercise.
William James

One man with courage makes a majority.
Andrew Jackson

You gain strength, courage and confidence by every experience in which you really stop to look fear in the face. You are able to say to yourself, "I lived through this horror. I can take the next thing that comes along." The danger lies in refusing to face the fear, in not daring to come to grips with it. If you fail anywhere along the line it will take away your confidence.

You must make yourself succeed every time. *You must do the thing you think you cannot do.*

Eleanor Roosevelt

Courage is often but the effect of despair, for we cease to fear when we have ceased to hope.

Lady Marguerite Blessington

A man who protects and hoards his life may lose it anyhow. Perhaps to protect it is to lose it in the most real sense of the word, for cowardice means spiritual death.

Sherman E. Johnson

I love the man who can smile in trouble, who can gather strength from distress, and grow brave by reaction. 'Tis the business of little minds to shrink, but he whose heart is firm, and whose conscience approves his conduct, will pursue his principles unto death.

Thomas Paine

Never be afraid to stand with the minority when the minority is right, for the minority which is right will one day be the majority; always be afraid to stand with the majority which is wrong, for the majority which is wrong will one day be the minority.

William Jennings Bryan

There are things which one must have the courage not to write.

Remy de Gourmont

The only thing we have to fear is fear itself.

Franklin D. Roosevelt

Courage is above bravery, as the head is above the body. Where the soul of bravery is daring, that of courage is nobility. Where the fruit of bravery is glory, that of courage is virtue.

Edward Coursin

Half the things that people do not succeed in, are through fear of making the attempt.

James Northcote

A ship in harbor is safe, but that is not what ships are built for.

William G. T. Shedd

"I Can't" sits moping at his work,
  His thoughts are just a crazy crew
Intent on shifty ways to shirk
  The thing he needs to do.
"I Can't" hangs by a feeble grip,
  "I Can" hold on with forceful hand;
"I Can't" lets all his chances slip,
  "I Can" bends all to his command.

Annie L. Muzzey

The soul little suspects its own courage. We have had to tear men's bodies to pieces, to burn, crush, strangle and crucify them to find that last wonderful drop of courage. Take even a common man, the commonest, and beat and bruise him enough and you will see his soul rise God-like.

Frank Crane

Knowledge without courage is sterile.

Baltasar Gracian

There is a famous statue in Mexico by Jesus Garcia, entitled "In Spite Of." The sculptor lost his right hand in the midst of his work on the statue. He determined that he would finish it. He learned how to carve with his left hand and finished it—and better, perhaps, than he would have done with his right hand. For a quality of life had gone into the statue. So they called the statue "In Spite Of."

E. Stanley Jones

Greatness, in the last analysis, is largely bravery—courage in escaping from old ideas and old standards and respectable ways of doing things. This is one of the chief elements in what we vaguely call capacity. If you do not dare to differ from your associates and teachers you will never be great.

James Harvey Robinson

It is good to remember that the tea kettle, although up to its neck in hot water, continues to sing.

Author Unknown

Education, whether of black man or white man, that gives one physical courage to stand up in front of a cannon and fails to give one moral courage to stand up in defense of right and justice, is a failure.

Booker T. Washington

Courage consists not in blindly overlooking danger, but in seeing it and conquering it.

Jean Paul Richter

An Arab folk tale relates that Pestilence once met a caravan upon the desert way to Bagdad. "Why," asked the Arab chief, "must you hasten to Bagdad?" "To take five thousand lives," Pestilence replied. Upon the way back from the City of the Caliphs, Pestilence and the caravan met again. "You deceived me," the chief said angrily. "Instead of five thousand lives you took fifty thousand." "Nay," said Pestilence. "Five thousand and not

one more. It was Fear who killed the rest."

Maurice Duhamel

For fourteen years I have not had a day of real health. I have wakened sick and gone to bed weary, yet I have done my work unflinchingly. I have written in bed and out of bed, written in hemorrhages, written in sickness, written torn by coughing, written when my head swam for weakness—and I have done it all for so long that it seems to me I have won my wager and recovered my glove. Yet the battle still goes on: ill or well is a trifle so long as it goes. I was made for a contest, and the Powers-That-Be have willed that my battlefield shall be the dingy, inglorious one of the bed and the medicine-bottle.

Robert Louis Stevenson

Nothing happens to any man which he is not formed by nature to bear.

Marcus Aurelius

The truth that many people never understand, until it is too late, is that the more you try to avoid suffering the more you suffer, because smaller and more insignificant things begin to torture you in proportion to your fear of being hurt.

Thomas Merton

A man in the right, with God on his side, is in the majority though he be alone.

Henry Ward Beecher

Nothing requires a rarer intellectual heroism than willingness to see one's equation written out.

George Santayana

Be not afraid of life. Believe that life is worth living and your belief will help create the fact.

William James

One ought never to turn one's back on a threatened danger and try to run away from it. If you do that, you will double the danger. But if you meet it promptly and without flinching, you will reduce the danger by half. Never run away from anything. Never!

Winston Churchill

To live well in the quiet routine of life; to fill a little space because God wills it; to go on cheerfully with a petty round of little duties, little avocations; to smile for the joy of others when the heart is aching —who does this, his works will follow him. He may not be hero to the world, but he is one of God's heroes.

Author Unknown

When moral courage feels that it is in the right, there is no personal daring of which it is incapable.

Leigh Hunt

What is more mortifying than to feel that you've missed the plum for want of courage to shake the tree?

Logan Pearsall Smith

Our nation was built by men who took risks—pioneers who were not afraid of the wilderness; brave men who were not afraid of failure; scientists who were not afraid of truth; thinkers who were not afraid of progress; dreamers who were not afraid of action.

Brooks Atkinson

I beg you take courage; the brave soul can mend even disaster.

Catherine of Russia

There is only one heroism and that is to see the world as it is and love it.

Romain Rolland

Truth is not only violated by falsehood; it may be equally outraged by silence.

Henri F. Amiel

My life might have been a complete failure if I had allowed the fact that I am supposed to walk in total darkness to interfere with my determination to search for the light.

Elsie Cowan

It is when we all play safe that we create a world of utmost insecurity.

Dag Hammarskjold

Fear is one of the passions of human nature of which it is impossible to divest it. You remember the Emperor Charles V, when he read upon the tombstone of a Spanish nobleman, "Here lies one who never knew fear," wittily said, "Then he never snuffed a candle with his fingers."

Samuel Johnson

Education consists in being afraid at the right time.

Angelo Patri

Why not go out on a limb? Isn't that where the fruit is?

Frank Scully

True courage is not built upon mental cleverness, or earthly power but it stands upon the solid rock of truth and spiritual power.

Lowell Filimore

God grant me the courage not to give up on what I think is right even though I think it is hopeless.
Chester W. Nimitz

He who would acquire fame must not show himself afraid of censure. The dread of censure is the death of genius.
William G. Simms

Facing it—always facing it—that's the way to get through. Face it! That's enough for any man!
Joseph Conrad

Keep your fears to yourself but share your courage with others.
Robert Louis Stevenson

Courage considered in itself or without reference to its causes, is no virtue, and deserves no esteem. It is found in the best and the worst, and is to be judged according to the qualities from which it springs and with which it is conjoined.
William Channing

Strength is born in the deep silence of long-suffering hearts; not amid joy.
Felicia Hemans

Bravery is fear sneering at itself.
Maxwell Bodenheim

To admit that there are questions which even our so impressive intelligence is unable to answer, and at the same time not to despair of the ability of the human race to find, eventually, better answers than we can reach as yet—to recognize that there is nothing to do but keep on trying as well as we can, and to be as content as we can with the small gains that in the course of ages amount to something—that requires some courage and some balance.
Elmer Davis

Courage is a special kind of knowledge: the knowledge of how to fear what ought to be feared and how not to fear what ought not to be feared.
David Ben-Gurion

However mean your life is, meet it and live it; do not shun it and call it hard names.
Henry David Thoreau

To be brave for one short instant is no hard matter; it is easier to die for a cause than to live for it.
Comtesse Diane

Perfect valor is to do unwitnessed what we should be capable of doing before all the world.
François Rochefoucauld

74. PATIENCE AND PERSEVERANCE

It is not necessary for all men to be great in action. The greatest and sublimest power is often simple patience.
Horace Bushnell

All the performances of human art, at which we look with praise and wonder, are instances of the resistless force of perseverance.
Ben Johnson

The principal part of faith is patience.

George Macdonald

Patience is bitter, but its fruit is sweet.

Jean Jacques Rousseau

There is no road too long for the man who advances deliberately and without undue haste; no honors too distant to the man who prepares himself for them with patience.

La Bruyere

Knowledge and timber shouldn't be much used till they are seasoned.

Oliver Wendell Holmes

Patience and fortitude conquer all things.

Ralph Waldo Emerson

The saints are the sinners who keep trying.

Robert Louis Stevenson

Learn to wait—life's hardest lesson
Conned, perchance, through blinding tears;
While the heart throbs sadly echo
To the tread of passing years.
Learn to wait—hope's slow fruition:
Faint not, though the way seems long;
There is joy in each condition;
Hearts through suffering may grow strong.
Thus a soul untouched by sorrow
Aims not at a higher state;
Joy seeks not a brighter morrow;
Only sad hearts learn to wait.

Author Unknown

How poor are they who have not patience!

What wound did ever heal, but by degrees?

William Shakespeare

I had no special sagacity, only the power of patient thought. I kept the subject constantly before me and waited until the first dawnings opened little by little into the full light.

Sir Isaac Newton

Endure and persist; this pain will turn to your good.

Ovid

The heights by great men reached and kept
Were not attained by sudden flight,
But they, while their companions slept,
Were toiling upward in the night.

Henry Wadsworth Longfellow

When you get into a tight place and everything goes against you, till it seems as though you could not hold on a minute longer, never give up then, for that is just the place and time that the tide will turn.

Harriet Beecher Stowe

Who persists in knocking will succeed in entering.

Moses Ibn Ezra

Levi Yitzhok asked a man, who seemed to be in a great hurry, why he rushed so. "I am in pursuit of my livelihood," replied the man. "And how do you know," asked the rabbi, "that your livelihood runs ahead of you? May be it is behind you, and what you need is to pause till it overtakes you."

Abraham Kahana

Patience is power; with time and patience the mulberry leaf becomes silk.

Chinese Proverb

Time was invented by Almighty God in order to give ideas a chance.
Nicholas Murray Butler

He that can have patience can have what he will.
Benjamin Franklin

We can best serve a desperate world by refusing to be desperate.
Author Unknown

Talent made a poor Appearance Until he married Perseverance.
Arthur Guiterman

Patience is the art of hoping.
Vauvenargues

Genius is eternal patience.
Michelangelo

The road to success is not to be run upon by seven-leagued boots. Step by step, little by little, bit by bit—that is the way to wealth, that is the way to wisdom, that is the way to glory.
Sir Thomas Fowell Buxton

Persistent people begin their success where others end in failure.
Edward Eggleston

What cannot be removed, becomes lighter through patience.
Horace

Excellence is never granted to man but as the reward of labor. It argues no small strength of mind to persevere in habits of industry without the pleasure of perceiving those advances, which, like the hand of a clock, whilst they make hourly approaches to their point, yet proceed so slowly as to escape observation.
Sir Joshua Reynolds

There is no grief which time does not lessen and soften.
Cicero

Patience and gentleness are power.
Leigh Hunt

Every noble work is at first impossible.
Thomas Carlyle

Time cures sorrows and squabbles because we all change, and are no longer the same persons. Neither the offender nor the offended is the same.
Blaise Pascal

There are but two roads that lead to an important goal and to the doing of great things: strength and perseverance. Strength is the lot of but a few privileged men; but austere perseverance, harsh and continuous, may be employed by the smallest of us and rarely fails of its purpose, for its silent power grows irresistibly greater with time.
Johann Wolfgang von Goethe

I hold a doctrine, to which I owe not much, indeed, but all the little I ever had, namely, that with ordinary talent and extraordinary perseverance, all things are attainable.
Sir Thomas Fowell Buxton

Sometimes nothing is harder in life than just to endure. There are two types of strength. There is the strength of the wind that sways the mighty oak, and there is the strength of the oak that withstands the power of the wind. There is the strength of the locomotive that pulls the heavy train across the bridge, and there is the strength of the bridge that holds up the weight of the train. One is active strength, the other is passive strength. One is the power to keep going, the other is the power to keep still. One is the strength by which we overcome, the other is the strength by which we endure.

Harold Phillips

There is strength of quiet endurance as significant of courage as the most daring feats of prowess.

H. T. Tuckerman

He who can endure all things may venture all things.

Vauvenargues

Great works are performed, not by strength, but by perseverance. He that shall walk, with vigor, three hours a day will pass, in seven years, a space equal to the circumference of the globe.

Samuel Johnson

Genius is only the power of making continuous efforts. The line between failure and success is so fine that we scarcely know when we pass it: so fine that we are often on the line and do not know it. How many a man has thrown up his hands at a time when a little more effort, a little more patience, would have achieved success. As the tide goes clear out, so it comes clear in. In business, sometimes, prospects may seem darkest when really they are on the turn. A little more persistence, a little more effort, and what seemed hopeless failure may turn to glorious success. There is no failure except from within, no really insurmountable barrier save our own inherent weakness of purpose.

Elbert Hubbard

To know how to wait is the great secret of success.

Joseph Marie De Maistre

The falling drops at last will wear the stones.

Lucretius

The difficult is just which can be done immediately; the impossible takes a little longer.

George Santayana

Perseverance is a great element of success. If you only knock long enough and loud enough at the gate, you are sure to wake up somebody.

Henry Wadsworth Longfellow

No great thing is created suddenly, any more than a bunch of grapes or a fig. If you tell me that you desire a fig. I answer you that there must be time. Let it first blossom, then bear fruit, then ripen.

Epictetus

When Abraham Lincoln was a young man he ran for the Legislature in Illinois and was badly swamped.

He next entered business, failed and spent seventeen years of his life paying up the debts of a worthless partner.

He was in love with a beautiful young woman to whom he became engaged—and then she died.

Later he married a woman who was a constant burden to him.

Entering politics again, he was badly defeated for Congress.

He failed to get an appointment to the U. S. Land Office.

He was badly defeated for the U. S. Senate.

In 1856 he became a candidate

for the Vice-Presidency and was again defeated.

In 1858 he was defeated by Douglas.

One failure after another—bad failures—great set-backs. In the face of all this he eventually became one of the country's greatest men, if not the greatest. When you think of a series of set-backs like this, doesn't it make you feel small to become discouraged, just because you think that you're having a hard time in life?

Author Unknown

And many strokes, though with a little axe, hew down and fell the hardest-timbered oak.

William Shakespeare

Misfortune may become fortune through patience.

Solomon Ibn Gabirol

Our real blessings often appear to us in shape of pains, losses and disappointments; but let us have patience, and we soon shall see them in their proper figures.

Joseph Addison

Heaven is not reached at a single bound,
We build the ladder by which we rise
From the lowly earth to the vaulted skies,
And we mount to its summit round by round.

J. G. Holland

When nothing seems to help, I go and look at a stonecutter hammering away at his rock perhaps a hundred times without as much as a crack showing in it. Yet at the hundred and first blow it will split in two, and I know it was not that blow that did it—but all that had gone before.

Jacob Riis

Patience is the support of weakness; impatience is the ruin of strength.

Caleb C. Colton

'Tis easy to be gentle when
Death's silence shames our clamor,
And easy to discern the best
Through memory's mystic glamor;
But wise it were for me and thee
Ere love is past forgiving
To take this tender lesson home—
Be patient with the living.

Author Unknown

Nothing in the world can take the place of persistence. Talent will not: nothing is more common than unsuccessful men with talent. Genius will not: unrewarded genius is almost a proverb. Education will not: the world is full of educated derelicts. Persistence and determination alone are omnipotent. The slogan "Press on," has solved and always will solve the problems of the human race.

Calvin Coolidge

By patience and time we sever
What strength and rage could never.

Jean de La Fontaine

The difference between perseverance and obstinacy is, that one often comes from a strong will, and the other from a strong won't.

Henry Ward Beecher

Failure is the line of least persistence.

Author Unknown

Perseverance gives power to weakness, and opens to poverty the world's wealth. It spreads fertility over the barren landscape, and bids the choicest fruits and flowers spring up and flourish in the desert abode of thorns and briers.

Samuel G. Goodrich

---

75. THE ART OF FAILING

No man succeeds in everything he undertakes. In that sense we are all failures. The great point is not to fail in ordering and sustaining the effort of our life.

Joseph Conrad

God will not look you over for medals, degrees or diplomas, but for scars.

Paul E. Holdcraft

We mount to heaven mostly on the ruins of our cherished schemes, finding our failures were successes.

Amos Bronson Alcott

Learn from your mistakes, but don't cry over them. We best redeem the past by forgetting it.

Elbert Hubbard

It is defeat that turns bone to flint, and gristle to muscle, and makes men invincible, and formed those heroic natures that are now in ascendancy in the world. Do not then be afraid of defeat. You are never so near to victory as when defeated in a good cause.

Henry Ward Beecher

Failures are divided into two classes—those who thought and never did, and those who did and never thought.

John Charles Salak

Failure changes to success when one acquires self-knowledge.

Louise A. Vernon

Failures are made only by those who fail to dare, not by those who dare to fail.

Louis Binstock

The only complete catastrophe is the catastrophe from which we learn nothing.

William Ernest Hocking

He that falls into sin is a man; that grieves at it, is a saint; that boasts of it, is a devil.

Author Unknown

Failures are necessary to human experience. A man usually learns more by his failures than by his moments of success. No man ever succeeded in any cause without his share of failures. . . . Our failures may sometimes be necessary in the sight of God to show us our own weakness, and that no man is sufficient unto himself.

Oliver Everette

The danger of failure is greatest at the beginning of an enterprise and not far from its consummation. Shipwrecks occur near shore.

Ludwig Boerne

We need to teach the highly educated person that it is not a disgrace to fail and that he must analyze every failure to find its cause. He must learn how to fail intelligently, for failing is one of the greatest arts in the world.

Charles F. Kettering

Develop success from failures. Discouragement and failure are two of the surest steppingstones to success. No other element can do so much for a man if he is willing to study them and make capital out of them. Look backward. Can't you see where your failures have helped you?

Dale Carnegie

Nothing succeeds like—failure.

Oliver Herford

The most important thing in life is not to capitalize on your gains. Any fool can do that. The really important thing is to profit from your losses. That requires intelligence; and it makes the difference between a man of sense and a fool.

William Bolitho

To make no mistakes is not in the power of man; but from their errors and mistakes the wise and good learn wisdom for the future.

Plutarch

Sometimes it is more important to discover what one cannot do, than what one can do.

Lin Yutang

No man ever became great or good except through many and great mistakes.

William Gladstone

Good education is not so much one which prepares a man to succeed in the world as one which enables him to sustain failure.

Canon Bernard Iddings Bell

I had rather be defeated in a cause that will ultimately triumph than triumph in a cause that will ultimately be defeated.

Woodrow Wilson

There is the greatest practical benefit in making a few failures early in life.

Thomas Huxley

Failure is instructive. The person who really thinks learns quite as much from his failures as from his successes.

John Dewey

They never fail who die
In a great cause.

Lord Byron

Failure is, in a sense, the highway to success, inasmuch as every discovery of what is false leads us to seek earnestly after what is true, and every fresh experience points out some form of error which we shall afterward carefully avoid.

John Keats

It happens very often that one tries to do something and fails. He feels discouraged, and yet he may discover years afterward that the very effort he made was the reason why somebody else took it up and succeeded. I really believe that whatever use I have been to progressive civilization has been accomplished in the things I failed to do rather than in the things I actually did do.

Senator George W. Norris

A success is one who decided to succeed—and worked. A failure is one who decided to succeed—and wished. A decided failure is one who failed to decide—and waited.

William A. Ward

There are some defeats more triumphant than victories.

Michel de Montaigne

The only failure a man ought to fear is failure in cleaving to the purpose he sees best.
George Eliot

Lord Byron and Sir Walter Scott were both lame. Byron was embittered by his lameness, brooded on it till he loathed it, never entered a public place but his mind reverted to it, so that much of the color and zest of existence were lost to him. Scott, on the other hand, never complained or spoke one bitter word about his disability, not even to his dearest friend. In the circumstances it is not so very surprising that Sir Walter should have received a letter from Byron with this sentence in it: "Ah, Scott, I would give my fame to have your happiness."
Robert J. McCracken

Our greatest glory is not in never falling, but in rising every time we fall.
Oliver Goldsmith

Failure sometimes enlarges the spirit. You have to fall back upon humanity and God.
Charles Horton Cooley

What is defeat? Nothing but education, nothing but the first step to something better.
Wendell Phillips

It ain't no disgrace for a man to fall; but to lay there and grunt is.
Josh Billings

The most important of my discoveries have been suggested to me by failure.
Sir Humphry Davy

In great attempts it is glorious even to fail.
Longinus

Because the stars are set so
high . . .
Shall I accept defeat?
What then would keep me looking
up
If they were at my feet?
Lillian Berdow

Every defeat is a Waterloo unless you have battalions of energy in reserve. Disraeli's first speech was a failure. When the old peers of England shook their double chins at him, he replied quietly, "The day will come when you will be glad to hear me."
John Homer Miller

---

76. DEATH AND BEYOND

Two children were overheard talking about the death of their grandmother. The five-year-old girl was asking her seven-year-old brother how "grandmother went to God." "Well," said the boy, "it happened this way. First Grandmother reached up and up and up as far as she could. Then God reached down and down and down. When their hands touched, he took her."
Gene E. Bartlett

I have never seen what to me seemed an atom of proof that there is a future life. And yet—I am strongly inclined to expect one.
Mark Twain

There is only one way to get ready for immortality, and that is to love this life and live it as bravely and faithfully and cheerfully as we can.

Henry Van Dyke

"Good-night! Good-night!" as we so oft have said,
Beneath this roof at midnight, in the days
That are no more, and shall no more return.
Thou hast but taken up thy lamp and gone to bed;
I stay a little longer, as one stays
To cover up the embers that still burn.

Henry Wadsworth Longfellow

I am a part of all whom I have met.

Alfred Tennyson

When at eve at the bounding of the landscape the heavens appear to recline so slowly on the earth, imagination pictures beyond the horizon an asylum of hope,—a native land of love; and nature seems silently to repeat that man is immortal.

Madame de Stael

I believe in my survival after death. Like many others before me, I have experienced "intimations of immortality." I can no more explain these than the brown seed can explain the flowering tree. Deep in the soil in time's midwinter, my very stirring and unease seem a kind of growing pain toward June.

Robert Hillyer

Men fear Death as children fear to go in the dark; and as that natural fear in children is increased with tales so is the other. . . . It is as natural to die as to be born; and to a little infant perhaps the one is as painful as the other.

Francis Bacon

Belief in immortality gives dignity to life and enables us to endure cheerfully those trials which come to us all. As the thought of immortality occupies our minds, we gain a clearer conception of duty and are inspired to cultivate character. Living for the future is no coward's philosophy, but an inspiration to noble and unselfish activity.

Samuel M. Lindsay

It is impossible that anything so natural, so necessary, and so universal as death should ever have been designed as an evil to mankind.

Jonathan Swift

Friendship between mortals can be contracted on no other terms than that one must some time mourn for the other's death.

Samuel Johnson

Whoever dies in the full tilt of his ambitions is buried alive, and whoever survives his hopes and fears is dead, unburied. Death for us is all we have missed, all the periods and planets we have not lived in, all the countries we have not visited, all the books we have not read, all the emotions and experiences we have not had, all the prayers we have not prayed, all the battles we have not fought. Every restriction, negation is a piece of death.

Israel Zangwill

I am a better believer, and all serious souls are better believers, in immortality than we can give grounds for.

Ralph Waldo Emerson

Nature is the most thrifty thing in the world; she never wastes anything; she undergoes change, but there's no annihilation—the essence remains.

Thomas Binney

The stars look down on the earth,
The stars look down on the sea.
The stars look up to the infinite God,
The stars look down on me.
The stars will live for a million years,
For a million years and a day.
But God and I will live and love
When the stars have passed away.

Harry K. Zeller, Jr.

Our lives are waves that come up out of the ocean of eternity, break upon the beach of earth, and lapse back to the ocean of eternity. Some are sunlit, some run in storm and rain; one is a quiet ripple, another is a thunderous breaker; and once in many centuries comes a great tidal wave that sweeps over a continent; but all go back to the sea and lie equally level there.

Austin O'Malley

What is lovely never dies, but passes into other loveliness.

Thomas Bailey Aldrich

I am fully convinced that the soul is indestructible, and that its activities will continue through eternity. It is like the sun, which, to our eyes, seems to set in night; but it has really gone to diffuse its light elsewhere.

Johann Wolfgang von Goethe

I know not when I go or where
From this familiar scene;
But He is here and He is there,
And all the way between;
And when I leave this life, I know,
For that dim vast unknown,
Though late I stay, or soon I go,
I shall not go alone.

Author Unknown

In old age life's shadows are meeting eternity's day.

Adam Clarke

The survivorship of a worthy man in his son is a pleasure scarce inferior to the hopes of the continuance of his own life.

Richard Steele

Were a star quenched on high,
For ages would its light,
Still travelling downward from the sky,
Shine on our mortal sight.
So when a great man dies,
For years beyond our ken,
The light he leaves behind him lies
Upon the paths of men.

Henry Wadsworth Longfellow

No one should fear death. I know, because I have come face to face with death several times. It is really a pleasant experience. You seem to hear beautiful music and everything is mellow and sweet and serene—no struggle, no terror, just calmness and beauty. When death comes, you will find it to be one of the easiest and most blissful experiences you have ever had.

Eddie Rickenbacker

Life seems to me like a Japanese picture which our imagination does not allow to end with the margin. We aim at the infinite and when the arrow falls to earth it is in flames.

Oliver Wendell Holmes, Jr.

Whence this pleasing hope, this fond desire,
This longing for immortality?
'Tis the divinity that stirs within us;
'Tis heaven itself that points out a hereafter,
And intimates eternity to man.

Joseph Addison

Our hope of immortality does not come from any religions, but nearly all religions come from that hope.

Ralph G. Ingersoll

The righteous are called alive in death; the wicked are called dead even when alive.

The Talmud

I know only scientifically determined truth, but I am going to believe what I wish to believe, what I cannot help but believe—I expect to meet this dear child in another world.

Louis Pasteur

Sleep and death—they differ in duration rather than in quality. Perhaps both are sojourns in the spiritual, the real world. In one case our carriage waits nightly to take us back from the entrance of slumber, while in the other, having arrived at our destination and with no further use for the carriage, it is dismissed.

John Bigelow

Cowards die many times before their deaths:

The valiant never taste of death but once.
Of all the wonders that I yet have heard,
It seems to me most strange that men should fear;
Seeing that death, a necessary end,
Will come when it will come.

William Shakespeare

Sleep on, O brave-hearted, O wise man that kindled the flame—
To live in mankind is far more than to live in a name.

Vachel Lindsay

Though inland far we be
Our souls have sight of that immortal sea
Which brought us hither.

William Wordsworth

Remind thyself that he whom thou lovest is mortal—that what thou lovest is not thine own, it is given thee for the present not irrevocably nor forever, but even as a fig or bunch of grapes at the appointed season of the year.

Epictetus

If I err in my belief that the souls of men are immortal, I err gladly, and I do not wish to lose so delightful an error.

Cicero

Life is the childhood of our immortality.

Johann Wolfgang Von Goethe

Many people seem to feel that science has somehow made "religious ideas" untimely or old-fashioned. But I think science has a real surprise for the skeptics. Science, for instance, tells us that nothing in nature, not even the tiniest particle, can disappear without a trace. Nature does not know extinction. All it knows is transformation.

Now, if God applies this fundamental principle to the most minute and insignificant parts of His universe, doesn't it make sense to assume that He applies it also to the human soul? I think it does. And everything science has taught me— and continues to teach me— strengthens my belief in the continuity of our spiritual existence after death. Nothing disappears without a trace.

Wernher von Braun

Death is not extinguishing the light; it is putting out the lamp because the dawn has come.

Sir Rabindranath Tagore

Life is a voyage that's homeward bound.

Herman Melville

If there were no future life, our souls would not thirst for it.

Jean Paul Richter

We sometimes congratulate ourselves at the moment of waking from a troubled dream: it may be so the moment after death.

Nathaniel Hawthorne

What we have done for ourselves alone dies with us. What we have

done for others and the world remains and is immortal.

Albert Pine

Life is real! Life is earnest!
And the grave is not its goal;
Dust thou art, to dust returnest,
Was not spoken of the soul.

Henry Wadsworth Longfellow

Fame is not popularity. It is the spirit of a man surviving himself in the minds and thoughts of other men.

William Hazlitt

I believe in the immortality of the soul, not in the sense in which I accept the demonstrable truths of science, but as a supreme act of faith in the reasonableness of God's work.

John Fiske

Still seems it strange, that thou shouldst live forever?
Is it less strange, that thou shouldst live at all?

Edward Young

Our Creator would never have made such lovely days, and have given us the deep hearts to enjoy them, above and beyond all thought, unless we were meant to be immortal.

Nathaniel Hawthorne

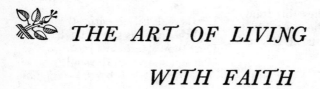

THE ART OF LIVING
WITH FAITH

77. WHAT IS RELIGION?

True religion is not a pie in which we put whatever ingredients we choose until it tastes just right to us, or, more often than not, produces spiritual indigestion. True religion is not a stew in which we drop a pinch of this or that until we have what seems to us to be the exact combination to make us happy and content. True religion is not a machine for which we assemble a great collection of cogs and wheels, put them together, and hope it will run. True religion is a tree that has life and growth and unity and roots which go down deep, drawing their power from the constant activity of God, the Creator.

George Gerald Parker

Religion makes easy and felicitous what in any case is necessary.

William James

What I mean by a religious person is one who conceives himself or herself to be the instrument of some purpose in the universe which is a high purpose, and is the motive power of evolution—that is, of a continual ascent in organization and power and life, and extension of life.

George Bernard Shaw

Your daily life is your temple and your religion.

Kahlil Gibran

Religion—that voice of the deepest human experience.

Matthew Arnold

The test of religion is whether it fits us to meet emergencies. A man has no more character than he can command in time of crisis.

Ralph W. Sockman

Religion is the first thing and the last thing, and until a man has found God and been found by God, he begins at no beginning, he works to no end.

H. G. Wells

The distinguishing mark of religion is not so much liberty as obedience, and its value is measured by the sacrifices which it can extract from the individual.

Henri F. Amiel

Selfishness is the only real atheism; aspiration, unselfishness, the only real religion.

Israel Zangwill

Religion is the reaching out of one's whole being—mind, body, spirit, emotions, intuitions, affections, will—for completion, for inner unity, for true relation with those about us, for right relation to the universe in which we live. Religion is life, a certain kind of life, life as it should and could be, a life of harmony within and true adjustment without—life, therefore, in harmony with the life of God himself.

Henry P. Van Dusen

Religion is the individual's attitude toward God and man as expressed in faith, in worship, in life, and in service.

Charles Foster Kent

The only religion that will do anything toward enriching your life is the religion which inspires you to do something toward enriching the life of others.

Author Unknown

The world is my country, all mankind are my brethren, and to do good is my religion.

Thomas Paine

Faith is more than praying
In humble solemn tone,
It is more than trusting
When weary and alone.

Faith is more than believing
In a well-ordered life;

It is more than victory
Over sin and strife.

Faith is more than planting
Seed beneath the sod,
Faith is daily walking
Hand in hand with God.

James Edmon Knowles

The question of bread for myself is a material question, but the question of bread for my neighbor is a spiritual question.

Nicolas Berdyaev

Religion is the everlasting dialogue between humanity and God.

Franz Werfel

We define religion as the assumption that life has meaning. Religion, or lack of it, is shown not in some intellectual or verbal formulations but in one's total orientation to life. Religion is whatever the individual takes to be his ultimate concern. One's religious attitude is to be found at that point where he has a conviction that there are values in human existence worth living and dying for.

Rollo May

The submergence of self in the pursuit of an ideal, the readiness to spend oneself without measure, prodigally, almost ecstatically, for something intuitively apprehended as great and noble, spend oneself one knows not why—some of us like to believe that this is what religion means.

Benjamin N. Cardozo

Science can tell us how to do more and more things; it cannot tell us what ought to be done.

Joseph Wood Krutch

The contours of old religions have been changed and their outlines blurred but religion remains and always will remain. I am speaking of religion as belief colored with emotion, an elemental sense of piety or reverence for life summing up man's certainty as to what is right and noble.

Lin Yutang

Religion is the best armour in the world, but the worst cloak.

John Newton

Your religion is good if it is vital and active. If it nourishes in you confidence, hope, love, and a sentiment of the infinite value of existence; if it is allied with what is best in you against what is worst, and holds forever before you the necessity of becoming a new man; if it makes you understand that pain is a deliverer; if it increases your respect for the conscience of others, if it renders forgiveness more easy, fortune less arrogant, duty dear, the beyond less visionary. If it does these things, it is good, little matter its name; however rudimentary it may be when it fills this office, it comes from the true source, it binds you to man and to God.

Charles Wagner

Those who make religion to consist in the contempt of this world and its enjoyments, are under a very fatal and dangerous mistake. As life is the gift of heaven, it is religion to enjoy it. He, therefore, who can be happy in himself, and who contributes all in his power toward the happiness of others, answers most effectually the ends of his creation, is an honor to his nature, and a pattern to mankind.

Joseph Addison

To serve God is not to pass our lives on our knees in prayer; it is to discharge on earth those obligations which our duty requires.

Jean J. Rousseau

If man's religion is of any importance, it is not just a garment of expression of unity with and security in the professed beliefs of a special group. It is rather an attitude of respect for himself, his God, his fellowman, which underwrites all his activity, which is allowed freedom of expression within the limitations of that respect.

Grace D. Yerbury

Religion is a hunger for beauty and love and glory. It is wonder and awe, mystery and majesty, passion and ecstasy. It is emotion as well as mind, feeling as well as knowing, the subjective as well as the objective.

It is the heart soaring to heights the head alone will never know; the apprehension of meanings science alone will never find; the awareness of values ethics alone will never reveal. It is the human spirit yearning for, and finding, something infinitely greater than itself which it calls God.

Waldemar Argow

A man cannot be religious without belonging to a particular religion any more than he can talk without using a particular language.

George Santayana

Art and religion are the soul of our civilization. Go to them, for there love exists and endures.
Frank Lloyd Wright

Superstition is the religion of feeble minds.
Edmund Burke

The purpose of science is to develop, without prejudice or preconception of any kind, a knowledge of the facts, the laws, and the processes of nature. The even more important task of religion, on the other hand, is to develop the conscience, the ideals, and the aspirations of mankind.
Robert A. Millikan

Religion should be the motor of life, the central heating plant of personality, the faith that gives joy to activity, hope to struggle, dignity to humility, zest to living.
William Lyon Phelps

Religion is a man's total reaction upon life.
William James

Men must beware of looking upon religion as an ideal to be yearned for, it should be an ideal to be applied.
Simon Dubnow

I would think of my religion as a gamble rather than think of it as an insurance premium.
Stephen S. Wise

Religion's all or nothing; it's no mere smile
Of contentment, sigh of aspiration, sir—
No quality of the finely tempered clay
Like its whiteness or its lightness; rather stuff

Of the very stuff; life of life, and self of self.
Robert Browning

And the essence of all faith it seems to me, for such a man as I, the essence of religion for people of my belief, is that man's life can be and will be better; that man's greatest enemies, in the forms in which they now exist—the forms we see on every hand, of fear, of hatred, slavery, cruelty, poverty and need—can be conquered and destroyed. In the affirmation of this fact, the continuance of this war, is man's religion and his living faith.
Thomas Wolfe

A man who puts aside his religion because he is going into society, is like one taking off his shoes because he is about to walk upon thorns.
Richard Cecil

Religion is the vision of something which stands beyond, behind, and within, the passing flux of immediate things; something which is real, and yet waiting to be realized; something which is a remote possibility, and yet the greatest of present facts; something that gives meaning to all that passes, and yet eludes apprehension; something whose possession is the final good, and yet is beyond all reach; something which is the ultimate ideal, and the hopeless quest.
Alfred North Whitehead

True religion is a profound uneasiness about our highest social values.
Reinhold Niebuhr

What a man believes may be ascertained, not from his creed, but from the assumptions on which he habitually acts.

George Bernard Shaw

Real religion is a way of life, not a white cloak to be wrapped around us on Sunday morning and then tossed aside into the 6-day closet of unconcern.

William A. Ward

True religion shows its influence in every part of our conduct; it is like the sap of a living tree, which penetrates the most distant boughs.

William Penn

Religion is what a man does with his solitariness.

Alfred North Whitehead

Let your religion be seen. Lamps do not talk, but they do shine. A lighthouse sounds no drum, it beats no gong; yet, far over the waters, its friendly light is seen by the mariner.

Theodore Ledyard Cuyler

At times in the lonely silence of the night and in rare lonely moments I come upon a sort of communion of myself with Something great that is not myself. Is it perhaps poverty of mind and language which obliges me to say that this universal scheme takes on the effect of a sympathetic person—and my communion a quality of fearless worship. These moments happen and are the supreme fact of my religious life to me, they are the crown of my religious experience.

H. G. Wells

---

78. THE ART OF BELIEVING

I have never discarded beliefs deliberately. I left them in the drawer, and after a while, I opened it, there was nothing there at all.

William Graham Sumner

Life is an adventure of faith, if we are to be victors over it, not victims of it. Faith in the God above us, faith in the little infinite soul within us, faith in life and in our fellow souls. Without faith, the plus quality, we cannot really live.

Joseph Fort Newton

We master fear through faith—faith in the worthwhileness of life and the trustworthiness of God; faith in the meaning of our pain

and our striving, and confidence that God will not cast us aside but will use each one of us as a piece of priceless mosaic in the design of His universe.

Joshua Loth Liebman

When all else is lost, the future still remains.

C. N. Bovee

What I admire in Columbus is not his having discovered a world, but his having gone to search for it on the faith of an opinion.

A. Robert Jacques Turgot

The heart will not long follow what the mind does not accept as true and trustworthy.

Costen J. Harrell

The old conceptions of religion can be overcome only through more religion, not through irreligion.

Berthold Auerbach

No ray of sunlight is ever lost, but the green which it wakes into existence needs time to sprout, and it is not always granted to the sower to live to see the harvest. All work that is worth anything is done in faith.

Albert Schweitzer

A man who bows down to nothing can never bear the burden of himself.

Dostoevski

It need not discourage us if we are full of doubts. Healthy questions keep faith dynamic. In fact, unless we start with doubts we cannot have a deep-rooted faith. One who believes lightly and unthinkingly has not much of a belief. He who has a faith which is not to be shaken has won it through blood and tears—has worked his way from doubt to truth as one who reaches a clearing through a thicket of brambles and thorns.

Helen Keller

That life is worth living is the most necessary of assumptions and were it not assumed, the most impossible of conclusions.

George Santayana

Fear builds prison walls around a man and bars him in with dreads, anxieties and timid doubts. Faith is the great liberator from prison walls. Fear paralyzes, faith empowers; fear disheartens, faith encourages; fear sickens, faith heals; fear puts hopelessness at the heart

of life, while faith sees beyond the horizon and rejoices in its God.

Lewis L. Dunnington

The plots of God are perfect. The universe is a plot of God.

Edgar Allan Poe

The notion that faith is going to help me to live "successfully" or to attain the kind of peace of mind that leaves me unruffled no matter how many refugees sleep on the streets of Hong Kong is far from the heart of our religious tradition.

Janet Harbison

If at some period in the course of civilization we seriously find that our science and our religion are antagonistic, then there must be something wrong either with our science or with our religion.

Havelock Ellis

There is no unbelief:
Whoever plants a seed beneath the sod,
And waits to see it push away the clod,
He trusts in God.

Whoever says, when clouds are in the sky,
Be patient, heart, light breaketh by and by,
Trusts the Most High.

Whoever sees 'neath winter's field of snow
The silent harvest of the future grow,
God's power must know.

The heart that looks on when the eyelids close,
And dares to live his life in spite of woes,
God's comfort knows.

There is no unbelief:
And day by day, and night, uncon-
    sciously,
The heart lives by the faith the lips
    deny:
God knoweth why.

John Tyndall

A belief is not merely an idea
the mind possesses; it is an idea
that possesses the mind.

Robert Bolton

Faith draws the poison from
every grief, takes the sting from
every loss, and quenches the fire
of every pain; and only faith can
do it.

J. G. Holland

There lives more faith in honest
    doubt,
Believe me, than in half the creeds.

Alfred Tennyson

He that has lost faith, what has
he left to live on?

Roger Bacon

The space of the whole universe
is emptied . . .
And frightening when there is
no God.

Zalman Shneor

Every man, either to his terror or
consolation, has some sense of religion.

James Harrington

Every tomorrow has two handles.
We can take hold of it by the
handle of anxiety or the handle of
faith.

Author Unknown

As human beings, we are so
made that we cannot help living
in two worlds, the "is" and the
"ought" the actual and the ideal.

Now the power which reaches out
into the "ought" and transforms it
into the "is" which lays hold upon
the possible and of it makes the
actual, is creative faith.

Harry E. Fosdick

He that will believe only what
he can fully comprehend, must
have a very long head or a very
short creed.

Caleb C. Colton

If you must tell me your opinions, tell me what you believe in.
I have plenty of doubts of my own.

Johann Wolfgang von Goethe

Faith affirms many things respecting which the senses are silent,
but nothing which they deny. It
is superior to their testimony, but
never opposed to it.

Blaise Pascal

Business is religion and religion
is business. The man who does
not make a business out of his
religion has a religious life of no
force, and the man who does not
make a religion of his business has
a business life of no character.

Maltbie Babcock

In actual life every great enterprise begins with and takes its first
forward step in faith.

August Von Schlegel

It is cynicism and fear that
freezes life: it is faith that thaws
it out, releases it, sets it free.

Harry E. Fosdick

Faith laughs at the shaking of
the spear; unbelief trembles at the
shaking of a leaf, unbelief starves
the soul; faith finds food in famine,
and a table in the wilderness. In
the greatest danger, faith says, "I

have a great God." When outward strength is broken, faith rests on the promises. In the midst of sorrow, faith draws the sting out of every trouble, and takes out the bitterness from every affliction.

Richard Cecil

Faith is kept alive in us, and gathers strength, more from practice than from speculations.

Joseph Addison

Faith is one of the forces by which men live, and the total absence of it means collapse.

William James

God moves in a mysterious way
His wonders to perform;
He plants his footsteps in the sea,
And rides upon the storm.

William Cowper

Not Truth, but Faith, it is
That keeps the world alive. If all
    at once
Faith were to slacken,—that unconscious faith
Which must, I know, yet be the corner stone
Of all believing—birds now flying fearless
Across would drop in terror to the earth;
Fishes would drown; and the all-governing reins
Would tangle in the frantic hands of God
And the worlds gallop headlong to destruction!

Edna St. Vincent Millay

Enter into the spirit of life, into the joy of living, and into the usefulness of being alive. For no one will grow tired and old if he has faith and enthusiasm.

Ernest Holmes

God who placed me here will do what He pleases with me hereafter, and He knows best what to do.

Lord Bolingbroke

We think we believe, but is our faith really awake, or is it lying bed-ridden in some dormitory of our souls?

William Ralph Inge

Nothing in life is more wonderful than faith—the one great moving force we can neither weigh in the balance nor test in the crucible!

Sir William Osler

To make anyone believe himself good is to make him, almost in spite of self, to become so.

Charlotte M. Yonge

Among all my patients in the second half of life—that is to say, over thirty-five—there has not been one whose problem in the last resort was not that of finding a religious outlook on life. It is safe to say that every one of them fell ill because he had lost that which the living religions of every age have given to their followers, and none of them has been really healed who did not regain his religious outlook.

Dr. Carl Jung

There is an old allegory of Knowledge the strong mailed knight, trampling over the great tableland, testing and making sure of the ground. Beside him, just above the ground, moved the white-winged angel of Faith. Together they came to the verge of a great precipice. Knowledge could go no farther. But the white-winged angel rose majestically and moved safely across the chasm.

J. Patterson Smyth

I respect faith, but doubt is what gets you an education.

Wilson Mizner

I think the greatest thing in the world is to believe in people.

John Galsworthy

What roots are to a tree, belief is to the soul. Great oak trees have great roots. Great souls have great faith. However, the faith that holds has spiritual qualities. The stable man has that intangible confidence in himself with capacities to be and to do, a recognition of God who may transform and empower his life, and a determined effort to realize man's highest ideals.

Author Unknown

It is recorded that a friend once said to Pascal: "I wish I had your belief, so that I might live your life." To which Pascal was swift to reply: "If you lived my life you would soon have my belief."

J. Trevor Davies

Faith, you can do very little with it, but you can do nothing without it.

Samuel Butler

Humanity will live by the faith and the hope, the love and the suffering, of a smaller number of men . . . who say: "Nevertheless and in spite of everything, and whatever may come, I believe."

Pierre Van Paassen

Faith is knowing there is an ocean because you have seen a brook.

William A. Ward

The person who has a firm trust in the Supreme Being is powerful in his power, wise by his wisdom, happy by his happiness.

Joseph Addison

In every seed to breathe the flower,
In every drop of dew
To reverence a cloistered star
Within the distant blue;
To wait the promise of the bow
Despite the cloud between,
Is Faith—the fervid evidence
Of loveliness unseen.

John B. Tabb

Life is the art of drawing sufficient conclusions from insufficient premises.

Samuel Butler

The smallest seed of faith is better than the largest fruit of happiness.

Henry Thoreau

I know not where His islands lift
Their fronded palms in air;
I only know I cannot drift
Beyond His love and care.

John Greenleaf Whittier

The turbulent billows of the fretful surface leave the deep parts of the ocean undisturbed; and to him who has a hold on vaster and more permanent realities, the hourly vicissitudes of his personal destiny seem relatively insignificant things. The really religious person is accordingly unshakeable and full of equanimity and calmly ready for any duty that the day may bring forth.

William James

On the wall of a cellar in Cologne, where a number of escaped prisoners hid out for the duration, there was found this inscription: "I believe in the sun, even when it is not shining. I believe in love, even when feeling it not. I believe in God, even when He is silent."

Louis Binstock

All I have seen teaches me to trust the Creator for all I have not seen.

Ralph Waldo Emerson

The first commandment is somewhat surprising. We would think that it would be. "Thou shalt believe in a God," a law against atheism. There is no such law. God took care of that in our creation. We do not teach a baby to hunger or to thirst, nature does that. However, we must train our children to satisfy their hungers and thirsts with the right things.

Charles L. Allen

Browning speaks of "grasping the skirts of God," but no man ever grasped the skirts of God by knowledge alone. Knowledge may have raised his arm, but faith moved his fingers and closed them in deathless grip.

R. O. Lawton

One must say, it seems to me, that a sound belief is always accompanied by a sane skepticism. It is only by disbelieving in some things that we can ever believe in other things. Faith does not mean credulity. It means a healthy skepticism by which life is measured, discriminated, weighed, and wheresoever it is found wanting dropped, disbelieved, discarded, denied. Faith without skepticism is not faith. It is superstition.

Samuel H. Miller

Faith is not something that we acquire once and for all. Faith is an insight that must be acquired at every single moment.

Abraham J. Heschel

Pessimism may often be a poison, and sometimes a medicine, but never a food.

G. K. Chesterton

The only faith that wears well and holds its color in all weathers is that which is woven of conviction and set with the sharp mordant of experience.

James Russell Lowell

An open mind is all very well in its way, but it ought not to be so open that there is no keeping anything in or out of it. It should be capable of shutting its doors sometimes, or it may be found a little draughty.

Samuel Butler

When God wants to punish a man, He deprives him of faith.

The Baal Shem

Dark as my path may seem to others, I carry a magic light in my heart. Faith, the spiritual strong searchlight, illumines the way. Although sinister doubts lurk in the shadow, I walk unafraid toward the Enchanted Wood where the foliage is always green, where life and death are one in the presence of the Lord.

Helen Keller

Faith is not trying to believe something regardless of the evidence. Faith is daring to do something regardless of the consequences.

Sherwood Eddy

You may be deceived if you trust too much, but you will live in torment if you do not trust enough.

Frank Crane

In a way, the greatest praise of God is his denial by the atheist who thinks creation is so perfect it does not need a creator.

Marcel Proust

Faith is not a stained-glass word reserved only for religious use, though it is essential to religion because it is essential to life. It is not something we can see on every street corner, but we dare not cross the street without it. If faith were removed for one day, our whole way of life would collapse.

V. Carney Hargroves

Faith is the daring of the soul to go farther than it can see.

William Newton Clarke

You believe easily that which you hope for earnestly.

Terence

Vital religious faith is the most important single thing in a man's personal health.

Kristofer Hagen

There need not be in religion, or music, or art, or love, or goodness, anything that is against reason; but never while the sun shines will we get great religion, or music, or art, or love, or goodness, without going beyond reason.

Harry Emerson Fosdick

Pray for a faith that will not shrink when it is washed in the waters of affliction.

Ernest M. Wadsworth

Faith will turn any course, light any path, relieve any distress, bring joy out of sorrow, peace out of strife, friendship out of enmity, heaven out of hell. Faith is God at work.

F. L. Holmes

If God is not, then the existence of all that is beautiful and in any sense good, is but the accidental and ineffectual by-product of blindly swirling atoms, or of the equally unpurposeful, though more conceptually complicated, mechanisms of present-day physics. A man may believe that this dreadful thing is true. But only the fool will say in his heart that he is glad that it is true. For to wish there should be no God is to wish that the things which we love and strive to realize and make permanent, should be only temporary and doomed to frustration and destruction. . . . Atheism leads not to badness but only to an incurable sadness and loneliness.

William Pepperell Montague

History is on the side of faith— not fear.

Author Unknown

Of two men who have no experience of God, he who denies Him is perhaps nearer to Him than the other.

Simone Weil

What is faith but a kind of betting or speculation after all? It should be, "I bet that my Redeemer liveth."

Samuel Butler

Saints are persons who make it easier for others to believe in God.

Nathan Soderblom

We live by Faith; but Faith is not
the slave
Of text and legend. Reason's voice
and God's,
Nature's and Duty's, never are at
odds.
John Greenleaf Whittier

My life is but the weaving
Between my God and me.
I only choose the colors
He weaveth steadily.
Sometimes he weaveth sorrow
And I in foolish pride,
Forget he sees the upper
And I the under side.
Author Unknown

It is among the profound convictions of a free society that the last word is never left with evil, that God never gets in a blind alley, and that even from the conspiracies of malevolence some good may be drawn, because importunity wins its consent even against the most reluctant.
James H. Robinson

Science without religion is lame, religion without science is blind.
Albert Einstein

Man lives by affirmation even more than he does by bread.
Victor Hugo

Belief is a truth held in the mind. Faith is a fire in the heart.
Joseph Fort Newton

Scepticism has never founded empires, established principles, or changed the world's heart. The great doers in history have always been men of faith.
Edwin Hubbell Chapin

Faith is to believe what we do not see, and the reward of this faith is to see what we believe.
St. Augustine

A religion based upon mystical intuition, unchecked by reason, is capable of all sorts of grossness and stupidities.
Milton Steinberg

Man is not master of the universe because he can split the atom. He has split the atom because he believed in his own unique mastery. Faith led to the material achievement, not the achievement to the faith.
Barbara Ward

The tragedy of the world is that men have given first-class loyalty to second-class causes, and these causes have betrayed them.
Lynn Harold Hough

Strong beliefs win strong men, and then make them stronger.
Walter Bagehot

To believe is to be strong. Doubt cramps energy. Belief is power.
Frederick Robertson

The dynamite of doubt is useful in wrecking old structures; but to build new buildings, we must have the dynamics of faith.
Joseph L. Baron

Faith keeps many doubts in her pay. If I could not doubt, I should not believe.
Henry David Thoreau

By far the greatest obstacle to the progress of science and to the under-taking of new tasks and provinces therein, is found in this

—that men despair and think things impossible.

Francis Bacon

We know not what the future holds, but we do know who holds the future.

Willis J. Ray

Galileo called doubt the father of invention; it is certainly the pioneer.

C. N. Bovee

He who has faith is never alone. But the atheist is always alone, even if from morning to night he lives in crowded streets.

Ignazio Silone

Faith reels not in the storm of warring words,
She brightens at the clash of "Yes" and "No,"
She sees the best that glimmers thro' the worst,
She feels the sun is hid but for a night,
She spies the summer thro' the winter bud,
She tastes the fruit before the blossom falls,
She finds the fountain where they wail'd "Mirage!"

Alfred Tennyson

---

79. PATHWAYS TO GOD

A humble knowledge of oneself is a surer road to God than a deep searching of the sciences.

Thomas à Kempis

I once was satisfied that the origin of life, and of the universe, could be explained by blind force and chance. My views changed as I grew older and more mature. The more I saw of that invisible world, teeming with its myriad forms of microscopic life, the more I became convinced that my original concept was wrong. The complexity and beautiful order of the microbiological world is so wonderfully constructed that it appears to be part of a divinely ordained system for check and balance in the regulation and continuation of all life.

Howard J. Shaughnessy

I could prove God statistically. Take the human body alone—the chance that all the functions of the individual would just happen is a statistical monstrosity.

George Gallup

There is a signature of wisdom and power impressed on the works of God, which evidently distinguishes them from the feeble imitations of men. Not only the splendor of the sun, but the glimmering light of the glowworm, proclaims his glory.

John Newton

And I have felt
A presence that disturbs me with a joy
Of elevated thoughts; a sense sublime
Of something far more deeply interfused,
Whose dwelling is the light of setting suns,

And the round ocean and the living air,
And the blue sky, and in the mind of man;
A motion and a spirit, that impels
All thinking things, all objects of all thought,
And rolls through all things.

William Wordsworth

God is the fact of the fact, the life of the life, the soul of the soul, the incomprehensible, the sum of all contradictions, the unit of all diversity; he who knows him, knows him not; he who is without him, is full of him; turn your back upon him, then turn your back upon gravity, upon air, upon light. He cannot be seen; but by him all seeing comes. He cannot be heard, yet by him all hearing comes. He is not a being, yet apart from him there is no being—there is no apart from him.

John Burroughs

God is a scientist, not a magician.
Albert Einstein

They serve God well,
Who serve his creatures.
Caroline Norton

Practical prayer is harder on the soles of your shoes than on the knees of your trousers.
Austin O'Malley

That is not faith, to see God only in what is strange and rare; but this is faith, to see God in what is most common and simple, to know God's greatness not so much from disorder as from order, not so much from those strange sights in which God seems (but only seems) to break His laws, as from those common ones in which He fulfills His laws.
Charles Kingsley

What can be more foolish than to think that all this rare fabric of heaven and earth could come by chance, when all the skill of art is not able to make an oyster? To see rare effects, and no cause; a motion, without a mover; a circle, without a center; a time, without an eternity; a second, without a first. These are things so against philosophy and natural reason that he must be a beast in understanding who can believe in them. The thing formed says that nothing formed it; and that which is made, is, while that which made it is not! This folly is infinite.
Jeremy Taylor

I pray every single second of my life; not on my knees, but with my work.
Susan B. Anthony

I see the marks of God in the heavens and the earth; but how much more in a liberal intellect, in magnanimity, in unconquerable rectitude.
William Channing

Men talk of "finding God," but no wonder it is difficult; He is hidden in the darkest hiding-place, your own heart. You yourself are a part of Him.
Christopher Morley

Men may tire themselves in a labyrinth of search, and talk of God; but if we would know Him indeed, it must be from the impressions we receive of Him; and the softer our hearts are, the deeper and livelier those will be upon us.
William Penn

Each cloud-capped mountain is a
   holy altar;
An organ breathes in every grove;
And the full heart's a Psalter,
Rich in deep hymns of gratitude
   and love.

Thomas Hood

One of the Godlike things of this
world is the veneration done to
human worth by the hearts of men.

Thomas Carlyle

I cannot conceive how a man
could look up into the heavens and
say there is no God.

Abraham Lincoln

The vastness of God's creation
should ever keep us humble. The
new telescope at Mt. Palomar enables man to photograph planets
over one billion light years away.
This distance in miles amounts to
a total of 186,000 (miles per second) × 60 seconds × 60 minutes ×
24 hours × 365 days × 1,000,000,-
000 (years). How many billions of
planets there are, no one can guess.
One astronomer, when asked how
he could believe in a God, replied,
"I keep enlarging my idea of God."

Obert C. Tanner

Whoever considers the study of
anatomy can never be an atheist.

Lord Edward Herbert

During World War II, a group of
Navy Chaplains were visiting a
hospital to view an operation. They
were all seated in the amphitheater.
As the doctor entered, an officer
asked the doctor if he would say a
few words. The doctor, with the
patient on the table before him,
looked at the crowd and around the
room and said, "This is my cathedral."

Harry D. Edgren

A man who has never had religion before, no more grows religious when he is sick, than a man
who has never learned figures can
count when he has need of calcula-
tion.

Samuel Johnson

I have learned more of experi-
mental religion since my little boy
died than in all my life before.

Horace Bushnell

Flower in the crannied wall,
I pluck you out of the crannies
I hold you here, root and all, in my
   hand,
Little flower—but if I could under-
   stand
What you are, root and all, and all
   in all,
I should know what God and man
   is.

Alfred Lord Tennyson

As the very atoms of the earth
and the stars of the sky seek harmony with the system which binds
them in a cosmic unity, so the souls
of men seek harmony with the
Spirit which makes them one.

John Haynes Holmes

An atheist cannot find God for
the same reason a thief cannot find
a policeman.

Author Unknown

If I give you a rose you won't
doubt God anymore.

Florens Tertullian

The mountains are God's majestic thoughts. The stars are God's
brilliant thoughts. The flowers are
God's beautiful thoughts.

Robert Stuart MacArthur

I see Thee in the starry field,
I see Thee in the harvest's yield,

In every breath, in every sound,
An echo of Thy name is found.
The blade of grass, the simple
flower,
Bear witness to Thy matchless
power.

Abraham ibn Ezra

The best proof of God's existence
is what follows when we deny it.

William L. Sullivan

Nature is the face of God. He
appears to us through it, and we
can read his thoughts in it.

Victor Hugo

One knows God, not so much
through reason, nor even through
the heart, but through one's feeling of complete dependence on
Him, akin to the feeling experienced by an unweaned child in the
arms of its mother. It does not
know who holds it, warms it, feeds
it; but it knows that there is this
someone; and more than merely
knows—it loves that being.

Leo Tolstoy

God needs no protectors. For
God lives in the open mind, in the
power of its thought, in the voice
of its truth, the inner impulse of its
honesty. He needs no protection.
Just give Him room.

A. Powell Davies

I believe in God the Father Almighty because wherever I have
looked, through all that I see
around me, I see the trace of an intelligent mind, and because in natural laws, and especially in the laws
which govern the social relations of
men, I see, not merely the proofs of
intelligence, but the proofs of be-
neficence.

Henry George

I believe in God as I believe in
my friends, because I feel the
breath of His affection, feel His
invisible and intangible hand,
drawing me, leading me, grasping
me; because I possess an inner consciousness of a particular providence and of a universal mind that
marks out for me the course of my
own destiny.

Miguel De Unamuno

In wonder-workings, or some bush
aflame,
Men look for God and fancy Him
concealed;
But in earth's common things He
stands revealed
While grass and flowers and stars
spell out His name.

Minot J. Savage

Artists are nearest God. Into their
souls he breathes his life, and from
their hands it comes in fair, articulate forms to bless the world.

Josiah Gilbert Holland

The soul of God is poured into
the world through the thoughts of
men.

Ralph Waldo Emerson

I hear and behold God in every
object, yet understand God not
in the least,
Nor do I understand who there can
be more wonderful than myself.
Why should I wish to see God better than this day?
I see something of God each hour
of the twenty-four, and each
moment then,
In the faces of men and women I
see God, and in my own face in
the glass,
I find letters from God dropped in
the street—and every one is
signed by God's name,

And I leave them where they are,
for I know that others will punc-
tually come forever and ever.

Walt Whitman

What are the sciences but maps
of universal laws; and universal
laws but the channels of universal
power; and universal power but the
outgoings of a supreme universal
mind?

Edward Thomas

God is within us: He is that inner
presence which makes us admire
the beautiful, which rejoices us
when we have done right and consoles us for not sharing the happiness of the wicked.

Eugene Delacroix

There is no substitute for firsthand experience in the spiritual
life. We must believe the explorers
of the high places of the unseen
world when they tell us that they
have been there, and found what
they sought. But they cannot really
tell us what they found; if we wish
to see what they have seen, we
must live as they have lived.

William Ralph Inge

To know the mighty works of
God; to comprehend His wisdom
and majesty and power; to appreciate, in degree, the wonderful
working of His laws, surely all this
must be a pleasing and acceptable
mode of worship to the Most High
to whom ignorance can not be
more grateful than knowledge.

Copernicus

We are still in the dawn of the
scientific age and every increase of
light reveals more brightly the
handiwork of an intelligent creator.

A. Cressy Morrison

Traditionally we think of God as
being "above." In childhood we got
the impression that God is up in the
sky somewhere. . . . I would have
you think of God as underneath,
like the foundation of a skyscraper,
or the concrete foundations of a
giant bridge. We do not have to
reach for love, courage, tolerance,
faith; they are foundation qualities.

Eilferd A. Peterson

Both the saint and the scientist
must possess the same qualities in
order to attain their ideals. But
these qualities are selfless devotion, a meticulous love of truth,
infinite patience, thoroughness, and
a depth of mind which does not
resent criticism. Without these
qualities neither of the two can
reach his goal. It is my firm belief
that the goal which both science
and religion reach by different
routes is one and the same.

B. C. Kher

Every new discovery must necessarily raise in us a fresh sense of
the greatness, wisdom, and power
of God.

Jonathan Edwards

God is in all that liberates and lifts,
In all that humbles, sweetens, and
consoles.

James Russell Lowell

God is that indefinable something which we all feel but which
we do not know. To me God is
truth and love, God is ethics and
morality, God is fearlessness, God
is the source of light and life and
yet He is above and beyond all
these. God is conscience. He is even
the atheism of the atheist.

Mohandas K. Gandhi

Nature has perfections, in order to show that she is the image of God; and defects, to show that she is only his image.

Blaise Pascal

The atheist acts as if the music coming from his radio were actually produced by the little box before him. He doesn't understand that in order for him to hear music in his room, somewhere there must be a studio and a transmitter and a man in tune with the Infinite to send out the beauty which he receives.

Roland B. Gittelsohn

Nature is but a name for an effect whose cause is God.

William Cowper

In contemplation of created things, by steps we may ascend to God.

John Milton

A little science estranges men from God, Much science leads them back to Him.

Louis Pasteur

God dwells wherever man lets Him in.

Mendel of Kotzk

God is better served in resisting a temptation to evil than in many formal prayers.

William Penn

To be alone with silence is to be alone with God.

Samuel Miller Hageman

Whenever I am prone to doubt and wonder,
I check myself, and say, the mighty One
Who made the solar system cannot blunder,
And for the best all things are being done.
He who set the stars on their eternal courses,
Has fashioned this strange earth by some sure plan.
Bow low—bow low to those majestic forces,
Nor dare to doubt their wisdom, puny man.

You cannot put one little star in motion,
You cannot shape one single forest leaf,
Nor fling a mountain up, nor sink an ocean,
Presumptuous pygmy, large with unbelief!
You cannot bring one dawn of regal splendor,
Nor bid the day to shadowy twilight fall,
Nor send the pale moon forth with radiance tender;
And dare you doubt the One who has done all?

S. A. Nagel

80. MAN AND GOD

Those people who are not governed by God will be ruled by tyrants.

William Penn

Unless there is within us that which is above us we shall soon yield to that which is about us.

Peter Forsythe

God may be either accompanying or pursuing you. It depends upon you.

Nicholai Velimirovic

How often we look upon God as our last and feeblest resource! We go to Him because we have nowhere else to go. And then we learn that the storms of life have driven us, not upon the rocks, but into the desired havens.

George MacDonald

It is hard to live in partnership with God. To attempt to live without him is to court certain spiritual bankruptcy.

Alexander A. Steinbach

If my religion's not all
That it ought to be,
The trouble's not with God,
The trouble's with me.

Author Unknown

God enters by a private door into every individual.

Ralph Waldo Emerson

The atheist does not deny God so much as he denies himself. A book is more enjoyable when we know the author. A symphony is more stirring when we know the composer. A painting is more meaningful when we know the artist. A poem is more personal when we know the poet. Life is more purposeful when we know the Creator.

William A. Ward

There is a difference between fear of God and being afraid of Him.

Maurice Samuel

"If you aren't as close to God as you once were," said a wise mother, "you can be very certain as to which one of you has moved."

Burton Hillis

In heaven it is always autumn, his mercies are ever in their maturity. We ask our daily bread, and God never says you should have come yesterday, he never says you must again tomorrow, but today if you will hear his voice, today he will hear you. . . . He brought light out of darkness, not out of a lesser light; he can bring thy summer out of winter, though thou have no spring; though in the ways of fortune, or understanding, or conscience, thou have been benighted till now, wintered and frozen, clouded and eclipsed, damped and numbed, smothered and stupefied till now, now God comes to thee, not as the dawning of the day, not as the bird in spring, but as the sun at noon to illustrate all shadows, as the sheaves in harvest, to fill all penuries, all occasions invite his mercies, and all times are his season.

John Donne

If one lives with Nature a little while, he soon recognizes the harmony of creation. He sees that each insect, each bird, each beast was given life for a purpose. Then, logically, man was created for the highest purpose. So it is our solemn duty to our Maker to develop whatever talents, in kind and in number, with which we have been blessed. Each of us is, therefore, an instrument of God. When one thinks of his humble self in this light, life takes on a more profound meaning.

Alden C. Palmer

Nature and revelation are alike God's books; each may have mysteries, but in each there are plain practical lessons for everyday duty.

Tryon Edwards

It is a most wanton presumption and pride for any man to dare to be sure that there is not some very important and critical place which just he and no one else is made to fill. It is almost as presumptuous to think you can do nothing as to think you can do everything. The latter folly supposes that God exhausted Himself when He made you; but the former supposes that God made a hopeless blunder when He made you, which is quite as impious for you to think.

Phillips Brooks

I find daily life not always joyous, but always interesting. I have some sad days and nights, but none that are dull. As I advance deeper into the vale of years, I live with constantly increasing gusto and excitement. I am sure it all means something; in the last analysis, I am an optimist because I believe in God. Those who have no faith are quite naturally pessimists and I do not blame them.

William Lyon Phelps

When a man says he can get on without religion it merely means he has a kind of religion he can get on without.

Harry E. Fosdick

He gives not best who gives most; but he gives most who gives best. If I cannot give bountifully, yet I will give freely, and what I want in my hand, I will supply by my heart.

Warwick

A little philosophy inclineth a man to atheism. Depth in philosophy brings a man back to God.

Francis Bacon

God gives every bird its food, but he does not throw it into the nest.

Josiah Gilbert Holland

Whether a man really loves God can be determined by the love he bears toward his fellow men.

Levi Yitzhok

God shall be my hope,
My stay, my guide and lantern to my feet.

William Shakespeare

Trust thyself. Accept the place the divine providence has found for you, the society of your contemporaries, the connection of events. Great men have always done so, and confided themselves childlike to the genius of their age, betraying their perception that the Eternal was stirring at their heart, working through their hands, predominating in all their being.

Ralph Waldo Emerson

So at the end of the long journey I have come to this: the first article of my creed is that I am a moral personality under orders.

William L. Sullivan

Service of God consists in what we do to our neighbor.

Leo Baeck

Progress—the onward stride of God.   *Victor Hugo*

Wherever you find man's footprints, there God is before you.

The Midrash

When God wants a great work done in the world or a great wrong righted, He goes about it in a very unusual way. He doesn't stir up his earthquakes or send forth his thunderbolts. Instead, He has a helpless baby born, perhaps in a simple home and of some obscure mother. And then God puts the idea into the mother's heart and she puts it into the baby's mind. And then God waits. The greatest forces in the world are not the earthquakes and the thunderbolts. The greatest forces in the world are babies.

E. T. Sullivan

God is the silent partner in all great enterprises.

Abraham Lincoln

Man cannot live all to this world. If not religious, he will be superstitious. If he worship not the true God, he will have his idols.

Theodore Parker

To think of God's name as a magic key to success in whatever we may undertake is both sacrilegious and silly. To think of him as an oracle who will solve for us whatever issues we pose to him in prayer is to misunderstand prayer. For God is quite as apt to create tensions within us as to relieve them, and he is more apt to prevent sleep than to induce it. He who makes us lie down in green pastures also searches out our paths and our lying down until we cry out, "Whither shall I go from thy Spirit, or whither shall I flee from thy presence?" Or, as Hosea discovered, sometimes "the Lord has a controversy with the inhabitants of the land."

Hunter Beckelhymer

God's textbook on economics starts out with the supposition that not only theoretically but very practically life belongs to him. This world is not God's by human courtesy; it's his by eminent domain.

Paul Scherer

The glory of God is, to a large extent, placed not merely within human reach, but under human control.

Israel Abrahams

Never undertake anything for which you wouldn't have the courage to ask the blessings of Heaven.

G. C. Lichtenberg

God is of no importance unless he is of supreme importance.

Abraham J. Heschel

O Lord, Thou knowest how busy I must be this day; if I forget Thee, do not Thou forget me!

Sir Jacob Astley

The great act of faith is when a man decides that he is not God.

Oliver Wendell Holmes, Jr.

Moral action is the meeting-place between the human and divine.

Leon Roth

A study was made by an agricultural college of the production of 100 bushels of corn on one acre of land. Man contributed the labor. God contributed a few things, too: 4 million pounds of water, 6800 pounds of oxygen, 5200 pounds of carbon, 1900 pounds of carbon dioxide, 160 pounds of nitrogen, 125 pounds of potassium, 40 pounds of phosphorus, 75 pounds of yellow sulphur, 50 pounds of calcium, 2 pounds of iron, and smaller amounts of iodine, zinc, copper, and other things. . . . 100 bushels of corn! Who made it?

Charles M. Crowe

From thee, great God, we spring; to thee we tend;
Path, motive, guide, original, and end.

Samuel Johnson

It is vain to ask God to make us good. He never makes any one good. We may ask Him to help us to become good; that He always does.

Washington Gladden

Man is not alone and neither his mind nor his conscience nor his creative powers can be truly understood if they are regarded as orphans without some universal Parent. I have come to feel that the whole human story, with all its tragedy and its triumph, is like a page torn from the middle of a book, without beginning or end—an undecipherable page, when cut out of its context . . .
The context of man is the Power greater than man. The human adventure is part of a universal sonnet—one line in a deathless poem.

Joshua Loth Liebman

God sleeps in the stone, breathes in the plant, moves in the animals, and wakes to consciousness in man.

Jonathan Brierly

The minority feel the need of God because they have got everything else, the majority, because they have nothing.

Leo Tolstoy

We and God have business with each other and in that business our highest destiny is fulfilled.

William James

We know of some very religious people who came to doubt God when a great misfortune befell them, even though they themselves were to blame for it; but we have never yet seen anyone who lost his faith because an undeserved fortune fell to his lot.

Arthur Schnitzler

"What did God ever make such a world for anyway?" one young person complained, adding, "I could make a better world than this myself." "That," a friend suggested, "is just the reason God put you into this world—to make it a better world. Now go ahead and do your part."

Charles L. Wallis

That belief which inspires a man to higher life, which moves him to trample down his besetting sins, to help his weaker brother, to rise into communion with God, is to him a Divine voice.

G. S. Merriam

To make our reliance upon providence both pious and rational, we should prepare all things with the same care, diligence, and activity, as if there were no such thing as providence for us to depend upon; and then, when we have done all this, we should as wholly and humbly rely upon it, as if we had made no preparation at all.

Robert South

God always leaves an unfinished task on the workbench of the world.

William Allen White

God can no more do without us than we can do without him.

Meister Eckhart

A boy was flying his kite and succeeded in letting it fly out of sight. A gentleman passing inquired, "What are you doing, my boy?" "I am flying my kite, sir," he answered. "But you must be mistaken," said the gentleman, "I cannot see any kite." "No more can I," said the boy, "but I know it's there, because I can feel it pull." No man hath seen God at any time, but every man some day will feel the "pull" of the infinite Spirit, and know that there is a God.

J. Tolefree Parr

When you have shut the doors and made a darkness within remember never to say that you are alone; for you are not alone, but God is within.

Epictetus

The human soul is a silent harp in God's quire, whose strings need only to be swept by the divine breath to chime in with the harmonies of creation.

Henry David Thoreau

Such as men themselves are, such will God appear to them to be; and such as God appears to them to be, such will they show themselves in their dealings with their fellow men.

William Ralph Inge

God, who loves the soul, cannot despise the body, so essential to the preservation of the individual and the species.

Jacob Anatoli

When men cease to be faithful to God, he who expects to find them so to each other will be much disappointed.

George Horne

Anything that makes religion a second object makes it no object. He who offers to God a second place offers him no place.

John Ruskin

A man who writes of himself without speaking of God is like one who identifies himself without giving his address.

Ben Hecht

How can he love God who loves not His works?

Ludwig Boerne

What is an offering to God? Charity to His children.

The Midrash

Fear only two: God and the man who has no fear of God.

Hassidic Saying

Thine is the seed time:
God alone beholds the end of what is sown;
Beyond our vision weak and dim
The harvest time is hid with Him.

John Greenleaf Whittier

Two men please God—who serves Him with all his heart because he knows Him; who seeks Him with all his heart because he knows Him not.

Ivan Panin

There is no room for God in him who is full of himself.

The Baal Shem

Some people think of business when they are in the House of God. Is it too much to ask them to think of God when they are at business?

Nahman of Kasovir

My own faith is that so marvelous is this human life of ours that (I say it reverently) God himself cannot save the world without us. This is for me a definitely sufficient explanation of why we are here.

Sir Wilfred Grenfell

Consecration is handing God a blank sheet to fill in with your name signed at the bottom.

M. H. Miller

God has two dwellings: one in Heaven, and the other in a meek and thankful heart.

Izaak Walton

Without the elements of chance and uncertainty, we could not develop faith and love. If everything were cut and dried in advance, there would be no adventure, no romance, no religion. God does not run this world like a factory where wage agreements are all signed ahead and pay envelopes are passed out every week. If He did run it thus, we could make things but we could not make men.

Ralph W. Sockman

I would not seek thee unless thou hadst already found me.

Blaise Pascal

God doth not need
Either man's work or his own gifts; who best
Bear his mild yoke, they serve him best; his state
Is kingly. Thousands at his bidding speed
And post o'er land and ocean without rest:
They also serve who only stand and wait.

John Milton

The hand that gives, gathers.

Ray

81. WORDS AND DEEDS

The world is blessed most by men who do things, and not by those who merely talk about them.

James Oliver

To look is one thing.
To see what you look at is another.
To understand what you see is a third.
To learn from what you understand is still something else.
But to act on what you learn is all that really matters.

Author Unknown

Loyal words have the secret of healing grief.

Menander

I would give nothing for that man's religion, whose very dog, and cat are not the better for it.

Rowland Hill

The only way to compel man to speak good of us is to do it.

Voltaire

A man of words and not of deeds is like a garden full of weeds.

Author Unknown

When men hold their peace, the stones will cry out.

Ferdinand Lassalle

For every word in *Mein Kampf*, 125 lives were to be lost; for every page, 4,700 lives; for every chapter, more than 1,200,000 lives. An expensive literary property.

Norman Cousins

Good words shall gain you honour in the market-place; but good deeds shall gain you friends among men.

Lao-tse

Of all commentaries upon the Scriptures, good examples are the best and the liveliest.

John Donne

We reform others unconsciously when we walk uprightly.

Mme. Soymonoff Swetchine

The feast of the sermon is always followed by spiritual indigestion unless followed by religious exercise.

Author Unknown

Beneath the yoke of barbarism one must not keep silence; one must fight. Whoever is silent at such a time is a traitor to humanity.

Stephen Zweig

Every man should be the author of good deeds, if not of good works. It is not enough to have one's talent in manuscript and one's nobility in parchments.

Joseph Joubert

Religion is action not diction.

Harry E. Fosdick

He who does not bellow the truth when he knows the truth makes himself the accomplice of liars and forgers.

Charles Peguy

Words without actions are the assassins of idealism.

Herbert Hoover

One example is worth a thousand arguments.

Thomas Carlyle

None preaches better than the ant, and she says nothing.

Benjamin Franklin

He who has much learning but no good deeds is like an unbridled horse, that throws off the rider as soon as he mounts.

The Talmud

The five most important words:
I am proud of you.
The four most important words:
What is your opinion?
The three most important words:
If you please.
The two most important words:
Thank you.
The least important word:
"I."

Author Unknown

It is the actions of men and not their sentiments that make history.

Norman Mailer

We try to do by agitation what We fail to do by demonstration.

Walter A. Jessup

Everyone who lives any semblance of an inner life thinks more nobly and profoundly than he speaks.

Robert Louis Stevenson

Conduct is three-fourths of our life and its largest concern.

Mathew Arnold

An acre of performance is worth the whole world of promise.

James Howell

"Drop a stone into the water—
In a moment it is gone,

But there are a hundred ripples
Circling on and on and on,
Say an unkind word this moment—
In a moment it is gone
But there are a hundred ripples
Circling on and on and on,
Say a word of cheer and splendor—
In a moment it is gone
But there are a hundred ripples
Circling on and on and on.

Author Unknown

It's quicker to act your way into right thinking than to think your way into right acting.

Stanley Jones

A pledge unpaid is like thunder without rain.

Abraham Hasdai

On wings of deeds the soul must mount
When we are summoned from afar,
Ourselves, and not our words, will count
Not what we said, but what we are.

William Winter

He does not believe who does not live according to his belief.

Thomas Fuller

In the conduct of life, habits count for more than maxims; because habit is a living maxim, becomes flesh and instinct. To reform one's maxims is nothing: it is but to change the title of the book. To learn new habits is everything, for it is to reach the substance of life. Life is but a tissue of habits.

Henri Frederic Amiel

The difference between the right word and the almost right word is the difference between lightning and the lightning bug.

Mark Twain

But words are things; and a small drop of ink,
Falling, like dew, upon a thought, produces
That which makes thousands, perhaps millions, think.

Lord Byron

The serene, silent beauty of a holy life is the most powerful influence in the world, next to the might of God.

Blaise Pascal

The ultimate test for us of what a truth means is the conduct it dictates or inspires.

William James

It is easier to fight for our principles than it is to live up to them.

Alfred Adler

Every man feels instinctively that all beautiful sentiments in the world weigh less than a single lovely action.

James Russell Lowell

Our deeds determine us, as much as we determine our deeds.

George Eliot

Not long ago I was reading the Sermon on the Mount with a rabbi. At nearly each verse he showed me very similar passages in the Hebrew Bible and Talmud. When we reached the words, "Resist not evil," he did not say, "This too is in the Talmud," but asked, with a smile, "Do the Christians obey this command?" I had nothing to say in reply, especially as at that particular time, Christians, far from turning the other cheek, were smiting the Jews on both cheeks.

Leo Tolstoy

A man's action is only a picture book of his creed.

> *Ralph Waldo Emerson*

Words are mighty, words are living;
Serpents with their venomous stings,
Or bright angels crowding round us
With heaven's light upon their wings.
Every word has its own spirit,
True or false, that never dies;
Every word man's lips have uttered
Echoes in God's skies.

> *Adelaide A. Proctor*

It is ever true that the life one lives speaks more loudly than the words one utters.

> *Gilbert L. Guffin*

The thought that leads to no action is not thought—it is dreaming.

> *Eliza Lamb Martin*

Who can protest and does not, is an accomplice in the act.

> *The Talmud*

If you want to get across an idea, wrap it up in a person.

> *Ralph Bunche*

My tastes are aristocratic; my actions democratic.

> *Victor Hugo*

One act of charity will teach us more of the love of God than a thousand sermons.

> *Author Unknown*

Go put your creed into your deed, Nor speak with double tongue.

> *Ralph Waldo Emerson*

Kind words are benedictions.

> *Frederick Saunders*

Your daily life is your temple and your religion.

> *Kahlil Gibran*

Loving words will cost but little,
Journeying up the hill of life;
But they make the weak and weary
Stronger, braver, for the strife.

Do you count them only trifles?
What to earth are sun and rain?
Never was a kind word wasted;
Never was one said in vain.

> *Author Unknown*

82. REWARD AND PUNISHMENT

When Rabbi Samuel visited Rome, he found a bracelet. The empress announced that she had lost a precious bracelet and offered a huge reward if it was returned in thirty days. Should the finder fail to return it in this time, he would forfeit his head.

Rabbi Samuel waited until the thirty days had passed before he returned the bracelet. He then ad-mitted to the empress that he had known of her promise and her threat.

In reply to the perplexed look on her face, the rabbi told her: "You must know that ethical conduct is inspired neither by hope of reward nor fear of punishment. It stems solely from the love of God and the desire to do His commandments."

> *The Talmud*

We are not punished for our sins, but by them.

Leon Harrison

The whole of what we know is a system of compensations. Every suffering is rewarded; every sacrifice is made up; every debt is paid.

Ralph Waldo Emerson

Let wickedness escape, as it may at the bar, it never fails of doing justice upon itself; for every guilty person is his own hangman.

Seneca

Divine Providence has granted this gift to man, that those things which are honest are also the most advantageous.

Quintilian

Who thinks of reward serves himself, not God.

Israel Salanter Lipkin

The law of consequence holds without variation or exception. "The day of reckoning is not far off," says the Jewish Agadah and men will learn that human action likewise reappears in their consequences by as certain a law as the green blade rises up out of the buried corn-seed.

John Haynes Holmes

I've seen much bread that was cast upon the waters, and that returned, buttered, covered with jam, wrapped in paraffin paper, and marked, "with love."

Channing Pollock

To be left alone, and face to face with my own crime, had been just retribution.

Henry Wadsworth Longfellow

Remorse is the pain of sin.

Theodore Parker

Nature is economic in her gifts: she will not give strength to those who will not expend it. These remain uninspiring and uninspired. She is lavish in her gifts to those who will use them, and especially to those who will devote them to nature's altruistic ends, for such ends harmonize the soul. The Sea of Galilee is fresh and blue and gives life to living creatures within its sunlit waters—not because it receives waters, but because it gives of them freely. The Dead Sea is dead, not because there is no supply of fresh water, but because it permits no outlet. It is a law of nature—a law of life—that only by giving shall we receive.

J. Arthur Hadfield

God says, "Take what you want and pay for it."

Spanish Proverb

The evening of a well-spent life brings its lamps with it.

Joseph Joubert

The best reward of a kindly deed
Is the knowledge of having done it.

Edgar Fawcett

The good life is not only good for one's conscience; it is good for art, good for knowledge, good for health, good for fellowship.

Lewis Mumford

What a sublime doctrine it is that goodness cherished now is Eternal Life already entered upon!

William Channing

It is one of the most beautiful compensations of this life that no man can sincerely try to help another without helping himself.

Ralph Waldo Emerson

They whose guilt within their bosom lies, imagine every eye beholds their blame.

William Shakespeare

Great is the conduct of a man who lets rewards take care of themselves—come if they will or fail to come—but goes on his way, true to the truth simply because it is true, strongly loyal to the right for its pure righteousness.

Phillips Brooks

Our rewards are never those we anticipate . . . but we are rewarded.

George Moore

There is no truth more thoroughly established, than that there exists in the economy and course of nature an indissoluble union between virtue and happiness.

George Washington

It has been well remarked, it is not said that *after* keeping God's commandments, but *in* keeping them there is great reward. God has linked these two things together, and no man can separate them—obedience and peace.

F. W. Robertson

What is vulgar, and the essence of all vulgarity, but the avarice of reward? 'Tis the difference of artisan and artist, of talent and genius, of sinner and saint. The man whose eyes are nailed, not on the nature of his act, but on the wages, whether it be money, or office, or fame, is almost equally low.

Ralph Waldo Emerson

There is no delusion more fatal, no folly more profound, than a man's belief that he can kick and gouge and scheme his way to the top—and then afford the luxury of being a good person; for no consequence is more certain than that we become what we do.

Sydney J. Harris

All human sin seems so much worse in its consequences than in its intentions.

Reinhold Niebuhr

He who lives for no one does not necessarily live for himself.

Seneca

I prefer to do right and get no thanks rather than to do wrong and get no punishment.

Marcus Cato

The man who lives to himself alone lives a little, dwarfed, and stunted life, because he has no part in this larger life of humanity. But the one who in service loses his own life in this larger life, has his own life increased and enriched a thousand or a million fold, and every joy, every happiness, everything of value coming to each member of this greater whole comes as such to him, for he has a part in the life of each and all.

Ralph Waldo Trine

Every man is his own ancestor, and every man is his own heir. He devises his own future, and he inherits his own past.

Frederick H. Hedge

There are loyal hearts, there are spirits brave,
   There are souls that are pure and true;

Then give to the world the best you
    have,
And the best will come back to
    you.

Give love, and love to your life will
    flow,
A strength in your utmost need;
Have faith, and a score of hearts
    will show
Their faith in your work and
    deed.

Give truth, and your gift will be
    paid in kind;
And honor will honor meet,
And the smile which is sweet will
    surely find
A smile that is just as sweet.

Give pity and sorrow to those who
    mourn;
You will gather in flowers again
The scattered seeds from your
    thought outborne,
Though the sowing seemed in
    vain.

For life is the mirror of king and
    slave;
'Tis just what we are and do;
Then give to the world the best you
    have,
And the best will come back to
    you.

Mary Ainge De Vere

It is not just when a villainous
act has been committed that it torments us; it is when we think of it
afterward, for the remembrance of
it lasts forever.

Jean Jacques Rousseau

Upon every face is written the
record of the life the man has led;
the prayers, the aspirations, the disappointments, all he hoped to be
and was not—all are written there;

nothing is hidden, nor indeed can
be.

Elbert Hubbard

This is the punishment of a liar:
he is not believed, even when he
speaks the truth.

The Talmud

An act of goodness is of itself an
act of happiness. No reward coming
after the event can compare with
the sweet reward that went with it.

Maurice Maeterlinck

Not sharp revenge, nor hell itself
can find a fiercer torment than a
guilty mind.

John Dryden

Punishment is lame, but it comes.

George Herbert

One lesson, and only one, history
may be said to repeat with distinct-
ness: that the world is built somehow on moral foundations; that in
the long run it is well with the
good; in the long run it is ill with
the wicked.

James Anthony Froude

To seek virtue for the sake of reward is to dig for iron with a spade
of gold.

Ivan Panin

Many a man thinks he is buying
pleasure, when he is really selling
himself a slave to it.

Benjamin Franklin

Foolish men imagine that because judgment for an evil thing is
delayed, there is no justice, but only
accident here below. Judgment for
an evil thing is many times delayed
some day or two, some century or
two, but it is sure as life, it is sure
as death!

Thomas Carlyle

Punishment is a fruit that, unsuspected, ripens within the flower of the pleasure that concealed it.

Ralph Waldo Emerson

The reward of such as live exactly according to the laws is not silver or gold, not a garland of olive-branches or of smallage, nor any such public sign of commendation; but every good man is content with the witness that his own conscience bears him.

Josephus

How can we expect a harvest of thought who have not had a seed-time of character?

Henry Thoreau

God hath yoked to guilt, her pale tormentor, misery.

William Cullen Bryant

For every action there is an equal and opposite reaction. If you want to receive a great deal, you first have to give a great deal. If each individual will give of himself to whomever he can, wherever he can, in any way that he can, in the long run he will be compensated in the exact proportion that he gives.

R. A. Hayward

A good deed is never lost. He who sows courtesy, reaps friendship; he who plants kindness, gathers love; pleasure bestowed upon a grateful mind was never sterile, but generally gratitude begets reward.

Saint Basil

Not less but more than Dante, we know for certain that there is a heaven and a hell—a heaven, when a good deed has been done, a hell, in the dark heart able no longer to live openly.

Edward Dowden

A man never gets what he hoped for by doing wrong; and if he seems to do so, he gets something more that spoils it all.

Author Unknown

The human mind is the richest unexplored area in the world. The mind, like land, does not care what we plant. Good or bad, it returns what's planted.

Richard R. Pharr

As no true work since the world began was ever wasted, so no true life since the world began has ever failed.

Ralph Waldo Emerson

Scientific truth is marvelous, but moral truth is divine; and whoever breathes its air and walks by its light has found the lost paradise.

Horace Mann

That is not virtue which looks for a reward.

Felix Adler

The conquered almost always conquer.

G. K. Chesterton

His gain is loss;
For he that wrongs his friends
    Wrongs himself more,
And ever has about him a silent
    court and jury
And himself, the prisoner at the
    bar ever condemned.

Alfred Tennyson

No man, who continues to add something to the material, intellectual, and moral well being of the place in which he lives, is left long without proper reward.

Booker T. Washington

The greatest penalty of evildoing is to grow into the likeness of bad men.

Plato

The dice of God are always loaded. Every secret is told, every crime is punished, every virtue rewarded, every wrong redressed, in silence and certainty. The thief steals from himself. The swindler swindles himself.

Ralph Waldo Emerson

What dungeon is so dark as one's own heart? What jailer so inexorable as one's self?

Nathaniel Hawthorne

Friendliness in the long run calls forth friendliness; kindness breeds kindness and active good will multiplies. The germ of love may not be as immediately powerful as that of hate, but in the crucible of time, it has greater survival value.

Sen. Paul Douglas

It would be an unspeakable advantage, both to the public and private, if men would consider that great truth, that no man is wise or safe but he that is honest.

Sir Walter Raleigh

Every man has a paradise around him till he sins, and the angel of an accusing conscience drives him from his Eden.

Henry Wadsworth Longfellow

He that does good to another, does good also to himself, not only in the consequences, but in the very act; for the consciousness of well doing is, in itself, ample reward.

Seneca

God is a sure paymaster. He may not pay at the end of every week, or month, or year, but remember He pays in the end.

Anne of Austria

The robber is robbed by his riches;
The tyrant is dragged by his chain;
The schemer is snared by his cunning;
The slayer lies dead by the slain.

Edwin Markham

He who wishes to secure the good of others, has already secured his own.

Confucius

What will be the punishment? Perhaps nothing else than, not having done thy duty, thou wilt lose the character of fidelity, modesty, propriety. Do not look for greater penalties than these.

Epictetus

Chain reaction is popularly associated with the atomic bomb, but it is no less gigantic a force in your daily life. Every word you speak, every action you perform sets up a chain of reaction that can end in a damaging explosion or in a shower of blessings.

Harold S. Kahm

What stronger breastplate than a heart untainted!
Thrice is he armed that hath his quarrel just;
And he but naked, though locked up in steel,
Whose conscience with injustice is corrupted.

William Shakespeare

As we are, so we do; and as we do, so it is done to us.

Ralph Waldo Emerson

Down in their hearts, wise men know this truth: the only way to help yourself is to help others.

Elbert Hubbard

Practicing the Golden Rule is not a sacrifice; it is an investment.

Clarence Edwin Flynn

What matters it to me if I am not at the oar when the little boat is pulled into harbor. To know that I have pulled at the oar, that is enough for me.

Olive Schreiner

The penalty of backsliding is not something unreal and vague, some unknown quantity which may be measured out to us disproportionately, or which, perchance, since God is good, we may altogether evade. The consequences are already marked within the structure of the soul. So to speak, they are physiological. The thing effected by our indifference or by our indulgence is not the book of final judgment, but the present fabric of the soul.

Henry Drummond

I fear that I am selfish, when I give a gift, or help a friend; I do it, not because I should but because it makes me feel so good.

Crystal Shoemaker

Act with kindness, but do not expect gratitude.

Confucius

Work and thou canst not escape the reward; whether thy work be fine or coarse, planting corn or writing epics, so only it be honest work, done to thine own approbation, it shall earn a reward to the senses as well as to the thought. No matter how often defeated, you are born to victory. The reward of a thing well done is to have done it.

Ralph Waldo Emerson

The liar's punishment is not in the least that he is not believed, but that he cannot believe anyone else.

George Bernard Shaw

History is a voice for ever sounding across the centuries the laws of right and wrong. Opinions alter, manners change, creeds rise and fall; but the moral law is written on the tablets of eternity. For every false word or unrighteous deed, for cruelty and oppression, for lust and vanity, the price has to be paid at last. . . . Justice and truth alone endure and live. Injustice and falsehood may be long-lived, but doomsday comes to them at last.

J. A. Froude

The world is a looking-glass, and gives back to every man the reflection of his own face. Frown at it, and it in turn will look sourly upon you; laugh at it and with it, and it is a jolly, kind companion.

William M. Thackeray

I would much rather that posterity should inquire why no statues were erected to me, than why they were.

Marcus Cato

Retribution is one of the grand principles in the divine administration of human affairs. There is everywhere the working of the everlasting law of requital: man always gets as he gives.

John Foster

He is well paid that is well satisfied.

William Shakespeare

We ought to love our Maker for

His own sake, without either hope of good or fear of pain.

Cervantes

The consequences of our crimes long survive their commission, and like the ghosts of the murdered forever haunt the steps of the malefactor.

Walter Scott

---

83. CONSCIENCE—THE STILL SMALL VOICE

A peace above all earthly dignities, a still and quiet conscience.

William Shakespeare

Yet still there whispers the small
  voice within,
Heard through Gain's silence, and
  o'er Glory's din:
Whatever creed be taught or land
  be trod,
Man's conscience is the oracle of
  God.

Lord Byron

Every man has a paradise around him till he sins and the angel of an accusing conscience drives him from his Eden. And even then there are holy hours, when this angel sleeps, and man comes back, and with the innocent eyes of a child looks into his lost paradise again— into the broad gates and rural solitudes of nature.

Henry Wadsworth Longfellow

A disciplined conscience is a man's best friend. It may not be his most amiable, but it is his most faithful monitor.

Austin Phelps

Insomnia gets most of the blame that conscience deserves.

Franklin P. Jones

A man's own conscience is his sole tribunal, and he should care no more for that phantom "opinion" than he should fear meeting a ghost if he crossed the churchyard at dark.

Edward G. Bulwer-Lytton

Courage without conscience is a wild beast.

Ralph Ingersoll

Nowhere in our literature is the power of conscience more superbly pictured than in Shakespeare. Think for instance of Macbeth immediately after the murder of Duncan. He hears the watchmen asking God to bless them, and he cannot say Amen. It is one of the profoundest touches in the drama, that Macbeth awakes to the discovery that he cannot say Amen. He feels that to say it would be a mockery, and he feels so because he is a murderer. Had he been saving Duncan's life instead of taking it, the word would never have stuck fast in his throat. It is Shakespeare teaching us through conscience that even villainy is conscious that God is on the side of what is good.

G. H. Morrison

The conscience is a thousand witnesses.

Richard Taverner

Labor hard to keep alive in your breast that little spark of celestial fire called conscience.

George Washington

Money dishonestly acquired is never worth its cost, while a good conscience never costs as much as it is worth.

J. P. Senna

Let no man be sorry he has done good because others have done evil. If a man has acted right, he has done well, though alone; if wrong, the sanction of all mankind will not justify him.

Henry Fielding

Fear is the tax that conscience pays to guilt.

George Sewall

Be master of your will and slave to your conscience.

Yiddish Proverb

I love to think of nature as an unlimited broadcasting station, through which God speaks to us every hour, if we will only tune in.

George W. Carver

He who sacrifices his conscience to ambition burns a picture to obtain the ashes.

Chinese Proverb

What the nations of the world need is a good loud-speaker for the still small voice.

Herbert V. Prochnow

Conscience is an elastic and flexible article, which will bear a great deal of stretching and adapt itself to a great variety of circumstances. Some people by prudent management and leaving it off piece by piece, like a flannel waistcoat in warm weather, even contrive, in time, to dispense with it altogether; but there be others who can assume the garment and throw it off at pleasure; and this, being the greatest and most convenient improvement, is the one most in vogue.

Charles Dickens

Man became the first implement-making creature not later than the beginning of the Ice Age, probably a million years ago. At the same time he became the first weapon-making creature. For perhaps a million years, therefore, he has been improving those weapons; but it is less than five thousand years since man began to feel the power of conscience to such a degree that it became a potent social force.

James H. Breasted

A person whose conscience tells him at fifty exactly what it told him at twenty has not grown up; he has kept his faculty of moral discernment out of the general development of his mind. We do not always learn the will of God by remembering what He told us yesterday, even when we are sure that we have heard Him rightly. Conscience is not memory. It is the power of discerning the moral relation of things.

T. E. Jessop

The only tyrant I accept in this world is the "still, small voice" within me.

Mahatma Gandhi

The soft whispers of the God in man.

E. J. Young

A good conscience is to the soul what health is to the body; it preserves a constant ease and serenity within us, and more than countervails all the calamities and afflictions that can possibly befall us.

Joseph Addison

Fear God by day, and you'll sleep soundly at night.

Joseph Zabara

The world stands or falls with the laws of life which Heaven has written in the human conscience.

Pierre Van Paassen

Conscience warns us as a friend before it punishes as a judge.

Leszinski Stanislaus

Conscience is a sacred sanctuary where God alone may enter as judge.

Lamennais

A man may have his conscience so well disciplined and trained, that instead of blazing a trail before him, it is like a pet dog which just trots obediently at his heels and never so much as barks.

E. L. Allen

Man's conscience is the supreme judge of what is true or false, good or evil. A person who lives professing a belief he does not hold has lost the only true, the only immutable thing—his conscience.

Dagobert D. Runes

We are obliged to do a good deal more than "follow our conscience." We are obliged to enlighten it and to keep it enlightened. It is just as liable to failure as our sight, just as liable to error as an uninformed and uninstructed intelligence. So far from being infallible, its verdicts are the measure of our moral capacity. That is why conscience varies so from man to man. Only when we develop it by constant discipline does it pass from adolescence to maturity, from the little to the big, from the relative to the absolute, from the provisional to the permanent.

Robert J. McCracken

What health can there be for him who is not whole with his Master?

Maimon ben Joseph

A good conscience: a soft pillow.

Author Unknown

My conscience is my crown,
Contented thoughts my rest;
My heart is happy in itself;
My bliss is in my breast.

Robert Southwell

Never esteem anything as of advantage to thee that shall make thee break thy word or lose thy self-respect.

Marcus Aurelius

The voice of conscience is so delicate that it is easy to stifle it; but it is also so clear that it is impossible to mistake it.

Madame de Stael

Civilization is simply applied conscience, and Progress is a widening conscience.

H. D. Lloyd

---

84. THE REVERENT MOOD

God hears no more than the heart speaks; and if the heart be dumb, God will certainly be deaf.

Thomas Brooks

Pray as if everything depended on God, and work as if everything depended upon man.

Francis J. Spellman

Lady Beaumont told me that when she was a child, previously to saying her prayers, she endeavoured to think of a mountain or great river, or something great, in order to raise up her soul and kindle it.

Samuel Taylor Coleridge

How marvellous that I, a filthy clod,
May yet hold friendly converse with my God!

Angelus Silesius

It is only when men begin to worship that they begin to grow.

Calvin Coolidge

The using up of strength is in a certain sense still an increase of strength; for fundamentally it is only a matter of a wide circle; all the strength we give away comes back to us again, experienced and transformed. It is so in prayer. And what is there that, truly done would not be prayer?

Rainer Maria Rilke

The best answer to all objections urged against prayer is the fact that man cannot help praying; for we may be sure that that which is so spontaneous and ineradicable in human nature has its fitting objects and methods in the arrangements of a boundless Providence.

Edwin Hubbell Chapin

Prayer has marked the trees across the wilderness of a skeptical world to direct the traveler in distress and all paths lead to a single light.

Douglas Meador

Is anything vital ever accomplished without persistent effort? Farmers plow and sow, and keep on plowing and sowing. Miners dig, and keep on digging, deeper and deeper. Musicians practice and keep on practicing. Scholars study, and keep on studying. And so must we—if we would know how prayer purifies, fortifies, enriches the inner life, we will have to persist.

Charles R. Brown

He who prays as he ought, will endeavor to live as he prays.

John Owen

It is good for man to open his mind to wonder and awe. Without science we are helpless children. But without a deep religion, we are blundering fools, reeling in our new and terrible cocksureness into one disaster after another.

J. B. Priestley

A man is never so noble as when he is reverent.

Thomas Carlyle

When we observe the needle of the mariner, without visible organ, or sense of faculty, pointing with a trembling and pious fidelity to the unseen pole, and guiding, no one favored people only, but all nations, at all times, across a wilderness of waters, so that a ship sails forth from one shore and strikes the narrowest inlet or bay on the other side of the globe, why ought we not to be filled with awe as reverential and as religious as though we had seen the pillar of cloud by day, and of fire by night, which led the children of Israel in their journey through the wilderness?

Horace Mann

Call on God, but row away from the rocks.

Indian Proverb

Pray to God at the beginning of thy works, that so thou mayest bring them all to a good ending.

Xenophon

My words fly up, my thoughts remain below:
Words without thoughts never to heaven go.

William Shakespeare

He prayeth well who loveth well
Both man and bird and beast.
He prayeth best who loveth best
All things, both great and small;
For the dear God who loveth us
He made and loveth all.

Samuel Taylor Coleridge

Many of us regretfully refrain from habitual prayer, waiting for an urge that is complete, sudden and un-exampled. But the unexampled is scarce, and perpetual refraining can easily grow into a habit. We may even come to forget what to regret, what to miss.

Abraham J. Heschel

Prayer is not a substitute for work; it is a desperate effort to work further and to be efficient beyond the range of one's powers.

George Santayana

Prayer should be the key of the day and the lock of the night.

George Herbert

Prayer is not the easy way out. Prayer is not an easy way of getting things done for us. So many people think of prayer as a kind of magic, a kind of talisman, a kind of divine Aladdin's lamp in which in some mysterious way we command the power of God to work for us. Prayer must always remain quite ineffective, unless we do everything we can to make our own prayers come true. It is a basic rule of prayer that God will never do for us what we can do for ourselves. Prayer does not do things for us; it enables us to do things for ourselves.

William Barclay

His daily prayer, far better understood
In acts than words, was simply doing good.

John Greenleaf Whittier

The purpose of prayer is to leave us alone with God.

Leo Baeck

We hear in these days of scientific enlightenment a great deal of discussion about the efficacy of prayer and many reasons are given us why we should not pray, whilst others are given why we should. But in all this very little is said of the reason why we do pray . . . The reason why we do pray is simply that we cannot help praying.

William James

Certain thoughts are prayers. There are moments when, whatever be the attitude of the body, the soul is on its knees.

Victor Hugo

If you are too busy to pray, you are too busy.

Author Unknown

God warms his hands at man's heart when he prays.

John Masefield

Does not every true man feel that he is himself made higher by doing reverence to what is really above him? No nobler or more blessed feeling dwells in man's heart.

Thomas Carlyle

Sometimes prayer is more than a light before us; it is a light within us. Those who have once been resplendent with this light find little meaning in speculations about the efficacy of prayer. A story is told about a Rabbi who once entered heaven in a dream. He was permitted to approach the temple of Paradise where the great sages of the Talmud, the Tannaim, were spending their eternal lives. He saw that they were just sitting around tables studying the Talmud. The disappointed Rabbi wondered,

"Is this all there is to Paradise?" But suddenly he heard a voice, "You are mistaken. The Tannaim are not in Paradise. Paradise is in the Tannaim."

Abraham J. Heschel

It can make all the difference to a day, if we pray about it in advance.

Stephen F. Winward

More things are wrought by prayer
Than this world dreams of.
Wherefore, let thy voice
Rise like a fountain for me night and day.
For what are men better than sheep or goats
That nourish a blind life within the brain,
If, knowing God, they lift not hands of prayer
Both for themselves and those who call them friends?
For so the whole round earth is every way
Bound by gold chains about the feet of God.

Alfred Tennyson

Prayer requires more of the heart than of the tongue.

Adam Clarke

To pray together, in whatever tongue or ritual, is the most tender brotherhood of hope or sympathy that men can contract in this life.

Madame de Stael

A few years' nightly view of the stars and other invariable arrangements, may give the soul a surprisingly lively twinge of what ages of faith have meant by the fear of God; the awesome suspicion that there is some sort of fundamental world order or control which cannot by any means be dodged or bribed to help you break its own laws. Who shall push the dragon or the great dog off his beat?

E. C. Montague

Prayer is nothing you do; prayer is someone you are. Prayer is not about doing, but about being. Prayer is about being alone in God's presence. Prayer is being so alone that God is the only witness to your existence. The secret of prayer is God affirming your life.

William Stringfellow

True worship is not a petition to God: it is a sermon to our selves.

Emil G. Hirsch

Once a mother heard her son praying. She noticed that what he was doing was telling God what he planned to do and seeking to direct God to help him. She said to him, "Son, don't bother to give God instructions; just report for duty."

Robert O. Smith

Do not lose the habit of praying to the unseen Divinity. Prayer for worldly goods is worse than fruitless, but prayer for strength of soul is that passion of the soul which catches the gift it seeks.

George Meredith

The fairest thing we can experience is the mysterious. It is the fundamental emotion which stands at the cradle of true art and true science. He who knows it not, can no longer wonder, no longer feel amazement, is as good as dead, a snuffed out candle.

Albert Einstein

The man who says his prayers in the evening is a captain posting his sentries. After that, he can sleep.

Charles Baudelaire

When a torpedo strikes a ship, or a bomb falls upon a crowd, the commonest and most instinctive cry is "My God!" All sorts of personal disasters and sorrows evoke the same outburst. Involuntarily and intuitively, man turns to thoughts of the Almighty when something befalls that is beyond the range of his normal experience or understanding. Even persons who do not commonly pray turn instantly to prayer in time of peril. The deepest impulses of the human heart lead naturally to God.

William T. Ellis

To pray is not the same as to pray for.

Claude G. Montefiore

Conviction brings a silent, indefinable beauty into faces made of the commonest human clay; the devout worshiper at any shrine reflects something of its golden glow, even as the glory of a noble love shines like a sort of light from a woman's face.

Honore de Balzac

Prayer is the very soul and essence of religion and therefore prayer must be the very core of the life of man, for no man can live without religion.

Mohandas K. Gandhi

A musician must practice by prearranged schedule, regardless of his inclination at the moment. So with the devout soul. It may not rely on caprice or put its hope in chance. It must work. The man on the other hand who folds his hands, waiting for the spirit to move him to think of God—who postpones worship for the right mood and the perfect setting, a forest or mountain peak, for example—will do little of meditating or praying. After all, how often does one find himself in a "cathedral of nature," and when he does who shall say that he will be in a worshipful temper?

Milton Steinberg

Serve and thou shalt be served. If you love and serve men, you cannot, by any hiding or stratagem, escape the remuneration.

Ralph Waldo Emerson

Prayer serves as an edge and border to preserve the web of life from unraveling.

Robert Hall

Genius, without religion, is only a lamp on the outer gate of a palace; it may serve to cast a gleam of light on those that are without, while the inhabitant is in darkness.

H. More

It is good for us to keep some account of our prayers, that we may not unsay them in our practice.

Matthew Henry

When thou prayest, rather let thy heart be without words than thy words without heart.

John Bunyan

All real joy and power of progress . . . depend on finding something to reverence, and all the baseness and misery of humanity begin in a habit of disdain.

John Ruskin

Prayer takes us beyond the self. Joining our little self to the selfhood of humanity, it gives our wishes the freedom to grow large and broad and inclusive. Our prayers are answered not when we are given what we ask, but when we are challenged to be what we can be.

Morris Adler

The right relation between prayer and conduct is supremely important and prayer may help it, but that prayer is supremely important and conduct tests it.

William Temple

Seven days without prayer makes one weak.

Allen E. Bartlett

Prayer digs the channels from the reservoir of God's boundless resources to the tiny pools of our lives.

E. Stanley Jones

Between the humble and contrite heart and the majesty of heaven there are no barriers; the only password is prayer.

Hosea Ballou

Prayer does not change God, but changes him who prays.

Sören Kierkegaard

To plow is to pray, to plant is to prophesy, and the harvest answers and fulfills.

Robert G. Ingersoll

Prayer is and remains the native and deepest impulse of the soul of man.

Thomas Carlyle

We need not perplex ourselves as to the precise mode in which prayer is answered. It is enough for us to know and feel that it is the most natural, the most powerful, and the most elevated expression of our thoughts and wishes in all great emergencies.

Arthur P. Stanley

We go hopelessly astray if we think of prayer as a selfish endeavor to persuade or inveigle, or browbeat God to do us a favor, or win us a victory, or even help us in some dire distress. He is not some kind of a divine bell-hop, to be summoned, as by the pressing of a button, to the service of our passing whims. God does not come to us, but we to Him—and prayer is the high road to His presence.

John Haynes Holmes

Who rises from Prayer a better man, his prayer is answered.

George Meredith

Prayer is governed by the same laws that govern the growth of the flower in the crannied wall. It is controlled by the same laws that control the flow of a stream, for, as God is in all things, so are his laws prevailing in all things. As prayer is life raised to the highest degree, so the laws of prayer are the laws of life raised to their highest expression. The man who learns and practices the laws of prayer should be able to play better, to work better, to love better, to serve better, for to learn how to pray is to learn how to live.

Glenn Clark

By benevolence man rises to a height where he meets God. Therefore do a good deed before you begin your prayers.

Ahai Gaon

The finest fruit of serious learning should be the ability to speak the word God without reserve or embarrassment. And it should be spoken without adolescent resentment, rather with some sense of communion, with reverence and with joy.

Nathan M. Pusey

He prays well who is so absorbed with God that he does not know he is praying.

St. Francis De Sales

Prayer should not be thought of as a time apart from our daily living, but should set the standard which is carried out in our every thought, word and deed.

Roselle Nutter

Prayer is the most powerful form of energy one can generate. The influence of prayer on the human mind and body is as demonstrable as that of secreting glands. Prayer is a force as real as terrestrial gravity. It supplies us with a steady flow of sustaining power in our daily lives.

Alexis Carrel

Those who always pray are necessary to those who never pray.

Victor Hugo

If you would have God hear you when you pray, you must hear Him when he speaks.

Thomas Brooks

The human heart will not tolerate forever an empty shrine. If God does not fill the heart of man something else will—there will be the worship of money, of power, the attraction of some other authority.

James Reid

Prayer is the soul's sincere desire,
Uttered or unexpressed,
The motion of a hidden fire
That trembles in the breast.

James Montgomery

The greatest happiness of the thinking man is to have fathomed what can be fathomed, and quietly to reverence what is unfathomable.

Johann Wolfgang von Goethe

No unsophisticated man prays to have that done for him which he knows how to do for himself.

George Santayana

The efficacy of prayer is not so much to influence the divine counsels as to consecrate human purposes.

John Stuart Blackie

The sovereign cure for worry is prayer.

William James

Worship is transcendent wonder; wonder for which there is now no limit or measure: that is worship.

Thomas Carlyle

Prayer is answered when it enables us to act as God desires.

Ernest Findlay Scott

85. THE GRATEFUL MOOD

Life owes me nothing. Let the years
Bring clouds or azure, joy or tears,
Already a full cup I've quaffed;
Already wept and loved and
laughed,
And seen, in ever endless days.
Life owes me naught. No pain that
waits
Can steal the wealth from memory's
gates;
No aftermath of anguish slow
Can quench the soul-fire's early
glow.
I breathe, exulting, each new
breath,
Embracing Life, ignoring Death.
Life owes me nothing. One clear
morn
Is boon enough for being born;
And be it ninety years or ten,
No need for me to question when.
While Life is mine, I'll find it good,
And greet each hour with gratitude.

Author Unknown

Thou has given so much to me
Give me one thing more—a grateful heart.

George Herbert

Let not your mind run on what you lack as much as on what you have already. Of the things you have, select the best; and then reflect how eagerly they would have been sought if you did not have them.

Marcus Aurelius

There is no lovelier way to thank God for your sight than by giving a helping hand to someone in the dark.

Helen Keller

I am grateful for the idea that has used me.

Felix Adler

You may believe anything that is good of a grateful man.

Thomas Fuller

Were there no God we would be in this glorious world with grateful hearts: and no one to thank.

Christina Rossetti

I am disposed to say grace upon twenty other occasions in the course of the day besides my dinner. I want a form for setting out upon a pleasant walk, for a moonlight ramble, for a friendly meeting, or a solved problem. Why have we none for books, those spiritual repasts—a grace before Milton—a devotional exercise proper to be said before reading THE FAERIE QUEEN?

Charles Lamb

The test of thankfulness is not what you have to be thankful for, but whether anyone else has reason to be thankful that you are here.

Author Unknown

Fear thoughts have a tendency to diminish our ability, but praiseful thoughts lift us up and give us power.

Lowell Fillmore

If one should give me a dish of sand and tell me there were particles of iron in it, I might feel for them with the finger in vain. But let me take a magnet and sweep through it, and how would that draw to itself the most invisible particles by the mere power of attraction! The unthankful heart, like my finger in the sand, discovers no mercies. But let the thankful heart sweep through the day, and as the magnet finds the iron, so it will find, in every hour, some heavenly blessings—only the iron in God's sand is gold.

Oliver Wendell Holmes

If we fasten our attention on what we have, rather than on what we lack, a very little wealth is sufficient.

Francis Johnson

No longer forward nor behind
I look in hope or fear;
But grateful, take the good I find,
The best of now and here.

John Greenleaf Whittier

He that receives a gift with gratitude repays the first installment on his debt.

Seneca

Gratitude takes three forms: a feeling in the heart, an expression in words, and a giving in return.

Author Unknown

John Henry Jowett said: "Gratitude is a vaccine, an antitoxin, and an antiseptic." This is a most searching and true diagnosis. Gratitude can be a vaccine that can prevent the invasion of a disgruntled attitude. As antitoxins prevent the disastrous effects of certain poisons and diseases, thanksgiving destroys the poison of faultfinding and grumbling. When trouble has smitten us, a spirt of thanksgiving is a soothing antiseptic.

Clinton C. Cox

One is tempted to accept life as it is and to forget the men and women of yesterday whose wisdom and sacrifices made it possible for us to have the privileges we now enjoy. Political liberty, universal suffrage, popular education, religious tolerance, trial by jury and the Bible in our own language are some of the blessings which were secured for us by the sacrifice of others. When one loses his sense of gratitude, it is wise to return and study the history of the centuries and seek to appraise the contribution which others have made to civilization.

Samuel Macaulay Lindsay

Live among men as if God were watching.
Talk to God as if men were listening.

Seneca

O God, if Thou shouldst chain me to a bed for the rest of my life, it would not suffice to thank Thee for the days I have lived. If these words are the last that I shall ever write, let them be a hymn to Thy goodness.

Frederick Ozanam

We can pay our debt to the past by putting the future in debt to ourselves.

John Buchan

Two kinds of gratitude: the sudden kind
We feel for what we take, the larger kind
We feel for what we give.

E. A. Robinson

Gratitude is the memory of the heart.

Jean Baptiste Massieu

No man is in true health who can not stand in the free air of heaven, with his feet on God's free turf, and thank his Creator for the simple luxury of physical existence.

T. W. Higginson

If you can't be thankful for what you receive, be thankful for what you escape.

Author Unknown

I have often thought it would be a blessing if each human being were stricken blind and deaf for a few days at some time during his early adult life. Darkness would make him more appreciative of sight; silence would teach him the joys of sound.

Helen Keller

People are always talking about originality: but what do they mean? As soon as we are born, the world begins to work on us and keeps on to the end. What can we call ours except energy, strength, will? If I could give an account of what I owe to great predecessors and contemporaries, there would be but a small remainder.

Johann Wolfgang von Goethe

We thank Thee, Lord, for giving us Thy gift of bread and meat.
We thank Thee, too—a little more—
That we are here to eat.

Leverett Lyon

Did you ever as a child come home bursting with some good news only to find the house empty, no one there to hear and share it? What a let down! The keen edge of joy is dulled if we have to keep it to ourselves. Thankfulness serves that same purpose of adding to the meaning and blessing of what we have received. If there were no one to thank, life would be poor indeed.

Peter H. Pleune

Don't believe the world owes you a living; the world owes you nothing—it was here first.

R. J. Burdette

Our thanks should be as fervent for mercies received, as our petitions for mercies sought.

C. Simmons

How much we owe to the labors of our brothers! Day by day they dig far from the sun that we may be warm, enlist in outposts of peril that we may be secure, and brave the terrors of the unknown for truths that shed light on our way.

Numberless gifts and blessings have been laid in our cradles as our birthright.

Union Prayer Book

For each new morning with its light,
Father, we thank Thee,
For rest and shelter of the night,
Father, we thank Thee,
For health and food, for love and friends,
For everything Thy goodness sends,
Father, in heaven, we thank Thee.

Ralph Waldo Emerson

---

86. THE SEARCH FOR MEANING

Some speak glibly of science "Conquering Nature." Nothing could be further from the truth. When a scientist conquers something, he abides by the fundamental laws and does so with Nature's permission. He has learned that conquering is submission.

Charles F. Kettering

A man has made at least a start on discovering the meaning of human life when he plants shade trees under which he knows full well he will never sit.

Elton Trueblood

The fact of the instability of evil is the moral order of the world.

Alfred North Whitehead

To say that everything happens according to natural laws, and to say that everything is ordained by the decree and ordinance of God, is the same thing.

Baruch Spinoza

A college student once remarked to his instructor that he believed the universe was nothing but a vast machine which made, repaired, and ran itself. The teacher asked him, "Did you ever hear of a machine without a pedal for the foot, a lever for the hand or any outlet for connection with some outside power?" The student of course admitted he had not. "Then," said the instructor, "we had better not think seriously of the universe as a machine."

Roger Hazelton

The beauty of the world and the orderly arrangement of everything celestial makes us confess that there is an excellent and eternal nature, which ought to be worshipped and admired by all mankind.

Cicero

The arc of the universe is long but it bends toward righteousness.

Theodore Parker

I cannot believe that God plays dice with the Cosmos.

Albert Einstein

Though the mills of God grind slowly, yet they grind exceedingly small.
Though with patience He stands waiting, with exactness grinds He all.

Fredrick von Logan

This is a good world. We need not approve of all the items in it, nor of all the individuals in it; but the world itself, which is more than its parts or individuals, which has a soul, a spirit, a fundamental relation to each of us deeper than all other relations—is a friendly world.

Jan C. Smuts

Hard as the world is to explain with God, it is harder yet without Him.

Claude G. Montefiore

It is good for man to open his mind to awe and wonder. Without science we are helpless children. But without a deep religion, we are blundering fools, reeling in our new and terrible cocksureness into one disaster after another.

J. B. Priestly

Behind the dim unknown,
Standeth God within the shadow, keeping watch above his own.

James Russell Lowell

If I, looking with purblind eyes upon a least part of a fraction of the universe, yet perceive in my own destiny some broken evidences of a plan, and some signals of an overruling goodness; shall I then be so mad as to complain that all cannot be deciphered? Shall I not rather wonder, with infinite and grateful surprise, that in so vast a scheme I seem to have been able to read, however little, and that little was encouraging to faith?

Robert Lewis Stevenson

To an astronomer the most remarkable thing about the universe is not its immense size, its great age, or even the violence of the forces operating within its borders. The thing which strikes an astronomer with awe is the element of perfect orderliness. From the tiny satellites of our solar system to the vast galaxies far beyond our own there is no trace of confusion. There is nothing haphazard, nothing capricious. The orderliness of the universe is the supreme discovery of science.

F. R. Moulton

The person who limits his interests to the means of living without consideration of the content or meaning of his life is defeating God's great purpose when he brought into existence a creature with the intelligence and godlike powers that are found in man.

Arthur H. Compton

The meaning of our life is the road, not the goal. For each answer is delusive, each fulfillment melts away between our fingers, and the goal is no longer a goal once it is attained.

Arthur Schnitzler

Roaming in thought over the Universe, I saw the little that is Good steadily hastening towards immortality,
And the vast all that is call'd Evil

I saw hastening to merge itself and become lost and dead.

Walt Whitman

Life can only be understood backwards, but it must be lived forwards.

Sören Kierkegaard

The man who regards his own life and that of his fellow creatures as meaningless is not merely unhappy but hardly fit for life.

Albert Einstein

A religious search is a lonely labor. It is like a flight over an ocean or a desert. Its main preoccupation is not the collecting of interesting episodes as one floats along, but the keeping of one's wings aloft and the reading of one's course by constant sun and steadfast stars. And at the end one's concern is to leave a few words of guidance, if one can, for other voyagers soon to take off upon a like adventure.

William L. Sullivan

What most people want—young or old—is not merely security, or comfort, or luxury, although they are glad enough to have these. Most of all, they want meaning in their lives. If our era and our culture and our leaders do not, or cannot, offer great meanings, great objectives, great convictions, then people will settle for shallow and trivial substitutes. This is a deficiency for which we all bear a responsibility.

. . . This is the challenge of our times.

Rockefeller Report on Education, 1958

Evil is necessary. If it did not exist, the good would not exist. Evil is the unique reason for the good's being. What would courage be far from peril? and what pity without pain? What would become of devotion and sacrifice if happiness were universal? It is because of evil and suffering that the earth may be inhabited and that life is worth living.

Anatole France

That the universe was formed by a fortuitous concourse of atoms, I will no more believe than that the accidental jumbling of the alphabet would fall into a most ingenious treatise of philosophy.

Jonathan Swift

Health alone does not suffice. To be happy, to become creative, man must always be strengthened by faith in the meaning of his own existence.

Stephen Zweig

He who is truly religious finds a providence not more truly in the history of the world than in his own personal and family history. The rainbow which hangs a splendid circle in the heights of heaven, is also formed by the same sun in the dew-drop of the lowly flower.

Jean Paul Richter

ACKNOWLEDGMENTS

The Editor wishes to acknowledge with warmest appreciation the devoted cooperation of Shirley Duffine who handled many of the technical aspects of preparing this volume with utmost efficiency. He is also indebted to Thelma Simmons and Elizabeth Wanicur who contributed their skill to the volume during the years that went into its preparation.

He is also indebted to the following publishers and authors who kindly granted permission to quote the items listed below:

Abingdon Press, from HERE'S A FAITH FOR YOU by Roy M. Pearson; from SPIRITUAL JOURNEY WITH PAUL by Thomas S. Kepler; from THAT IMMORTAL SEA by Leslie D. Weatherhead; from QUESTIONS GOD ASKS by Hunter Beckelhymer.

Association Press, from LIFE'S MEANING by Henry P. Van Dusen; from PUBLIC SPEAKING by Dale Carnegie.

Atlanta Constitution, from SO MANY by Frank L. Stanton; passages by Ralph McGill.

Beacon Press, from THE INDIVIDUAL AND THE STATE by Richard Ballou.

Better Homes and Gardens magazine, for passages from its feature, THE MAN NEXT DOOR by Burton Hills, copyright by Meredith Publishing Company, Des Moines, Iowa.

The Bobbs-Merrill Co. Inc. from IN TUNE WITH THE INFINITE by Ralph Waldo Trine, copyright 1908, 1936, 1957, reprinted by permission of the publishers; from FATHERS AND MOTHERS by George Herbert Betts, copyright 1915, 1942 by Mrs. Anna Betts, reprinted by permission of the publishers; from THE MEASURE OF MAN by Joseph Wood Krutch, copyright 1953, 1954, reprinted by permission of the publishers; from BUT WE WERE BORN FREE, by Elmer Davis, copyright 1952, 1953, 1954, reprinted by permission of the publishers.

Broadman Press, poem—IN TIME OF TROUBLE by Leslie Savage Clark from WITH ALL THY HEART.

Columbia University Press, from AGING SUCCESSFULLY by George Lawton.

W. B. Conkey & Co., poem WILL, by Ella Wheeler Wilcox.

Thomas Y. Crowell Company, from GUIDEPOSTS IN CHAOS by Channing Pollock.

Devin-Adair Company, passages by Austin O'Malley.

Doubleday & Company, Inc., from MADAME CURIE by Eve Curie; from THE STRATEGY OF DESIRE by Ernest Dichter; from ADVISE AND CONSENT by Alan Drury; from THE SUMMING UP by W. Somerset Maugham; from STRICTLY PERSONAL by W. Somerset Maugham.

Duell, Sloan & Pearce, Inc., from THE GREAT LITTLE THINGS by George Matthew Adams.

Reverend L. L. Dunnington, from HANDLES OF POWER.

E. P. Dutton & Co., Inc., from THE ULTIMATE BELIEF by A. Clutton-Brock; from MARRIAGE by William Lyon Phelps.

Wm. B. Eerdmans Publishing Co., from FEELING LOW? by Harold E. Kohn.

Evangelical Publishers—poem, WHAT GOD HATH PROMISED by Annie Johnson Flint.

Farrar, Straus & Cudahy, Inc., from THE TEMPTATION TO BE GOOD by A. Powell Davies.

Field Newspaper Syndicate, passages by Sydney J. Harris.

Harry Emerson Fosdick for passages from many of his publications.

Harcourt, Brace & World, Inc., from A POCKETFUL OF PEBBLES by Jan Struther; from MODERN MAN IN SEARCH OF A SOUL by Dr. C. G. Jung; from BASIC JUDAISM by Milton Steinberg; from IN THE NAME OF SANITY by Lewis Mumford; from THE CONDUCT OF LIFE by Lewis Mumford; from A FAITH FOR LIVING by Lewis Mumford.

Harper & Brothers, selection from INTERIM from COLLECTED POEMS by Edna St. Vincent Millay, copyright 1917-1945; permission of Norma Millay Ellis.

Rabbi Richard C. Hertz, passages from PRESCRIPTION FOR HEARTACHE.

Houghton Mifflin Company, from ACCEPTING THE UNIVERSE by John Burroughs.

Ladies Home Journal, quotations by Marcelene Cox.

J. P. Lippincott Co., from LET'S READ ALOUD by Ruth Gagliardo; from FROM THESE NERVES by George Lincoln Walton; from RIVER OF YEARS by Joseph Fort Newton.

Longmans, Green & Co., Ltd., from PERSONAL RELIGION and THE LIFE OF DEVOTION by William Ralph Inge.

Macmillan & Co., from KEYS TO RICHER LIVING by Lewis L. Dunnington; from SCIENCE AND THE MODERN WORLD by Alfred North Whitehead; from MEMOIRS OF CHILDHOOD AND YOUTH by Albert Schweitzer; from WHO SPEAKS FOR MAN? by Norman Cousins; from THE PSYCHOLOGY OF POWER by J. Arthur Hadfield; from GOD: A COSMIC PHILOSOPHY OF RELIGION by J. E. Boodin.

Virgil Markham, for permission to quote from poems by Edwin Markham.

David McKay Co., Inc. from WITHIN OUR POWER by Raymond B. Fosdick.

Douglas Meador, from his column TRAIL DUST, in the Matador Tribune.

New York Sun, from GOD, YOU HAVE BEEN TOO GOOD TO ME by Charles Wharton Stork.

W. W. Norton & Company, Inc., from MAN'S SEARCH FOR HIMSELF by Rollo May; from THE MATURE MIND by Harry A. Overstreet.

Mrs. Celeste Phelps Osgood, for permission to quote from AUTOBIOGRAPHICAL LETTERS by William Lyon Phelps.

Prentice-Hall, Inc., from SECRETS OF A HAPPY LIFE by David O. McKay; from MAN IN NATURE by Marston Bates.

G. P. Putnam's Sons, from AT LARGE by Arthur Christopher Benson.

The Saturday Review, for passages by Norman Cousins.

Simon & Schuster, Inc., a passage by Madame Chiang Kai-Shek from WORDS TO LIVE BY, edited by William Nichols; a passage by Henry King from WORDS TO LIVE BY, edited by William Nichols; from A CHILD OF THE CENTURY by Ben Hecht.

The Society of Authors, for excerpts from the works of George Bernard Shaw.

Ralph W. Sockman, for permission to quote several of his passages.

MELVIN POWERS SELF-IMPROVEMENT LIBRARY

ASTROLOGY

ASTROLOGY: HOW TO CHART YOUR HOROSCOPE *Max Heindel*	3.00
ASTROLOGY: YOUR PERSONAL SUN-SIGN GUIDE *Beatrice Ryder*	3.00
ASTROLOGY FOR EVERYDAY LIVING *Janet Harris*	2.00
ASTROLOGY MADE EASY *Astarte*	3.00
ASTROLOGY MADE PRACTICAL *Alexandra Kayhle*	3.00
ASTROLOGY, ROMANCE, YOU AND THE STARS *Anthony Norvell*	4.00
MY WORLD OF ASTROLOGY *Sydney Omarr*	5.00
THOUGHT DIAL *Sydney Omarr*	4.00
WHAT THE STARS REVEAL ABOUT THE MEN IN YOUR LIFE *Thelma White*	3.00

BRIDGE

BRIDGE BIDDING MADE EASY *Edwin B. Kantar*	7.00
BRIDGE CONVENTIONS *Edwin B. Kantar*	7.00
BRIDGE HUMOR *Edwin B. Kantar*	5.00
COMPETITIVE BIDDING IN MODERN BRIDGE *Edgar Kaplan*	4.00
DEFENSIVE BRIDGE PLAY COMPLETE *Edwin B. Kantar*	10.00
GAMESMAN BRIDGE — Play Better with Kantar *Edwin B. Kantar*	5.00
HOW TO IMPROVE YOUR BRIDGE *Alfred Sheinwold*	5.00
IMPROVING YOUR BIDDING SKILLS *Edwin B. Kantar*	4.00
INTRODUCTION TO DEFENDER'S PLAY *Edwin B. Kantar*	3.00
SHORT CUT TO WINNING BRIDGE *Alfred Sheinwold*	3.00
TEST YOUR BRIDGE PLAY *Edwin B. Kantar*	5.00
VOLUME 2 — TEST YOUR BRIDGE PLAY *Edwin B. Kantar*	5.00
WINNING DECLARER PLAY *Dorothy Hayden Truscott*	4.00

BUSINESS, STUDY & REFERENCE

CONVERSATION MADE EASY *Elliot Russell*	3.00
EXAM SECRET *Dennis B. Jackson*	3.00
FIX-IT BOOK *Arthur Symons*	2.00
HOW TO DEVELOP A BETTER SPEAKING VOICE *M. Hellier*	3.00
HOW TO MAKE A FORTUNE IN REAL ESTATE *Albert Winnikoff*	4.00
INCREASE YOUR LEARNING POWER *Geoffrey A. Dudley*	3.00
MAGIC OF NUMBERS *Robert Tocquet*	2.00
PRACTICAL GUIDE TO BETTER CONCENTRATION *Melvin Powers*	3.00
PRACTICAL GUIDE TO PUBLIC SPEAKING *Maurice Forley*	3.00
7 DAYS TO FASTER READING *William S. Schaill*	3.00
SONGWRITERS' RHYMING DICTIONARY *Jane Shaw Whitfield*	5.00
SPELLING MADE EASY *Lester D. Basch & Dr. Milton Finkelstein*	3.00
STUDENT'S GUIDE TO BETTER GRADES *J. A. Rickard*	3.00
TEST YOURSELF— Find Your Hidden Talent *Jack Shafer*	3.00
YOUR WILL & WHAT TO DO ABOUT IT *Attorney Samuel G. Kling*	3.00

CALLIGRAPHY

ADVANCED CALLIGRAPHY *Katherine Jeffares*	7.00
CALLIGRAPHER'S REFERENCE BOOK *Anne Leptich & Jacque Evans*	7.00
CALLIGRAPHY— The Art of Beautiful Writing *Katherine Jeffares*	7.00
CALLIGRAPHY FOR FUN & PROFIT *Anne Leptich & Jacque Evans*	7.00
CALLIGRAPHY MADE EASY *Tina Serafini*	7.00

CHESS & CHECKERS

BEGINNER'S GUIDE TO WINNING CHESS *Fred Reinfeld*	3.00
CHECKERS MADE EASY *Tom Wiswell*	2.00
CHESS IN TEN EASY LESSONS *Larry Evans*	3.00
CHESS MADE EASY *Milton L. Hanauer*	3.00
CHESS PROBLEMS FOR BEGINNERS *edited by Fred Reinfeld*	2.00
CHESS SECRETS REVEALED *Fred Reinfeld*	2.00
CHESS STRATEGY— An Expert's Guide *Fred Reinfeld*	2.00
CHESS TACTICS FOR BEGINNERS *edited by Fred Reinfeld*	3.00
CHESS THEORY & PRACTICE *Morry & Mitchell*	2.00
HOW TO WIN AT CHECKERS *Fred Reinfeld*	3.00
1001 BRILLIANT WAYS TO CHECKMATE *Fred Reinfeld*	4.00
1001 WINNING CHESS SACRIFICES & COMBINATIONS *Fred Reinfeld*	4.00
SOVIET CHESS *Edited by R. G. Wade*	3.00

COOKERY & HERBS

_____	CULPEPER'S HERBAL REMEDIES *Dr. Nicholas Culpeper*	3.00
_____	FAST GOURMET COOKBOOK *Poppy Cannon*	2.50
_____	GINSENG The Myth & The Truth *Joseph P. Hou*	3.00
_____	HEALING POWER OF HERBS *May Bethel*	3.00
_____	HEALING POWER OF NATURAL FOODS *May Bethel*	3.00
_____	HERB HANDBOOK *Dawn MacLeod*	3.00
_____	HERBS FOR COOKING AND HEALING *Dr. Donald Law*	2.00
_____	HERBS FOR HEALTH — How to Grow & Use Them *Louise Evans Doole*	3.00
_____	HOME GARDEN COOKBOOK — Delicious Natural Food Recipes *Ken Kraft*	3.00
_____	MEDICAL HERBALIST *edited by Dr. J. R. Yemm*	3.00
_____	NATURAL FOOD COOKBOOK *Dr. Harry C. Bond*	3.00
_____	NATURE'S MEDICINES *Richard Lucas*	3.00
_____	VEGETABLE GARDENING FOR BEGINNERS *Hugh Wiberg*	2.00
_____	VEGETABLES FOR TODAY'S GARDENS *R. Milton Carleton*	2.00
_____	VEGETARIAN COOKERY *Janet Walker*	4.00
_____	VEGETARIAN COOKING MADE EASY & DELECTABLE *Veronica Vezza*	3.00
_____	VEGETARIAN DELIGHTS — A Happy Cookbook for Health *K. R. Mehta*	2.00
_____	VEGETARIAN GOURMET COOKBOOK *Joyce McKinnel*	3.00

GAMBLING & POKER

_____	ADVANCED POKER STRATEGY & WINNING PLAY *A. D. Livingston*	5.00
_____	HOW NOT TO LOSE AT POKER *Jeffrey Lloyd Castle*	3.00
_____	HOW TO WIN AT DICE GAMES *Skip Frey*	3.00
_____	HOW TO WIN AT POKER *Terence Reese & Anthony T. Watkins*	3.00
_____	SECRETS OF WINNING POKER *George S. Coffin*	3.00
_____	WINNING AT CRAPS *Dr. Lloyd T. Commins*	3.00
_____	WINNING AT GIN *Chester Wander & Cy Rice*	3.00
_____	WINNING AT POKER — An Expert's Guide *John Archer*	3.00
_____	WINNING AT 21 — An Expert's Guide *John Archer*	5.00
_____	WINNING POKER SYSTEMS *Norman Zadeh*	3.00

HEALTH

_____	BEE POLLEN *Lynda Lyngheim & Jack Scagnetti*	3.00
_____	DR. LINDNER'S SPECIAL WEIGHT CONTROL METHOD *P. G. Lindner, M.D.*	1.50
_____	HELP YOURSELF TO BETTER SIGHT *Margaret Darst Corbett*	3.00
_____	HOW TO IMPROVE YOUR VISION *Dr. Robert A. Kraskin*	3.00
_____	HOW YOU CAN STOP SMOKING PERMANENTLY *Ernest Caldwell*	3.00
_____	MIND OVER PLATTER *Peter G. Lindner, M.D.*	3.00
_____	NATURE'S WAY TO NUTRITION & VIBRANT HEALTH *Robert J. Scrutton*	3.00
_____	NEW CARBOHYDRATE DIET COUNTER *Patti Lopez-Pereira*	1.50
_____	QUICK & EASY EXERCISES FOR FACIAL BEAUTY *Judy Smith-deal*	2.00
_____	QUICK & EASY EXERCISES FOR FIGURE BEAUTY *Judy Smith-deal*	2.00
_____	REFLEXOLOGY *Dr. Maybelle Segal*	3.00
_____	REFLEXOLOGY FOR GOOD HEALTH *Anna Kaye & Don C. Matchan*	3.00
_____	YOU CAN LEARN TO RELAX *Dr. Samuel Gutwirth*	3.00
_____	YOUR ALLERGY — What To Do About It *Allan Knight, M.D.*	3.00

HOBBIES

_____	BEACHCOMBING FOR BEGINNERS *Norman Hickin*	2.00
_____	BLACKSTONE'S MODERN CARD TRICKS *Harry Blackstone*	3.00
_____	BLACKSTONE'S SECRETS OF MAGIC *Harry Blackstone*	3.00
_____	COIN COLLECTING FOR BEGINNERS *Burton Hobson & Fred Reinfeld*	3.00
_____	ENTERTAINING WITH ESP *Tony 'Doc' Shiels*	2.00
_____	400 FASCINATING MAGIC TRICKS YOU CAN DO *Howard Thurston*	4.00
_____	HOW I TURN JUNK INTO FUN AND PROFIT *Sari*	3.00
_____	HOW TO WRITE A HIT SONG & SELL IT *Tommy Boyce*	7.00
_____	JUGGLING MADE EASY *Rudolf Dittrich*	2.00
_____	MAGIC FOR ALL AGES *Walter Gibson*	4.00
_____	MAGIC MADE EASY *Byron Wels*	2.00
_____	STAMP COLLECTING FOR BEGINNERS *Burton Hobson*	3.00

HORSE PLAYERS' WINNING GUIDES

_____	BETTING HORSES TO WIN *Les Conklin*	3.00
_____	ELIMINATE THE LOSERS *Bob McKnight*	3.00
_____	HOW TO PICK WINNING HORSES *Bob McKnight*	3.00

____ HOW TO WIN AT THE RACES *Sam (The Genius) Lewin*		3.00
____ HOW YOU CAN BEAT THE RACES *Jack Kavanagh*		3.00
____ MAKING MONEY AT THE RACES *David Barr*		3.00
____ PAYDAY AT THE RACES *Les Conklin*		3.00
____ SMART HANDICAPPING MADE EASY *William Bauman*		3.00
____ SUCCESS AT THE HARNESS RACES *Barry Meadow*		3.00
____ WINNING AT THE HARNESS RACES — An Expert's Guide *Nick Cammarano*		3.00

HUMOR

____ HOW TO BE A COMEDIAN FOR FUN & PROFIT *King & Laufer*	2.00
____ HOW TO FLATTEN YOUR TUSH *Coach Marge Reardon*	2.00
____ HOW TO MAKE LOVE TO YOURSELF *Ron Stevens & Joy Grdnic*	3.00
____ JOKE TELLER'S HANDBOOK *Bob Orben*	3.00
____ JOKES FOR ALL OCCASIONS *Al Schock*	3.00
____ 2000 NEW LAUGHS FOR SPEAKERS *Bob Orben*	4.00
____ 2,500 JOKES TO START 'EM LAUGHING *Bob Orben*	3.00

HYPNOTISM

____ ADVANCED TECHNIQUES OF HYPNOSIS *Melvin Powers*	2.00
____ BRAINWASHING AND THE CULTS *Paul A. Verdier, Ph.D.*	3.00
____ CHILDBIRTH WITH HYPNOSIS *William S. Kroger, M.D.*	5.00
____ HOW TO SOLVE Your Sex Problems with Self-Hypnosis *Frank S. Caprio, M.D.*	3.00
____ HOW TO STOP SMOKING THRU SELF-HYPNOSIS *Leslie M. LeCron*	3.00
____ HOW TO USE AUTO-SUGGESTION EFFECTIVELY *John Duckworth*	3.00
____ HOW YOU CAN BOWL BETTER USING SELF-HYPNOSIS *Jack Heise*	3.00
____ HOW YOU CAN PLAY BETTER GOLF USING SELF-HYPNOSIS *Jack Heise*	3.00
____ HYPNOSIS AND SELF-HYPNOSIS *Bernard Hollander, M.D.*	3.00
____ HYPNOTISM *(Originally published in 1893) Carl Sextus*	5.00
____ HYPNOTISM & PSYCHIC PHENOMENA *Simeon Edmunds*	4.00
____ HYPNOTISM MADE EASY *Dr. Ralph Winn*	3.00
____ HYPNOTISM MADE PRACTICAL *Louis Orton*	3.00
____ HYPNOTISM REVEALED *Melvin Powers*	2.00
____ HYPNOTISM TODAY *Leslie LeCron and Jean Bordeaux, Ph.D.*	5.00
____ MODERN HYPNOSIS *Lesley Kuhn & Salvatore Russo, Ph.D.*	5.00
____ NEW CONCEPTS OF HYPNOSIS *Bernard C. Gindes, M.D.*	5.00
____ NEW SELF-HYPNOSIS *Paul Adams*	4.00
____ POST-HYPNOTIC INSTRUCTIONS — Suggestions for Therapy *Arnold Furst*	3.00
____ PRACTICAL GUIDE TO SELF-HYPNOSIS *Melvin Powers*	3.00
____ PRACTICAL HYPNOTISM *Philip Magonet, M.D.*	3.00
____ SECRETS OF HYPNOTISM *S. J. Van Pelt, M.D.*	3.00
____ SELF-HYPNOSIS A Conditioned-Response Technique *Laurence Sparks*	5.00
____ SELF-HYPNOSIS Its Theory, Technique & Application *Melvin Powers*	3.00
____ THERAPY THROUGH HYPNOSIS *edited by Raphael H. Rhodes*	4.00

JUDAICA

____ HOW TO LIVE A RICHER & FULLER LIFE *Rabbi Edgar F. Magnin*	2.00
____ MODERN ISRAEL *Lily Edelman*	2.00
____ SERVICE OF THE HEART *Evelyn Garfiel, Ph.D.*	4.00
____ STORY OF ISRAEL IN COINS *Jean & Maurice Gould*	2.00
____ STORY OF ISRAEL IN STAMPS *Maxim & Gabriel Shamir*	1.00
____ TONGUE OF THE PROPHETS *Robert St. John*	5.00

JUST FOR WOMEN

____ COSMOPOLITAN'S GUIDE TO MARVELOUS MEN Fwd. by *Helen Gurley Brown*	3.00
____ COSMOPOLITAN'S HANG-UP HANDBOOK Foreword by *Helen Gurley Brown*	4.00
____ COSMOPOLITAN'S LOVE BOOK — A Guide to Ecstasy in Bed	4.00
____ COSMOPOLITAN'S NEW ETIQUETTE GUIDE Fwd. by *Helen Gurley Brown*	4.00
____ I AM A COMPLEAT WOMAN *Doris Hagopian & Karen O'Connor Sweeney*	3.00
____ JUST FOR WOMEN — A Guide to the Female Body *Richard E. Sand, M.D.*	5.00
____ NEW APPROACHES TO SEX IN MARRIAGE *John E. Eichenlaub, M.D.*	3.00
____ SEXUALLY ADEQUATE FEMALE *Frank S. Caprio, M.D.*	3.00
____ YOUR FIRST YEAR OF MARRIAGE *Dr. Tom McGinnis*	3.00

MARRIAGE, SEX & PARENTHOOD

____ ABILITY TO LOVE *Dr. Allan Fromme*	5.00
____ ENCYCLOPEDIA OF MODERN SEX & LOVE TECHNIQUES *Macandrew*	5.00
____ GUIDE TO SUCCESSFUL MARRIAGE *Drs. Albert Ellis & Robert Harper*	5.00

____	HOW TO RAISE AN EMOTIONALLY HEALTHY, HAPPY CHILD *A. Ellis*	4.00
____	SEX WITHOUT GUILT *Albert Ellis, Ph.D.*	5.00
____	SEXUALLY ADEQUATE MALE *Frank S. Caprio, M.D.*	3.00

MELVIN POWERS' MAIL ORDER LIBRARY

____	HOW TO GET RICH IN MAIL ORDER *Melvin Powers*	10.00
____	HOW TO WRITE A GOOD ADVERTISEMENT *Victor O. Schwab*	15.00
____	MAIL ORDER MADE EASY *J. Frank Brumbaugh*	10.00
____	U.S. MAIL ORDER SHOPPER'S GUIDE *Susan Spitzer*	10.00

METAPHYSICS & OCCULT

____	BOOK OF TALISMANS, AMULETS & ZODIACAL GEMS *William Pavitt*	5.00
____	CONCENTRATION — A Guide to Mental Mastery *Mouni Sadhu*	4.00
____	CRITIQUES OF GOD *Edited by Peter Angeles*	7.00
____	EXTRA-TERRESTRIAL INTELLIGENCE — The First Encounter	6.00
____	FORTUNE TELLING WITH CARDS *P. Foli*	3.00
____	HANDWRITING ANALYSIS MADE EASY *John Marley*	3.00
____	HANDWRITING TELLS *Nadya Olyanova*	5.00
____	HOW TO INTERPRET DREAMS, OMENS & FORTUNE TELLING SIGNS *Gettings*	3.00
____	HOW TO UNDERSTAND YOUR DREAMS *Geoffrey A. Dudley*	3.00
____	ILLUSTRATED YOGA *William Zorn*	3.00
____	IN DAYS OF GREAT PEACE *Mouni Sadhu*	3.00
____	KING SOLOMON'S TEMPLE IN THE MASONIC TRADITION *Alex Horne*	5.00
____	LSD — THE AGE OF MIND *Bernard Roseman*	2.00
____	MAGICIAN — His Training and Work *W. E. Butler*	3.00
____	MEDITATION *Mouni Sadhu*	5.00
____	MODERN NUMEROLOGY *Morris C. Goodman*	3.00
____	NUMEROLOGY — ITS FACTS AND SECRETS *Ariel Yvon Taylor*	3.00
____	NUMEROLOGY MADE EASY *W. Mykian*	3.00
____	PALMISTRY MADE EASY *Fred Gettings*	3.00
____	PALMISTRY MADE PRACTICAL *Elizabeth Daniels Squire*	4.00
____	PALMISTRY SECRETS REVEALED *Henry Frith*	3.00
____	PROPHECY IN OUR TIME *Martin Ebon*	2.50
____	PSYCHOLOGY OF HANDWRITING *Nadya Olyanova*	5.00
____	SUPERSTITION — Are You Superstitious? *Eric Maple*	2.00
____	TAROT *Mouni Sadhu*	6.00
____	TAROT OF THE BOHEMIANS *Papus*	5.00
____	WAYS TO SELF-REALIZATION *Mouni Sadhu*	3.00
____	WHAT YOUR HANDWRITING REVEALS *Albert E. Hughes*	3.00
____	WITCHCRAFT, MAGIC & OCCULTISM — A Fascinating History *W. B. Crow*	5.00
____	WITCHCRAFT — THE SIXTH SENSE *Justine Glass*	4.00
____	WORLD OF PSYCHIC RESEARCH *Hereward Carrington*	2.00

SELF-HELP & INSPIRATIONAL

____	DAILY POWER FOR JOYFUL LIVING *Dr. Donald Curtis*	3.00
____	DYNAMIC THINKING *Melvin Powers*	2.00
____	EXUBERANCE — Your Guide to Happiness & Fulfillment *Dr. Paul Kurtz*	3.00
____	GREATEST POWER IN THE UNIVERSE *U. S. Andersen*	5.00
____	GROW RICH WHILE YOU SLEEP *Ben Sweetland*	3.00
____	GROWTH THROUGH REASON *Albert Ellis, Ph.D.*	4.00
____	GUIDE TO DEVELOPING YOUR POTENTIAL *Herbert A. Otto, Ph.D.*	3.00
____	GUIDE TO LIVING IN BALANCE *Frank S. Caprio, M.D.*	2.00
____	GUIDE TO PERSONAL HAPPINESS *Albert Ellis, Ph.D. & Irving Becker, Ed.D.*	5.00
____	HELPING YOURSELF WITH APPLIED PSYCHOLOGY *R. Henderson*	2.00
____	HELPING YOURSELF WITH PSYCHIATRY *Frank S. Caprio, M.D.*	2.00
____	HOW TO ATTRACT GOOD LUCK *A. H. Z. Carr*	4.00
____	HOW TO CONTROL YOUR DESTINY *Norvell*	3.00
____	HOW TO DEVELOP A WINNING PERSONALITY *Martin Panzer*	3.00
____	HOW TO DEVELOP AN EXCEPTIONAL MEMORY *Young & Gibson*	4.00
____	HOW TO OVERCOME YOUR FEARS *M. P. Leahy, M.D.*	3.00
____	HOW YOU CAN HAVE CONFIDENCE AND POWER *Les Giblin*	3.00
____	HUMAN PROBLEMS & HOW TO SOLVE THEM *Dr. Donald Curtis*	4.00
____	I CAN *Ben Sweetland*	5.00
____	I WILL *Ben Sweetland*	3.00
____	LEFT-HANDED PEOPLE *Michael Barsley*	4.00

_____ MAGIC IN YOUR MIND *U. S. Andersen*		5.00
_____ MAGIC OF THINKING BIG *Dr. David J. Schwartz*		3.00
_____ MAGIC POWER OF YOUR MIND *Walter M. Germain*		5.00
_____ MENTAL POWER THROUGH SLEEP SUGGESTION *Melvin Powers*		3.00
_____ NEW GUIDE TO RATIONAL LIVING *Albert Ellis, Ph.D. & R. Harper, Ph.D.*		3.00
_____ OUR TROUBLED SELVES *Dr. Allan Fromme*		3.00
_____ PSYCHO-CYBERNETICS *Maxwell Maltz, M.D.*		3.00
_____ SCIENCE OF MIND IN DAILY LIVING *Dr. Donald Curtis*		5.00
_____ SECRET OF SECRETS *U. S. Andersen*		5.00
_____ SECRET POWER OF THE PYRAMIDS *U. S. Andersen*		5.00
_____ STUTTERING AND WHAT YOU CAN DO ABOUT IT *W. Johnson, Ph.D.*		2.50
_____ SUCCESS-CYBERNETICS *U. S. Andersen*		5.00
_____ 10 DAYS TO A GREAT NEW LIFE *William E. Edwards*		3.00
_____ THINK AND GROW RICH *Napoleon Hill*		3.00
_____ THINK YOUR WAY TO SUCCESS *Dr. Lew Losoncy*		5.00
_____ THREE MAGIC WORDS *U. S. Andersen*		5.00
_____ TREASURY OF COMFORT *edited by Rabbi Sidney Greenberg*		5.00
_____ TREASURY OF THE ART OF LIVING *Sidney S. Greenberg*		5.00
_____ YOU ARE NOT THE TARGET *Laura Huxley*		4.00
_____ YOUR SUBCONSCIOUS POWER *Charles M. Simmons*		5.00
_____ YOUR THOUGHTS CAN CHANGE YOUR LIFE *Dr. Donald Curtis*		5.00

SPORTS

_____ BICYCLING FOR FUN AND GOOD HEALTH *Kenneth E. Luther*		2.00
_____ BILLIARDS—Pocket • Carom • Three Cushion *Clive Cottingham, Jr.*		3.00
_____ CAMPING-OUT 101 Ideas & Activities *Bruno Knobel*		2.00
_____ COMPLETE GUIDE TO FISHING *Vlad Evanoff*		2.00
_____ HOW TO IMPROVE YOUR RACQUETBALL *Lubarsky, Kaufman, & Scagnetti*		3.00
_____ HOW TO WIN AT POCKET BILLIARDS *Edward D. Knuchell*		4.00
_____ JOY OF WALKING *Jack Scagnetti*		3.00
_____ LEARNING & TEACHING SOCCER SKILLS *Eric Worthington*		3.00
_____ MOTORCYCLING FOR BEGINNERS *I. G. Edmonds*		3.00
_____ RACQUETBALL FOR WOMEN *Toni Hudson, Jack Scagnetti & Vince Rondone*		3.00
_____ RACQUETBALL MADE EASY *Steve Lubarsky, Rod Delson & Jack Scagnetti*		3.00
_____ SECRET OF BOWLING STRIKES *Dawson Taylor*		3.00
_____ SECRET OF PERFECT PUTTING *Horton Smith & Dawson Taylor*		3.00
_____ SOCCER—The Game & How to Play It *Gary Rosenthal*		3.00
_____ STARTING SOCCER *Edward F. Dolan, Jr.*		3.00
_____ TABLE TENNIS MADE EASY *Johnny Leach*		2.00

TENNIS LOVERS' LIBRARY

_____ BEGINNER'S GUIDE TO WINNING TENNIS *Helen Hull Jacobs*		2.00
_____ HOW TO BEAT BETTER TENNIS PLAYERS *Loring Fiske*		4.00
_____ HOW TO IMPROVE YOUR TENNIS—Style, Strategy & Analysis *C. Wilson*		2.00
_____ INSIDE TENNIS—Techniques of Winning *Jim Leighton*		3.00
_____ PLAY TENNIS WITH ROSEWALL *Ken Rosewall*		2.00
_____ PSYCH YOURSELF TO BETTER TENNIS *Dr. Walter A. Luszki*		2.00
_____ SUCCESSFUL TENNIS *Neale Fraser*		2.00
_____ TENNIS FOR BEGINNERS *Dr. H. A. Murray*		2.00
_____ TENNIS MADE EASY *Joel Brecheen*		3.00
_____ WEEKEND TENNIS—How to Have Fun & Win at the Same Time *Bill Talbert*		3.00
_____ WINNING WITH PERCENTAGE TENNIS—Smart Strategy *Jack Lowe*		2.00

WILSHIRE PET LIBRARY

_____ DOG OBEDIENCE TRAINING *Gust Kessopulos*		4.00
_____ DOG TRAINING MADE EASY & FUN *John W. Kellogg*		4.00
_____ HOW TO BRING UP YOUR PET DOG *Kurt Unkelbach*		2.00
_____ HOW TO RAISE & TRAIN YOUR PUPPY *Jeff Griffen*		3.00
_____ PIGEONS: HOW TO RAISE & TRAIN THEM *William H. Allen, Jr.*		2.00

*The books listed above can be obtained from your book dealer or directly from
Melvin Powers. When ordering, please remit 50¢ per book postage & handling.
Send for our free illustrated catalog of self-improvement books.*

Melvin Powers
12015 Sherman Road, No. Hollywood, California 91605

NOTES